ZOLA, CÉZANNE, AND MANET

ZOLA, CÉZANNE, and MANET

A Study of L'Oeuvre

By Robert J. Niess

Ann Arbor
THE UNIVERSITY OF MICHIGAN PRESS

Library of Congress Catalog Card No. 68-16443
Published in the United States of America by
The University of Michigan Press and simultaneously
in Rexdale, Canada, by Ambassador Books Limited
United Kingdom agent: The Cresset Press
Manufactured in the United States of America

Published with the assistance of a grant from the
Horace H. Rackham School of Graduate Studies

To Martha

Contents

I. The Origins of *L'Oeuvre*—The Literary Tradition 1
II. The Secondary Figures 26
III. Pierre Sandoz 62
IV. Lantier—Cézanne 78
V. Cézanne: the Novel and the Biography 87
VI. Lantier—Manet 113
VII. Lantier—Zola 151
VIII. Lantier and the Others 170
IX. The Novel—Its Genesis and Development 192
X. The Novel as Fiction 211
XI. Theses and Messages 234
Notes 251
Select Bibliography 287
Index 297

I

The Origins of L'Oeuvre—*the Literary Tradition*

Of the twenty novels of the *Rougon-Macquart* series, *L'Oeuvre* has surely been one of the most controversial. Within days of its publication in April 1886, it came under criticism from various quarters as a roundabout attack on Impressionism in art and within a decade and a half the idea was widely accepted that it contained a savagely distorted portrait of one of Zola's intimates, either Édouard Manet or Paul Cézanne. Since about 1900 every historian of Impressionism has dwelled at greater or lesser length on Zola's "incomprehension" of his contemporaries' artistic theories and practices and his supposedly dishonorable intentions in writing the book, and every critic of his novelistic accomplishment has spent more or less time summing up the biographical information the work contains. Yet with all this attention—and the subject seems as fresh today as it did in 1900 or in 1925, judging by the eagerness with which recent historians of art have approached it—*L'Oeuvre* has never been one of the most successful books of the series, either with the critics or with the public. Only a few critics have rated it highly and public response has left it well below the median of the *Rougon-Macquart* series in total sales. It has never enjoyed the popularity of *Germinal, L'Assommoir, Nana,* or *La Débâcle,* and not even the success of *La Faute de l'Abbé Mouret* or *Pot-bouille.*[1]

If Zola could know how divided opinion on the novel has been in the eighty-odd years since its publication, he would surely be disappointed, for it is probable that no other work of the series, save perhaps *La Joie de vivre,* contained more of himself. At all events, *L'Oeuvre* was one of his oldest conceptions, dating as far back in his designs for writing as *L'Assommoir* itself or *La Curée* or *Nana.* When he entered into negotiations with the publisher LaCroix in the winter of 1868-69 he brought him, along with the manuscript of *La Fortune des Rougon,* a series of brief plans for the ten novels he then envisaged as composing the series. Among them was this one:

> A novel which will have the art world as its frame and for its hero Claude Dulac, another child of a working-class family. Curious effect of heredity, transmitting genius to a child of illiterate parents. Nervous influence of the mother. Claude has intellectual appetites which are irresistible and unbridled, as certain members of his family have physical appetites. The violence he employs in satisfying the passions of his mind drives him to impotency. A picture of the artistic fever of the period, of what is called decadence but which is only a product of the mad activity of minds. The poignant physiology of an artistic temperament in our time, and the terrible drama of an intelligence which devours itself.[2]

It was not until some fifteen years later, after the enormous sensation of *Germinal* and before the bombshell of *La Terre*, that he sat down, on May 12, 1885, to begin the work projected so long before. Nine months later—a little less perhaps than the usual gestation time of his novels[3]—on February 23, 1886, he wrote to his old friend Henry Céard that he had just finished the novel, which had turned out to be longer than he had expected.[4] Faithful to his usual practice, Zola had sold first publication rights for the very substantial sum of 20,000 francs[5] to *Le Gil Blas*, where it began appearing on December 23, 1885, and continued until March 27, 1886. Almost immediately after the conclusion of the *Gil Blas* serialization, Charpentier released the volume, which was registered with the Ministry of the Interior on April 2 and announced in *La Bibliographie de la France* for April 15, 1886.

Critical response, while not overwhelming, was at least considerable, for by 1886 Zola was a figure to be reckoned with. In *Le Figaro* of April 5 Philippe Gille spoke well of the novel (he saw *L'Oeuvre* as a reflection of the good old days he and Zola had known in the Batignolles), Jules Lemaître was disturbed in *La Revue bleue* for April 17, Armand de Pontmartin was horrified and disgusted in *La Gazette de France* for May 15, and Gustave Geffroy was sympathetic in *La Justice* for May 12.[6] A sour note in the chorus was struck by a number of critics who implied or openly charged that *L'Oeuvre* was a plagiarism of Balzac's *Le Chef-d'oeuvre inconnu*; this accusation was discussed at considerable length by Maurice Français (who had previously reviewed the book) in *Le Voltaire* for May 3. Critical reaction, while certainly not wholly unfavorable, made it apparent from the outset that *L'Oeuvre* was not going to be a real hit. But how could it have been? *Germinal* was still fresh in the public memory, and unflattering comparisons between that rich and bloody masterpiece and the gray and slightly monotonous study of artistic frustration were inevitable. Again, *L'Oeuvre* had some very stiff competition to face: Drumont's notorious *La France juive* appeared almost simultaneously with it and immediately seized the headlines. More—just as Zola's novel was coming to an end in *Le Gil Blas* and was appearing in the booksellers' windows, Pierre Loti began publishing *Pêcheur d'Islande,* one of the nineteenth century's really considerable popular successes, in Mme Adam's *Nouvelle Revue; Pêcheur d'Islande* appeared in book form in June 1886 and was received with acclaim by all critics. Zola's novel apparently never recovered from the blow.

The comparatively active press response had been prepared somewhat in advance, as was—and is—usual in the Parisian literary world, by a series of teasing references to the subject matter of the novel, its autobiographical importance, and its character as a *roman à clef.* Zola told the Italian critic Edmondo de Amicis of his plans as early as 1880 and De Amicis was not slow to divulge what the novelist had said to him.[7] In the same year Zola mentioned in an interview with the journalist Fernand Xau that he was planning a study on art, centering on Claude Lantier,[8] but by far the most effective advance reference was made in 1882 by Paul Alexis, who of course got his information straight from Zola himself:

> A work for which he will have less trouble collecting the documents is the novel which he intends to write on art. Here he will have only to remember what he saw in our circle and what he felt himself. His principal character is all ready: it is that painter, in love with modern beauty, who is glimpsed in *Le Ventre de Paris:* it is that same Claude Lantier. His project is to recount in this novel his years in Provence, that early youth of his which was so singular, so special. . . . I know that he intends to study in Claude Lantier the frightful psychology of artistic impotence. Around the central man of genius, a sublime dreamer paralyzed in production by a flaw, other artists will move, painters, sculptors, musicians, men of letters, a whole band of ambitious young men who have also come to conquer Paris: some failing in their projects, others succeeding more or less; all of them cases of the malady of art, varieties of the great contemporary neurosis. Naturally, Zola in this work will be obliged to levy upon his friends, to gather their most typical traits.[9]

On the whole, Alexis' pages were not a bad bit of *réclame,* just the right note of mystery, just the proper hint of interesting biographical revelations and disloyalty to old friends. Zola could not have done better if he had written it himself. Perhaps he did.

As the novel began to take form in Zola's mind, more direct bits of information trickled from Médan. Zola's unfortunate young friend Louis Desprez, for example, declared that in the "novel on art" Zola would call up his memories, his youthful struggles, and would even give his friends a role in the book, which would study some curious cases of impotence in the world of painters and writers.[10] In an interview with an anonymous reporter of *Le Matin* (March 7, 1885) Zola stated that after *Germinal* it was probable that he was going to write a short work, with few characters, laid in an artistic milieu, and added that it was possible that he would employ Claude Lantier, of *Le Ventre de Paris*, as his central figure.[11] On May 2 *Le Figaro* published a fairly detailed description of the book and on June 9 Charles Chincholle (who signed only Charles) speculated on the real identity of the painter who was to figure as Claude Lantier.[12] As the campaign progressed Zola released a squib to *La Vie moderne*, which published on June 27 a page of Zola's notes containing a brief background sketch of Claude Lantier and indicating that the novel would surely have its conclusion after 1870, contrary to the original plan of the *Rougon-Macquart* series.

The most interesting episode of the little publicity campaign came toward the end of July 1885, nearly three months after Zola had begun writing the novel. On July 22 the well-known reporter "Parisis" (Émile Blavet) published an interview with Edmond de Goncourt in *Le Figaro* which contained an unfortunate sentence implying that the "Grenier" was growing concerned about *L'Oeuvre* and was ready to accuse Zola of plagiarizing *Manette Salomon*. Goncourt had never made such an accusation and indeed said flatly in the interview that *L'Oeuvre* and *Manette Salomon* would have little in common. Declaring that he knew all about Zola's plans, he said that Zola would describe in his novel the little army of painters becoming a legion, classic painting attacked and dethroned by "naturalistic" art, the special parasitical world of merchants and collectors, and the whole picturesque world of the Hôtel des Ventes. He pointed out further that the period to be treated in Zola's novel would be far different from that of *Manette Salomon* (he was right) and that Zola's painters would be far different from the artists of his own novel (he was right again).

In spite of this disclaimer, Zola was sufficiently exercised by the interview to write a sharp rejoinder, dated July 22, 1885, and published in *Le Figaro* on July 24, in which he denied that *L'Oeuvre* would have even the remotest similarity to *Manette Salomon* and that it would really be nothing more than a study of a profound passion. But even this did not calm Zola's mind, for some days later, on July 26, he wrote Alphonse Daudet at length about the matter, protesting sharply at the charge of plagiarism and disloyalty to his old friends and urging Daudet (and by implication his friends) to close ranks with him in the face of public hostility instead of quarreling among themselves.[13] Zola's suspicions of Goncourt were of course well founded, for even if Goncourt never openly and publicly accused him of plagiarism, his *Journal* makes it only too clear that he thought that plagiarism was exactly what Zola had committed.

With all this advance publicity—and there is no bad publicity where book sales are concerned—Zola was now ready to begin composition of the novel. His private letters provide an interesting little history of the progress of the work. On July 6, 1885, he wrote his Dutch admirer J. Van Santen Kolff that he had begun the novel and that in it he had recounted his own youth and had put his friends and even himself in its pages. His goal, he said, was to study how a work of art takes root and develops, but he also added that he had included a "drama of passion" which he thought would be interesting,[14] saying that Provence would have but little place in the novel, giving the definitive title, and indicating that the book was a kind of history of a work of art, its genius and "drama" in the artistic mind.[15] A month later, on August 23, he revealed to Céard that he had contracted with *Le Gil Blas* for the serial publication of the novel[16] and on September 25 told another Dutch admirer, Frans Netscher, that the novel, which he calls "a story of passion in a literary and artistic milieu," was causing him a good deal of trouble.[17] The same note is accentuated two months later in a letter to Alphonse Daudet, in which Zola unconsciously reveals that part of the reason for *L'Oeuvre*'s stylistic and compositional deficiencies was the fact that *Le Gil Blas* had made him accept too early a publication date and that he had consequently to work too rapidly.[18] The only other letters available in which Zola speaks of his novel are those addressed to Kolff, of February 14, 1886, where he indicates he will have completed *L'Oeuvre* within about ten days,[19] and to Céard, in which he tells his old friend that he has just finished the writing.[20] These half-dozen letters, brief and simple as they are, are the only first-hand sources of information about *L'Oeuvre;* they indicate clearly that the novel has autobiographical elements, but they do not, unfortunately, give any but the vaguest clues as to the identity of the persons, living or dead, who might have served as models for the figure of Claude Lantier or the other characters in the book. And that is the very problem that has most interested the art historians and the literary critics who have devoted themselves to the work.

Nor are these letters of any aid in attempting to discover which literary works, if any, Zola called upon as sources in the composition of *L'Oeuvre.* Original or not, Zola's novel was in a literary tradition, the tradition of the artist as hero, which was already some eighty years old and which could boast, besides *Le Chef-d'oeuvre inconnu* and *Manette Salomon*, Nodier's *Le Peintre de Saltzbourg*, the first example of the type (1803), Balzac's *La Maison du Chat-qui-pelote, La Bourse, Pierre Grassou* and *La Rabouilleuse,* Musset's *Le Fils du Titien,* Mürger's *Scènes de la vie de bohème,* Gautier's *Le Berger,* Flaubert's *Éducation sentimentale,* and Daudet's *Les Femmes d'artistes.*[21] How much *L'Oeuvre* owes to this tradition has been a moot question for three-quarters of a century, and the chances are that it will remain just that in the future. No references to literary works are to be found in the notes for the novel, but it is also true that this does not necessarily mean that Zola wrote *L'Oeuvre* without benefit of example.

The source first and most frequently suggested for *L'Oeuvre* is of course Balzac's brilliant *Le Chef-d'oeuvre inconnu,* though in his interview with Maurice Français in *Le Voltaire* for May 3, 1886, Zola seemed to deny appropriating anything important from Balzac and claimed that he could remember only vaguely the subject of the famous short story. He made no bones about admitting that he always gathered a certain stock of specialized information to serve as the basis of each of his novels, but quickly added that he never borrowed plots; he also conceded that his work and Balzac's might have some details in common and that his novel might contain some reminiscences of Balzac's story, but at all events they would be much more developed in *L'Oeuvre* than in *Le Chef-d'oeuvre inconnu.*

How seriously is this denial, if it is a denial, to be taken? Was Zola merely speaking *pro forma*, defending his literary practice as any author would when placed in his position? Or did he really mean that he had taken nothing of major importance from his favorite author? The question is impossible to answer, but it is not at all difficult to point out some very striking resemblances between *L'Oeuvre* and *Le Chef-d'oeuvre inconnu.*

There are, to begin with, marked similarities of plot and intrigue: both works deal with an artist's endless attempt to fix on canvas a certain vision of female beauty and both conclude with his suicide when he discovers his inability to render his ideal. Moreover, both provide a parallel to the main plot by the introduction of a living woman who gradually comes to regard the ideal beauty of the canvas as her arch enemy and both thus reinforce the intellectual meaning of the story by a dramatic subplot, the rivalry of the woman of flesh and blood with the imaginary woman for the artist's affection. It is true that this aspect of the story is only hinted at in *Le Chef-d'oeuvre inconnu*, but its presence is undeniable. In *L'Oeuvre* it is the subplot which gives the work most of its human interest.

But not only are the plots of both works basically similar, there is a close resemblance of theme, inasmuch as both *L'Oeuvre* and Balzac's story treat as their major subject the quest for the absolute in art, a quest taking the form of an unceasing search for perfection in a single work, which eventually becomes the painter's one and only true love, then his obsession and at last the symbol of his imperfection as an artist. Both Frenhofer, Balzac's hero, and Claude Lantier, his somewhat paler brother in Zola's novel, spend years pursuing their inner vision of beauty, and in both cases this desperate pursuit takes the form of constant retouches and changes of detail in a single work, changes which reveal only too clearly the deep though unconfessed self-doubt that harries each painter. For both of them, in spite of their dogged efforts, are doubters, and it is their mute suspicion that they are incomplete which renders their lives miserable and fruitless. Near the climax of his sufferings Frenhofer cries out that his very accumulation of knowledge has made him doubt his work,[22] and his friend, Porbus, himself a painter, notes that by dint of searching, Frenhofer has come to doubt the very object of his researches. It is unnecessary to point out how great a role this same kind of doubt plays in *L'Oeuvre*, for Zola actually makes it the principal psychological force of the whole last half of the book—the real motive that brings Claude to failure and destruction.

Both Frenhofer and Claude, and this is one of the closest similarities in the two works, push the doubt-impelled process of change and retouching so far that they end by almost completely obliterating their original genial conceptions—almost, for in both paintings one detail miraculously escapes the constant reworking, to let us glimpse the masterpiece that we have lost by their long and blind pursuit. When Frenhofer's friends at last see the unknown masterpiece they discover nothing but a mass of lines and colors which betrays its original beauty only by the perfection of a woman's foot, the sole detail that has been spared in the rage for perfection, and in Claude's painting there remains, besides the huge, bejeweled, and horrible nude, only the group of longshoremen unloading sacks of plaster.[23] It is probably not without significance that both Balzac and Zola quite clearly make their heroes' self-doubt stem directly from an intellectualizing tendency to reason too much about their art, to seek the perfect formula when perfection is not of this world, to meditate and contemplate too much, to the detriment of the actual practice of their art.

In both *L'Oeuvre* and *Le Chef-d'oeuvre inconnu* the paintings that bring the artists to failure are executed essentially without model. Frenhofer has never found the perfect beauty he has long dreamed of, and Claude, after years of searching among the models of Paris and further years of forcing his wife, Christine, to pose for him, finally turns to the vision of his inner eye alone and ceases any pretence that an earthly beauty can satisfy his hunger for perfection. So both tales are reworkings, somewhat distant, it is true, of the ancient Pygmalion legend. Frenhofer is passionately in love with his Belle-Noiseuse, his "wife," as he calls her; he has lived with her for ten years, she has been his pride, his consolation, his passion. She has smiled at him with every stroke of the brush, she has a soul which he has given her, she would blush if any other eyes were to fall upon her.[24] And Claude goes so far in the same direction that Christine can justly reproach him for making real mistresses out of his oil and canvas nudes, for abandoning her in favor of a painted image, for pressing an illusion in his arms.[25] It is here, in the strangely erotic nature they give their paintings, in their fruitless attempt to render some unconfessed and unsatisfied sexual desire, that Frenhofer and Claude resemble each other most fundamentally.

The similarity between the subplots dealing with the rivalry of woman and art is less marked, though not negligible. Zola, of course, makes much of it, while Balzac does not do much more than hint at the subject, but the experience of Gillette, Poussin's mistress, is a kind of sketchy prophecy of Christine's long struggle in *L'Oeuvre*, that is, a preliminary victory of love over art, then a gradual but definitive defeat as the intellectual and emotional forces of art grip the painter ever more tightly, leaving no strength for any fleshly love.

There are one or two other similarities between *L'Oeuvre* and Balzac's story, none of them very important but interesting and perhaps significant in their ensemble. In both stories the dénouement is brought about by the device of a second person who reveals to the artist how and to what extent he has ruined his work. Frenhofer overhears Poussin's cry that sooner or later he will perceive that there is nothing on his canvas[26] and immediately realizes what he has done—or has not done. And Zola causes Claude to be awakened from his long dream by Christine, who, in disgust and agony at his long abandonment of her in favor of his painted women, cries out that he must at last see what a fool he has been for falling in love with anything so lamentably grotesque as the nude of the last painting and urges him roughly to awaken from his long dream and embrace life at last.[27]

Then there is at least an apparent similarity of philosophical conclusion in each work, a conclusion drawn in each case by the author's spokesman from the painter's failure. Balzac, it seems, intends us to realize that art, by definition, contains the seeds of its own destruction: the search for the absolute, implicit in all artistic effort, must lead to failure.[28] Sandoz, in *L'Oeuvre*, utters what seems to be an echo of this same belief when he says to Bongrand, over Claude's grave in the cemetery of St. Ouen that creation is not within mankind's power and that since we can only be feeble copyists, we might as well crack our heads open and be done with it without delay.[29]

Do these similarities, some of which are significant and all of which add up to a strong argument, mean that Zola patterned *L'Oeuvre* on Balzac's fine story? Perhaps they do. At all events, they make it impossible to dismiss easily the hypothesis of an influence and may point to something more than Zola was willing publicly to concede.[30]

There remains another possibility, that Zola found the original idea for his novel not in Balzac at all but in an imitator of Balzac. Henry James's short story, "The Madonna of the Future," clearly a reworking of *Le-Chef-d'oeuvre inconnu,*[31] appeared in translation as "La Madone de l'avenir" in the *Revue des deux mondes* for April 1, 1875,[32] and could easily have supplied Zola with a source for his novel.[33]

"The Madonna of the Future" concerns a poor American expatriate in Florence, Theobald, who has spent years in seeking the formula for the ideal beauty he has so long conceived but not achieved, so as to put it on canvas, for he has never passed the stage of dreaming, meditating, and theorizing. Only once—and the detail is significant—has he succeeded in creating a work attracting any attention whatsoever and that was when he painted a portrait of the dying child of his friend and model Serafina. Theobald spends much time talking to the narrator, H. (who sounds very much like James himself), exposing his idealistic doctrines, theorizing on the concept of a perfect beauty, justifying in every way his own lack of production and his fundamental sterility. At last H. manages to see the object of his adoration, the beloved and beautiful Serafina, who is the inspiration and occasional model for the great new Madonna Theobald is constructing, and when he sees her he is shocked to find that she is an undistinguished woman of middle age who has nothing to offer the artist now but the remains of a vanished beauty. When H. reveals the truth to Theobald and tells him bluntly that he has been deluding himself and wasting his time, Theobald is crushed and overwhelmed with shame, disillusionment, and something like remorse. Finally, he dies of a broken heart and is buried quietly by a handful of fellow expatriates; H. manages to seize the great painting—which is nothing but a "mere dead blank, cracked and discoloured by time"[34]—to keep it from the eyes of the mockers who have suspected all along that Theobald is nothing but a theorist and a poseur.

There are a good many details in the story that make it look like a source for *L'Oeuvre:* the endless quest for perfection in a single canvas; years of contemplation and theorizing; the bohemian condition of both Theobald and Claude, living outside society, obsessed with their monomania and devoting their entire existence to it, to the exclusion of all human and fleshly love; the portrait of the dead child (James makes it a dying child, but Zola is more dramatic and "plastic");[35] the great canvas, awaited so long by the painter's friends, some of whom at least think him a genius, and which turns out to be an almost laughable failure; the longtime reputation as a great figure, at least potentially, and the gradual turning away of friends, tired of waiting and hoping for the perfect formula; the painter's belief in a kind of conspiracy against him; the fact that both Theobald and Claude, near the end of their lives, come to paint almost completely without model, directly from the inner vision of ideal beauty; the revelation by a second person that the painter has deluded himself, and the artist's terrible awakening from his long dream; the painter's death brought about by heartbreak and disillusionment; the quiet little funeral (which neither Serafina nor Christine attends), so symbolic of society's lack of patience with the dreamers, the weak; the concluding detail, where the friend seizes the canvas to keep it from profane eyes; the contrast between the failure of an idealist and the success of a cynic, depicted by Zola in the prosperity of his Fagerolles and by James in the comfortable life of Serafina's lover, who makes a good living selling obscene animal figures.

But actually the similarities of idea are much more significant than the resemblances of plot and detail, however close the latter may be. It is here that Zola's novel, with its emphasis on a kind of philosophy of art, is much closer to James's work than to Balzac's story, which, while it contains an incredibly accurate forecast of what some modern artists, especially Cézanne and his followers, have attempted, gives less specific attention to the broadest questions of idealism versus observation, theory versus practice, and meditation versus production.

Theobald, like Claude (and of course like Frenhofer, though more vocally), is a monomaniac, a perfectionist, and a fiercely uncompromising idealist, and, again like his French cousin, is capable of the greatest self-deception in his search for perfection.[36] Perhaps, as in Claude's case, it is partly this blinding idealism (Zola calls it Romanticism, but they are talking of the same tendency) that makes it impossible for Theobald to carry out the artist's normal functions of observation and production. At any rate Theobald is conscious at the end of the story that he is incomplete and paralyzed and puts into words the awful thoughts that must have passed through Claude's mind before he hanged himself, thoughts of great conceptions and imperfect realizations, thoughts of time and effort wasted in preparing to work and not in working, despairing thoughts of a paralyzed hand and of a wasted life. The whole long speech sounds like nothing so much as a blueprint for Claude's life and death. And could it be that H.'s words of advice to Theobald before he has discovered his terrible error lay as a distant source in Zola's mind when he formed the figure of Sandoz and gave him his role as steady worker and faithful producer? The possibility is certainly not too remote. And it is not impossible that Zola duplicated, consciously or unconsciously, the relationship between Theobald, the "eye," the "brain," and Serafina's lover, the "hand," when he contrived the figure of the slick and successful Fagerolles as contrast to the dreaming Claude.

Another American work—this one by Poe—that may also have given Zola important ideas for his novel is the short sketch, "The Oval Portrait," which Baudelaire translated as "Le Portrait ovale" in his *Nouvelles histoires extraordinaires.* The story is, briefly, that a poet, visiting a lonely and deserted chateau, sees a curiously vital portrait of a young woman with an expression so completely rendered as to be absolutely adequate to life itself. The young girl had married an austere, passionate, studious painter who had already found a spouse in his painting; she had gradually come to hate art, her rival, with a hatred so bitter that it soon filled her life. She came to fear the palette and brush, to detest hearing her husband speak of art, but so great was her love that she patiently posed for him day after day as the portrait advanced toward completion. His passion for his art was so absorbing that he could not see that the light falling in the tower where he painted was sapping the health and the spirits of his wife, who lived for nothing but him.[37] When at last the portrait is finished, the painter, not seeing that its colors were drawn from the very lifeblood of the girl, gives the final touch and then, in a moment of fearful realization, cries out that he has created life itself![38] It may have been here, and not in Balzac or in Goncourt, that Zola first found the idea of the struggle between art and love and here also that he may have come upon the notion of the painter's fatal attempt to render life itself in oil and canvas and of his "draining" of his beloved's life to give vitality to the work of art. But a creator of Zola's experience and an observer of his skill had no need to look to Poe or Baudelaire for the primary thematic elements of his novel—he must have drawn these from himself, from his long career in the world of letters, and from the pessimistic and not always compassionate view he had formed of the men he saw around him.

The only other major possibility of a source for *L'Oeuvre* is the Goncourt brothers' *Manette Salomon* of 1867. Professor Bowie, in *The Painter in French Fiction*, has noted a long series of what might be called "synthetic" similarities between the two novels, that is, resemblances of structure and conception, that may be the products of the same way of thinking and looking at the world, the same manner of conceiving the novel, rather than of direct imitation on Zola's part. He points out that of all the works that compose the literary tradition of the painter in fiction in the nineteenth and twentieth centuries (he lists more than forty novels and short stories), only *Manette Salomon* and *L'Oeuvre* contain all of the stock devices which give the works of this tradition their common character. These are, briefly, an account of the painter's early days and training in art school; a description of his milieu, embracing his studio, points of contact with nature (an open-air studio or the motif he chooses, such as Fontainebleau or Paris) and points of contact with other artists, such as cafes; the notation of shop talk with painters, models, and dealers; long discussions of aesthetic and technical questions, presented by an artist or by the author's spokesman; criticism of the academic tradition and "official" art; accounts of exhibitions and Salons and the operation of the jury system; the introduction of literary figures as foils to the painter; involvement of the artist in sentimental complications, the rivalry of woman and art; the introduction of actual painters, either under their own names or in transparent disguise, to serve the ends of the plot and also to provide verisimilitude, and their use as elements of composite portraits.[39] This is a considerable list of general similarities, and even though it does not prove a direct filiation, it does establish a remarkable likeness of conception between the two novels. But Bowie has more to add, notably that Claude passes through almost exactly the same phases of development as the Goncourts' unfortunate hero, Naz de Coriolis, moving from the study of wild nature to the revelation of Paris, with its modern and "human" quality;[40] that Zola, like the Goncourts, lays heavy stress on Claude's personality as the key to his painting;[41] that both Zola and the Goncourts are much interested in dramatizing situations and exploiting their emotional content and that consequently they are more concerned with the emotional nature of their heroes than with their intellectual ability, to the point, indeed, where both condemn the artist philosopher;[42] and that both Lantier and Coriolis are self-doubters who come eventually to suffer from a kind of paralysis.[43]

One of Bowie's most interesting points is that Zola quite clearly adapted the Goncourts' "quasi-medical" definition of genius to his own "pseudo-scientific" treatment of the principle of heredity. He points out that not only does Claude have all the qualities of a genius, he is highly conscious of having them, and this consciousness keeps him steadfast amid the most discouraging conditions of poverty, bad luck, and lack of recognition. He is of very tough fiber and resists all his trials manfully until, like Coriolis, he ventures into experiments with light and color, and at this point he begins to lose self-control and to reveal symptoms of a kind of madness. His intellectual interest becomes a physical obsession, which in turn degenerates into a disease or madness of the eye, which finally affects his mind.[44] Is this really true, or does Claude's innate flaw drive him to these experiments? It is heredity which leads him into the error of his final years. It would seem that he errs because he is a born failure, not that his error drives him to failure, for it is fate, genes, that destroy Claude, not his technical searches, which at most are evidences of his madness. But at all events it is this search for constantly more vivid color which provides the only important outward similarity in *Manette Salomon* and *L'Oeuvre;* a brilliant passage in *Manette Salomon,* in which Coriolis' growing mania is described, may well have inspired Zola in the final descriptions of Lantier's great painting, where he covers his nude with jewels and gold, pure yellows and reds, and where he reveals the final destruction of his sense of reality.[45]

Coriolis visits mineralogical displays, seeks out chemicals, dreams of rediscovering the famous *amatito*, the lost color of the Renaissance, the true Roman purple; he collects strange shades of blue, green, gold, yellow, passes from minerals to seashells, seeks out all the changing shades of the sea and its products, and finally comes to believe that to paint at all he needs all that gleams, all that burns in heaven, earth, and sea.[46]

It is difficult to find any other elements of *Manette Salomon* which might have served Zola directly. And while it is true that the resemblances observed by Bowie are important ones, resemblances of basic conception, for instance, and of outlook and structure, they merely demonstrate again that Zola learned something of his technique from his older colleagues, and they certainly do not bear on the immediate conception of the novel's plot, details, or characters.

As demonstrated by Robert Ricatte,[47] the role of anecdote is more extensive in *Manette Salomon* than in Zola's novel, and the atmosphere of the two works is very different. Lantier's *bohème*, for instance, is certainly a step down and a step or two to the left of the one frequented by Coriolis. The essentially tragic tone of Zola's work is far removed from the Goncourts', which is ironic, and there is far more drama in Zola's narrative. What is more, the central idea of the two books is completely different: *Manette Salomon* is a combination of a novel of ideas and an anti-Semitic tract, written obviously to give the brothers' ideas concerning the art of their own time and the art of the future,[48] and to demonstrate their belief that women and art do not mix; as a consequence of the latter notion and their anti-Semitism, their painter is destroyed by a Jewess, while Zola makes woman impotent in the face of the challenge of art.

It is true also, as François Fosca points out, that the Goncourts' work seems more knowledgeable, professionally, than Zola's, written more from the inside of the artistic world and perhaps more accurate as a document than *L'Oeuvre*. The Goncourt brothers, he points out, were themselves artists and had lived among artists, whereas Zola had to brief himself about art as he had about mining, and his book reveals that the documentation was essentially external to the novel.[49] His argument, on the whole, is not without merit, though it contains a serious injustice to Zola, who understood more than a little of the nature of painting, as his marvelous record of rightness in selecting the enduring art of his time from the vast mass of dross surrounding it amply testifies. Nor was he completely devoid of firsthand knowledge of the studios, for his first decade in Paris was spent, as Fosca must have known, with Manet, Fantin-Latour, Cézanne, and others of the artistic world. Yet Fosca is right in his main contention: by 1885-86 Zola was no longer in direct contact with the painters—save Cézanne—with whom he had spent his youth and *L'Oeuvre* certainly betrays the fact that the details of *métier* which appear so frequently are by now only documentation and not living experience.[50]

Another novel of the Goncourt brothers, although it deals with a writer and not a painter and consequently does not figure in the tradition properly speaking, may also have contributed certain ideas to the formation of *L'Oeuvre*. This is *Les Hommes de lettres*, better known as *Charles Demailly* (1860). Like *Manette Salomon, Les Hommes de lettres* concerns the destruction of a talent by an unscrupulous and unfeeling woman, and hence has a different intention from *L'Oeuvre*, but it does contain some passages which may have given Zola an idea or two for his discussion of the rivalry of woman and art. In *L'Oeuvre,* one of the chief reasons for Christine's ultimate unhappiness with Claude is his persistence in refusing to regard her, after the first years at Bennecourt, as a real woman, and in looking upon her as a beautiful object devoid of human sensibilities, a fascinating assemblage of lines, planes, and tones. Toward the end of his life he carries this tendency so far that he ceases all conjugal relations with Christine and reduces her quite simply to the status of unpaid model. This conduct, according to Zola, is explained, if not justified, by the special passion of artists like Claude, who remain artists always, in all the situations of life, and never become men like other men. The same idea is expressed in *Les Hommes de lettres,*[51] which also contains a great many reflections on the jealousy woman naturally feels for art as it steals her lover from her, or tries to, but none of this seems particularly close to any specific passage of *L'Oeuvre.*

It is true, of course, that Zola may have been impressed by these discussions in his predecessors' two novels and may have decided to show the reverse face of the medal, the victory of art over woman, as a kind of answer to them, and in this case the influence would be real, though pervasive rather than immediate. But there is a passage in *Les Hommes de lettres* that seems very much like an advance sketch of Claude's indifference to his child and his complete inability to play the role of father. Charles Demailly declares to a friend that marriage is forbidden to artists, and when his friend asks him why, he answers that artists are men outside the social law and the conjugal role—their books are their children.[52] There is only one more detail in *Les Hommes de lettres* which seemingly could have served Zola: one of its characters, a member of the staff of *Le Scandale* and a thoroughgoing hypocrite, is called "le père Malgras." It may have been from him that Zola took the name of his art dealer,[53] who, according to Zola's notes, was a composite of Martin and Aubourg, two comparatively well-known dealers of the 1860's and 1870's.

Among the other works which formed the tradition of the painter in literature before *L'Oeuvre,* no other can be said to be a really major source, though it is possible that one or more provided Zola with important ideas for individual passages of his work. Chief among these is the novel *Grave imprudence,* by his friend the art critic Philippe Burty, a former frequenter of the Café Guerbois and an early supporter of the Impressionists. *Grave imprudence,* constructed around the artist Brissot, chief of a movement which closely resembles Impressionism and obviously a composite of Manet, Monet, and others, first appeared in *La Nouvelle revue* in 1880[54] and then was published by Charpentier in the same year. It is a somewhat rambling novel of artistic life and high society, the kind of piece which would appeal to the readers of *La Nouvelle revue* and hence about as different in tone from *L'Oeuvre* as a novel can be, but nevertheless it contains elements that seem to announce Zola's work.

There is, for example, Brissot's vision of the Seine and the Ile de la Cité from the Pont d'Austerlitz, which is something like Claude's obsessive vision as he faces the Ile. Zola may have been impressed with Burty's rendition of the Ile as a prow and he may have taken from it the original idea for Claude's great unfinished painting. There is also the evident attempt to make a painting of the scene and to render it in Impressionistic terms (exactly as Zola does in *L'Oeuvre* and even more so in the notes he used in its composition), the same emphasis on clouds, smoke, the bridges and the traffic on them, the fleeting vision of the Left Bank, the view of Paris in its specifically modern aspects, and the vision of the city as the symbolic city, the "Ville suprême."[55] Curiously, this view prompts Brissot to the same kind of frantic efforts as Claude's in the last half of *L'Oeuvre,* efforts ending in the same kind of failures,[56] but finally, happier than Claude, he discovers the technical means of rendering what he wishes, and when he does so it is the Impressionistic technique full blown. But he often does act like Claude: the same point of view, the same attempts to sketch on the spot and complete in the studio, the same fruitless efforts, the same spoiled canvases, the same stubbornness, and the same sense of urgency. But where Burty made of these things a paragraph, Zola made of them half a novel.

Moreover, *Grave imprudence* shows the painter passing through the same evolution as Claude, from landscapes to Parisian scenes, becoming a convinced modernist who seeks out workmen in their shops to observe their movements and attitudes; he goes so far in his modernism as to paint a socialistic "Mineurs" and a highly original "Gare de chemin de fer." And there are one or two other resemblances with *L'Oeuvre,* for example, Brissot's desire to paint a nude in the open air, "a healthy and spontaneous woman," a new Giorgione, even as Claude does in his first important painting; and his inspiration to paint a picture of a nude woman in a small boat approaching a French warship in a Japanese harbor. The latter is a little far from the conception Claude has of his last nude, but it is possible, nevertheless, that Burty's scene impressed Zola, who could have taken its central idea and transposed it into modern, Parisian terms.

Two or three other novels offer possibilities of sources for

L'Oeuvre, details or scenes or broad conceptions that Zola may have made his own as he composed his work on the world of art. One of them is *La Femme d'Henri Vanneau* (1884), by Zola's disciple, Édouard Rod.

La Femme d'Henri Vanneau is a reworking of a short story of Rod's, "La Nuit vendue," which appeared in 1880 in *Les Allemands à Paris,* and it is possible that the short story could also have been a source for *L'Oeuvre.* The two works by Rod share the same plot, more or less, and neither is really close to *L'Oeuvre* in this respect, but both of them contain details which are like some details of Zola's novel. The essential story line of both "La Nuit vendue" and *La Femme d'Henri Vanneau* is provided by the struggles of an artist to break from an academic style in order to attain modernism, his gradual realization that he cannot completely uproot his early habits, his attempt to become a kind of naturalist-symbolist and his eventual madness and death, after long efforts at a single canvas; but the story is developed somewhat differently in the two works. The painter of "La Nuit vendue," Maurice Wehland, a dreamer come to Paris from Munich, begins his career as a painter of religious subjects, then changes to mythology, in the mid-nineteenth century manner, but finds that his Venuses show a distressing resemblance to the madonnas of his first period. Gradually, he loses his religious convictions and in spite of the solid success which his inoffensive paintings have brought him, determines to become a modernist and so evolves a philosophy of modernist painting, stressing "truth" and seriousness, which often resembles the philosophy of Claude and Sandoz in *L'Oeuvre.*[57] Little by little, Maurice evolves toward the Impressionist position, although he had always criticized the Impressionists; he is attracted particularly by their modernism, their desire to "see" their own times and under their influence he determines to depict modern society in all its multiple forms, its beauties and its uglinesses. So he is compelled to break with his past, to seek truth, and it is clear that his intention is as naturalistic as Claude's, for what he wishes to depict is the "immense field of reality," from which nothing can be excluded by the artist who wishes his work to live, breathe, and speak.

Maurice's wife reproaches him for his new manner (Christine is not convinced that Claude's way is the best, either), saying that he now paints like Courbet and Manet, but to him this is high praise, for these men saw clearly and rendered their own time. Like them he rejects the classic ideal of an absolute beauty in favor of another ideal, more modern, closer to man, the beauty of life itself, and from here he is led to a philosophy of art which neither Claude nor Sandoz would reject, the belief that the artist must above all create, that he must snatch from the gods the secret of life. In his passion for modernism, Maurice turns against the very bourgeoisie which had given him his early success and condemns it in terms which recall Sandoz' words at the first Salon, pointing out that "good" people have opposed every reform, every attempt at change in art and that when today's revolutionaries have been accepted, the very people who most condemn them now will be their defenders against tomorrow's innovators. Finally, Maurice arrives at the conception of the painting, "La Nuit vendue," which will be a symbolic depiction of vice in modern society. But soon he finds, like Claude, that the conception is too difficult for him: he is not truly a naturalist, any more than Claude is, and his dreamy, generalizing tendencies make it impossible for him, in spite of protracted efforts, to bring the canvas to completion. And like Claude he finds that he is a victim of a kind of automatism that keeps bringing him back to the same techniques, the same results. Like Claude again, Maurice drifts away from his wife as his struggles with the painting intensify, and at last he devotes himself entirely to his work in a way which recalls Claude's fierce attempts to complete the "Apotheosis of Paris," and finally he goes mad under the pressure of his failure and in his madness dreams that he is called to revive modern art. But at last he dies with his painting looking down at him, the painting that had absorbed all his spirit and all his strength. He dies before the phantoms of his imagination, the only beings to whom he could give the life of which he dreamed.

With many of the same essentials, *La Femme d'Henri Vanneau* is quite a different work, but one which also could have contributed to Zola's conception of *L'Oeuvre.* The painter, transformed from a German dreamer into a French provincial, displays an early passion for art, which his father opposes unsuccessfully, for at last Henri comes to Paris to make his name. Too timid and too afraid of women to work in a studio, he begins by copying at the Louvre and eventually meets a girl, Marguerite, who becomes his ideal woman. An inheritance leaves him free to paint as he wishes, and like his predecessor Maurice he begins by painting madonnas, to whose faces the same automatism brings the same expression. He marries Marguerite, who like Christine Hallegrain is lacking in artistic intelligence, and a daughter is born to them who recalls the poor little Jacques of *L'Oeuvre;* like Claude, Henri is incapable of loving the child and she soon dies. And like Claude again, he is a victim of the indifference of the crowd at the Salon, where his "Sainte Élisabeth" is ignored in favor of a painting by Vollon. This failure convinces him that he must become a modernist, so he sets out to discover a "motif" which will permit him to synthesize his ideas in symbolic form, and he spends much time describing the details of the projected canvas, just as Claude spends many hours discussing the details of the "Apotheosis" with Christine. Then he begins work and immediately encounters terrible difficulties—his struggles recall Claude's in their duration and intensity. But gradually doubt grows within him and paralyzes him until at last he goes insane. But still he continues working in the belief that the canvas is almost finished, though only big spots of crude color, such as a child would make, cover the canvas. Finally, lost in madness, he dies.[58]

There is no evidence that Zola knew either of these works of Rod's, though it is certainly possible, even probable that he did, given the close relationship between the two writers at the time. But at all events it is undeniable that they bear a certain likeness to *L'Oeuvre*, so good a likeness indeed that some pages of that novel sound a great deal like reminiscences, and not so distant reminiscences either.

Another possibility is Joris-Karl Huysmans' *En Ménage*, which appeared in 1881 and which Zola almost certainly knew.[59] *En Ménage* is a somewhat desultory novel, mostly concerned with the private life of one Cyprien Tibaille, a painter in search of a little peace and comfort at home; its plot has nothing to do with that of *L'Oeuvre*, few details could be said to show even the slightest resemblance to Zola's novel, and its characters are as far from Zola's as it is possible to imagine. But occasionally certain themes show some similarity to the themes of *L'Oeuvre*, and it is not impossible that they provided the point of departure for one or two of Zola's ideological developments. One of these is the theme of modernism, so much stressed in *L'Oeuvre*. Cyprien, in the course of long disquisitions on Paris, expresses ambitions and desires that are not far from Claude's as the latter contemplates modern Paris; but where Cyprien seems really to be a kind of distant model for Zola's artist is in the explanation he gives of modern painters' inability to be themselves, to see modern life clearly for what it is, a great source of serious art.[60] And like Sandoz, he complains of the terrible effects of what he calls the "gangrene of romanticism," which makes it so difficult for today's artists to seize the beauty of the modern world. Was Huysmans the master's master here? Or was his Cyprien simply expressing a commonplace of Zola's group, did the two authors arrive at the same conclusion from the observation of the same circumstances, from the application of the same principles, from the same point of view on their time and from the same theory of art evolution? There is, of course, no answer here, but it is not at all impossible that the more original Huysmans gave his mentor food for thought by having his Cyprien discourse on the failure of modern painting to find its true path.

Another possible source, though it is far from certain that Zola had even heard of the book, much less read it, is *Le Quartier Pigalle* (1883), by Georges Duval, whose pen name was Harry Allis. This third-rate novel, a kind of continuation *en noir* of Mürger's *Scènes de la vie de bohème,* is a bitter satire of the world of art, letters, and journalism, with heavy stress on the terrible rivalries between cliques of artists, the "politics" of art, venal journalism, and the machinations and combinations of those who wished to succeed in the Paris of the 1870's and 1880's. As a picture of the underside of the world of creators and intellectuals of the time, *Le Quartier Pigalle*[61] has a certain documentary interest—it has some scenes from typical cafes of the period, the Chat Noir and the Nouvelle Athènes, it contains some portraits of living people, Maurice Rollinat and Rodolphe Salis, for instance, and offers a full-length view of the famous Nina de Villars, whom Zola called on more than once for elements of his "destroying" women—but the looseness of its structure, the lack of recognizable truth in the characters' psychology, and the exaggeration of its tone considerably obscure its serious intentions and blunt its point.

The essential subject of *Le Quartier Pigalle* (and there are several subjects) is the rivalry between two artists, Marius Valard and Théophile Lasarus. Valard resembles the Fagerolles of *L'Oeuvre* (and indeed it is possible that Zola found the latter's name in Duval's novel, for the musician Fragerolles appears in its pages); like Fagerolles, Valard attains a brief notoriety in spite of his lack of talent, using every device of corrupt journalism, politics, and female influence in his climb to fame; like Fagerolles he has an elegant studio on the Avenue de Villiers, and, like him again, he finds himself caught in a liaison with one of the well-known demimondaines of the time. On the whole the portrait Duval gives of him—and it is to be supposed that he is something of a composite portrait, like Fagerolles, representative of a broad tendency of the art world then—is rather effective, with its discussion of the devices such a man could and would use to succeed.

In sharp contrast to him is the figure of Lasarus, the "Claude" of *Le Quartier Pigalle.* Lasarus is not only poor and unsuccessful, he is solitary and defenseless in the savage world he inhabits, just as Claude is, incapable of the compromises and machinations that are the surest way to popular reputation. A man of unrecognized genius, a truly original talent, he lives in poverty and dignity, the complete antithesis of the corrupt and conscienceless Valard. In his innocence Lasarus makes the error of sending to the Salon a painting which attracts the attention of one critic and which promises to be the beginning of true fame for him and so provokes the jealousy of Valard and his "little band" (which somewhat resembles the one in *L'Oeuvre,* being composed of a painter, a sculptor, a journalist, and a writer) that they destroy his reputation and eventually do him to death by means of a duel. Significantly, it is only after his death that Lasarus gains any recognition and exerts any influence, and he does so—as Claude does—through the very painters who "pillaged" his work. Lasarus has another similarity to Claude: he is a doubter. As he prepares to send his "Vue de Loisy" to the Salon he is seized by such scruples that at the last minute he almost withdraws from the competition. But send it he does, and the Salon scenes that ensue are not far different from the Salon scenes of *L'Oeuvre.* First, there is a kind of overall view, resembling the ones given in chapters V and X of Zola's novel, including the same emphasis on the physiognomy of the crowd, the protests of the artists at their location on the walls of the Salon, snatches of conversation, portraits of individual types, the social success of the artist *en vue;* then, and, more significantly, the contrast between Valard's success with the crowd and Lasarus' almost complete anonymity. His "Vue de Loisy" is exactly the same kind of failure as Claude's "L'Enfant mort," and he expresses the same chagrin as Claude as he sees his inferior win the applause of the crowd and the recognition of the critics. And to complete the similarities the merit of Lasarus' painting is recognized by his rival, even as Fagerolles recognizes the merit of "Plein-Air" while the crowd mocks it.

All this recalls so well the situation and events of the Salon scenes of *L'Oeuvre* that the idea is inescapable that Zola must have seen *Le Quartier Pigalle* at some time before he composed his own work on the art world.

But these scenes are not all. *Le Quartier Pigalle* is full of the same kind of protest at official domination of art and letters as can be found on a score of pages of *L'Oeuvre,* the relationship between Marie des Seigles and Lasarus strongly resembles the relationship between Claude and Christine (she is his model and mistress), and *Le Quartier Pigalle* ends with the funeral of the artist, as *L'Oeuvre* does, so it is evident that a fair case for influence can be made. But there is no certainty here at all, no evidence that Zola knew Duval's work or that he imitated any part of it if he did know it. It may well be that the resemblances, striking as some of them are, were the products of a similar view of similar circumstances, no more. But it is intriguing to think of a Zola being in the debt of a Georges Duval, all the same.

Another novel, one which Zola unquestionably knew, since he had praised it in *L'Événement* for June 29, 1866, may have furnished some ideas and scenes for *L'Oeuvre*. The novel is Alexandre Dumas *fils*'s *Affaire Clémenceau*,[62] a partly autobiographical study of the art world and not a bad performance of an old-fashioned kind. The subject of the book has little to do with *L'Oeuvre*, for it deals with the murder by a sculptor, Pierre Clémenceau, of his wife and model, Iza, a good rendition of the familiar literary type of the heartless woman infatuated with her own beauty and completely inaccessible to the appeals of love or loyalty. Pierre Clémenceau has not much in common with Claude Lantier, since he is a successful sculptor and quite worldly, but he does resemble him in his adoration of living flesh and in a complete lack of paternal feeling—he is devoted solely to his art and to Iza—and his relationship with an older sculptor may have given Zola some ideas for the almost filial affection which Lantier feels for Bongrand. And Iza is by no means Christine, she is far too self-centered and vain for that, but throughout the novel she is Pierre's model, his only model after he encounters her, and like Christine she is absolutely devoid of any maternal instinct. It is true that Dumas motivates this lack of feeling in her by fear that child-bearing will ruin her beauty, while Christine's inability to love her son is produced by her overwhelming passion for her husband, but the result is nearly the same in both novels. It is possible also that Zola may have recalled from his distant reading of *Affaire Clémenceau* the attitude of the sculptor toward his model, one dominated almost wholly by aesthetic considerations, which keep him from regarding her, as she poses, as anything more than a beautiful object. But if it is true that Zola did remember this detail from his early reading, he dramatized the attitude considerably more than Dumas did and made of it the basis of one of the best scenes of the novel, the scene in which Claude calmly tells Christine how age and time have damaged her beauty. It is also possible, though perhaps not likely, that the excellent early scene in *L'Oeuvre* where Claude sketches the head of the sleeping Christine had its origins in a somewhat similar scene in *Affaire Clémenceau*, where the young sculptor makes a drawing of the sleeping Iza. The circumstances are a good deal different, but memory may have prompted Zola here to one of his most successful pages. The same may be true of still another little scene, the one in which the young Christine deliberately decides to pose nude for Claude when he reaches the point of desperation in the composition of "Plein-Air." It is quite clear that Christine does so partly out of jealousy of other possible models, partly out of love for Claude, while Iza offers herself to Pierre Clémenceau out of vanity and a desire to see herself immortalized in stone, though the element of a kind of jealousy or possessiveness also enters here; but the fact remains that it is the young woman who takes the initiative, not the artist, and so the two small scenes have somewhat similar psychological consequences.

In spite of the close resemblances the probabilities are that it was not in *Affaire Clémenceau* that Zola found the inspiration for this scene, if he found it anywhere but in his own imagination. If he did not create it himself out of whole cloth, it seems much more probable that he borrowed the central idea and some of the details from the work of one of his own disciples, George Moore. In 1883, Moore published a long, rambling—and not very good—novel which he called *A Modern Lover.* That Zola knew of the existence of this work is beyond doubt, for on September 17, 1883, Moore wrote him about the novel's success and told him he would be in Paris the following spring.[63] It is not certain, of course, that Zola knew what the book contained, for he did not read English well enough to handle a difficult text, but there is at least a good possibility that he did know something of its contents, for he and Moore were old friends by 1885—their acquaintance dated from the Bal de l'Assommoir, where Manet introduced them—and Moore may well have read parts of the book to him when he saw him in 1884 at Médan.

At all events, *A Modern Lover* has as its central figure a certain Lewis Seymour (modeled in part on Moore's Parisian friend Lewis Weldon Hawkins), a young provincial artist who is starving in London as he seeks fame and fortune and who shows signs of becoming an Impressionist. At the opening of the book Lewis is down to his last shilling, for in London he has met only failure and oblivion; he is overcome with melancholy and is contemplating suicide. But in the nick of time he recalls that a young working girl who lives in his apartment building, Gwynnie Lloyd, is about to be paid, and he imagines that she will surely help him in his distress. As it happens, Gwynnie is in love with Lewis—but he is not in love with her—and she is about to agree to lend him the money he needs when their conversation is interrupted by a messenger who tells Lewis that he has been given a commission to finish some decorative panels for a dealer, who had given his pledge that they would be ready by a given date and who now finds that he cannot keep his promise because of the illness of the artist on whom he had counted. The messenger refuses to give Lewis any advance on the three pounds which the panels will bring, so Lewis tries to complete the panels without a model, by copying some of his old academic studies. He tries to fit the legs of one study to the torso of another and to patch up the panels so that they will be acceptable to the prospective buyer (Claude Lantier does much the same thing as he works at "Plein-Air," using several models simultaneously in a vain effort to achieve the effect he wants), but he soon discovers that the method will not work. Try as he will, he cannot make the figure come out right and as the light fades, he realizes that the panel is becoming steadily worse. Finally, bitterly disappointed, he scrapes the panel clean and is on the point of giving up the whole project. But then again he remembers Gwynnie and her paycheck and determines to ask her for the money to hire a model. But alas! some heartless thief has picked her pocket and she has nothing left.

Lewis then begs her to pose, but her strict Methodist training exerts its force and she refuses again and again, even in the face of his threats of suicide, his fears of starvation, and his promises for the future. But at last he overcomes her resistance and she consents.[64] Zola's handling of the theme is far better than Moore's, but the circumstances surrounding the central idea of the pose—the artist's desperation, the last-minute nature of the affair, the modesty of the model—are so similar that they surely suggest more than coincidence. And once again, it is amusing to think of Zola in debt to Moore.[65]

It is not impossible that "L'Atelier," one of Edmond Duranty's short stories in *Le Pays des arts,* gave Zola the idea of introducing technical terms into his novel, descriptions of brushes, knives, the processes of painting and sculpture, and so on, for Duranty's story is not much more than a catalogue-description of a studio. But it seems more probable that Zola decided on the incorporation of such material as a perfectly normal bit of local color and needed no inspiration here.

Again, it may be that he took the basic idea of his suicide scene from Baudelaire's vivid prose poem, "La Corde," which appeared in both *Le Figaro* and *L'Artiste* in 1864 and again in *L'Événement,* for which Zola was then writing a regular series of book reviews, in 1866. "La Corde" is a very short description of the suicide of a boy (it is said that his model was one of Manet's *rapins,* who had posed for the famous "Enfant aux cerises"), with strong emphasis on the picturesque and horrible elements. But once more, Zola, at this point of his career, hardly needed anyone else's inspiration for the creation of scenes of great emotional impact, and while it is probable that he knew of Baudelaire's piece, or had known of it at one time, there is no necessity to find a source in it. The same is true of *L'Éducation sentimentale,* where, toward the end, Rosanette has Frédéric call in the painter Pellerin to capture a last view of her son. But in addition to the fact that Zola might have found this same idea in Henry James's "Madonna of the Future," it is also possible that the scene, as he gives it, is a transposition of an event from the life of Claude Monet,[66] or a literary treatment of a painting Zola may have seen. So while Flaubert's work might have provided Zola with the model of this little scene, there is no certainty that it did.[67]

The only other significant detail which Zola may have borrowed from another author is provided by the figure of the art dealer, Malgras, who, according to Charles Beuchat, while taking his name from *Charles Demailly,* as noted above, was actually based on père Samuel of Champfleury's *Chien-Caillou.*[68] But while it is true that Malgras resembles Samuel (both bring the artist articles of food for his still lifes and leave them with him as part payment for the pictures they extort from him) the probabilities are that Zola based his portrait on the dealer Aubourg. In the notes for *L'Oeuvre* Zola mentions Aubourg as engaging in this very practice.[69]

In all these possible sources Zola obviously had material from which he could draw, and it is probable that the major concepts of the novel were influenced by one or more of his predecessors. Yet *L'Oeuvre* is far from a mere copy of any of the works discussed, and it is not a mosaic of other men's inventions. Whatever Zola's debt to those who went before him, the treatment of any material he may have borrowed is surely his own, for the Zola signature is on every page. It is his own "temperament," as he said of Manet, that gives the novel its tone, its meaning and its originality.

II

The Secondary Figures

In the structure of *L'Oeuvre,* there are four major elements: the struggle of Claude Lantier to achieve self-fulfillment; the rivalry of his wife, Christine, with the "demon of art" for Claude's love; a summary history of the artistic "moment" of the 1860's and 1870's; and a study of the constitution and ultimate breakup of an artistic school. The first of these, partly fictional, partly autobiographical, and partly based on some painter or painters Zola had known, is the most important of these elements and so deserves separate treatment. The second, possibly fictional but perhaps deriving from the literary tradition or from some case observed by Zola or indeed from his own experiences,[1] is scarcely amenable to the processes of literary research, for it offers little in the nature of a "document" and gives almost no clués to its origins in its creator's mind. The third, the little history of the artistic movement of Zola's time, anecdotal and incomplete and containing some distortions of chronology, is unquestionably the product of the notes given him by his friends of the literary and artistic worlds, together with his own firsthand observations. The last is certainly based on events and people Zola himself had known, though like the others it also contains a large measure of fictional embellishment. This chapter will be devoted to a discussion of the last element and will be an attempt to measure with some exactness the scope of the biographical elements of the book and to assay its "real life" content, excluding for the time being the complex question of the origins of Claude Lantier and Pierre Sandoz.

L'Oeuvre opens on a stormy July night in 1862 and closes on a bleak November in the late 1870's. It is not easy to fix the terminal date exactly, for references to the lapse of time are not always specific, but Zola causes Claude's son, born in February 1864, to die at the age of twelve, slightly more than six months before his father's suicide, thus making the final year 1876.[2] That the action goes so far beyond 1870 points up the rather slim connection of the novel with the series as a whole. Of the two-dozen or so people who appear in *L'Oeuvre,* only Claude Lantier figures in any other novel of Zola's and the whole tone and character of the work are essentially different from the rest of the works which recount the history of the Rougons and the Macquarts.

Because this is so and because the novel does not fit into the set chronology of the series but perhaps most of all because of certain pronouncements of Zola's, the idea has steadily grown that *L'Oeuvre,* far from being a work of pure fiction, is in reality a *roman à clef,* a more or less malicious caricature of certain persons whom Zola knew well and with whom he was still on a basis of intimacy when he wrote the book.

The first hint that *L'Oeuvre* was to contain personages based on real people came from Zola himself, though indirectly, through the medium of Paul Alexis' *Émile Zola, notes d'un ami* (1882); Alexis flatly declared that Zola would call on his friends as models.[3] Immediately after the novel appeared Zola gave implicit confirmation to Alexis' "inspired" prophecy when he declared to Maurice Français, who was interviewing him for *Le Voltaire,* that "the failures I have known would have been failures even without the women they had with them."[4] The context in which this phrase was spoken made it apparent to every reader that the creator of Naturalism was admitting that his book contained real—and harsh—portraits, and ever since these words were uttered his critics have made a game of discovering who his models were and how he employed them.

These researches have led to a quite general agreement that the characters of the novel had living, real people as their origins, but at the same time two widely different views have emerged: the first, held by about half the critics who have touched on the question, is that the characters of the novel are either composite portraits or almost complete transformations or transpositions of reality; the other, sometimes expressed with a certain heat, is that Zola directly and consciously put into the work real portraits of real people and did not bother with such fancy work as transposing or combining.

The first group of critics echoes in more or less detailed form the statement made in 1924 by Emile Solari, Zola's godson, that even if Zola called on the comrades of his youth for physical and moral traits, not one of his characters is a complete reconstitution.[5]

But this eminently moderate view, which has much more than just moderation to recommend it, is not by any means held by all the historians of *L'Oeuvre.* Many commentators believe that the book contains real portraits, and some argue that these portraits prove that Zola thought his friends failures. The most exaggerated version of the "direct" thesis is that of Fernand Doucet, who apparently thought that each of the major figures was exactly copied from life and who declared flatly that *L'Oeuvre* was a real key novel.[6] The most modest exponents of the same general theory are Joachim Gasquet, Cézanne's friend, who believed that in the first part of the novel the figures were modeled directly on living persons but that in the last part their evolution was purely a product of Zola's imagination,[7] and Maurice LeBlond, Zola's son-in-law, who found that the people of *L'Oeuvre* were indeed exact imitations of living beings, but were all subjected in the novel to circumstances markedly different from the real-life situations their prototypes had known, and thus were radically changed.[7a] All these variations of the same original opinion have some justification, and enough evidence can be adduced in support of any of them to render very difficult the task of coming to a single satisfactory conclusion with respect to Zola's general method of drawing characters in this particular novel.

The problem is made more difficult by the fact that, with one or two exceptions, we do not know very much about any of Zola's early intimates, the ones on whom he must have called if he wished to write a real key novel dealing with the first half of his own career. The Aix group is almost completely unknown, except for Cézanne (and how much of even his biography remains in the realm of speculation and conjecture!) and it is very nearly impossible to discover anything solid and informative about such men as Anthony Valabrègue, Baptistin Baille, or even Paul Alexis. Of the other groups that Zola might have used for his model, one, the famous "groupe de Médan," did not apparently provide much material for *L'Oeuvre*, at least if the *Dossier* is a good guide; if it had, researches into the nature and origins of the novel would have been a great deal easier than they are. The other, the "groupe des Batignolles," certainly must have given him anecdotes and situations and personalities, but it is very difficult to estimate how far he went in using this material. And how much do we know of the private lives and personalities of the men of this group? To top off the difficulty posed by the comparative obscurity of most of Zola's friends among the litterateurs and the painters, we have no idea of Zola's private opinion of the men who were his intimates. What do we really know of what he thought of Alexis or Chaillan, of Monet or even of Cézanne? There are few telling references in his correspondence, no diary, no journal, no memoirs to help us discover his opinion of any of these old friends. It is for such reasons as this that any serious attempt to seek out the originals for the characters of the novel seems almost completely vain.

But it is not wholly vain, for the immensely detailed *Dossier* of sketches, plans, and notes which accompanies the manuscript of *L'Oeuvre* gives clues and leads of many kinds, and the novel itself contains enough hints to permit one or two fairly certain identifications and some guesses that may be—but are not demonstrably—exact.

The *Ébauche*, the very earliest form of the novel, its primordial form, so to speak, makes it clear that at least at the beginning Zola had in mind four principal living models, in addition to himself and Cézanne and Manet: Antony Valabrègue, Baptistin Baille, Paul Alexis, and Henri Gervex, that is, three members of the Aix group and one man he had come to know during his Batignolles days. Of these, Valabrègue and Gervex were apparently "basic" figures, that is, were essential to Zola's conception of what his novel should be. Gervex, who like Valabrègue appears very early in the *Ébauche*, was evidently chosen to represent one side of the fundamental contrast the novel was to set forth, between the true artist and the copier, the genius and the success hunter; it is not certain that Gervex remained the only model for Fagerolles as the character was elaborated in the novel, but it is certain that he was Zola's point of departure for the portrait of Claude's moral and artistic opposite.

Valabrègue's role was a little different, for he became, as the *Ébauche* progressed and as the novel was written, the most important source of failures. He first appears in the *Ébauche* as a man of large ambitions and insignificant accomplishment, and as an inveterate woman chaser and, finally, as a "tame" married man; here, of course, he resembles Jory in the novel. But a little later he begins to resemble Mahoudeau, the sculptor with a love of force and power but with an ineluctable grace in his fingers which condemns him to the small and the delicate. Still later he is presented as the type of the radically impotent man, like Chaîne. For a moment, he becomes the painter who turns against Claude and blames him for his own lack of success, but then he becomes a sculptor once again and is largely replaced by Solari as model for the figure of Mahoudeau. Then, still in the *Ébauche*, Zola seems to fall into a kind of confusion and cannot make up his mind whether he wants Valabrègue to serve as the model for the man of ambition who declines into insignificance or as the original of the man who is radically impotent. Finally, he solves the matter by using Valabrègue as a partial source for three of his failures, Mahoudeau, Chaîne, and Jory. His case is unique in the *Dossier*, for he is a model on whom not one complete figure is modeled but who serves as a partial original for three. Baille and Alexis also appear fairly early in the *Ébauche*, but is is clear that neither of them was, in the manner of Gervex and Valabrègue, a really "primary" type for Zola. No single living model for any other character is given in the *Ébauche* save for Claude and Sandoz, though it is apparent that Zola was not at first sure of what his own role should be, and it is interesting to note that such an important figure as Christine does not seem to stem from any individual. That no living models for these characters are mentioned in the *Ébauche* does not mean that they have no models, it may simply be that Zola felt no need to remind himself of their originals in life.

The most important conclusion to arise from a close study of the *Dossier* and the novel is that no statement about the origins of the characters can be devised that will be applicable to all of them, for it is plain that Zola followed no one, invariable method in drawing them. There seem to be four kinds of people in the book, excluding for the moment both Claude Lantier and Sandoz. There are, to begin with, figures that are obviously and indubitably drawn from life and presented unchanged; these are the least numerous and perhaps the least important of all. Then there are the personages who have recognizable characteristics of real people or who pass through situations that are historically verifiable but who are not exact or complete copies of any individual; these are the most numerous and by far the most important and it is their presence in *L'Oeuvre* which gives it its reputation as a key novel. Again, there are some characters who offer no really good clues as to their identity, either in the *Dossier* or in *L'Oeuvre* itself, but about whom fairly good guesses may be made on the basis of more or less vague indications in the pages of the novel, chronological likelihood, and the like; all these are the most minor figures. Lastly, there is a comparatively important group of characters which seem to be entirely fictional, with no traceable connection to people Zola had known and no basis in reality save in that general human reality upon which the realistic novelist, with his habits of observation and documentation, constantly draws.

The only two people of the first group, that is, the characters who are undoubtedly based completely on real individuals, with little admixture of fiction and no transposition of characteristics from other people, seem to be Henriette Sandoz and Madame Sandoz *mère* (again Pierre Sandoz and Claude Lantier are excluded here). Neither of them is at all important in the novel, and it might even be said that the latter figure is not a real character at all, since she never speaks, indeed, never even appears on stage. But the details of her life make it apparent that she represents Madame François Zola: her widowhood after a brief married life with a foreign-born inventor, her departure from Plassans (Aix), harried by creditors, confused by lawsuits, angered by the ill-will of her former compatriots in the little southern city, her life in Paris with her only son, who supports and shelters her, her long illness, her last years with her son and daughter-in-law, and her death just as the novelist gains recognition.[8] The identification of Henriette Sandoz with Madame Alexandrine Zola, while supported by fewer similarities with the real person, seems equally certain. At her first appearance she is described as an orphan, a beautiful and intelligent girl, daughter of small merchants, and this is not fiction, for the handsome and intelligent Alexandrine Meley, who lost her mother early in life, was the daughter of small commercial people. A little later we see her as she actually was after her marriage, "tall, with a calm and gay face, beautiful brown hair,"[9] occupying herself with the management of the house and taking very tender care of her young husband, who promised such prosperity to come, spoiling him with her cooking and generally making his life as comfortable as possible. Her very way of living, once Sandoz has made his way, recalls Madame Alexandrine Zola's, for her salon is a fairly tightly closed one, with no literary "clients," no reporters, and no poetry readings. There is no mistaking it, the two women who surround Pierre Sandoz with their love and their attentions are taken from life.[10]

The principal group of personages, those who possess characteristics which recall specific persons of Zola's acquaintance or who pass through circumstances which are identifiable but who are not complete representations of any persons, comprises the figures which give the book its atmosphere and physiognomy, Dubuche, Chaîne, Bongrand, Fagerolles, Jory, Mahoudeau, Chambouvard, Malgras, Naudet, and, perhaps, though not certainly, Gagnière (most of the very minor characters are excluded from consideration—Madame Vanzade, little Jacques, the various professional models). These are the personages who give point to Zola's claim in his interview with Maurice Français of *Le Voltaire* in 1886 that his characters were not taken from life.

A good deal of speculation has surrounded most of these and various interpretations, some of them fairly fantastic, have been made. It is nearly impossible to formulate any comprehensive statement about them, taken as a group, but the *Dossier* makes it plain that all but one of them, Dubuche, were conceived as composite figures, combining details from several real persons, with a substantial share of fictional embellishment. Dubuche, as far as the testimony of the *Dossier* goes, seems to have been centered on a single individual, but he differs from Madame Sandoz *mère* and Henriette in that he is nothing like a true or complete reconstitution of the person who served as the point of departure.

Most of the critics who have touched on the question identify Dubuche with Zola's boyhood friend, Baptistin Baille, and make no reservations as to the identification.[11] They seem to be justified in doing so, for the *Ébauche* makes it perfectly clear that Zola intended from the very first to call upon Baille as the model for one of his three young "inseparables." The *Ébauche* mentions him by name four times, and the first reference makes it apparent that Zola saw him as a type character, a representative of a large class, those who abandon art for more bourgeois concerns.[12] Zola also mentions him, along with Cézanne and himself, in the list of memories which follows the *Ébauche* and which evokes the pranks and wanderings of the three young friends in the countryside around Aix.[13] But in the *Personnages* of the *Dossier*, where he discusses the character (here named Louis Baude—Zola probably realized later that a sculptor named Charles Baude was on the scene), there is no mention of Baille, though it is still true that some of the characteristics attributed to him seem to come from the real Baille. In the notes on architecture, where Dubuche's name occurs frequently, Zola never refers to Baille. It is possible, though there is no evidence to prove it, that the details of Dubuche's career as a student of architecture were taken by Zola from the life of Joseph Huot, another Aixois come to conquer Paris and an early friend of Zola's in the capital. It would seem that in the first idea for the character, advanced in the *Ébauche*, Zola planned to give something like a real portrait of his friend,[14] but that as the character took shape in his mind it evolved rather sharply away from the original conception and became either a "contamination" or a truly fictional entity.

This impression is strengthened by the general nature of the figure of Dubuche in *L'Oeuvre*. The architect is generally shown in a disagreeable light, as a serious, mediocre, and ambitious young *petit bourgeois*, a climber impressed by academic conventions and distinctions, at bottom shocked by and hostile to the experimental art of his young friends, devoid of talent and of any real interest in the things of art and so anxious to win a comfortable place in society that he sacrifices his integrity—and incidentally his happiness—to attain it. It is impossible to say how close this is as a portrait of the real Baille or how accurately it reflects Zola's opinion of him, though there are good signs in Zola's early correspondence of a growing irritation with his friend because of his bourgeois outlook and petty ambitions. Zola even goes so far in one instance as to declare that Baille talks like a "rich grocer,"[15] and it is possible that the figure in the novel may reflect Zola's real, if somewhat exaggerated, judgment of Baille's personality and character. There is evidence that the two had drifted apart after 1880 or thereabouts,[16] but there is no sign of any hostility between them.[17]

But however much the personality of Dubuche, in the novel, may reflect Zola's personal judgment of Baille, the events of Dubuche's life do not in general parallel the events of Baille's career; the latter was not an architect, for instance, and though he made a financially good marriage, there is no evidence that he sold his soul for money, as Dubuche does. It is probable that Baille stood in Zola's mind for the type of man who abandons his early and not very deep interest in art for other concerns and other pursuits as he grows older and who gives up a kind of youthful, imitative bohemianism for a more conservative and middle-class outlook on life. The impression that Zola did consider him as something of a type-figure is heightened by the fact that in each of the four references made to Baille in the *Ébauche*, Zola uses the term "le Baille" or "un Baille." All in all, it seems that Dubuche represents the best example in the novel of a character which, with its point of departure given by a real person, changes quite completely as the book progresses and becomes almost entirely fictional.

The minor figure of Justin Chaîne, the untalented peasant painter of Saint-Firmin who is sent up to Paris on a scholarship and who finishes his career as a lottery operator in a fair, probably represents something like the same case, though it is difficult to say with any assurance since almost nothing is known of the man who is generally supposed to have been his original, Jean-Baptiste-Mathieu Chaillan.[18] Again, the critics who mention him believe him to be a direct image of the latter,[19] basing their opinion on such references as these in the *Dossier:* "all of Chaillan's story," and "a comrade who will be Chaillan."[20] But once more it is not certain that Zola meant to give anything like a complete picture of the man he had known in his youth in Paris, though it is certainly true that the general contempt with which Chaîne is depicted in the novel seems to reflect Zola's true feelings about Chaillan, if the Aix letters are a good indication. There are a half-dozen references to Chaillan in letters of 1860 which show clearly that Zola regarded him as a presumptuous simpleton, almost a fool,[21] and the tone of these remarks is exactly the same as in the descriptions of Chaîne in *L'Oeuvre.* It is perhaps significant that Chaîne is the only figure treated with real contempt and disparagement in the work and that Chaillan is the only person for whom Zola's early letters betray the same spirit. But from the way in which Zola refers to Chaîne in the *Dossier* it seems on the whole that he intended him to be less a depiction of a man he had once known than a symbol of the poor provincial painter sent to Paris by an indulgent city administration only to meet defeat because of his radical lack of talent. If that is what he is, he may well stand for another figure of Zola's acquaintance also, for Zola mentions in the *Ébauche* a certain Valentin, sent to Paris by the Aixois art teacher, Dejulienne, and apparently a failure like his friend; if the Valentin mentioned here is the same one who appears in Zola's correspondence, he is Fernand Desmoulin, the engraver who aided Zola during his exile in England in the late 1890's. It is thus possible that Desmoulin was one of the models for Chaîne, though nothing could be less certain than such an assumption.[22] The *Dossier* also shows that Zola originally intended Chaîne to be a student of Corot's[23] but the novel indicates that he finally sketched him as a crude primitive, capable of creating something like good "images d'Épinal," but no more. Such a change as this points to the probability that there is more fiction in the character than the critics appear to believe, and again Chaîne seems to represent Zola's tendency to form fictional type figures on the basis of an observed youthful reality for the purpose of expressing a form of the disillusionment he was apparently experiencing at this period of his life; but the lack of documentary sources here leaves the whole question in the realm of speculation. It is clear from the *Ébauche* that Antony Valabrègue contributed something to the character of Chaîne, but the references are so vague that it is impossible to measure his contribution. It might be added that at least one element of Chaîne's life as it is given in *L'Oeuvre* seems to be borrowed from Zola's own experiences. In the description of the miserable existence of Chaîne and Mahoudeau, Zola notes that the former, having received a cask of olive oil from home, had tried unsuccessfully to peddle it to former southerners living in Paris and had finally been driven to consume it himself as his only means of subsistence. It is possible that this small incident reflects Zola's own extreme misery at the beginning of his career, when, according to Maupassant, he was driven to the very same expedient.[24]

The most interesting characters of the group of artists surrounding Claude are unquestionably Paul Jory and Henri Fagerolles, both because Zola gave them so much attention and because of their formation. Paul Jory is frequently identified as Paul Alexis,[25] and indeed the public had already been prepared for his appearance in the novel by Alexis' own words in *Émile Zola, notes d'un ami*. The *Dossier* indicates that Alexis' advance information was exact, for his name appears there a half-dozen times, generally but not always with the usual "I' " which seems to indicate that Zola thought of his friends as types for the novel rather than as individuals.[26] But though it is certain that Zola intended, as early as the last part of the *Ébauche*, to employ Alexis' character and personality to some end in *L'Oeuvre*, it is also clear that he did not know at first what he would do with him. Alexis appears later in the *Ébauche* than Gervex or Valabrègue, and in his first role as painter takes over some of the functions originally assigned to Valabrègue, which were eventually given to Chaîne. As a painter Alexis is to be presented as "dramatized, made evil,"[27] and when he makes his definitive appearance as journalist it is apparent that Zola, while changing his vocation, has not altered his conception of the way Jory's character should be presented. In the *Personnages* Zola again refers to a changed Alexis, this time saying "Alexis transformed," and indicates that he is thinking of having Sandoz write his first articles for him, perhaps recalling some similar service he had rendered Alexis or another beginner of his acquaintance; this plan was ultimately dropped.

So it is plain that Zola wanted to employ Alexis as a model, or part of a model, for one of his characters, but once more it is not clear how accurately he sketched his portrait, for though we know more about Alexis than about any member of the Aix group except Cézanne, it is still true that we do not know him well. Unlike some of Zola's later friends, Alexis possesses no well-known physiognomy which we might compare with Jory's, and in addition to this, we know almost nothing of Zola's personal view of his most faithful friend.

It is certain, nevertheless, that some of the details of Jory's life and character were selected by Zola from what he knew of Alexis. At the beginning of the novel, for instance, he is shown as a young man of good southern family arriving in Paris with a small baggage of sonnets and proceeding immediately to become the despair of his well-situated father by his adventures in the bohemian world of the 1860's. These details seem to be accurate reflections of the beginnings of Alexis' own career, for his unpublished correspondence with Zola indicates that his early wild life in Paris deeply troubled his conservative family, and, of course, the matter of the sonnets is a direct reminiscence of the elaborate hoax arranged by Alexis to introduce his *Vieilles plaies*, and incidentally himself, to the Parisian literary world. But aside from the fact that Jory soon became a journalist, these are about the only details of his life that can be said with any certainty to have been taken from Alexis'. Some elements of his character, though, seem to come directly from Alexis, for Jory is repeatedly shown as an inveterate noctambulist and woman-chaser, and there is some reason for believing that Alexis was those things too. Denise LeBlond-Zola describes him in very similar terms, but it is possible that her article on him, which never mentions Jory or *L'Oeuvre*, was based in good part on the novel itself and so may have had little or no documentary value.[28] But it is quite possible that Jory's worst traits—his lying, his unscrupulousness and cynicism, his commercial interest in art, and so on—may be something like reflections of the reality of Alexis' personality; Henry Céard, in his letters to Zola, draws a picture of Alexis, whom he detested, which somewhat resembles Jory, but his unsupported testimony, obviously in part the result of a bitter dislike, is not sufficient to let us think that Alexis was the kind of individual Jory turns out to be. It must not be forgotten that Valabrègue was the distant model for Jory before Alexis was thought of, apparently, and at least one detail of his life, his marriage and consequent subjugation by a shrewish wife, occurs in the description of one of the early, nameless characters stemming out of Valabrègue. How much of the real Valabrègue entered into Jory's composition it is impossible to say.

Whatever Jory's origins, Alexis did recognize himself in the journalist, for after reading *L'Oeuvre* he cried in a letter of March 26 (1886): "Poor Duranty! and Flaubert! and Cézanne, and I and all of us. *Our* youth, all of us, in this book."[29] But why was there no note of protest? Why no reproach that his old friend, his idol, had shown him in such a disagreeable light?

The answer, probably, is that Alexis knew, as no one else could know, that his portrait under the name of Paul Jory was presented but in part and that Jory not only represents a fictional being, but that many of the details of Jory's life did not come from his own life at all. The incident of the near duel in which Jory is challenged because of one of his articles in *Le Tambour* is a case in point; when Zola included this small incident he was probably thinking of the Manet-Duranty duel in which he was a second and which he mentions in the list of memories which follows the *Ébauche*.[30] Moreover, the fact that Jory is responsible in large part for Fagerolles' popular success seems to be borrowed from the relationship of Albert Wolff, the influential critic of *Le Figaro*, and Antoine Guillemet, for in the first plan of Chapter VII Zola notes: "Jory, the press, advertising, effect on painters. Comradeship. Fragerolles (sic) made by Jory. I made Claude. Guillemet and Wolff."[31]

Most of all, it is apparent that Jory, in many of his experiences, is Zola himself, as some of the more recent critics of the novel have recognized.[32] Jory, like Zola, begins his real career as art critic of a small but noisy newspaper (*Le Tambour* has replaced *L'Événement*);

one of his articles, devoted to a canvas of Claude's, stirs up an enormous scandal because in it he sacrifices the consecrated glories of the time to the new artists, just as Zola did in his articles on Manet; he sets Claude up as master of the new plein air school, as Zola had done, in some measure at least, with Manet;[33] some of his articles attack the jury system of the Salon, as Zola's did in *L'Événement* in 1866, and he promises to write an article in praise of Mahoudeau's "Vendangeuse," just as one of Zola's pieces in his *Salon* of 1868 praised Solari's "Nègre endormi," which may have been the original of Mahoudeau's second statue, the collapsing "Baigneuse." Moreover, Jory is shown from the first as a nonprofessional art critic who for the most part repeats the theories of the group to which he belongs, as Zola undoubtedly was compelled to do at the beginning of his experiences with the Salon. Again, Jory is attacked by various members of the band after he has achieved eminence as a critic because he does not mention them any more in his articles, very probably a reflection of some of the reproaches from the Impressionists that Zola must have heard after he had succeeded in capturing an audience with his first *Salon*. Like Zola, Jory rises rapidly in the journalistic field and soon becomes a power, though it is hardly likely that Zola is reflecting his own experiences when he has Jory traffic in influence and conclude shady deals with the painters in exchange for favorable mention. Actually, in Jory's career there are more precise, verifiable details from Zola's own life than from Alexis' and though the journalist's personality and character certainly do not resemble Zola's, still it may be said that he is a kind of autobiographical figure—which is not to say that there is not a great deal of fiction in him.

The case of the successful artist Henri Fagerolles is somewhat similar, although here there is no admixture of details from Zola's life. That Zola intended Fagerolles to be a really major figure in the novel is indicated, first, by the frequency of his appearance, and then, by his being the most clearly marked contrast to Claude. He is also charged with expressing, by indirection at least, one of the novel's pessimistic conclusions: that great geniuses are often denied immediate popular success, which goes usually to those of lesser, more easily comprehensible talent. Moreover, he was clearly intended, in Zola's plan, to stand as a representative of a group of painters to whom Zola paid very frequent attention in his successive Salons, the artists who were skillful and unscrupulous enough to adapt the findings of men of genius to bourgeois taste and thus to make fortunes, while the great inventors starved amid middle-class ridicule. As such, Fagerolles has been unusually interesting to the critics who have written on *L'Oeuvre*, and many of them have attempted to discover the identity of his original, for nearly everyone seems agreed that he is a real portrait of some painter Zola had known. Even before the novel appeared there had been a certain amount of speculation on the model who had served Zola for Fagerolles' figure, and the painter Roybet was so often suggested that Zola felt obliged on two different occasions to deny that Roybet was to be the model for his central figure. He did so in a letter to Charles Chincholle, the *Figaro* reporter who had openly proposed Roybet's name,[34] and again in an interview in *Le Voltaire* for May 3, 1886, in which he said that his Fagerolles was not at all "the portrait of a very popular young painter whose exhibition at the Salon has alerted all the columnists." This was certainly Roybet.

But, at the same time, Zola did not reveal whom Fagerolles represented, if he represented any painter specifically. Since the novel's appearance, most critics argue that it was Zola's old friend and adviser in things artistic, Antoine Guillemet, who sat for the portrait, and some of them feel that Zola's treatment of Guillemet was anything but charitable, since Guillemet had supplied him with the major portion of his technical documentation for *L'Oeuvre*. Fosca, Bowie, and Perruchot declare that Fagerolles is modeled on Guillemet, while Doucet and LeBlond also believe him to be the original, though conceding that Fagerolles also displays traits borrowed from Paul Bourget.[35]

There is a good deal of reason for this identification. Guillemet was the right age for the figure of Fagerolles, being almost exactly of the generation of Zola and Cézanne, and he had something of a reputation as a malicious gossip, as Fagerolles had, if we are to judge by a remark made about him by Henry Céard, who once referred to him as "that exquisite back-biter."[36] Moreover, it is undeniable that the whole scene of the *charité* in which Fagerolles finally consents to accept Claude's "Enfant mort" on his own responsibility, is quite plainly taken from an experience of Guillemet's. In the discussion of the jury's operations in the *Dossier*, where Zola notes down Guillemet's observations for later use in the novel, the scene of the *charité* is described in words which are repeated almost textually in the novel, save that Gervex and Guillemet exchange places.[37]

Guillemet himself believed, for a time at least, that Zola had copied him without saying anything about it, for in March 1886, Camille Pissarro wrote his son Lucien to this effect:

> Guillemet, who is furious about the book, . . . wrote to Zola, but only to complain that Fagerolles is too easily identifiable. They are telling a charming anecdote in this connection; Guillemet,

> who worships Zola, and with good reason, wanted his name to appear in this book, which he was certain would add to Zola's renown. He wrote Zola, requesting that the book be dedicated to him. Zola, very embarrassed, as you can imagine, by this expression of admiration, replied that he was reserving all dedications until the whole *Rougon-Macquart* series appeared. But since *His Masterpiece* was published, Guillemet's ardor has melted like butter in the sun; he wrote Zola a long letter of complaint.[38]

But Guillemet's pique did not last long, apparently, for a very cordial unpublished letter to Zola after the *Manifeste des cinq* indicates that they were on excellent terms by 1887.[39]

Of course, it is perfectly plain from the *Dossier* that Fagerolles was a composite figure, as Philippe Gille suggested,[40] and it is very possible that Guillemet came, with time, to realize it. The *Dossier* shows that as Zola projected the character he thought of several different men of his acquaintance, notably Maupassant and Bourget. There are two references to Maupassant, neither very flattering. The first of them, in the *Personnages*, links his name with Gervex' (Maupassant and Gervex were friends and sometimes traveled together),[41] and the second does the same, but much more harshly.[42] Bourget seems to have been only a passing idea, and it appears that Zola used him as the type of man who succeeds by the influence of fashionable women.[43] In the novel Fagerolles succeeds through the machinations of Naudet, though his relationship with Irma may be a reflection of Zola's original idea. Moreover, in spite of Zola's denials that he had called on Roybet for his model, the *Dossier* indicates that the relationship of Fagerolles with Naudet was copied from the connection between Roybet and the dealer Brame in the early and middle 1880's. In the notes provided him by Guillemet on "Les Marchands de tableaux," Zola describes how Brame won the painter over to join his stable of painters by urging him to raise his prices and restrict his production and especially by promising him a lavish town house if he would cooperate. After recounting how Brame thus won Roybet over, Zola adds: "to be repeated with Fagerolles."[44]

But Guillemet, Maupassant, Bourget, and Roybet were at best secondary models for Fagerolles. Incontestably, the artist of whom Zola was thinking most as he sketched Claude's rival and imitator was the famous and successful Henry Gervex, disciple of Cabanel, friend of Manet, brilliant example of the successful artist of the 1880's who has joined the legion of the forgotten. The *Dossier* makes it clear that Zola regarded him—or perhaps what he stood for—as a real *donnée* of his novel, a primordial figure in the manner of Valabrègue. Of about twenty references in the *Dossier* to the character who came ultimately to bear the name Fagerolles (perhaps borrowed from the composer Auguste Fragerolles, mentioned in Duval's *Le Quartier Pigalle* and famous for his patriotic songs, or from the painter Mazerolles, who had two portraits in the Salon of 1884), no less than seventeen are to Gervex by name, usually as "le Gervex," to point up his role as type. It seems nearly incredible that Maurice LeBlond, who had first access to the *Dossier*, could have come to the conclusion that it was Guillemet whom Zola had in mind [45] and that so many others have reflected his error. The evidence is plain. In the *Ébauche* Zola says, for example: "I have Gervex, who uses everyone and then betrays."[46] Again: "Gervex is inevitably a painter, very academic at first, a product of the School; then, stealing his idea from Claude and applying to it a flabby and bourgeois technique which wins success."[47]

Perhaps LeBlond suffered from the same error as Fernand Doucet in this instance: Doucet seems to have believed that Gervex was a name invented by Zola, which Zola hesitated to use because the initial too easily recalled Guillemet. Besides the two uses of Gervex' name quoted above, there are over a dozen more,[48] and, aside from the *Personnages*, in which Zola speaks of the character as Fagerolles, there are only two cases where he uses that name; all the rest are as Gervex. It is beyond doubt, then, that Gervex was the starting point for Fagerolles.[49]

Was he more than that? It is difficult to say, for though the facts of Fagerolles' career bear some resemblance to those of Gervex'—the friendship with Claude, for instance, recalls the friendship of Gervex for Manet—it is not likely that the character of the fictional painter was anything like Gervex', for there is no evidence that the real painter was the kind of liar, thief, and hypocrite which Fagerolles becomes. More than that, we have no idea of Zola's intimate opinion of Gervex; all we know is what he said of him in his *Salons*, and that opinion is public and "official."

What seems most likely is that Gervex simply stood in Zola's mind for a kind of painter he saw more and more frequently around the Salon with the increasing affluence of the country, which made it possible for artists to make large sums of money with comparative ease by perfecting a relatively painless commercial technique. That financial success was becoming more and more the goal of painters is evident in the criticisms of a good many contemporary observers, typical of whom is Albert Wolff, whose comments in the *Figaro-Salon* for 1883 on the recent rise of the painter in search of success may be the distant origin of the character of Fagerolles.[50]

That Zola was concerned by the activities of such profiteers is clearly evident in his *Salons*, and like some of the other critics he thought that most of them were imitators of Manet; the *Salons* make it apparent that he saw Gervex as one of the new band.[51]

But it was by no means only Gervex whom Zola saw in the role of imitator and adapter. The criticism leveled at Gervex in the *Salons* is nowhere nearly as biting as the observations Zola makes of the work of both Bastien-Lepage and Carolus Duran; that he sees them as imitators of Manet and the Impressionists makes it possible that he also had them in mind as he composed the figure of Fagerolles. Moreover, he says of both of them what he does not say of Gervex, that they made money and reputation quickly, and largely by means of concessions to middle-class taste, and here surely they are closer to Fagerolles than is either Gervex or Guillemet who is never mentioned in the *Salons* as either an *arriviste* by imitation or as a moneymaker in the manner described by Albert Wolff. This seems to indicate that Guillemet's role as the original of Fagerolles is considerably less than might appear from what the critics have said about it, and that both Bastien-Lepage and Carolus Duran must be considered as components of this undoubtedly composite character.

At all events, what Zola says of Bastien-Lepage in some of his *Salons* sounds remarkably like some of the pages of *L'Oeuvre* consecrated to Fagerolles, and some of the charges brought against Carolus Duran are even closer in tone and content to the pages of *L'Oeuvre*.[52] So it would seem that Fagerolles is Guillemet and Gervex and Bastien-Lepage and Carolus Duran, but he is also none of them, a type figure of a race that Zola, with his theories of originality and temperament, detested: the epigoni. And he seems to be very largely a fictional figure, for though his role is modeled on the careers of these men, his personality is surely not a reflection of theirs; in making Fagerolles a liar, a cheat, a humbug, and a hypocrite, Zola was yielding to his taste for the exaggerated and the violent, was pouring on him his contempt for the noncreative of the world of art and was indulging his baroque taste for the extremes of mankind.[53]

Another member of the "little band" is the sculptor Charles Mahoudeau (Zola may have found the name on a bust shown by A. d'Halou in 1884), who, though playing only a minor part in *L'Oeuvre*, has been the subject of considerable speculation.

Rewald and Marcel Provence identify him as Zola's old friend from Aix, Philippe Solari; the compilers of the Bibliothèque Nationale catalogue declare that Solari "provided some traits" for the character of Mahoudeau, and Ernest Vizetelly thinks he is "in a measure" Solari. But François Fosca, Angus Wilson, and Maurice LeBlond see Mahoudeau as a mixture of traits from Solari and Anthony Valabrègue, and LeBlond further declares that he seems closer to the latter than to the real sculptor Solari.[54] The *Dossier* indicates beyond all doubt that his view is correct, though it is not strongly enough stated.

The *Personnages* give no hint whatsoever of the identity of the model Zola chose for this minor character, but the *Ébauche* abounds in evidence that it was chiefly Valabrègue whom Zola had in mind as he constructed the figure of this other failure. Of about a dozen references to the sculptor in the *Ébauche*, only one is to Mahoudeau; all the others use the name Valabrègue, or, more frequently, "le Valabrègue." The first reference is typical: "I have, finally, a kind of Valabrègue who, with enormous and naive ambitions, falls to the level of the little insignificant painting."[55] The idea of making Mahoudeau a painter, while employing the basic character of Valabrègue as his foundation, evidently persisted for some time in Zola's mind as he drew up the *Ébauche*, but eventually Zola saw that he had enough painters with Claude, Gagnière, Fagerolles, and Chaîne and that sculpture was not represented by any major figure at all. He came to the opinion that he should call upon Solari as his model, and it is this sentence—one of the two in which Solari is mentioned— that seems to be the basis for the critics' opinion that it was the real sculptor and not the transformed journalist whom Zola had in mind as he created Mahoudeau. But immediately after deciding to call on Solari as his model, Zola once again refers to the figure as Valabrègue and does so in every other case but one in which the sculptor is mentioned. Zola's final decision with respect to the character is contained in a sentence or two near the end of the *Ébauche*, where he seems to exclude Solari and to speak only of Valabrègue.[56] The contention that Solari was a model is based, as will be seen, on other considerations.

Nothing in the *Dossier* indicates that Zola considered Valabrègue as the special kind of failure represented by Mahoudeau, but two significant letters from Paul Alexis, in which Valabrègue's name figures, certainly show that some people in Zola's entourage thought of him as just such a failure as the fictional character represents, and it is not at all impossible that Zola shared the opinion. As early as September 28, 1871, Alexis mentions Valabrègue's impotence and, referring to his own self-doubts and hesitations, conjures up what he calls "the spectre of Valabrègue,"[57] and in 1875, just before his twenty-eighth birthday, Alexis, meditating on his own lack of accomplishment, says:

"Already I feel old and empty. I don't want to be a Valabrègue. . . ."[58] Such statements do not constitute any kind of proof that Zola felt the same way about his younger compatriot, but there is an excellent chance that if Alexis believed this of Valabrègue, it was at least partly because Zola thought so too. Moreover, there is some possibility that Zola had been deeply disappointed in Valabrègue's career and that his portrait of Mahoudeau is a direct reflection of this disappointment. In *La Tribune* for January 17, 1869, Zola had spoken in the highest tone of Valabrègue, calling him one of "tomorrow's masters" and urging his readers to remember his name, for this was a young man with a future. When his great expectations are contrasted with the undistinguished reality of Valabrègue's career, the character of Mahoudeau, at least in its origins, becomes comprehensible.[59]

Apparently, then, Mahoudeau is really Valabrègue in character, symbol of grace and prettiness and coquettishness—of everything Zola disliked in art.

But the details of Mahoudeau's life probably do not come from Valabrègue's career, and in the events of his unhappy attempt to reach the public Mahoudeau seems much closer to Solari than to the original model. In the early part of his career, for instance, Mahoudeau is made to turn out statuettes of saints at so much per hour, just as Solari writes Zola that he is compelled to do in 1868;[60] the heartrending incident of the collapse of the "Baigneuse" before the Salon is also doubtless sketched from an incident in Solari's early career, if Joachim Gasquet[61] is a reliable witness. But to illustrate the impossibility of drawing definite conclusions on such details as this, it might be pointed out that precisely the same incident of a collapsing statue had occurred to the sculptor Louis Brion, who, like Mahoudeau, saw the work of years ruined in one freezing night. Eugène Pelletan, in an article entitled "Les Morts inconnus" in *La Tribune* for August 8, 1869, tells of the affair, and Zola was certainly in a position to know of his story, for he published a "causerie" in the same issue of *La Tribune.*

Other details, for example, the transformation of the fallen "Baigneuse" into a reclining figure (Solari exhibited his "Nègre endormi" in 1868 and Zola mentioned it in his *Salon* of that year), may well be taken from Solari's life, for which no good biographical source exists, but these suffice to show that Mahoudeau represents a well-defined case of a character formed around the general idea Zola had of one man's life and one man's nature and yet taking some outward details from another and far different life. Mahoudeau is a fictional personage and cannot be completely identified with anyone; but to the extent that such declarations are ever true, it can be said that Zola meant him to represent the essence of his view of Valabrègue.[62]

The minor character whom Zola himself apparently found most interesting and sympathetic was not properly one of "la petite bande" at all, but a predecessor of theirs in the art world, the painter Achille Bongrand. If not a front-rank figure in *L'Oeuvre*, he does play a considerable role, and much of the reason for his importance undoubtedly is that Zola based the character on a person or persons whom he had greatly liked and admired in his youth and in the process of literary elaboration was carried along by the memories and emotions which the beloved figure called up.

Once again the critics are divided as to the living original of the figure. Bowie says flatly that it was Manet,[63] while Philippe Gille saw Flaubert's traits in Bongrand.[64] Ernest Vizetelly, whose sources of information were excellent, expressed an idea shared by no other critic when he declared in the preface to the first English translation of *L'Oeuvre:*

> Bongrand is a commingling of Courbet, Cabanel, and Gustave Flaubert. For instance, his so-called "Village Wedding" is suggested by Courbet's "Village Wedding;" his friendship for Claude is Cabanel's friendship for Manet; whilst some of his mannerisms, such as his dislike for the praise accorded to certain of his works, are simply those of Flaubert, who . . . almost invariably lost his temper if one ventured to extol *Madame Bovary* in his presence.[65]

But on the other hand Fernand Doucet advances the opinion that Bongrand is for the most part made up of traits borrowed from Flaubert and Manet;[66] Maurice LeBlond, while expressing no opinion himself, simply cites the line from the *Dossier* on which Doucet's view is based: "I call him the old boy, but he must not be more than fifty. A very *chic* Manet, rather, a Flaubert."[67] This is the only good indication given in the entire *Dossier* of the identity of Zola's model for this character. When speaking of Bongrand in the *Dossier*—which contains evidence that Zola was at first uncertain whether Bongrand should be a writer or a painter—Zola never refers to him by the name of a living person, as he does with both Mahoudeau and Jory, for example, but nearly always calls him simply "le vieux." This might mean that Zola was thinking only of Flaubert as he composed the figure, for he and the men of his generation had been fond of calling Flaubert that, but it may be that "vieux" here has its literal meaning and that Zola used it only to keep in mind that Bongrand represented an earlier generation and so had to be a man somewhat older than the members of the "little band."

In the novel some of the details of Bongrand's career might have come from the experiences of either Manet or Flaubert. He is a well-to-do artist, for instance, spared the necessity of producing for a commercial market by the comfortable fortune he enjoys, and here Zola might have had either Flaubert or Manet in mind. Again, the striking quality of his work, for Claude, is its amazing simplicity, and the work of both Manet and Flaubert has a kind of surface simplicity which conceals a highly developed technique. But most of all the "formula" which Bongrand brings to art might be considered as Zola's opinion of the contribution of either of his old friends.

> From this painting (i.e., "La Noce au village") an evolution dated, for it had brought a new formula. After Delacroix and parallel with Courbet, it was a Romanticism tempered with logic, with more exactness in observation, more perfection in form, though nature was not yet approached head-on, in the crude light of the open air. Yet, the whole new school called on this art as its authority.[68]

Though this idea is expressed in painterly terms, it applies equally well either to Manet and his relationship to the Impressionists or to Flaubert and the naturalists. Perhaps Zola had them both in mind.

There is a certain amount of evidence in the *Dossier* that Zola originally thought of Manet as his model for Bongrand. In the *Personnages* he notes that his artist has passed through a period of intense absorption in Spanish life and art and that he has brought back some excellent canvases from Spain; this may be, quite possibly, a reflection of Manet's career. Again, also in the *Personnages*, he says that he will have Fagerolles steal ideas and techniques from Bongrand, and here it is possible that he was thinking of the relationship of Manet and Gervex, who Zola thought may have borrowed a little too heavily from his friend. However, neither of these details appears in the novel, indicating perhaps that Zola quite early dropped the idea of calling on Manet as his chief source here.

What seems to have happened is this: thinking first of both Manet and Flaubert as possible models, elaborating the character in his early sketches on the basis of both these originals, Zola eventually came, as he wrote *L'Oeuvre*, to think only of Flaubert, and it is almost certain that he alone is the true model for Bongrand. Most of the details of Bongrand's life and career are taken from Flaubert's. Bongrand is named Achille, like Flaubert's brother, and like Flaubert is a bachelor, forty-five years old at the opening of the novel and nearly sixty at its close, not very far from Flaubert's real age if the dates of the novel are considered as exact; he is thus closer to the generation which Zola needed for contrast with the plein air artists than the younger Manet would have been. Bongrand's physical size and loud voice also recall Flaubert much more than the slight, aristocratic, sarcastic Parisian that a dozen contemporaries have described under the name of Manet. Nor did the latter, at least as far as those same contemporaries indicate, possess Bongrand's talent for mimicry, while there are numerous testimonies that Flaubert could be an excellent and cruel mimic on occasion. Flaubert too seems to have been widely liked, while Manet's personality was less engaging; surely Bongrand's position in the art world of the 1870's was closer to the reality of Flaubert's than to that of Manet's. Again, the *Ébauche* emphasizes Bongrand's constant need for "beginning again," a trait that may well have come from Flaubert's character (although Zola may have been reflecting his own *affres* here); and at the same time Zola stresses Bongrand's fear of beginning each new canvas—a fear which stands in paradoxical but entirely human relationship with the need for new experiments—and this fear was certainly typical of Flaubert, as his hesitations and researches testify only too well. Zola himself had just such fears, and Bongrand may be in no small measure a reflection of his own intimate life as artist.

Certainly, Bongrand's first great painting, "La Noce au village," seems to have been designed by Zola as a kind of analogue in oil and canvas of *Madame Bovary*—indeed, Zola himself says so, for in the second plan of Chapter III he notes that "they will talk to him of his masterpiece (his *Madame Bovary*)."[69] The details of its subject (a wedding party in a field, some peasants) and the presence of the fiddler seem like reflections of the wedding scene from Flaubert's novel, and Bongrand's touchiness on the subject of his great canvas is an echo of a trait Zola mentioned in "Mes Souvenirs sur Gustave Flaubert"—that Flaubert became so tired of hearing the book praised that on one occasion he declared that if he could afford it, he would withdraw all copies from the market.[70] It is also possible that "La Noce au village" was imitated from Courbet, as Vizetelly contends, and this view is seemingly supported by the fact that the last painting of Bongrand's described in *L'Oeuvre* is entitled "Enterrement au village," just as Courbet's most famous painting was called "Enterrement à Ornans." The only other specifically mentioned painting by Bongrand is a small indoor scene of two women sewing in a sunny window;[71] this may be taken from a water color by Fantin-Latour, "Les Couseuses,"[72] and in any case does not seem to come from either Courbet or Manet.

The special costume worn by Bongrand while at work certainly recalls Flaubert's working dress[73] and Zola, in "Mes Souvenirs sur Gustave Flaubert," describes Flaubert's costume in very nearly the same terms as in the novel. Some other details seem to come from Flaubert, at least as Zola saw him. When Naudet asks Bongrand for another *Noce,* he is undoubtedly reflecting a detail of Flaubert's career, for Zola declares that every work of Flaubert's after *Madame Bovary* was either attacked or ignored, and the public kept insisting that he give it another masterpiece in the manner of the great success of 1857. Again, when Bongrand accompanies Claude home after one of Sandoz' dinners, he is duplicating Flaubert's habits, for Zola says that after the dinners of "Les Auteurs sifflés" and their interminable discussions, Flaubert accompanied him home, philosophizing at every street corner, so that Zola could rarely get to bed before three in the morning. Flaubert also hated the prying by newspapermen into the private lives of artists, just as Bongrand hates the practice when it is applied to Fagerolles, whom the press seeks to make into a young master.

But the connection between Bongrand and Flaubert goes far beyond these simple details of mise-en-scène and extends to the essence of the artist's career. Bongrand is shown from the beginning of *L'Oeuvre* as a man past his peak and clearly on the decline, and here it is highly likely that Zola was thinking of the Flaubert of the 1870's, after the great triumphs of *Madame Bovary* and *L'Éducation sentimentale,* a Flaubert already on the downgrade, at least to his eye, and incapable of reaching the heights of 1857 again. It is significant that Bongrand never accomplishes anything so important or so excellent as "La Noce au village," and again Zola is probably reflecting a private opinion that Flaubert never wrote anything to compare with *Madame Bovary.* Such details as these seem to rule out Manet as the essential model, for Zola had the opportunity to observe the painter through almost the whole of his career, not merely during his decline, and it cannot be established that any single work by Manet (with the possible exception of "Olympia") occupied a position similar to *Madame Bovary's* in Flaubert's works. Moreover, Bongrand's later manner is described on more than one occasion as characterized by a certain dryness and lack of spontaneity; his "Enterrement au village" is "stiff," "dry,"[74] and here the reminiscence is almost certainly of Flaubert, whose *Trois contes* and *Bouvard et Pécuchet* may well have appealed to Zola as being a little stiff, dry, and overtechnical, especially lacking in the kind of warmth which appealed so deeply to the readers of the time in

Madame Bovary. In "Mes Souvenirs sur Gustave Flaubert" Zola emphasizes a kind of progressive dehumanization of Flaubert's novels, a constantly increasing stress on pure rhetoric, a growing domination by form, technique: "slowly, from legs to torso, Flaubert was becoming a statue."

His search for perfection, like Bongrand's, became a real malady, and as he became more and more preoccupied with pure form he gradually lost the sense of humanity.[75] It is certain that much of Bongrand's temperament comes from Zola's observation of Flaubert, for the "Souvenirs" shows him as a man of unusual sensitivity to criticism, as Bongrand is, as very proud and touchy, as a kind of provincial, detesting the Parisianism he saw around him, quickly violent and quickly calmed, with a kind of naiveté or innocence which made the great man often seem childlike; all of these traits appear in Bongrand. It is true that the detail of Bongrand's "self-survival" might be taken from the career of either Manet or Flaubert, both of whom saw new and radically different schools grow up to displace their own, and it is also possible that the detail of a lingering romanticism in outlook and execution might be borrowed from the career of either man, but it is almost certain that the disillusionment with fame and glory that Bongrand expresses is an echo of ideas which Flaubert had uttered on one of his Sunday afternoons in the rue Murillo. And surely the deep pessimism of the end of his career comes from Flaubert's own bitter view of life and man; Bongrand's speech in the closing pages of the novel might have come—perhaps did come—from the lips of Flaubert himself.[76] At all events, a good witness, one who knew both Flaubert and Manet, Paul Alexis, recognized Flaubert in Bongrand and did not see Manet. The simple testimony of his letter to Zola is worth a dozen pages of proof: "Poor Duranty! And Flaubert!"[77] And to this implicit testimony should be added the all-important fact that Bongrand, alone of all the male characters of *L'Oeuvre,* is beloved by everyone; that this universal affection was a reality of Flaubert's life is made explicit in Zola's "Souvenirs," one of the most sincere and loving tributes Zola ever paid to the character and temperament of a fellow artist.[78]

Bongrand's opposite number in the novel, the sculptor Victor Chambouvard, is far less important and interesting. He makes only two appearances and is obviously dragged in to serve as a contrast to Bongrand, the tormented self-doubter, and as a further contrast to Mahoudeau, who lacks his strength and productive force. The *Personnages* give no hint of the identity of the model for this character, but two references in the *Ébauche* make it clear that Zola was thinking especially of Gustave Courbet, with Victor Hugo in the immediate background. On the first occasion he says: ". . . don't forget, in the background, the artist of genius, immobile, satisfied, the monster bloated with his own personality, without critical sense, and who has become a god: Courbet, Hugo."[79] A few pages further on, Zola's expression makes it evident that his choice has settled on Courbet: "I shall make of my god, my Courbet, a sculptor. . . ."[80]

In his two appearances in *L'Oeuvre,* Chambouvard is presented as a powerful physical specimen, whose peasant background is clearly indicated by his physique (could Zola have been thinking of Carpeaux, in whom he had been much interested at the time of Carpeaux's death in 1875?), an artist of irresistible creative force, completely lacking in self-doubt and with an enormous, naive vanity which is allied to an almost incredible stupidity and lack of critical sense. He is, as Zola puts it, "a worker of genius, without refinement." Allowing for a good deal of exaggeration, we have a fairly exact portrait of Courbet, as the latter's contemporaries depicted him and as he depicted himself in his letters and other writings. It is true, however, that such traits are so general that they might equally well represent Zola's opinion of Victor Hugo (perhaps it is no accident that Chambouvard's first name is Victor, just as it probably was not entirely coincidental that Jory's name was Paul and Fagerolles' was Henri). Hugo, with more refinement, subtlety, and intelligence, was much this same kind of "god," and the fact that Chambouvard's first statue in the novel is called "Le Semeur," recalling "Saison des semailles—le soir," seems to increase the possibility that Hugo was at least partly the model. At all events, if Zola did take Courbet and Hugo as models for the vain, blind genius, he was on solid ground, for Edmondo de Amicis observed that only two artists of the time, Hugo and Courbet, never had the slightest doubt that they could do anything less than perfectly in their respective domains.[81]

But Ernest Vizetelly thought that as far as disposition was concerned, Chambouvard undoubtedly was Courbet, though he also added that the sculptor's career was based on that of the enormously prolific Clésinger,[82] and there may be some truth in his contention, for Clésinger's reputation for vanity and scorn of his contemporaries has come down to us even today. There is no evidence in the *Dossier,* however, to support Vizetelly's view. Actually, the only detail in the presentation of Chambouvard which can be certainly traced to a real person comes from the life of Courbet. Chambouvard's habit of looking at his creations with a smile of self-satisfaction and repeating "it's comical" was not only borrowed from Courbet but had actually been observed by Zola himself at some point in his career. Edmond de Goncourt, writing in 1882, quotes Zola as repeating the phrase textually from Courbet.[83] It is also possible that Chambouvard's second appearance in the novel, at the Salon of 1876, is a reflection of Courbet's triumph in 1866, a triumph all the greater because Manet had been rejected and did not appear at all. It will be recalled that in the novel Bongrand does not show any paintings in this second Salon, thus pointing up Chambouvard's success.

On the whole, Chambouvard, despite his resemblance to Courbet, is too exaggerated and lacking in nuance to be a portrait of any single man. Rather, he seems, like most of the figures of the "little band," to summarize a whole artistic temperament, one which Zola—who for many of his contemporaries was a kind of Chambouvard himself—could not help viewing with a kind of amused irritation.

Another pair of characters, the art dealers *père* Malgras and Jules Naudet, likewise are probably types based on more than one individual. Malgras, who represents the old school of art dealers in contrast with the new group of the period of Durand-Ruel, occupies somewhat the same position in the novel as Bongrand, for his function, besides providing handy local color, is mainly to demonstrate the integrity and soundness of the older personalities and their methods and thus to point up the latter decline in quality, exemplified both by Naudet and his protégé, Fagerolles. Malgras is shown as a shoe-string operator of excellent taste and real devotion to art, contenting himself with a minimum profit on a few carefully chosen and really successful canvases, a connoisseur and an authentic bohemian in dress and manner. As such, it is probable that he represents a whole era and a whole tendency rather than a single individual, and the impression that he has a composite basis in Zola's observation is confirmed by the *Dossier*, where Zola describes Malgras from the first as "a compromise between Martin and Aubourg."[84]

In the notes on "Les Marchands de tableaux" that he got from Guillemet, Zola reveals that *père* Aubourg was also called *la Crasse*. Like Malgras, he had a great deal of taste and flair and was satisfied with small profits on good canvases; he too was badly dressed, and his dealings with the painters were characterized by an insulting attitude which surely gave Zola the idea for Malgras' behavior toward Claude. Like Malgras again, Aubourg retired with a small income after having contributed materially to the success of several distinguished artists, among them Corot, Jongkind, and Pissarro.

It is apparent that Malgras resembles Aubourg a great deal, and the impression that the latter may have been Zola's chief model is heightened by the fact that Zola expressly says of him that he practices "the business of the roast of lamb," promising the artist a roast on condition that he make a study of it for him in return. This is the origin of the scene in *L'Oeuvre* in which Malgras promises Claude a lobster in return for a still life of it, one of the best short bits in the work.

But these similarities do not make it certain that Aubourg was the chief model. The other dealer mentioned by Zola, Martin, practiced the same system of dealing in only a few excellent paintings and taking a modest profit, and like Aubourg he found his greatest satisfaction in discovering new talents. The *Dossier* shows that the rather brutal technique of bargaining adopted by Malgras with Claude came from Martin's practices, for Martin is specifically named.[85]

It was apparently such similarities as this which led the compilers of the Bibliothèque Nationale catalogue to list only Martin as the model for Malgras.[86] Their point of view is certainly strengthened by the brief sketch of Martin given by Théodore Duret in his edition of the letters of Manet and Sisley;[87] here Martin looks so much like Malgras in general outline that it is difficult to believe Zola could have had any other model.

The best possibility, however, is that Malgras was a composite in origin. Zola chanced to have in the notes Antoine Guillemet gave him descriptions of two men—really three, since he also mentions Beugnet, "a large-scale Martin, operating in exactly the same way"[88]—whose careers resembled each other closely in essentials and who were of approximately the same character and disposition. He probably took what he wanted from each and finished with a type figure which strongly resembles those of the "little band" in that it is mainly representative and not specific or complete.

Jules Naudet, while entirely different in personality and temperament from Malgras, resembles him closely in origin, for he too is a composite character, drawn from at least two living models, and as such is a type character charged with representing the new—and to Zola completely hateful—commercial tendencies of the art world. There is no hint of his original or originals in either the *Personnages* or the *Ébauche*, but the notes Zola got from Guillemet on "Les Marchands de tableaux" clearly show that Naudet was mainly based on the figures of Georges Petit and Brame, with Charles Sedelmayer contributing at least one important detail of characterization.

Naudet, who appears in the novel more frequently than Malgras and who occupies an important if secondary position in the economy of the work, is depicted as the dealer who sets in motion the revolution in sales technique which completely upsets the art world and makes possible the prodigious success of such painters as Fagerolles. He is shown as quite a gentleman and something of a dandy, wearing the latest thing in sport jackets, with a carriage, a stall at the Opéra, and a terrifically expensive way of life. Because he lives so well Naudet is constantly in need of money and so becomes a speculator in art, with no true interest in painting but with a remarkable gift for discovering and exploiting the kind of fake realists pleasing to the bourgeois public and thus enabling him to charge fantastic prices and to make fantastic profits. As his affairs develop Naudet (whose first profits come from the sale of canvases by established figures like Courbet, Millet, and Rousseau) gradually abandons the old practice of dealing with authentic amateurs and begins to concentrate on the rich but naive collector who can be persuaded to pay high prices either because he knows nothing at all of art or because he regards pictures as a solid investment, like stocks or bonds. Naudet also practices the technique of persuading his chosen painter to produce only for him and in order to protect his market keeps the artist from painting more than a strict minimum of works each year. In addition, he invents the clever short-term device of selling canvases with a guarantee to repurchase at a higher price at the end of a stated time, thereby allaying any fears the collector may have at buying a painting by a comparatively unknown artist. As his affairs prosper Naudet sets up a huge gallery, where he holds numerous private exhibitions and gradually develops the American trade as his chief source of revenue after the exhaustion of the European market. One of his most successful tricks in gulling the Americans is to set up a single painting in a gallery, like a relic in a shrine, and to refuse to show it except to a chosen few; when the American has succeeded in persuading him to show the painting, he then declares that the canvas is simply too expensive for anyone to buy, whereupon the foreigner, piqued, determines to have it at any cost for his collection.

But toward the close of the novel, Naudet, in spite of all his techniques and devices, begins to find himself in trouble (just as the dealers of the Parisian art world began to have difficulties about 1885 as the result of the financial crash of 1882 and as a consequence of their imprudent speculations). Forced to set up a syndicate of dealers to help carry the financial burden which has grown too heavy for him, he resorts to shady tricks, such as fictitious sales; he is driven to repurchase paintings at a heavy loss and eventually faces bankruptcy, just as some dealers did at about the time *L'Oeuvre* was being written. In his last appearance in the novel, Naudet is on the point of bringing suit against Fagerolles to recover his investment in the tapestries, furniture, and bibelots with which he had furnished the painter's palace on the avenue de Villiers as a means of guaranteeing his continued loyalty and submission to the harsh necessities of the new technique of selling.

All of these details appear, and in almost exactly the same form, in Guillemet's notes on Brame, Petit, and Sedelmayer. Brame is shown as the elegant gentleman in the English jacket, with his stall at the Opéra, who revolutionizes standard sales practices by dealing only with rich collectors who know nothing of art. Like Naudet, he perfects the technique of acquiring a tame painter who will agree to produce only for him and to limit his yearly production carefully in order to keep the market high. His chosen painters are the kind of false realists, according to Guillemet, who will be sure to appeal to his rich middle-class clientele. Brame's dealings with the painter Roybet, as noted, are certainly the origin of Naudet's relationship with Fagerolles.

From Petit, who is described in the notes as operating in much the same way as Brame but on a larger scale, Zola took the idea of an enormously expensive way of life ("wife, mistress, eight horses, chateau, hunting grounds"[89]) leading to the necessity of constantly expanding his operations. Where Brame is described as the man who revolutionized selling techniques, Petit is shown in the notes as the first important centralizer, setting up a large gallery, conducting many private expositions, and cultivating the American trade for the first time on a large scale. Like Naudet, Petit made his first important profits on well-known figures like Delacroix, Courbet, Corot, Millet, and Rousseau, and also like him he was forced to establish a syndicate to help carry the burden of his operations; again, faced with bankruptcy, like Naudet, because of the small number of rich amateurs, he is compelled to make fictitious sales and to repurchase paintings at a loss when things begin to go badly. But as in the case of Naudet, bankruptcy seems inevitable because of the very nature of his operations.

Sedelmayer's career, as outlined in the notes, seems to have provided Zola with a single detail, the device of persuading the American to purchase by hinting that he was not rich enough to afford the "painting of the year." His technique as described in the notes is much the same as it appears in Naudet's final attempt to cover his losses by trapping the American.[90]

Curiously, although there are fairly ample notes on him, Durand-Ruel provided nothing in the composition of the figure of Naudet; indeed, the *Dossier* makes it clear that Zola rejected the idea of calling on Durand-Ruel for anything in creating Naudet.[91] This is strange, for of all the dealers of the 1870's and 1880's Durand-Ruel was by far the most interesting, and Zola might have done better to call on him than on the lesser figures he chose to employ as his models.

The question must, of course, arise as to whether or not Zola presented anything like a fair or accurate picture of the new art dealer of his time in the person of Naudet. There is some evidence that he is systematically unfair to Georges Petit, for instance, in refusing him any positive virtues and in declining to recognize his important role in the final public acceptance of the Impressionists, and it is possible that he is equally unjust to Brame. Guillemet's notes are anything but comprehensive and indeed are so one-sided that they give the very clear impression that Zola sent him out specifically to find unfavorable aspects of the art dealer's trade in order to point up the integrity and flair of the older operators, symbolized by Malgras, and thus to strike one more blow in favor of the past as against the present. Also, his description of the creation of the new selling techniques is slightly out of phase with the chronology of the novel as a whole, for while almost exactly the process he describes in *L'Oeuvre* did come about—the replacement of the old-style dealer by the commercial operator—it occurred a little later than the novel seems to indicate. The near bankruptcy of the new businessmen-dealers, for instance, began at about the time Zola was composing *L'Oeuvre*, not before 1876, as the work indicates.

But more important than such considerations is the undeniable fact that the very composition of Naudet's figure proves beyond doubt that Zola knew almost nothing of art dealings of the 1870's and 1880's and was forced into a complete dependence on others for his documentation. Whatever he might have known of the techniques and practices of the 1860's, it is clear that by 1885, and apparently much before that, he had lost touch and was unable or unwilling to document himself by his own observation or research. Because of his lack of direct, personal knowledge Zola was forced to make Naudet the most completely identifiable figure in the book, the person who with *Mère* Sandoz and her daughter-in-law, is demonstrably closest to contemporary reality and the furthest from fictional existence—which does not at all mean that he is the poorest character in the novel.

The figure of Gustave Gagnière, who appears in the novel on the fringe of the "little band," is quite different. Gagnière (whose name, incidentally, may be a Gallicized form of Wagner or may have been taken by Zola from the name of an art historian who published several books in the 1880's) was probably modeled on a living individual or individuals of Zola's acquaintance, but not enough details of his character and personality are given to permit easy identification. As presented in the novel, Gagnière is a minor landscape painter living in Melun and visiting Paris only rarely to meet the members of the "band." Although nominally a graphic artist—his small landscapes are gray, precise, and unexceptionable—he is most deeply interested in music, and indeed figures in the novel as the type of personality in which one art gradually kills another, rendering the figure impotent in both his original vocation and in his later avocation. Eventually, Gagnière marries a pianist, retires to Melun, and abandons painting altogether. He is thus another type of failure for Zola's gallery, but is perhaps a little more significant than some of the more developed characters in that he symbolizes a profoundly important artistic movement of the time, the progressive encroachment of music on the other arts.

There is nothing in the *Personnages* to give any clue to Gagnière's original, but in the *Ébauche* Zola does reveal the identity of at least one of his models for the character, the painter Edouard Béliard.[92] But there is no indication of the extent to which Zola employed the physiognomy of the painter in composing the character; unfortunately, the matter must rest there, for little biographical information is available on Béliard. A letter of Paul Alexis', written on September 2, 1886, seems to offer some proof that the essence of Gagnière came from Béliard, who, incidentally, lived at Étampes and visited Paris only occasionally in the latter part of his life. Alexis stresses Béliard's idleness, his lack of interest in art, his detachment from life, in short he offers a portrait which could have been the model for Gagnière.[93]

It is also true that Zola's description of Béliard's paintings in his "Russian" letter of 1876 offers a marked resemblance to the description of Gagnière's canvases in *L'Oeuvre:*

> Béliard is a landscape artist whose distinguishing characteristic is meticulousness. One feels in him the studious copyist of nature. Having studied it deeply, he has acquired a great solidity of workmanship which makes each one of his pictures an erudite and exact translation of nature. Some of his landscapes: "Rue de Chanfour à Etampes," "Les Bords de l'Oise," "La Rue Dorée à Pontoise," are excellent things, perfectly drawn, faithful in tone and absolutely true. The only fault I find in him is the absence of originality. I would like to see an inner flame consume his scruples, even if that fire were to burn at the expense of exactness.[94]

In the Salon where Claude meets his final defeat with *L'Enfant mort,* Gagnière exhibits "his usual landscape, the banks of the Seine that he had sent for fifteen years, of a pretty gray tone, conscientious and so discreet that the public had never noticed it."[95]

It seems certain, then, that Béliard was the principal model for Gagnière, and at least one critic, Fernand Doucet, sees him in the fictional figure.[96] But it is nonetheless possible that, as in the case of some of the other characters, Gagnière is a composite figure to which Béliard contributed only the essential outline. Gagnière's marriage to the pianist, for instance, might be a reminiscence of Manet's marriage to the Dutch pianist, Suzanne Leenhoff. Again, it might have been from Fantin-Latour's life that Zola got the idea of incorporating two competing arts in the same figure, for Fantin was a devotee of the new music and defended the revolutionary composers with as much vehemence as any of the young painters, going so far as to paint a "Scène du Tannhäuser."[97] Likewise, Zola could have been thinking of his brilliant and unfortunate friend, the gifted painter Frédéric Bazille, who died in the first days of the Franco-Prussian War and who served him in *Le Rêve* as the original of the engaging figure of Félicien d'Hautecoeur. Bazille was more passionately fond of music than almost any painter of the period, it appears, and was especially impressed by the advanced music of Berlioz and Wagner; he was a steady patron of the Concerts Pasdeloup and made frequent visits to the Conservatoire, where he crossed swords with the critics of Wagner and the new tendencies.[98] It is notable, however, that Bazille's appearance and personality do not at all resemble Gagnière's and the possibility that he was a serious model for the character is rather slight.

But another friend of Zola's—he appears with him in Fantin-Latour's "Un Atelier aux Batignolles"—might well have been the original, at least as far as appearance and manner are concerned, Edmond Maître. He was an amateur musician and, like Bazille, an ardent defender of Wagner. Bazille's portrait of him, as described by Gaston Poulain, makes him resemble Gagnière to a considerable degree:

> From the white collar his sharp profile emerges, with a blond beard, and his oval head, round at the back, has smooth hair with glints of steel. It is an admirable face of a disillusioned intellectual, or of a convalescent threatened by a relapse and whose emaciated face, very pale, stands out against the tan background.[99]

The best possibility after Béliard, however, is certainly the strange, vague, and dreamy musician called Cabaner (Jean de Cabanes), a pillar of the Nouvelle-Athènes during the time when Duranty, Manet, and Cézanne were often seen there,[100] and a friend and defender of the Impressionists and especially of Cézanne.[101] Cabaner, who died of tuberculosis at the age of forty-eight in 1881, is described by a friend, who writes of "the cenacle of modern bohemianism," as "the Schaunard of the group, the musician."[102] His dreamy, idealistic, somewhat sickly personality and manner surely recall Gagnière, as does his appearance, at least as one acquaintance rendered it: "A little thin man, old in features, young in glance, his long hair over his neck and a little thin on top, gentle without being sad."[103] For Henri Perruchot he is almost the type of the self-confessed failure, with a fertile imagination and an original talent, but without the courage to keep at work steadily, a man of curious temperament.[104] There is no doubt that Zola knew Cabaner—though there is little evidence that he knew him well—for in 1881 he wrote the preface for the catalogue of a benefit sale organized for him, and so the possibility of his being a model,[105] at least a partial model, for Gagnière, seems a very good one.

There may be numerous other possibilities as originals, for Gagnière is so vaguely rendered as to make it very difficult to link him with anyone of Zola's acquaintance. One of the best of these possibilities might be the poet-musician Maurice Rollinat. Here it is significant that the *Dossier* indicates that Zola had at first intended to make Gagnière a Parnassian poet; perhaps it was Rollinat or someone like him whom he originally had in mind.

One curious detail offered by Gagnière is that he is employed in *L'Oeuvre* to express some of the rare technical ideas that the work contains. His theories of complementary colors were taken directly by Zola from a letter written him by a painter named Léo Gausson and now forming part of the *Dossier*. Gagnière is in some respects the least likely character in the novel to advance such ideas, based as they are on the theories of the physicist Chevreul and leading directly to the neo-impressionism of 1886 and later. Zola apparently considered Gagnière as a kind of catch-all character who could symbolize not only the vast new popularity of music and its quickening invasion of the other arts, but also the decline of landscape painting[106] and the rise of the theories which in time were to bring about profound modifications in the nature of Impressionism and of pictorial art in general. But as presented in the novel, Gagnière is a long way from being up to his multiple tasks.

Of the other figures in *L'Oeuvre,* again excluding Claude Lantier and Pierre Sandoz, only one, the classic painter Mazel, can be identified with any certainty. In both the *Personnages* and in the second plan of Chapter IX Zola indicates clearly that his model for this figure was the academic painter Cabanel, who seems to have stood in his eyes for all that was old-fashioned and conventional in the "successful" art of the middle of the nineteenth century.[107] M. Hue, the slightly eccentric collector who is one of the few patrons of the "little band" in the novel, has been identified as the early patron of the Impressionists, Victor Chocquet,[108] but this identification has no documentary support and depends on an interpretation of Claude Lantier as Paul Cézanne and of the "band" as the young Impressionists. But M. Hue might equally well have been modeled on Dr. Paul-Ferdinand Gachet or on the novelist Eugène Murer or even on the ruined millionaire turned art critic, Hoschedé, for all these men were, like M. Hue, early and passionate defenders of the new movement. It is probable that in Hue, Zola was simply creating a representative character who would stand for all the impoverished but enthusiastic amateurs Zola had seen around the studios when he was in close contact with the art world; at all events there is no evidence that he had any specific individual in mind here.

The retired landscape painter Courajod (a Louis Courajod was on the staff of the Louvre in the 1880's), who does not actually appear in *L'Oeuvre* but who is mentioned on several occasions, has been identified with Corot,[109] and there is some slight reason for the identification. In the novel Courajod is described as "one who invented landscape art"[110] and his most famous painting is "La Mare de Gagny," which seems to recall Corot's studies of the pond at Ville-d'Avray. Moreover, "La Mare de Gagny" is described by Claude in 1863 as dating from about thirty years back, which would put its composition in the years when Corot was at the height of his talent; Courajod is said to be about seventy at the time of the Salon des Refusés, which again would be almost exactly right for Corot. But nothing in the *Dossier* supports this circumstantial evidence, so there is little certainty in the identification.

The case of Mathilde Jabouille, who becomes Jory's wife in the novel, is somewhat different. The *Ébauche* makes it clear that she had an original among Zola's acquaintances,[111] but does not indicate with any clarity who she may have been, though perhaps Zola meant the mistress of Antony Valabrègue. There is no possibility of confirming whether or not he actually did create Mathilde on such a model, if one existed in reality, but if he did, he must have "romanced" the figure considerably, for Mathilde is surely the most repugnant character in *L'Oeuvre*. Her relationship with Jory, though, may have had a purely literary origin, for in "Mes Souvenirs sur Gustave Flaubert" Zola cites a project of Flaubert's last years which strangely resembles the marriage of the two worthless people in the novel:

. . . he had finally found a subject, but he described it to us in too confused a fashion for me to speak clearly of it here; it was the story of a passion put under control, of vice becoming bourgeois and satisfying itself beneath very honorable appearances.

No one else in the novel has any demonstrable connection with reality, save the Margaillan family[111a] and perhaps Irma Bécot in her last incarnation as the rich and dignified courtesan who ruins Fagerolles; this aspect of Irma comes from one of Zola's favorite figures of the demimonde, Valtesse de la Bigne.[112] But this is true only of the later Irma, not of the younger girl, who is a "flower of the streets" and probably almost completely fictional, as will be seen. Madame Vanzade, little Jacques, the professional models—all these were, so far as we know, from Zola's stock of memories and apparently owe little or nothing to individuals specifically observed for the purposes of the novel.

Surprisingly enough, this seems true for one of the three major characters of the book, Claude's wife, Christine Hallegrain. Several not very satisfactory attempts have been made to identify her with a real person. John Rewald thinks she represented Hortense Fiquet, Cézanne's wife,[113] but her personality and role are so different from the real Hortense—at least as she appears in Cézanne's letters—that the possibility seems slight indeed. Ernest Vizetelly believed that she might have come from the wife of the engraver Belot (the model himself, incidentally, for Manet's "Bon Bock"),[114] but Emile Solari, who had as much inside knowledge as Vizetelly and surely more than Rewald, says flatly that Christine was, like most of Zola's heroines, entirely created.[115] His view is almost certainly right, for there is no evidence of any kind either in the work itself or in the *Dossier* or in any other source that in this figure Zola employed any model other than the ideal woman he carried in his head—or in his heart (could Louise Solari be the distant model?)—and on whom he fashioned so many of his young women, from Ninon to the "Abisaïg" of *Le Docteur Pascal.* The *Dossier* indicates with the greatest clarity that Christine Hallegrain (her name resembles the family name, Allegrain, of a number of artists of the sixteenth and seventeenth centuries) had no model, that she was a work of pure imagination; as such her creation offers an unusually interesting sample of Zola's creative tendencies and methods.

Christine first appears in the *Ébauche* as a *rouleuse,* picked up at night by Claude but untouched by him. She leaves his apartment but returns some time later as a kept woman; it is evident that Zola meant her from the beginning to be in love with Claude, though he is not at first in love with her. Zola's next idea was that she should be picked up at a carnival, drunk; here he adds the idea that Christine should have some artistic inclinations and that she should be more amorous than Claude. They live together briefly, then Claude abandons her because she comes to represent for him reality attained. Then, as he elaborates the *Ébauche,* the conception of the "ideal" woman enters: Claude glimpses her one day, falls in love with her romantically, and eventually possesses her. Then Zola abandons the idea of a rivalry between the "real" woman and the "ideal"; but when he writes the novel he returns to it in two different ways: the rivalry of Christine with the two nudes of Claude's two great paintings, and the rivalry of Christine and Irma, both of whom stem out of his original figure of the mistress. Irma's figure emerges vaguely after Zola has hit upon the idea of the "ideal" woman; she is not "primordial" in the sense that Christine is, but she evidently intrigues him, for he sees in her another Nana, perhaps, and then proceeds to develop her character. As she emerges from his gropings, the previous idea that the "ideal" woman should satisfy Claude's passion becomes Claude's brief *passade* with Irma.

In the *Ébauche* Christine becomes Claude's mistress before the Salon des Refusés, and Zola continues to think of her as originally "impure," not a virgin, for she is depicted as being very fickle, and he says of her that she has had adventures very young. At one point he thinks of having her deceive Claude—the opposite happens in the novel —and it might be said in general that the original portrait makes her out to be more active than she appears in *L'Oeuvre,* for she supports Claude by working for a time. Fairly late in the *Ébauche* Christine still resembles the figure who will eventually become Irma, but signs of her final character keep appearing: she is an orphan, she lives with an aunt, and so on. Eventually, Zola decides that he must make some kind of selection among the qualities and defects he has given her, so he divides her into two people, Christine and Irma. The latter is to be the mistress of "le Baille," "l'Alexis," and "le Gervex," but it is clear that some of her role is eventually taken over by Mathilde Jabouille, and at the end it becomes apparent that she will be modeled in part on Valtesse de la Bigne. In the *Ébauche* Zola is clear that Christine will be jealous only of the painted nudes, not of Irma, and he thinks of having her openly desire that Claude have an affair with Irma so that he may forget himself and the phantasmagoria of his art in her. He suppresses entirely the concept of the "ideal" woman, but in the novel she reappears in the form of the painted nudes. Thus from the original idea of a woman who is to be Claude's mistress stem three women: a "good" woman, Christine, an "evil" woman, Irma, and an "ideal" woman, the painted nude of the "Apotheosis of Paris." This is fiction at its most fictional.[116]

This long discussion indicates clearly that while Zola evidently borrowed numerous events and details from the lives of people he knew, *L'Oeuvre* is far from being as much of a key novel as some critics have thought.[117] In only a few instances can it be said with any certainty that he deliberately depicted the character or personality of a living individual, though it is often certain that he did make use of the outward facts of his life and career. When he did borrow events and details or even personal characteristics from his friends and acquaintances, he so combined, transposed, and modified them that it is almost impossible to recognize any of them surely. And most of all, of course, he invented, as every good novelist must do, so that the people of *L'Oeuvre,* whatever their point of departure in living individuals, remain essentially fictional. No formula for his creation of character can be set down that is completely satisfactory here. But the closer the character stands to the three central figures—Claude, Sandoz, Christine—the more likely it is that Zola has some real person as his point of departure, however far he may depart from the reality as the story develops. This is true in nearly every case, the only important exceptions being the art dealers Malgras and Naudet, and here Zola's ignorance of the contemporary art world drove him to rely on other men's observations. Thus, from the point of view of character portrayal, the novel appears as a core of central figures, surrounded closely by imitations, close or remote, of people Zola had known, who are in turn surrounded by a second group of almost completely fictional figures. It is also true, and to a degree not remarked by the critics, that most of the characters of *L'Oeuvre* represent clearly marked types, not individuals. They all have sharp, clear attitudes and postures, but they do not have much inner life and they do not much depart from their inflexibility as frieze figures. They produce in the long run the impression that Zola did not really care deeply for any of them, except perhaps Sandoz, and that he kept them rigorously at arm's length as a sign of his lack of sympathy for what they represented. On the whole they well illustrate Henry James's opinion that Zola was the writer who, better than anyone else, gave an excellent imitation of observation.

III

Pierre Sandoz

If there is one aspect of *L'Oeuvre* on which opinion approaches unanimity, it is that the character of Pierre Sandoz is a direct and exact self-portrait of Zola himself. Some contemporary critics, already alerted by Alexis' prophecies, recognized Zola behind the figure of his novelist and proclaimed the personal nature of *L'Oeuvre* from the very first. Philippe Gille, for instance, who knew Zola well, was sure that his friend had given a detailed self-portrait in the novel,[1] and both Denise LeBlond, Zola's daughter, and Maurice LeBlond, her husband, agree with him.[2] They are joined by nearly every historian or critic who has touched on Zola's work, from Jules Lemaître to Armand Lanoux.[3]

There is excellent evidence to back this opinion, both in the novel and in the *Dossier*. In the *Ébauche* of the work, there are nearly a dozen instances where he uses the pronoun "I" to refer to the friend and confidant of Claude Lantier.[4] In the sketchy little preliminary plan by chapters which seems to have followed the *Ébauche* as Zola plotted the course of the novel there are a half-dozen more such references,[5] and in the detailed plans, which appear to have immediately preceded the actual composition of the work, there are two or three others,[6] though it is notable that as Zola draws closer to the moment of writing he tends to replace "I" by the name Sandoz, perhaps indicating that the figure of the novelist was now beginning to take on something of its final aspect and was departing a little from its first conception as a strictly personal portrait.

Not only does the *Dossier* make it perfectly clear that Zola himself was to be the starting point for the character of Sandoz, it spells out in some detail just what aspects of his life and career Zola intended to incorporate into the structure of the work. It shows that he wanted from the beginning to include somewhere a conversation between Sandoz and Claude which would be a reflection of his own long discussions with Cézanne after the latter's failures in his early years;[7] that he intended Sandoz to be a novelist and journalist, like himself;[8] that he planned to have him born in Paris and live his youth in Plassans, where he would be a schoolmate of Lantier and the architect Dubuche, as Zola himself had been a schoolmate of Cézanne and Baille;[9] that the three soirées at which the group would meet should be reflections of similar gatherings at his own house;[10] that Sandoz should pose for Claude, as Zola himself had posed for Manet and Cézanne;[11] and that the cottage at Bennecourt rented by Lantier and Christine should be a copy of one he himself had occupied before success came to him with *L'Assommoir*.[12] Each of these details appears in the novel. Then, as the list of memories at the end of the *Ébauche* makes clear, he wished especially to evoke his childhood and early youth, the years from about 1850, say, to 1862 or 1863,[13] and the impression that it was especially his youth which he first wished to render in the pages of the novel is heightened by the description he gives of Sandoz in the *Personnages* of the *Dossier:*

> My portrait modified. Spanish origins, Spanish father having married a Burgundian girl. Very dark, strong without being big, at the beginning. Round and willful head. Square chin, square nose. Soft eyes in the energetic face. Full black beard. Have him live first with his mother (the mother ill, not appearing), whom he supports by a position in a city hall (in birth records). Later, he will marry and the receptions will continue on Thursdays.
>
> Mother ruined by the death of the father, engaged in industry. Inventor, builder. A paper mill, for instance, with models of new machines.[14]

It is clear enough that Sandoz was conceived originally as a static background figure, not much more than a *porte-parole,* and not as a true actor of the drama at all, and that his principal connection with lived reality was to be only with the young and struggling Zola, not with the mature and successful novelist who conceived and wrote *L'Oeuvre* in 1885. This is almost certainly why the description of Sandoz in the *Personnages* of the *Dossier* is so short; it is indeed the shortest given to any major character of the book (with the exception of Claude Lantier, who has virtually none at all, only a brief sketch of his chronology and of his connection with the Rougon-Macquarts), shorter even than the description of such minor figures as Irma Bécot and Justin Chaîne.

But if Zola originally conceived his fictional novelist as nothing more than a mouthpiece and as a partial re-creation of his own youth, he soon came, without doubt consciously, to widen Sandoz' role greatly and to make of him much more than the young and immobile theorist he seems to have first imagined. As he did so, he gave the novel a far different importance and meaning from what he had apparently first intended and made it, instead of a study of an unsuccessful artist, something like a real autobiography spanning the years 1850 to 1880 and even after.

This is borne out by a host of situations and ideas in the work, all of them taken directly from Zola's own experiences and all of them directly verifiable either from other autobiographical sources or from the biographies written by those who knew him.

First, in the physical details of his life Sandoz is depicted as being a close friend of Claude Lantier, but one who suffers a prolonged absence from his old companion and consequently a cooling of affection when Lantier goes to Bennecourt; this separation may represent one of the quarrels which separated Zola and Cézanne during their early years in Paris and which are reflected in Zola's correspondence. Again, Sandoz lives in three different lodgings in Paris and at least two of these are identifiable with actual apartments or houses Zola occupied at one time or another. The first, rue d'Enfer, is not surely identifiable, but, as described, seems somewhat like an apartment that Zola rented in 1863 on the fourth floor of number 7, rue des Feuillantines.[15] If there is doubt about the identification of this first lodging, there is none about the second and third. As Sandoz finds increasing success he leaves the rue d'Enfer for an unpretentious house in the Batignolles, rue de Nollet, a small *pavillon* behind a larger house. Robert Sherard has identified this as Zola's house on the rue Truffaut,[16] and Philippe Gille, who lived on the same street, corroborates the identification.[17] The last dwelling of Sandoz' in the novel is a sumptuous, if tasteless, private residence, rue de Londres, almost certainly an exact copy of Zola's longtime lodgings on the rue de Bruxelles (now rue Ballu). The description which he gives of the salon of this house, with its antiques, its tapestries, its bibelots, tallies so accurately with the accounts given by Maupassant[18] and by a half-dozen reporters who came there at various times for interviews that there can be no doubt that Zola, as he described his salon in the novel, was actually looking out his study door and noting the bizarre and romantic furnishings he saw before him. There are a dozen similar details: the dog Bertrand, image of the line of faithful Bertrands—they actually bore the name—who gave Zola such pleasure and such pain when they died; the stupendous final dinner given by Zola in 1882 and described by Edmond de Goncourt in his *Journal*;[19] Sandoz' *gourmandise*, a reflection of Zola's own tendencies before he took to dieting; the funeral of Claude Lantier, the details of which are handled by Sandoz as Zola took charge of the interment of Edmond Duranty; perhaps most important of all, Sandoz' work habits—steady, regular, inexorable—and the extent to which work captures him, dominates him, keeps him from life. This aspect of Sandoz' professional life perhaps identifies him most closely with Zola, for from the beginning of his writing career Zola had worked with such tenacity that by the time he had achieved success he had come very nearly to detest the grinding labor that composition meant; from about the middle of the 1870's, nearly every reference to Zola in the Goncourt *Journal* mentions the complaints he kept uttering about his lack of freedom, the constant pressure on him, his sense of imprisonment in his vast series. Here is a far different Zola from the one the public saw, and here again *L'Oeuvre* has great value as a confession; if this part of the novel is an accurate reflection of Zola's intimate life, and there is every reason to think it is, then Zola was no great copy machine after all, as legend had it, but a sufferer from the "terrors of style."

But these details, important as they are, are by no means all. There is also Sandoz' family situation, which in every main detail is almost an exact reflection of Zola's. Sandoz' father, a Spanish inventor who had taken refuge in France after certain political difficulties, had set up a paper mill in Plassans, where he used several of his own machine inventions; it does not take much of a stretch of the imagination to see here clear reflections of the life of François Zola, the Italian officer who had come to France after some difficulties with the Austrian occupiers of his homeland, who had invented some ingenious earth-moving equipment, and who had put his talents to good use in the planning and construction of the canal which now bears his name. Sandoz' father dies embittered, followed by local spitefulness,[20] and this is almost certainly a hint of Zola's bitterness about the ill will, stubbornness, and general malevolence of a certain portion of the population of Aix, against whom he seems to have maintained his rancor almost to the end of his life. The elder Sandoz leaves his wife in financial difficulties, just as François Zola did, with a series of obscure and tangled lawsuits on her hands; and the widow (a Burgundian girl—Zola's mother was a Beauceronne), tired of trouble with the people of Plassans, moves to Paris with her only son, who supports her by a small job, his brain haunted by dreams of literary glory.[21] All these events occurred in the life of Zola, just as he recounts them in the novel. The story is complete, even to the long illness of Madame Zola, the little attentions paid her by her son, and her death, events which surely reflect the domestic incidents of Zola's own life from 1875 to 1880, the year of his mother's death. The presence of the mother in the menage alongside Sandoz' young wife, Henriette, recalls that Madame Zola lived for some fifteen years with her daughter-in-law (Sandoz' marriage takes place at almost exactly the same period of his career as the beginnings of Zola's own liaison did, just at the opening of his brilliant journalistic career), though the family situation was not in actuality always as tranquil as Zola depicts it in *L'Oeuvre*.[22]

The events of Sandoz' youth, as he recalls them with Claude Lantier in Chapter II, the memories of the pranks at the dingy *collège* at Plassans, the teachers and their manias, their nicknames, their foibles, are surely sketched from life, as are the descriptions of the wanderings of the three "inseparables" through the hills around Plassans-Aix, as a dozen writings of Zola's testify, notably the preface to the *Nouveaux contes à Ninon*. And Sandoz' love of the Romantics, of Hugo and Musset, his need to declaim thunderous verses in the rain out of hatred for the crass cafe life of the schoolboys of the time, his passionate love of nature in the rough, his dreams of an ideal woman (Ninon?), these, too, are out of Zola's past. Even the detail of the clarinet and cornet serenades beneath the window of the two young girls comes from that time—the only time?—when Zola was happy.

And then there are memories of another kind and of another period, the account of the wanderings of the friends in the suburbs of Paris, Verrières, the valley of the Bièvre, Bellevue, Meudon, wanderings imitated, if early journalistic efforts of Zola are a good guide, from his long walks with Cézanne, ever in search of "*le motif*"—and wanderings on which Zola discovered the melancholy charm of the new suburbs long before Huysmans made them his own. There is no need to add that the persistent theme of wandering in Paris in the novel, in which we find the whole "band" on occasion, Claude alone sometimes or with Sandoz, is directly out of Zola's past, as shown by the essay he published on Anthony Valabrègue's *Petits poèmes parisiens* in *Le Voltaire* on June 29, 1880, an essay which reads like a preliminary sketch of certain parts of *L'Oeuvre:*

> We were then a whole little group, isolated, unknown, walking the pavement with the most absolute confidence in our future triumph. It's fine, youth is. Since that time, I have accomplished some of my dreams, but I have never experienced the joy in fulfillment that I had promised myself, and I still miss the time of hope, which had so much sweetness. It is not glory that intoxicates, it is the desire for glory.
>
> Blessed years when the world was ours and when we dined

> in the cheap restaurants of the Latin Quarter! Does Anthony Valabrègue remember our long walks in the streets, those promenades on the quays, up to the esplanade of the Invalides, all of us lost in literary theories, in discussions which brought us back to the quarter by the outer boulevards, without our being conscious of the distance we had traveled? Later, we went to bury ourselves in a corner of Normandy. Well! I found all that again on reading the *Petits poèmes parisiens*. There is a little of my youth in these verses and that is why I yield to the desire of talking about them.

The literary career of Sandoz is obviously another in this long series of memories. His first book is a nameless collection of short stories, a handful of "pleasant sketches, brought up from Plassans, in which a few harsher notes were the only indication of the rebel, the man passionate for truth and power"[22a]—after all, did not the *Contes à Ninon* include *Le Sang* and *Soeur des pauvres*? Sandoz likewise proposes a Dantesque poem on the genesis of the universe, with one section on the creation, a second on the history of humanity, taking its place in the great chain of being, and a third on the future, with its hope in work and life; no one has provided a more accurate description of Zola's own early vision of a vast poem, of which, happily, only fragments survive. Like Zola in 1865, Sandoz leaves his small position in the city administration (converted from Zola's place with Hachette) to try his hand at journalism and at almost exactly the same age as did his creator; he enters journalism for the same reasons that impelled Zola to abandon his position with Hachette for the more active and rewarding life of a journalist, where he could exert the power he felt growing in him as he matured. Sandoz, like Zola, has no intention of growing old in journalism, for he has a project worth ten of that, "a creation big enough to kill me with work, something I'm going to plunge into, perhaps never to emerge."[23] This first transparent reference to the *Rougon-Macquart* series is amplified later when Sandoz describes his intentions to Claude:

> I am going to take a family and I shall study its members, one by one, where they come from, where they go, how they react upon each other; in short, humanity in little, the way humanity grows and acts. . . . Moreover, I shall put my characters in a defined historical period, which will give me the milieu and the circumstances, a bit of history. Eh? you understand, a series of books, fifteen, twenty books, episodes which will have connections, while each one has its separate framework, a series of novels to build me a house for my old age.[24]

And not only do the outward details of Sandoz' series resemble those of the *Rougon-Macquart,* the spirit of his books is also amazingly similar to the pervasive philosophy of Zola's great creation:

> Eh? to study man as he is, not their metaphysical puppet, but physiological man, determined by his surroundings, acting according to the play of his organs. . . . Isn't it a farce, this continuous and exclusive study of the function of the brain, under the pretext that the brain is the noble organ? . . . . Thought, thought? By God, thought is the product of the entire body. Make a brain think all by itself, see what becomes of the nobility of the brain when the belly is sick! No, there's no science or philosophy in it, we are positivists, evolutionists, and we should keep the literary mannequins of classic times, and we should continue to unwind the tangled hair of pure reason? He who says "psychologist" says "traitor to the truth." Moreover, physiology, psychology, all that means nothing: one interpenetrates the other, both of them are only one today, man's mechanism boiling down to the sum total of his functions. . . . Ah! the formula is there, our modern evolution has no other basis; it means the inevitable death of the old society, it means the birth of a new society, and it necessarily means the growth of a new art in this new terrain . . . yes, they'll see, they'll see the new literature which is going to spring up for the coming century of science and democracy.[25]

And again:

> . . . the all-powerful role given back to the environment, vast nature eternally in creation, life, in a word, total, universal life which goes from one end of animality to the other, without high or low, without beauty or ugliness; and the audacities of language, the conviction that everything must be said, that there are abominable words necessary as branding irons, that a language comes out enriched from these strength-giving baths; and especially the sexual act, the origin and continuous completion of the world, taken from out of the shame where it is hidden, put back into its place of glory, beneath the sun.[26]

No better short descriptions have been written of the *Rougon-Macquart* series in its general aspects, intentions, and spirit. And if these were not enough, there is Zola's specific statement in the second and definitive plan for Chapter II: "A vast work, still confused, the Ark, men, beasts, nature, with a soul, with life everywhere. *A work of art is a bit of nature seen through a temperament.*"[27]

The first novel, again nameless, of Sandoz' series appears to be a composite of *Thérèse Raquin* and *La Fortune des Rougon*. It is described as the opening volume of the monumental creation, as *La Fortune des Rougon* was, and it appears in October, as the latter did, but the year assigned to it in *L'Oeuvre* seems to be 1867, the true year of *Thérèse Raquin* (the first edition of which actually bore the date of 1868). Moreover, although the novel is not described in *L'Oeuvre*, the attacks on it by the critics certainly recall Zola's battle with Louis Ulbach over the question of "putrid literature," as represented by *Thérèse Raquin*.[28] Two other novels of Sandoz' series are mentioned, though not many details are given about either. The first of them attains a sudden popular success at about the time of the death of the novelist's mother, a success which permits Sandoz to move to the rue de Londres. If Zola is in effect following the chronology of his own life here, this novel would be either *L'Assommoir*, his first important financial success, or *Nana*, which appeared in the year of Madame François Zola's death. The chronology of *L'Oeuvre*, with its terminal date in 1876, seems to favor the former, though the death of Sandoz' mother indicates how freely Zola treated the events of his own life as he romanced them here. The other novel, mentioned toward the end of *L'Oeuvre*, may be a reflection of *Germinal*, which seems to have been the first of Zola's works to obtain any real acclaim from the general body of critics. No details of the novel are given in *L'Oeuvre*, but it is described as stirring up "that rumor of success which consecrates a man, even amidst the persistent attacks of his enemies."[29]

In addition to the numerous reflections of Zola's own life and career and the fact that Sandoz plays the central figure in the "band," as Zola did with the Aix group of Cézanne, Alexis, Solari, Baille, Roux, and Valabrègue, and as he did in the Médan group, the figure of the novelist in *L'Oeuvre* has many other psychological and ideological resemblances to his creator. The *Dossier* contains abundant proofs that Zola intended to do far more than simply sketch in a figure which would resemble him as a young man and express certain of his own theories on art and literature. There are too many pronouncements throughout the *Dossier* like the one in the *Personnages* ("My character, my ideas") and the other in the preliminary plan ("All my ideas . . . . All my theories")[30] to doubt that Sandoz gradually came to represent in Zola's own mind something very much like a complete intellectual and psychological, as well as a physical, self-portrait. At all events, *L'Oeuvre* demonstrably contains, in addition to a developed physical, chronological, and social portrait of Zola, important elements of his philosophy of life, some of his favorite ideas, and a bit of his personality transferred to the character of Sandoz.

The *Dossier* makes it clear that the general view of life advanced by Sandoz, filled as it is with a kind of vague and slightly Germanic pantheism and partaking of the notion of a great chain of being, is Zola's also. In the *Ébauche,* for instance, he declares that he will transfer his own *Weltanschauung* to Sandoz:

> If I appear on stage, I should like either to complete Claude or to be his opposite. First, all the philosophical side: a new psychology, a soul in all of nature, no longer considered as apart, but everywhere, man no longer seen in his brain alone, but in all his organs; animals beloved, depicted; surroundings completing the being, explaining it, etc. In a word, the vast creation, taken up and set in a work. Boldness of language, to say everything and to know everything. The sexual act, origin and continuation of the world, the most important thing. Then, the two questions, lyricism, the upward flight that sums up the synthesis, sweeps it along, widens it. Then pessimism: but faith also, the generative act glorified after all.[31]

In the novel he is as good as his word:

> Ah, how fine it would be if one could give his entire existence to a work where he would try to put things, beasts, men, the whole immense Ark! And not according to the order given in the philosophy manuals, according to the idiotic hierarchy which tickles our pride; but in the full flow of universal life, a world where we men would be only an accident, where the passing dog, even the stone on the road, would complete us, explain us, in a word, the Great Whole, with neither high nor low, dirty nor clean, just as it functions. . . . Certainly, novelists and poets must now address themselves to science, which is today the only possible source. But what to take from science, how walk in company with her? Immediately, I feel myself floundering. . . . Ah! if I knew, if I knew, what a series of books I'd hurl at the heads of the public![32]

Here is Zola the autodidact speaking—the autodidact who was the first to turn to science for his method and for his justification. A little later in the book he is more lyric, even more personal; as Sandoz lies in the grass at Bennecourt he cries:

> Ah! good earth, take me, you, the common mother, the only source of life! you, the eternal, the immortal, in whom circulates the world soul, that essence which rises even in the stones and which makes of the trees our great immobile brothers! . . . Yes, I would lose myself in you, it is you I feel there, beneath my body, embracing me and enkindling me, it is you alone who will be the

> prime force in my work, the means and the end, the immense Ark where all things are animated by the breath of all beings.
>
> But begun as a joke in the rhetoric of his lyric exaggeration, this invocation ended in a cry of ardent conviction, that a profound poetic emotion made tremble, and his eyes moistened, and to hide this emotion he added in a rough voice, with a wide gesture which embraced the whole horizon:
>
> Isn't it stupid, a soul for each of us, when there is this great soul![33]

Surely this cry is not Sandoz' alone, but Zola's also, the Zola who created Le Paradou and so many other passages in which the Romantics' own animism betrays his belief in a world spirit and a "great soul" that links us all, stones, beasts, and men in an indissoluble whole.

Certain specific ideas advanced by Sandoz seem to confirm the impression that he not only speaks for his creator but *is* his creator to the life. When, for instance, Sandoz pleads the cause of logic before Claude's great, unsuccessful canvas, his "Apotheosis of Paris," to use Ima Ebin's phrase, it is clear that he is voicing the very objections of Zola himself to the concept of a pure pictorial art, careless of truth to nature or logic. But far more important than this is the bitter attack Sandoz launches, very near the close of the novel, on the influence of Romanticism on his own generation, the kind of bastard Romanticism which endured after the school had died and which was in great part responsible for Claude's failure:

> Our generation is too deeply soiled with romanticism to give the world healthy works. A generation, two generations perhaps, will be necessary before men paint and write logically, in the high and fine simplicity of the truth . . . truth, nature is the only possible basis, the necessary guard beyond which folly begins; and let man not fear that his works will be spiritless, for temperament is there which will always sweep the creator along. Does anyone think of denying the personality, the involuntary movement that deforms the statue and constitutes our poor human creation![34]

There can be no doubt at all that here Zola is speaking directly, for not many years before, in his "Revue dramatique et littéraire" in *Le Bien public* for April 8, 1878, he had used very nearly the same terms:

> I have already made a confession and I shall repeat it: all of us today, even those of us who are passionate for exact truth, are

> gangrened to the marrow with romanticism, we drank it in in school behind our desk tops when we read the forbidden poets; we breathed it in the poisoned air of our youth. . . . Often, when I think of us, I am clearly conscious of what romanticism has done to us. A literature remains long troubled by such a fit of madness. All logic, all basis in serious philosophy, all scientific method, all analytical knowledge of men and things were swept away in this sudden access of lyricism, and since that time we have been unable to recover our balance. In such matters, the ill generation does not carry its malady away with it; the virus passes to the following generations, it has to wear itself out in several generations in order to disappear completely. We, the first to come along after 1830, we are the most deeply infected; our children will be less and less so, and I have already observed better health in many young people. But the attack was so violent that at least fifty years will be necessary to rid our literature of that leprosy.

And the remarks on the relative roles of observation and personality in Sandoz' diatribe could have come from none other than the aesthetician of "homo additus naturae," in more recent terms, "nature seen through a temperament."

Again, when Sandoz speaks with a curious insistence on marriage as the only possible state for the creator he is quite obviously expressing a belief of Zola's own, that at this point in the century it was time to abandon Romantic bohemian life once for all and to settle into the routine of family life, the only life that could guarantee stability, clarity of mind, and freedom from temptation.[35] Perhaps here Zola is reflecting some of the debates he himself had on the question with his friends of the artistic world; certainly, he is pleading *pro domo*, arguing for the kind of life which had been such a vital element in his own success.

It is more difficult to trace the elements of Zola's personality and character in Sandoz, for however much we know of Zola, we still do not know his inner life very well, his true view of himself. Nonetheless, some aspects of Sandoz' nature are exact reflections of Zola's, at least as Zola saw himself, and here again the literary figure is more than just a literary image, cut from the whole cloth of the imagination.

Two aspects of Sandoz' personality are stressed in the two phases of his career in which he appears in *L'Oeuvre*. In the first, generally in the first half of the book, he is shown on the street, so to speak, a young revolutionary in art and letters, surrounded by a group of rebels of his own age and determined to help lead the "little band" to triumph in Paris. Here he is a young man on the rise, and insofar as we know the young Zola he seems a faithful reflection of his creator. His chief characteristics are those clearly marked in Zola's newspaper articles, correspondence, and novels between 1865 and 1870: hatred of the past and of tradition in art and ideas, rebellion against fixed academic standards in any realm of art, great combativity and aggressiveness, and whole-hearted contempt for the bourgeoisie and its influence in politics, art, and society. His whole attitude toward the world is summarized in his disdain for the rich Margaillan family, into which his friend Dubuche marries at the price of his integrity and happiness. Régine Margaillan and her mother and father are cousins of all the hateful bourgeois figures of *Pot-bouille,* of *La Conquête de Plassans,* and of *La Joie de vivre,* and when Sandoz condemns them in bitter terms he speaks for Zola himself—and not only as a young man.[36]

But as Sandoz grows older and attains widening popular success his character undergoes a change, perhaps just such a change as Zola experienced between 1875 and 1885. In this second role, where he appears "at home," and which figures chiefly in the second half of the novel, his revolutionary fervor has given way to a quieter acceptance of life and only a single major quality characterizes his personality, loyalty. For through thick and thin he is loyal to the "little band," unquestionably, blindly, sometimes exasperatingly loyal. It is significant of Zola's intentions with respect to the mature Sandoz, who seems to have acquired some of the same bourgeois qualities he so detested as a young man (and did not Zola also?), that the only time in the *Dossier* that he mentions Sandoz as "I" in connection with the group he does so in terms which reflect the same kind of unseeing devotion to his friends.[37]

Whatever the reasons for this newly exclusive dependence on one quality to characterize the older Sandoz, he maintains an almost invariable physiognomy throughout the last half of the book, in marked contrast to the fairly rapid evolution of Claude Lantier toward insanity and suicide. As *L'Oeuvre* progresses toward its dénouement, the same note is struck more and more frequently: Sandoz is the only member of the "little band" to visit Claude in his frightful atelier on the rue Tourlaque, and even when it is apparent to everyone that no further harmony is possible among the old companions he sets his heart on a splendid dinner that will reunite them again and eradicate all the jealousies and rivalries that have destroyed their friendship. It is only very late in the novel, at the conclusion of this dinner, with its quarrels and gossip and hatred, that Sandoz realizes how wide and how deep the split really is, that he comes to see the enormity of his error in dreaming of eternal loyalty and constant friendship.[38] The dinner is the end of his long dream, the end of his youth.

It is impossible to know just how far Sandoz' situation toward the close of the novel reflects the realities of Zola's own life, but the tone of such confessions as this, with the rather desperate emphasis on Sandoz' unwavering constancy, makes it appear that here again Zola is speaking directly and is recounting certain experiences of his own more or less recent past. By 1885 the Aix group had pretty completely faded from his life: he was living in comparative isolation for long periods of each year at Médan; Cézanne had definitively returned to the Midi, with only brief visits to Paris; Baille was hopelessly lost in the business world; Valabrègue was sinking lower and lower into the depths of journalism; Solari was frequently absent; Roux had disappeared; and only Alexis was in constant attendance to recall the good old days of camaraderie and courage. It is undeniable that Zola had been not only the intellectual leader but the social center of this group—there is evidence that his Thursdays began early in his career and continued almost uninterrupted for a very long period—and it is entirely possible that Sandoz' loyalty may be a quite human reflection of Zola's deeply held belief that only he had remained always faithful as his group began to break up under the stresses of individual ambitions, rivalries, jealousies, and aims. If this is true, then *L'Oeuvre* is from one point of view at least an attempt to prove that it was the others, not he, who had changed, that success had not altered him, and that his heart and his door were still as open as ever to his less fortunate friends, whatever they might think and whatever the newspapers might say of him and his success.

But more than that, Sandoz' final awakening to the facts of life may well be an expression of Zola's own sadness at the passing of time and the changes life brings. Full of honors and glory, rich, influential, the most important figure in the intellectual battle of his time, Zola seems to have felt alone, abandoned, and his search for love in the arms of Jeanne Rozerot may have had other causes than his desire for children. Perhaps it was that he felt that all his ambitions had been achieved, that the battle was won. *L'Oeuvre* is his cry of nostalgia.

The impression that Zola was in serious psychological difficulties at the time he composed *L'Oeuvre* is heightened by the manifest lack of self-confidence on the part of Sandoz, who almost certainly speaks for him here. The signs are numerous in the work that at this period Zola was still in a crisis of grave self-doubt and dissatisfaction with his own efforts, a crisis which had lasted at least since the middle

1870's. In the *Ébauche*, speaking of himself as "I," the only explanatory note is: "A novelist who would provide literary work, continual doubt, a rage for production";[39] a little farther on, he says once more of "I":

> Combatted by the critics, but producing all the same, without the logic of Claude, who kills himself. Knowing that his work is imperfect, and resigning himself to the fact, with great sadness. Going always straight ahead, brief joys, continual anguish. Casting off his works, going to the goal, without wanting to stop, without looking back, not being able to reread himself. My whole confession.[40]

In the novel itself, this is hardly changed from the notes, indicating that the *Ébauche* expressed in something like final form his own view of his career at this stage.[41] Sandoz, then, is only another name for the man who, a half-dozen years before, had written in *Le Voltaire*: "For my misfortune, I still weep with rage over my manuscripts; I call myself an idiot a score of times every morning, I don't publish a book without believing it inferior to its predecessors."[42] And he is only another form of the man who described to Edmondo de Amicis everything he had written as "horrible," who confided that "I kill myself working, and I don't succeed in doing what I want," who cried that he cannot reread his own books, for when he does they seem so idiotic that tears come to his eyes.[43]

But the most significant of these evidences of some kind of growing complex of failure on Zola's part comes in Chapter X in the conversation between Lantier and Sandoz which takes place before Claude's nearly completed painting; this conversation is probably intended to be the philosophical climax of the book, or at least to draw the artistic lesson. That Sandoz' words represent Zola's intimate view of his own accomplishment is beyond doubt, for in the definitive plan of Chapter IX, referring directly to this conversation, he calls for "a superb page" and adds: "my confession."[44] It is not without significance that the same idea of personal and artistic failure should reappear in the very last pages of the novel, when Claude has been buried and Sandoz and Bongrand pause a moment before returning to their toil. "Yes, we really must lack pride and resign ourselves to approximations, play unfairly with life," Sandoz says at this supreme moment. "I who push my books to their limit, I scorn myself for feeling them incomplete and false, in spite of my effort."[45] And then when he and the old painter are about to part, he adds: "Since we cannot create anything, since we are only weak imitators, we might just as well crack our heads open right away."[46] This is not the final note of the novel, but it is so close to the final word that we can have no doubt that it was this idea which Zola wished to leave as the signature of his artistic testament.

Actually, this discontent and self-doubt are only two manifestations of some deeper and wider feeling on Zola's part, a feeling which gives the book its tone and which stamps it as one of the important documents in the pessimistic current of the end of the century. It is clear that Zola, at this point of his career, was beginning seriously to doubt that the game was worth the candle, that the rewards were in any sense commensurate with the killing struggle of artistic production. In another part of the same conversation-confession of Sandoz with Lantier before the huge unsuccessful painting the novelist, replying to an unspoken complaint of Lantier's, cries out all the bitterness that his life of labor has brought him, the oppressiveness of toil, the solitude, the unpopularity that success has meant.[47] *Nulla dies sine linea*—and no day without its rage.

And this was no mere literary rage, as a score of pages from the Goncourt *Journal* testify, as Edmondo de Amicis could guarantee—Zola had told him of his "continual doubt," his fatigue, his fear and resentment at the spreading legend about him, that he was a man without conscience, faith, or modesty, a lost soul.[48] And there is Zola's confession in the preface to *Nouveaux contes à Ninon* of a dozen years before *L'Oeuvre*. Its pages are like an advance notice of the general spirit of the later novel: Memory is the only joy his heart now finds, he confides to Ninon, ten years have passed since their love blossomed in the wild gorges of Provence, and all he knows is disgust and disillusionment, solitude, emptiness of heart, and sadness.[49]

Thus *L'Oeuvre* emerges as one of the capital documents for an intimate knowledge of Émile Zola, the man and the creator. The novel does not tell much about the "little band"—is it the Aix group, the Médan group, or the Batignolles group, or all of them?—nor does it even tell much directly about Zola's opinion of his early friends. But it does tell us a great deal, directly and demonstrably, about him. The taste of success had proved less sweet than the taste of struggle, his youth was gone, Jeanne had not yet appeared, he was childless, attacked on every side as a public poisoner, most of his old friends had left him, the road before him seemed to lead only down. Perhaps because the book had to be written so hastily, but even more because he felt himself in crisis, he was led to put more of himself into its pages, to render more and more directly the obscure torment that was making his life wretched, the torment which had already produced

La Joie de vivre and *Germinal* and which was yet to produce *La Terre* before it was swept away by an autumn love. True enough, the portrait Zola gives of himself is not uniformly attractive—Sandoz is too good to be true, he speaks with an irritating sententiousness, he has no sense of humor at all—but its very limitations and distortions are revealing as glimpses of what Zola thought of himself. But more than that, it is interesting as testimony that even this robust worker, this tireless creator, this younger Balzac lived in discouragement, in doubt, and in discontent and that like many others of his kind he found it best to "shed his sickness in books."

IV

Lantier—Cézanne

Over the years the chief interest of *L'Oeuvre* for most critics has been the identity of the model chosen by Zola for the figure of Claude Lantier. Beginning with the publication of the novel and continuing even today, many attempts have been made to name the real-life person or persons Zola had in mind as he put together the fictional character. In the course of this investigation, Paul Cézanne and Édouard Manet have emerged as the most probable models, both close friends of his and companions of his youthful struggles for recognition. From the beginning Cézanne has been the more frequently mentioned and by now it is firmly accepted by many critics of art and literature that he provided Zola with the essentials of the character of Claude Lantier and that *L'Oeuvre* was not only a key novel but an unforgivable attack on the personality and artistic attainment of the man who was Zola's oldest friend.[1]

Three kinds of evidence have been brought to support the argument that Zola intended Claude Lantier as a portrait of Cézanne: biographical or other extraliterary data tending to establish probabilities, if not certainties; references to Cézanne in the *Dossier*; and similarities in *L'Oeuvre* to the known facts of Cézanne's life, career, and personality.

Undeniably, some extraliterary evidence supports the belief that Lantier is a portrait of Cézanne. For instance, *L'Oeuvre* seems to mark a complete and final break in the relationship between Zola and Cézanne, for there is no evidence that the two ever met or corresponded after its appearance. It is presumed by some critics, such as Rewald,[1a] that Cézanne either recognized himself in the character or was told that Zola had meant to caricature him in the book. If it could be established that Cézanne saw himself in Lantier, this would be a powerful argument for accepting him as a true portrait of the master of Aix. Curiously enough, though the claim that *L'Oeuvre* caused the two men to separate is implicit in the argument of nearly everyone who has looked into the matter, almost no one lays the blame wholly or even chiefly on the novel, and nearly every historian of the affair has erected some theory about the general relationship of Zola and Cézanne before 1885 to help explain the break between the two old friends. Some see a growing separation between the two based on differences of personality; others ascribe the break to some specific incident, such as a condescending smile on Zola's part; Armand Lanoux, with a kind of cavalier disregard for probability, thinks that Cézanne had once been Mme Zola's lover and that Zola's resentment finally boiled up in a quarrel with the partner, while Angus Wilson's view is that the separation was caused by Zola's deep envy of Cézanne for having "realized" himself at Aix, whence the Zola family had been driven in bankruptcy.[2]

Even Rewald, the most persuasive spokesman for the belief that the novel estranged Cézanne from Zola, has doubts. He has to admit that the divergence of the two temperaments, the different place acquired by each man in society, and Cézanne's resentment of Zola's pity and increasing doubts about his friend's ability to realize himself, all played a part in the separation. In spite of his conviction about *L'Oeuvre*'s role in disturbing the old friendship, Rewald does not lay all the blame on it and feels compelled to place it in a psychological context where even the slightest similarities to his own life could make Cézanne leap to the conclusion that the book was intended as a judgment of him both as man and as artist.[3]

It should be pointed out that this speculation on the pre-1885 relationship of Zola and Cézanne has little evidence to support it. The record indicates the contrary of a growing divergency between the two: Cézanne was a frequent visitor to Médan just before and even during the composition of *L'Oeuvre*; he called on Zola for help of all kinds, practical and moral; and Zola apparently complied with each of his requests with good will and equanimity. There is no sign that Cézanne was shocked by Zola's supposed vulgarity and pretention, no hint of a growing divergence of temperament or view; the two seem excellent friends and that is all there is to it, so far as we know.

The question then rises, if a break came between the two friends, was it solely the fault of the novel or did it come about because of a quarrel over entirely different matters some time in the period immediately following the publication of the work? Or, was the fault solely Cézanne's? The painter seems to have been notably touchy, especially in later years when diabetes profoundly affected his personality, and it is possible that he took offense at something quite different from *L'Oeuvre* and broke off the friendship as a consequence. Perhaps the rupture was the result of some kind of intimate crisis on Cézanne's part, for we possess no letters from him to anyone for the period May 1886 to July 1889; it may be that the separation came about because of something he did to Zola, not because of what Zola did to him. Furthermore, there may never have been any real quarrel or break at all, as Théodore Duret argues;[4] the two may have simply drifted apart.

What little we know of the relationship of the two men after the publication of *L'Oeuvre* is of no help in solving the problem. Probably for lack of concrete information on their relationship between 1885 and Zola's death, some critics have made a good deal of the last letter known to have been written by Cézanne to Zola:

> *Gardanne, April 4, 1886*
>
> I have just received *L'Oeuvre*, which you have been kind enough to send me. I thank the author of the *Rougon-Macquart* for this good witness to our memories, and I ask him to let me press his hand while thinking of the years gone by.
>
> All yours
> under the impulse of past days,
> Paul Cézanne[5]

It is obvious, when this note is compared to the other letters written by Cézanne to Zola before 1886, that there is a certain difference of tone in it, and Rewald, to take one example, argues from this difference that Cézanne was deeply hurt and offended by the book and was here writing a letter of farewell to his old friend. He also stresses that Cézanne speaks only of the past and gives no slightest mark of interest or friendship and concludes that Cézanne surely meant this letter to be the last.[6]

On the other hand, Denise LeBlond-Zola does not think that the note foreshadows a break in any sense[7] and Mack believes that Cézanne's acknowledgment of the book is at least presumptive evidence that he was not deeply hurt by it.[8]

It seems that Mme LeBlond-Zola and Mack are right, for while the letter certainly differs from the others from Cézanne to Zola, it still does not justify, either in tone or content, the assumptions of Rewald and Lanoux. A certain reserve is evident, but that may have been due to something in Cézanne's personal situation, not to the effect of the novel itself; certainly there is nothing like open unfriendliness and nothing portending a final break. If Cézanne was as angry as he is made out to be, would he have written such a note at all? It does not seem likely that he would, and the conclusion appears to be that the letter has been used—and abused—as evidence to hold up a case that is none too strong.

Then what about their relationship after the publication of *L'Oeuvre*? What do we know of it that would support the case for an open break between them? Unfortunately, almost nothing. Nearly everyone in a position to know anything about the matter emphasizes that the two, while never seeing each other again after 1886, did not lose their affection for each other and kept alive the memory of their years together in Aix and Paris and Médan. Denise LeBlond-Zola says that her father always cherished the memory of his old friend and that he never went to see him in their later years because of Cézanne's difficult character and the impossibility of getting him to change his mind.[9]

Actually, about all that is certain is that each man had had at least one definite opportunity to see his old friend after *L'Oeuvre*, and both declined flatly. Zola was in Aix to visit Numa Coste in 1896 but did not see Cézanne, and two years later the painter refused to accompany Gasquet and Maurice LeBlond to Zola's apartment. That is all that is surely known, and no conclusions can be drawn save that ten years after the novel the two seem to have been on bad terms, but not so bad that they had become enemies in the proper sense of the word. This conclusion seems to be supported by an unpublished letter from Paul Alexis to Zola, dated February 13, 1891, in which Alexis gave a half-comic account of Cézanne's difficulties with his wife and son.[10] If Zola and Cézanne were on really bad terms, would Alexis have written such a letter? True enough, Cézanne does not come off very well in Alexis' account, and it is possible that Alexis was pandering to Zola's spite in recounting a host of petty details, but it seems rather that Alexis is passing on a little gossip to an old friend who might have kept an amused interest in the affairs of his companion who was so "weak in life." It is true that such an interest, if it existed, may have died when Zola learned of Cézanne's conservative and Catholic opinions during the Dreyfus case and that the great *affaire* of the 1890's might well have been the wedge which finally drove the two old friends apart.

But if little can be found in the relationship of Cézanne and Zola after 1886 to support the contention that Lantier was in a real sense Cézanne, two other bits of evidence, one of them circumstantial, the other negative, seem to back it. The first is contained in a letter from Zola's Dutch friend and supporter, J. Van Santen Kolff, who on frequent trips to see Zola in Paris and Médan obtained material for articles in Dutch and German journals on the *Rougon-Macquart* series. In an undated letter written just before the appearance of *Lourdes*, Kolff tells Zola that in Richard Müther's *History of Art* the final chapter of the second volume opens with a discussion of *L'Oeuvre* as an introduction to the Impressionists. Kolff then adds: "Only, the author does not seem to know Paul Cézanne; he speaks only of Edouard Manet as having inspired *L'Oeuvre*."[11] As Zola spoke quite frankly and fully to Kolff of his plans, his intentions, and his actual accomplishments, it seems probable that he must have told him that he had called on Cézanne to provide the essential traits of the fictional character. It is possible that Kolff had merely seen the *Dossier* and had noted the remarks on Cézanne, but it is also possible that Zola had told him something concrete about the actual execution of the novel.

Perhaps more significant is the fact that in the fifteen years or so that Zola lived after the publication of *L'Oeuvre*, he never gave any sign, any statement to contradict the growing belief that Cézanne had been his chief model. Surely he must have been aware of what people were saying and even writing about *L'Oeuvre*; that he never made any comment in opposition seems to indicate that his old friend had been called upon in important ways in the construction of the figure of Claude.

This then is the extraliterary evidence supporting the claims of those who see in Lantier a more or less modified portrait of the master of Aix. It is good evidence and the case is almost convincing. Unfortunately, the case is not quite that, for there is a good, though not so large, body of opposing evidence that contradicts it in important ways.

First of all, no painter who knew Cézanne well—and with all his disappearances, his seclusion, his solitude, there were people in Paris who knew him well—seems to have recognized him in the figure of Lantier. Camille Pissarro, with whom he had spent years at Auvers and who might have been expected to identify him if anyone could, says nothing of him in his letters to his son Lucien. Indeed, on February 5, 1886, Pissarro wrote Lucien to the effect that he had been present with Cézanne at a meeting in the home of Robert Caze, where *L'Oeuvre* had been hotly criticized by the friends of the Impressionists as an attack on the school, but he says nothing at all about the novel (then appearing in *Le Gil Blas*) as a portrait of his friend.[12] Nor does Monet mention any resemblance when he writes Zola to complain that the novel will do the Impressionists no good with the general public,[13] nor does anyone else, so far as is known, and such a silence makes it seem that whatever Zola's intention had been, the portrait of the fictional painter departed so far from reality that it ceased to be recognizable to those who knew its supposed model best. Also, it is curious, if *L'Oeuvre* really does deal with a living painter, that such a skillful and informed gossip as Edmond de Goncourt makes no mention of any model, that Léon Daudet, always anxious to find an excuse to attack Zola, says nothing about it, that George Moore, who knew the backstairs of the Parisian art world as well as anyone of the time, makes no reference to Cézanne in connection with it. And it must be emphasized again that Cézanne, so far as we know, made no complaint to Zola, although he saw the novel in the very process of composition. Certainly, he was a good enough friend to have dared to protest, if he had seen himself in the book. But there is no sign that he ever did, either to Zola or to anyone else, and his supposed remarks to Vollard toward the close of his life simply cannot be taken as evidence. Again, does a hidden attack by Zola have psychological verisimilitude on its side? Is it possible that Zola could have ambushed his oldest and one of his most valued friends? There is not the slightest sign of cooling friendship before 1885, though they were not constantly in contact, and to attribute to Zola the intention of presenting such a radically unfavorable picture of a man he had known so intimately and so long seems to deny Zola's traits of loyalty and constancy.

The evidence from the *Dossier* contains very clear indications that Zola was thinking of Cézanne as he planned the novel, but gives no incontrovertible proof that Cézanne was the sole or even the major model for Claude Lantier. Most of the references to Cézanne are found in the *Ébauche*, where there are six mentions of Cézanne by name and another sentence which may, but does not surely, refer to him. Near the beginning, Zola says: "Claude and his friends on their return (i.e., from the Salon des Refusés), Cézanne and I on our return,"[14] and a little later: "Don't forget the despair of Paul, who always believed he was discovering painting. Once, an absolute discouragement, Paul ready to abandon everything, then a masterpiece, a portion of a study only, which saves him from his depression."[15] The first of these references indicates that Cézanne served to evoke certain incidents of a young painter's life in the early 1860's, and the second seems much the same. It is not clear, given Zola's way of talking to himself in the *Ébauche*, that "an absolute discouragement" refers to a real event in Cézanne's life or whether it simply indicates Zola's intention to describe such a period in the life of his fictional painter.

Somewhat later, speaking of the Impressionists, Zola remarks that "Claude will rise up against their hasty work,"[16] but this is not surely a reference to Cézanne, for though the painter had a rather low opinion of the techniques and accomplishments of the Impressionists, so did

Zola, whose sense of method and desire for "finish" made him rebel at the very idea that a painting could be anything like an impression, as the *Dossier* reveals on more than one occasion. Toward the end of the *Ébauche,* there are several references to Cézanne by name: "My youth in school and in the fields—Baille, Cézanne,"[17] "In Paris. New friends. School. Arrival of Baille and Cézanne,"[18] "Cézanne's studios. All the traits of his character. My poses for him."[19]

It is interesting that almost all these references are to Cézanne's youth and early career, and his name seems to be mentioned here more as a starting point for some episodes of the novel than for any other purpose. Moreover, the subject in every case is Zola himself and he appears to want to re-create his state of mind at specific periods of his own life rather than to evoke Cézanne as a person; Cézanne seems merely to serve as part of the background and is not cited for his own sake. The phrase "all the traits of his character" is certainly important, for it seems to indicate that Claude Lantier was meant to incarnate Cézanne in small as well as important aspects. But does it really mean that, or is the phrase intended as a kind of *aide-mémoire* to help Zola as he composed the figure, a phrase to trigger in his mind the appearance of a list of traits from which he would select certain ones for the creation of the fictional figure of Lantier? The answer is difficult to find, for not only have we little real idea of Cézanne's character and personality and almost no notion at all of what Zola thought of him in 1885 and 1886, but there are frequently, in Zola's practice, wide differences between *ébauche* and execution. One example of this is the phrase quoted above concerning Cézanne's studios. These seem intended as points of departure for descriptive passages, but the *Dossier* later shows that when it came time to describe the artist's milieu, Zola employed a description that came from Guillemet, or indeed described Guillemet's own studio, and does not certainly refer to Cézanne's first installation.[20] Later, Béliard's studio on the rue de Douai was his point of departure for the description of Lantier's last location.[21]

But there is one reference to Cézanne in the *Ébauche* which seems, at first glance, absolutely conclusive and which has been much cited as evidence that Zola based Claude Lantier on him: "I add that he has produced some absolutely marvelous bits, a Manet, a dramatized Cézanne, closer to Cézanne."[22] But again it must be noted that there was, in Zola's usual practice, a wide difference between the loose, preliminary discussion of the *Ébauche* and the actual planning and composition of the novel. It seems certain that he originally intended to make Claude Lantier into something like a dramatized Cézanne, but it is also probable that as the plan progressed he departed more and more from that idea. Again, it must be noted that at the very most

Cézanne is cited as only one model, not at all as the sole figure on whom Claude Lantier was to be based, and that Zola, even in this reference, declares that he will only be closer to Cézanne than to Manet. Far from being conclusive, this sentence merely increases the doubt and confusion which now surround the whole question. It must be emphasized again that the *Ébauche* seems rarely to have been for Zola anything like a definitive plan of any novel, for actual planning—that is, division into chapters, arrangement of plot, description of characters and setting, and so on—took place after the writing of the *Ébauche;* there are many evidences in all Zola's novels that the *Ébauche* was often quite far from the finished product and that the ideas expressed in it were frequently much changed and sometimes omitted entirely. These things are true of *L'Oeuvre,* as a later chapter will demonstrate, and the important differences that can be found between the original sketch and the final execution of the work seem to lessen the importance of any statement in the *Ébauche* as a certain indication of what Zola actually accomplished when he sat down to write.

Nevertheless, other references in the *Dossier* that are not in the *Ébauche* support the claim that Cézanne served, at least in part, as a model for Lantier. In the brief two- or three-line sketches for the chapters that precede the detailed plans Zola mentions "all our friendship at Plassans"[23] and in the final plan of the second chapter he indicates that the fictional painter will be a student at the Atelier Suisse, as Cézanne was.[24] In a kind of preliminary note to the description of the characters of the novel he refers to his painter as a youth in Plassans and adds: "Down there, knew Sandoz and Baille"[25] and a few lines further on says that he will "take the physical portrait in *Le Ventre de Paris.*"[26] If the portrait of Claude Lantier in *Le Ventre de Paris* is really that of Cézanne, and Zola's notes to that novel indicate that it is, then there is good reason for thinking that at first, at least, he intended to make the Claude Lantier of *L'Oeuvre* look much like Cézanne. Actually, however, this indication is not so conclusive as it might seem, for while the physical description of Claude Lantier given in *L'Oeuvre* does resemble that of *Le Ventre de Paris,* the resemblance is a general one, and no significant details can be matched up to indicate that Zola carried out his plan. Moreover, the portrait in *Le Ventre de Paris* is that of the young Cézanne; any imitations of it in *L'Oeuvre* do not necessarily indicate that Zola had the later Cézanne in mind as he portrayed his protagonist.

Only one other reference in the *Dossier* is clearly to Cézanne: the discussion, in the description of the Salon, of Guillemet's *charité* of 1882, when Guillemet took in one of Cézanne's paintings on his own responsibility. Cézanne is mentioned by name here, and there is no doubt that the episode in which Claude Lantier's portrait of his dead son is accepted by the jury because of Fagerolles' action is based on a real event from Cézanne's life. This is only an incident in the novel; it does not prove in any way that Claude Lantier is a portrait of Paul Cézanne or that he was so intended by Zola.

The *Dossier* contains no other valid evidence that Cézanne could have been the model for Lantier, but it does contain one or two indications that he may not have been that at all. In the first place the names Cézanne and Lantier are never used interchangeably in the *Dossier,* as they are in the case of Zola-Sandoz, Alexis-Jory, Gervex-Fagerolles, and others; this detail seems to indicate that Zola always considered Lantier and Cézanne as separate entities and that Cézanne was nothing more than a source of certain traits for the painter in the novel and that his life gave Zola the opportunity to describe scenes and episodes which he considered typical of the artists of his time. Again, the portrait of Claude Lantier given in the *Personnages* of the *Dossier* is different from any other in that it gives no significant details of the character's background, previous life, and so on, and is far shorter than any of the sketches devoted to the other major figures of the book. Of the ten lines Zola devotes to Claude Lantier here—as against about four times that number for Jory, Dubuche, or Fagerolles—six are given to his age and one to the briefest mention of his mother and aunt. The rest indicates that the figure is to be a fictional one, a member of the Rougon-Macquart family: "Eldest son of Gervaise and Lantier, born at Plassans in 1842. Fusion mixture. Moral preponderance of the mother and physical resemblance to her. Heredity of a neurosis turning to genius."[27] No physical portrait was necessary here, for Zola had already expressed his intention of transferring to *L'Oeuvre* the portrait established in *Le Ventre de Paris,* but it is curious that there is no mention whatsoever of the moral traits to be attributed to the artist in the novel. Does this mean that Zola was so familiar with the person he was to use as a model that he needed no indications? Or does it mean that there was to be no single model, that the figure was to be made up of a host of memories and impressions, that it was to be, in sum, a fictional character? The absence of any reference to Cézanne or to any other of Zola's friends makes the latter seem more probable.

It is clear that Cézanne figured in Zola's calculations as he planned *L'Oeuvre,* but it is far from clear how far and in what manner he figured in the actual execution of the book. Was he *the* model, *a* model, or only a point of departure? The evidence from his biography seems to indicate that he was the second, probably not the first and almost surely not the third.

V

Cézanne: the Novel and the Biography

In *L'Oeuvre* Lantier is depicted as a difficult and complex personality whose chief characteristic is a constant alternation between confidence and discouragement. One moment he is hopeful, enthusiastic, courageous, ambitious—he even has a kind of *idée fixe* about his genius and his eventual triumph—but the next he is despairing, doubting, almost suicidal. And because he doubts he is driven to endless retouchings and changes which in every case destroy the original genial conception; even in the midst of a successful session on "Plein-Air" he cannot desist, driven by his special torment, and Sandoz, who witnesses his pain, cannot stop him before it is too late. It becomes clear from his first appearance as a painter that his great gifts will never find full expression, that he is condemned never to succeed as real geniuses succeed. A dark force constantly works in Claude to choke his inspiration, a kind of radical impotency, the product of his evil inheritance, the devil he took from the whole line of sick and crazed forebears. As his career progresses, the torment becomes worse, the tare more evident, until his life becomes a long torture.

But it is not the "lesion" alone, the hereditary taint, which keeps Claude from complete genius, it is the influence of his time of transition —his milieu—when romanticism, dead, is not quite dead, and chimeras of the past, not yet exorcised by science, realism, and truth, rise to blind the artist's eye and corrupt his vision of his world. Over and over Zola repeats that Claude comes at the confluence of the work of Delacroix and Courbet, when romanticism has not yet gone and realism has not fully come. He is a product of his times as surely as he is a product of his diseased parentage and his corrupt ancestors, and his times, as much as his psychological and physical limitations, will be responsible for the catastrophic philosophic error he will commit when he conceives his final painting as a synthesis of the real and the dream.

Claude himself knows he is a Romantic, just as he knows he is ill of his "lesion"; as he works on "Plein-Air" and as the figures steadily refuse to come out with the splendor he dreams of, he cries: "Damn it all, it's still black! I've got that confounded Delacroix in my eye. And that, that hand is out of Courbet. Ah! we're all steeped in the romantic sauce. Our youth paddled too much in it, we're soaked up to the chin. We'll have to have a famous cleaning."[1] But the "cleaning" will never come, for his generation at least, and he is doomed by the germ from within and the moral atmosphere from without to live a life of fierce, unending labor, of rage against himself and of anger against art, which he comes to execrate with the execration of a betrayed lover. His only relief in his disequilibrium is in quarrels and discussions with his friends and in long wanderings through the Paris he would paint but which remains forever beyond his powers.

Yet, knowing that he will never be free and that he will never create, this artist of pure integrity and unbelievable stubbornness continues on his path, always working, always retouching, forever spoiling his attempts in an endless search for the perfection that is not of this world. He emerges at last as a sketcher of genius, endowed with superb technical gifts and a powerful vision, but limited always to the first draft, the great conception which will never take full form but which, in the vice of his temperament, he strives to push to finish and perfection. Complicating his life, as if it were not complicated enough with his temperamental and philosophical vices, is a failing of sexual origin. The root of the whole second plot of the novel, the struggle between woman and art for mastery of his soul, is his unconquerable timidity toward women and the sublimation of his desires in the painted flesh which is the focal point of his two great canvases. Over and over Zola stresses this aspect of Claude's nature, "his chaste man's passion for woman's flesh,"[2] having him proclaim: "I have no other religion. I'd fall on my knees before it for my whole life."[3] His preference for the creations of his brush over actual, breathing women is nowhere better seen than toward the close of the book where in a fine scene he calmly and brutally compares Christine to the painted figure of his first large canvas, for which she had posed in such dramatic circumstances; the comparison, coming from this man whose chastity is the psychological crux of the subplot, is all to the advantage of the creation of his brain and hand, and such is his absorption in his art that he does not perceive the hurt he inflicts on the woman who has served him with such abnegation. This is, in Zola's catalogue of sins, one of the blackest, the sin against life, and Venus will exact her revenge in front of the very canvas where he had glorified her.

But actually, this timidity, this morbid chastity, is only another sign of Claude's "differentness," only another indication that he is born to live as an outcast, apart from men, from women, for art and art alone. Because he is such a loner, Claude is, inescapably, the wildest of bohemians, hating all that is not art, execrating any form of commerce in painting, any surrender to public taste, any concession, scorning the Beaux-Arts and all convention, all tradition, mocking the imitators in the Louvre, but saving his finest fury and his finest irony for the bourgeoisie, which he holds essentially responsible for the artist's decline, for the fall in taste, for the ugliness of modern life, and for his own lack of public success. This idealist, this revolutionary, this bohemian—so bohemian that he will commit the most heinous of French crimes, spending his capital in order to paint—knows he is apart from his world, out of touch with the dominant elements of its society. Knowledge of his alienation drives him to supreme efforts, to an eccentricity of conduct which toward the end of his life brings him the reputation of being an arrogant madman, a painter ignorant of his own trade but contemptuous of the work of others, of being a bellicose and moody failure. But in spite of his position as outcast and outsider, Claude believes firmly—more and more firmly as his failures multiply—in the necessity of public success and recognition. He must not only paint great paintings, he must conquer Paris and the Salon, he must impose his vision of the world. He knows that in France the artistic revolution of which he dreams will never be accomplished without the sanction of the very bourgeoisie he detests, and he is aware that his painting will have been for nothing if he does not attain official recognition and public acceptance. In spite of the absolute and mocking rejection he finds from the crowd, the critics, and from his fellow artists, he continues unceasingly, driven by his *idée fixe* of a new art and his consciousness of his role as prophet. The great irony of his life, the punishment for his "lesion" and his romanticism, his violence and his revolutionism, is that when his art finally does triumph, it does so in attenuated form, watered down for the detestable bourgeois and his silly wife and daughter by the agents of the new commercialism and the artists of small conscience and little faith.

How closely does this portrait render the real Cézanne, if indeed it renders him at all? The problem is complicated by three major difficulties: it requires a nearly impossible comparison of a fictional life with a real existence; the insufficiencies of the biographies of Cézanne; and our almost total ignorance of what Zola thought of him and his accomplishment in his middle years, from about 1870 to 1885-86. The greatest difficulty is lack of knowledge of the true Cézanne. Not only do we know very little of his temper, moods, passions, ambitions, joys, and sorrows, but in nearly every biography we pick up we have one of the most romanticized figures in French painting, a man whose intellectual, moral, and physical physiognomy has been more distorted than most and whose varying portraits are about as contradictory as can be found for any famous figure.[4] We know something of his late years, less of his middle period, and still less of his youth, which, in spite of Zola's letters to and about him, is still virtually unknown ground.

Everything written on the Cézanne of the years before 1890 has been based either on *L'Oeuvre* as a direct biographical source, on his letters to Zola, on Zola's letters, or on a small handful of testimonies written by men who knew him more or less well and who left descriptions of him, factual or fictional, which may perhaps—but do not surely —render some part of the truth.

Claude Monet, for instance, told Gustave Geffroy some years after Cézanne's death that he remembered him as a bohemian in dress and manner, always wearing a worker's red sash, and Duranty in his bitter satire, "Le Peintre Louis Martin," of *Le Pays des arts*,[5] presented him as a real madman, a crude and savage revolutionary, painting with a spoon and constantly encouraged by his parrot, who would cry periodically: "Martin is a great painter!" Catulle Mendès, writing in *Le Rappel* in 1874 under the pseudonym of Jean Prouvaire, offered another portrait of Cézanne as bohemian, carrying his own paintings on his back to the Impressionist exhibition of the Boulevard des Capucines.[6] About the only variation is provided by Cézanne's friend Marion, who refers on one or two occasions to the "black moral and temperamental despair" that he often suffered[7] and who describes Cézanne's long efforts to discipline his temperament and to impose on it some rule of calm knowledge.[8]

The only near-contemporary portrait of any serious value is that of Théodore Duret, who has this to say of Cézanne in his early *Histoire des peintres impressionnistes:*

> Cézanne was a man of serious and reflective mind, inclined to turn in on himself. The restraint that is seen in his painting existed, at bottom, in his way of acting and expressing himself. He let himself go, in the first moment, under the impulse of his sensations, like a real Southerner, with a kind of impetuousness, of quivering accompanied by oaths, exclamations, sharp words, but after that, if he was talking with friends or serious people, one could see the man of judgment and reflection.[9]

Duret goes on to stress the contrast between the public image and the reality of Cézanne. For most of those who had ever heard of him,

Cézanne was a Communard, an anarchist, a social and artistic revolutionary of the most repellent type, but in fact he was a bourgeois, a rich and conservative Catholic. Duret's observations, especially the latter ones, are undoubtedly exact; the only difficulty is that they may —probably do— represent only the latter reality and do not take much account of the young Cézanne of the years before *L'Oeuvre*. That he was, even in early maturity, just such a bohemian as legend had it seems undeniable if Edmond Duranty's eyewitness testimony is exact. In a letter to Zola written some time before the death of Edouard Manet, Duranty told Zola that Cézanne had reappeared in "the little café on Place Pigalle" and that he was dressed in his usual costume, all covered with daubs of paint and wearing an old battered hat.[10] Duranty's portrait of him as Martin does not seem to have been exaggerated, and it may be that Claude's marked external bohemianism did come from Cézanne's example.

Perhaps the best evidence that Lantier's personality and general social role were based on Cézanne's is given by John Rewald in his *Cézanne, Geffroy et Gasquet*.[11] He quotes a portion of an essay by Geffroy, who knew Cézanne well and was in a position to give a valid assessment of the man:

> For a long time, Paul Cézanne had a strange artistic fate. He could be defined as a personage unknown and famous at the same time, having only rare contacts with the public and considered as an influence by the restless and the seekers in painting, known by a few only, living in a fierce isolation, reappearing, disappearing suddenly before the eyes of his intimates. From all the poorly known facts of his biography, from his half-secret production, from the variety of his canvases, which did not seem to be controlled by any of the accepted laws of publicity, there came to him a sort of bizarre renown, already distant; a mystery surrounded his being and his work. Those in quest of the new, who liked to discover things not yet seen, spoke of Cézanne's paintings with an understanding air, gave indications about him as though they were giving passwords.
>
> In fact, encounters with Cézanne's pictures were rare in ordinary life. . . . In artistic circles, Cézanne's reputation has become more solid, has visibly increased. Cézanne has become a kind of precursor.[12]

This is, *grosso modo*, the way Claude Lantier appears in *L'Oeuvre*, and Geffroy's remarks are a powerful indication that the fictional artist really was intended by his creator to be a portrait of Cézanne. This impression is heightened by a letter from Monet to Geffroy, quoted by Rewald in the same book:

> I hope that Cézanne will still be here and that he will be one of us, but he is so strange, so fearful of seeing new faces that I am afraid he will disappoint us, in spite of his desire to meet you. What a misfortune that this man has not had more support in his existence! He is a real artist and one who has come to doubt of himself too much.[13]

Mary Cassatt contributes, in a letter to her friend Mrs. Stillman in the same collection, to the impression that Zola remained fairly faithful to the truth of Cézanne's personality as he sketched Claude Lantier:

> On me, he made the impression of a kind of brigand, with big, red, bulging eyes which gave him a ferocious air . . . and such a violent way of speaking that he literally made the dishes echo. I discovered later that I had let myself be deceived by appearances, for, far from being ferocious, he has the gentlest possible temperament, like a child. . . .[14]

Whereas Cézanne's correspondence is of no help at all—seldom has a great man written letters which give so few insights into his heart and mind—Zola's is somewhat better, for it contains many letters to Cézanne from 1858 to the 1880's and offers dozens of references to him in letters to other men. If the letters of the years 1858 to about 1865 are to be relied on, Zola apparently considered the chief characteristic of his old friend to be a propensity to discouragement and felt called upon to encourage him on numerous occasions. In June 1860, he remarks that Cézanne has talked of throwing his brushes "against the ceiling," and he urges him to accept life as it is rather than to give up as he discovers that reality is different from what he had thought it to be before coming to Paris.[15] In July of the same year he encourages him again,[16] and a year later, in August 1861, he tells Baille that Cézanne is once more in the depths and that he is having trouble keeping him from leaving Paris in despair. Cézanne has just run his fist through a portrait of Zola that the latter had persuaded him to paint in order to keep at work (Lantier, too, has a propensity to destroy works on the easel), and Zola is beginning to wonder about his own ability to prevent him from abandoning art once for all in some fit of despondency.[17]

As late as 1867, when it might be supposed that Cézanne had

finally found his path, Zola again remarks, this time to Valabrègue, that their mutual friend is having difficulties with himself.[18] The slightest obstacle makes him despair, it seems, and this propensity to discouragement is not made easier to bear by his fantastic and capricious nature. The painter was about as illogical in his ideas and behavior as one could be, from what Zola says of him, and to prove anything to this "excellent whimsical fellow"[19] is like trying to prove to the towers of Notre-Dame that they should execute a quadrille. "He might say yes, but he wouldn't budge an inch."[20] Paul is the stubbornest of men, "all of a piece, stiff and hard to the touch; nothing bends him, nothing can get a concession out of him."[21] And like many stubborn men, he hates argument and discussion, fearful that he will be made to change his mind; age and experience have not changed him at all and he is just as he was back in Aix. Sensitive and easily offended, touchy and hot tempered, he has to be handled with extreme care. The partial and incomplete portrait that emerges from these letters allows us to glimpse a generally difficult man, an "original," one with whom it was not easy to live and who required constant encouragement and comfort from his oldest friend, who seems to have felt at times that the task was a little burdensome.

How close, then, is the moral portrait of Lantier to the living Cézanne of the years 1860-85? Rewald says that they have only a few traits in common,[22] and given our meager knowledge of the real painter in his early and middle career, there can be no other certain declaration. But there is little doubt that Zola had his oldest friend in mind as he sketched the personality of Lantier, for the two certainly offer a general similarity of nature: both are bohemians, difficult, capricious, stubborn, hot-tempered, and easily offended, given to frequent fits of discouragement, even despair, but kept afloat always by the power of the *idée fixe*.[23]

It is scarcely possible to be more conclusive about the external events of Lantier's life (distinct from his artistic career) as it is recounted in *L'Oeuvre*. Unquestionably, the young Lantier's experiences are modeled in some part on those of the young Cézanne: he is a Provençal who comes to Paris, his wanderings over his native hills are like Cézanne's, he has an adolescent affair with an apprentice hatmaker (Cézanne's father had been a hatmaker before he went into banking, and Paul had undoubtedly flirted with the young employees of the factory), there is a reference to the Jas de Bouffan. Lantier even has a small income that keeps him from starving, just as Cézanne did, though here Zola was possibly not copying reality but was arranging a situation to explain his hero's lack of commerical production and to establish a justification for the long period of experimentation and groping in which he indulges.

Surely, the early wanderings of Lantier in the Parisian suburbs reflect Cézanne's long search for the motif in the hills along the Seine, and the cooling of his friendship for Dubuche recalls the decline of Cézanne's friendship for Baille, a cooling described in Zola's letters both to Cézanne and to Baille. Even Lantier's brief quarrel with Sandoz and his fairly prolonged separation from him are probably based on real incidents, and the Bennecourt episode may reflect a certain coolness between Zola and Cézanne in the 1860's. The closest extensive similarity to reality may lie in the general relationship between Lantier and Sandoz, one which is almost certainly translated from reality. Sandoz' role vis-à-vis Lantier is always to encourage, to give moral and artistic support in the bad days, and this surely represents the real situation between the novelist and the painter, as it is again reflected in the correspondence of Zola and Cézanne.

It may also be that the general attitude of Lantier toward women reflects a fact of Cézanne's life, for the painter was profoundly disturbed by nude models and displayed a curious combination of violence and timidity toward them, a combination which Zola may have dramatized and exaggerated into Claude's sexual malady—painted flesh becomes infinitely preferable to human flesh. This is, of course, no more than speculation.

Beyond this we cannot venture, for again our lack of knowledge of Cézanne's life between 1860 and 1885 makes any detailed comparison impossible. All in all, it seems probable that only the life of the young Cézanne, the man of about eighteen to twenty-five, provided actual details and situations for the life of Lantier. Certainly, nothing in the record justifies us in thinking that *L'Oeuvre* contains anything like a dependable biography of Cézanne as a mature man. Zola never thought of Cézanne as a madman, however eccentric he might have found him at times, and it must not be forgotten that Lantier is a madman, only incipiently at first, but a real madman at the end.

Does the novel offer any solid evidence that Claude Lantier's artistic career, as distinct from his life as an individual, is based directly on Cézanne's? Some details seem to be based on Cézanne's experiences, but by no means as many as some of the critics have found. It is undeniable that the young Lantier is meant to represent Cézanne, for he comes to Paris, as Cézanne did, with a fairly long background of sketching in the hills of Provence, and his first studio, as described in the novel, may well represent Cézanne's on the rue

Beautreillis. Rewald has identified the two studios but, as noted, some doubt remains, for in the *Dossier* Guillemet's name appears where the first studio is described, indicating either that Zola had Guillemet's studio in mind or that Guillemet had sketched a typical bohemian studio of the 1860's or 1870's for him. If Zola was evoking Cézanne's first studio here, the description represents a considerable effort of memory, for a quarter of a century had intervened between the time he frequented it and the time he described it. But Lantier's early painting surely seems to recall Cézanne's, "rough, dazzling, with a violence of tones which offended like a trucker's oath,"[24] full of "great strokes of pastel slashing the shadows,"[25] just as his desire to create vast paintings almost certainly is a reflection of Cézanne's early desire, recorded by Zola in his correspondence, to embark on canvases five meters in dimension.[26] It also seems likely that Zola's description of Lantier as having his eye from Delacroix, his hand from Courbet,[27] is a more colorful rendition of his idea, expressed in his *Salon* of 1880, that Cézanne "remains closer (i.e., than the other realists) to Courbet and Delacroix."[28] Then, too, the important change that began to manifest itself in Lantier's manner after his happy experience in Bennecourt is possibly intended by Zola to represent in modified form the same kind of change that took place in Cézanne after the fertile years in Auvers with Pissarro—and perhaps Zola meant the relationship of Lantier and Bongrand to reflect the friendship between Cézanne and Pissarro. In any event, no such dramatic change from violent scenes of the imagination to a calmer and more balanced, almost objective, view of nature can be found in the career of any other artist whom Zola knew well. Certainly, the scene of the *charité* described in chapter X of *L'Oeuvre* is based on an incident of Cézanne's career, when Guillemet forced the jury of 1882 to accept a canvas against its wishes. The *Dossier* indicates clearly here that Zola was depending strictly on reality for his inspiration.[29]

Again, Claude's long, fruitless search for the motif which will at last enable him to develop all his powers and his equally frustrating pursuit of the magic formula of art whereby he will be able to express his personality and view of the world may also be reflections of Zola's opinions of Cézanne's career, indeed of the reality of his career until the mid-1870's. There is no evidence in Zola's writings that he ever considered that his friend had found either the subject matter or the way of treating it that would allow him to bring his undoubted genius to full expression, but there are fairly numerous signs that he was never convinced, before writing *L'Oeuvre,* that Cézanne had found himself in any real sense. There is of course the famous remark of 1861 to the effect that Cézanne had the genius of a great painter but not the talent to become one;[30] there is the letter to Duret of 1870, in which he described Cézanne as still struggling to find his way;[31] and there are some public pronouncements which give a clear idea of his unchanging opinion, the first of them published in Cézanne's home territory in the *Sémaphore de Marseille* in 1877:

> Next, I shall cite M. Paul Cézanne, who is surely the greatest colorist of the group (i. e., of the Impressionists). At the exhibition there are Provençal landscapes of his that are of the most beautiful character. This artist's paintings, so strong and so true to life, may make the bourgeois smile, but it is none the less true that they display the elements of a great painter. The day when M. Paul Cézanne possesses himself entirely, he will produce completely superior works.[32]

Add to that the *Salon* of 1880, where he declares that his friend is "still struggling in technical research,"[33] and his notorious article "Peinture," of 1896, where he could say of Cézanne that he is a "grand peintre avorté,"[34] and the evidence becomes clear that the novelist thought quite sincerely that his friend never had discovered the formula so long and so furiously sought. That Zola was not entirely wrong in his assessment of Cézanne's career, at least in its early and middle stages, is borne out by the testimony of some who knew Cézanne. Duret, who was acquainted with him and knew a good deal about his career, stresses this long search for the proper motif,[35] and there is Gauguin's mocking letter of 1881 in which he asks Pissarro if his rival has at last found the formula he has been looking for, a prescription for compressing the expression of all his sensations into a unique procedure.[36] If Zola thought that Cézanne was condemned to a long groping and if he depicted this aspect of his friend's career in Lantier's fruitless quest in the novel, he was no more than reflecting the truth of the matter—with the difference, of course, that Cézanne did find the motif and the formula, Lantier did not.

The general situation of Claude Lantier, almost beyond a doubt, also reflects something like a reality of Cézanne's life, or at least a reality as Zola saw it. The gradual separation of Claude from the Baudequin group in the middle and late chapters of *L'Oeuvre* very probably recalls Cézanne's withdrawal from the Impressionist *chapelle* after about 1877—if it does not reflect a reality of Zola's own life, his increasing solitude after the great successes of his middle career. Moreover, Lantier is accused, both implicitly and openly, by the members of the "little band" of being their Jonah, of bringing public scorn and derision on them and essentially of barring the road to success. Cézanne likewise—and Zola surely knew this because of his relations with various Impressionists—was occasionally accused of delaying the school's triumph by his intransigence and violence. By 1869 only he of the entire group had never been accepted by the Salon, and by 1874, when it was decided to hold separate exhibitions, the Impressionists were so generally opposed to Cézanne, both as man and as artist, that Pissarro, the organizer, had considerable difficulty in persuading Degas and Monet to exhibit alongside the "madman"; others, like Manet, Fantin-Latour, and Guillemet, refused flatly, at least partly on the grounds of a possible proximity to Cézanne. It might also be pointed out that the scorn of the Baudequin group is matched by Lantier's contempt for their hasty methods and lack of integrity, just as the Impressionists' hostility was balanced by Cézanne's low opinion of them as a "gang." The gradual development of a kind of legend around Lantier as the novel progresses seems to be a direct transposition of the reality of Cézanne's career.

Lantier is regarded by everyone as a man of enormous genius, but genius coupled with some fatal flaw, as a creator who might revolutionize painting but whose incompleteness will keep him forever from success, as a lone wolf whose very friendship is damning but whose sketches contain within them a mysterious power and are the clear sign of the exceptional brain and hand. Some such legend seems to have grown up around Cézanne after 1870, when nearly all his friends appear to have lost faith in his ability ever to find his way. The tales of his eccentricity that are accredited by Duranty and the others who knew him undoubtedly reflected some part of this aura, and such expressions as "monster" and "ogre," as used by Duret in his *Histoire des peintres impressionnistes,* certainly were only pale renditions of stronger language in the mouths of both critics and public. When Catulle Mendès wrote of Cézanne after the first Impressionist exhibition that "of all the juries, not one, even in a dream, has glimpsed the possibility of accepting him,"[37] when Georges Rivière, commenting on the third Impressionist exhibition three years later called Cézanne "the most attacked, the most abused artist in the past fifteen years," when he added that there was no epithet that was not connected with his name, when he declared that his works obtained only the same "success of hilarity" as before,[38] they expressed a truth that Zola did not forget when he set down on paper the situation of his cursed hero. And when Zola has the members of the Baudequin group whisper that Claude, with all his arrogance and contempt for less gifted men, does not even know his craft, he almost certainly is echoing one of the criticisms most frequently addressed to Cézanne in the 1870's and early 1880's. But the same thing was said often enough of Manet, of Monet, and of every Impressionist, so the detail can hardly constitute real evidence.

L'Oeuvre further contains a number of events pertaining to Lantier's career which may be, but are not certainly, taken from Cézanne's own experiences. In these cases it is possible to find real origins other than those offered by Cézanne's life; they may come in large part from the career of Édouard Manet or some other painter of Zola's acquaintance or from the life of Zola himself. An example is Lantier's project, advanced early in the novel, for illustrating a book of Sandoz'. It is known that there was some casual talk of such a project between Zola and Cézanne early in Zola's career, but there is no evidence that either man took any steps to carry it out. It is more probable that Zola is referring to a similar project he formed with Manet.[39] About the same may be said of the fact that Sandoz poses as one of the figures in "Plein-Air"; Zola sat for Cézanne, but it seems more probable that this detail was borrowed from his relationship with Manet.[40] Lantier's art education offers something of the same case. He first studies with a père Belloque in Aix and later, in Paris, at the Atelier Boutin, one of the so-called "free studios" which were fairly common at the time. This undoubtedly recalls the Atelier Suisse which Cézanne frequented with Pissarro and Guillaumin, inasmuch as Zola mentions it in the *Dossier*.[41] But between père Belloque and the Atelier Boutin, Claude also studies with a certain Berthou, who, the *Dossier* makes clear, was intended to represent Couture, one of Manet's teachers. It seems probable, then, that Claude's training is a combination of Cézanne's and Manet's; perhaps it is simply meant to be typical of the avant-garde painters of the time and does not refer to any individual.

It has also been suggested that Lantier's employment of his mistress (later his wife) as his model indicates that Zola had Cézanne in mind, since Hortense Fiquet was practically the only woman who posed for him over a long period of years. Perhaps Zola was thinking of Cézanne here, but it is possible that this detail is from the career of Claude Monet, who likewise employed his mistress (later his wife) for this ungrateful task. Surely the practice must have been common enough among other painters of Zola's acquaintance, so that again this bit of evidence seems less conclusive than it is sometimes made out to be. Perhaps one aspect of the relationship between Fagerolles and Claude may reflect the relationship of Cézanne and Paul Gauguin. Fagerolles clearly and openly copies some facets of Claude's work, as Claude knows very well, and here Zola may have had in mind Cézanne's fear that Gauguin, in the first part of his career, was stealing his "little sensation."[42] More probably, however, Zola had in mind the relationship between Manet and Gervex or Guillemet or some other watered-down and popular realist or Impressionist. Again, it may be that Claude's persistent desire to conquer the Salon was borrowed from Cézanne's long efforts in the same direction. Cézanne's career gave a fine example of stubbornness, since he tried for more than two decades before he gained entrance through Guillemet's help, but both Manet and Monet expressed the same kind of desires and gave the same example of persistence in the face of a hostile officialdom; moreover, Zola himself was a great believer in the necessity of storming the citadels of official art—witness his long and fruitless quest for election to the Academy.

Another example of the same kind of evidence is the mockery of Claude at the Salon des Refusés, where his painting, "Plein-Air," is greeted by the hoots and jeers of the public.[43] Quite possibly Zola was here recalling, in a symbolic scene, the kind of reception Cézanne's paintings nearly always received at the Impressionists' exhibitions, but as the scene is clearly laid at the Salon des Refusés (where Cézanne did indeed exhibit, though his name does not appear on the program of exhibitors) it is more probable that the incident was to represent specifically the horror and amusement of the bourgeoisie before Manet's "Le Déjeuner sur l'herbe." Of course, Zola may have intended the episode to be a general one, recalling the usual reaction of the public to all the Impressionists' early efforts. It does not seem probable, in spite of Cézanne's terrible reputation and the guffaws that always greeted his work, that Zola was thinking of him specifically here.

In a different realm, the philosophy of art, Claude Lantier is frequently described as an impentitent romantic. As he ruins attempt after attempt, he becomes furious at the "romantic gangrene which grew in him in spite of everything; that was his disease, perhaps, the false idea whose weight he sometimes felt in his head,"[44] and Sandoz is careful, at the end of the novel, to ascribe Claude's failure at least partly to the influence of romanticism. It is possible that Zola had in mind the early Cézanne of "L'Enlèvement" and "Le Jugement de Pâris" and that Claude's sickness is a transposition of a flaw which Zola saw, or imagined he saw, in his old friend. But more probably he was rendering a truth about himself, for he made it clear in a dozen public confessions that he regarded himself as cursed by a resurgent romanticism, even in the last years of his career; or possibly this aspect of Claude's makeup was intended to represent what Zola thought to be the truth about his whole generation.

Likewise, the question of Claude's use of brush and knife, as described in *L'Oeuvre,* gives no sure indication that Zola was recounting Cézanne's practices. It is well established that Cézanne frequently applied colors with a knife, but he was by no means the only one to do so. He was fondest of the practice in his earliest years and almost abandoned it in his middle period. Moreover, the *Dossier* contains a long passage—given to Zola by Guillemet—on the brushes and knives in use, and it is obvious that Zola simply transposed these notes; there is no evidence in the *Dossier* that Guillemet was referring in the material to Cézanne's practice; rather, he was only describing the general practice of some painters.

Lastly, it can be argued that Claude's nature as an incomplete genius may well reflect Zola's opinion of Cézanne's situation as artist. Throughout the novel he emphasizes Claude's enormous ability as a sketcher and the nearly perfect details he creates from time to time, details which spring from his brush just often enough to keep up his hopes that some day he may be able to bring them together to create the great canvas which is almost within reach. But each time the picture is ruined by his inability to marshal all his forces, to go beyond the sketch to the finished creation, and this Tantalian torture ultimately drives him to suicide. It is impossible to say how far this particular detail of Lantier's character reflects Zola's opinion of Cézanne. While we are reasonably sure that he regarded his old friend as suffering from a limitation which recalls Lantier's, it is even more certain that he regarded Manet as incomplete,[45] so there is no good reason to suppose that in this trait of the fictional painter he was recalling a specific truth, or what he may have considered to be a truth, of Cézanne's nature.

Such is the evidence, certain and doubtful, which supports the contention that Lantier and Cézanne share a blood relationship. It clearly indicates that Cézanne was in some measure a model for the tragic figure of Lantier, but, unfortunately, it does not establish to just what extent he was a model, and *L'Oeuvre* contains strong evidence in the form of Lantier's total career that points away from the mature Cézanne. If it was wholly the Cézanne of the 1870's and 1880's whom Zola depicted as Claude Lantier, then he so completely misunderstood the career and accomplishment of his friend as to make himself out to be nothing short of artistically and intellectually blind.

Claude is shown throughout the novel as a revolutionary, a rebel against the art of convention and tradition, willing to throw the whole history of French painting overboard for the sake of one or two geniuses among his immediate predecessors. But his revolutionary talk could hardly have come from the example of the taciturn and conservative Cézanne, who, far from burning the Louvre, spent endless hours there copying the masters, and whose ambition was to be the Poussin of his time and whose very originality was built on a profound knowledge of the past, of the evolution of French art from classics to romantics. These rebellious cries of Lantier's are the cries of a school, of a time, they are reflections of Zola's own early defense of Manet. They have little to do with Cézanne. It is not possible to think that Lantier's "confounded series of paintings" could be a reflection of Cézanne's practice, confined as it was largely to nonurban scenes.

Again, about midway in the novel Lantier becomes a theorist of color and light and advances certain ideas which were becoming popular among artists in the 1880's and which had their origins in the physical sciences. But Zola did not get these theories from Cézanne. They came to him, rather, from a young and unknown painter, Léo Gausson, who took the trouble to compose for Zola, quite gratuitously it seems, a kind of manual of contemporary art theories and physical hypotheses out of Chevreul. There is no evidence that Cézanne even knew of the existence of these theories, and if he arrived at doctrines resembling them it was through his own researches and discoveries. But we do not know much about Cézanne's theories in art, for every commentator has given a different version of them, and in ignorance of the theoretical substructure of his works, we can only conclude that Claude Lantier, who becomes an Impressionist for a time, is not the Cézanne of the biographies.

Nor is he Cézanne in his eternal inability to let well enough alone, in his mania for retouching, changing, adding, which appears from beginning to end of *L'Oeuvre*. This kind of self-torture does not seem to have been characteristic of Cézanne. Legend has it that he was anything but a constant retoucher. If the stories of the paintings abandoned along the Seine and left to disintegrate on Sainte-Victoire are true, then it appears that he was far from being the same kind of artist as Lantier. He practiced such a diametrically opposite method that he was quite capable of leaving sections of a canvas entirely bare of paint and, far from agonizing over a canvas, simply progressed to another when he found insuperable technical or philosophical difficulties barring his way.

Much the same might be said of the general imitation of Claude that Sandoz observes in the Salon toward the close of the novel. As he passes through the halls with Claude he points out to him that in his very failure he has won the battle, for all the young artists now imitate him, he has conquered vicariously, his tone, his color, his manner are triumphant. Undoubtedly, this observation by Sandoz was based on the one made by Zola in a visit to the Salon before the writing of *L'Oeuvre*, the notes of which are in the *Dossier*. He had unquestionably seen the same general lightening of tone, the same disappearance of historical and traditional themes, the same blond sun. But Zola could never have believed that these profound changes were the product of Cézanne's practice and the result of his example, for he was as aware as anyone that Cézanne was beyond the pale in 1885 and 1886 and was simply too unknown to have exerted much influence at that date, even on the men who knew him best. His day was to come later, a good deal later, and if Zola observed a lightening of tone in the Salon, a broad change in matter and technique, it must have been because of the influence of Manet and Monet and Bastien-Lepage, not of Cézanne. What Zola is doing in this passage and in others like it, is reflecting the general influence of the Impressionists on contemporary art, he is not attributing to Cézanne a revolution which Cézanne did not accomplish and which Zola knew he had not accomplished.

Above all, it is Claude Lantier's artistic evolution that argues against an identification with Cézanne. A considerable number of paintings by Claude Lantier are mentioned in *L'Oeuvre*, but only a few are described sufficiently to give them anything like a definite appearance and to permit us to have any real idea of the subject matter on which they are constructed or of the technique. The earliest mentions of Claude's first paintings are too vague and general to allow us to make any certain identification either with Cézanne's work or with the work of any known artist:

> . . . there were sketches hanging on the walls, without frames, a thick flood of sketches which descended to the floor, where they were heaped up in a landslide of canvases thrown down pell-mell. Never had she seen such terrible painting, rough, dazzling, with a violence of tones that offended like a trucker's oath heard on the steps of an inn.[46]

Claude's first sketch of Christine is equally vague:

> In spite of herself, she glanced around the studio, at the terrifying sketches with which the walls flamed; and in her clear eyes a trouble reappeared, an anxious astonishment at this brutal painting. From a distance, she saw, wrong way to, the study which the painter had sketched of her, so perturbed by the violent tones, the great strokes of pastel slashing the shadows, that she did not dare ask to look at it closely.[47]

The only conclusion that may be drawn from these brief statements is that Claude is a revolutionary, willfully departing from conventional styles to seek an effect of shock. Certainly, this was true of the early Cézanne, but it was also true of so many of the young avant-garde of the 1860's that it may be assumed that Zola is only reflecting a general truth of the artistic moment he came to know at the time of *Édouard Manet* and *Mes Haines.* At all events, it is impossible to identify this early painting of Claude's with Cézanne's first efforts in Paris and equally impossible to put any other painter's name on it.

The first recognizable canvas by Claude Lantier in *L'Oeuvre* is his "Plein-Air," the painting that begins his reputation:

> It was a canvas five metres by three in size, completely covered, but of it only a few bits emerged from the sketch. This sketch, put down in one sitting, showed a superb violence, an ardent life of colors. In an opening in a forest, with thick walls of greenery, fell a downpour of light; to the left, only a shaded lane stretched into the background, with a distant spot of light on it. There, on the grass, amidst the June verdure, a nude woman was lying, an arm under her head, swelling her breast; and she was smiling, eyelids closed, in the rain of light that bathed her. In the background, two other female figures, small, one brunette, the other a blonde, were wrestling and laughing; they set off, amid the greens of the foliage, two adorable tones of flesh. And, as the painter needed a dark contrast in the foreground, he had quite simply satisfied himself by placing a male figure there, dressed in a simple velvet jacket. The man turned his back to the public, all that could be seen of him was his left hand, on which he was leaning, in the grass.[48]

Rewald believes that "Plein-Air" is a fusion of Manet's "Olympia" and "L'Enlèvement,"[49] basing his inclusion of "L'Enlèvement" on the resemblance of the small nude figures in the background to the small female figures in Claude's painting.[50] On the other hand the compilers of the Bibliothèque Nationale catalogue see in "Plein-Air" a clear reminiscence of Cézanne's "Pastorale" (circa 1870).[51] Ebin gives still another identification. She regards the canvas as a fusion of Manet's "Le Déjeuner sur l'herbe" and "Olympia," slightly modified under the influence of Cézanne's "L'Enlèvement" and "La Nouvelle Olympia,"[52] but argues that the basic model was "Le Déjeuner sur l'herbe." Whatever the facts may be, the logic of the situation seems to require that Zola should have called on Manet's first great revolutionary painting as the model for Claude's first major attempt to overturn traditional art rather than on a minor work of Cézanne's, itself in part an imitation of Manet. Since Zola wished to describe a typically revolutionary work in the first part of the novel, it seems highly likely that he would have chosen the work which above all others was scoffed at in the Salon des Refusés and which has come to be regarded as the very symbol of that salon. There is the possibility that "Plein-Air" was not imitated from any painting and that it was simply a creation of Zola's own mind, though the general similarity of the subject to Manet's "Déjeuner" argues against that possibility. In any event, "Plein-Air," as it now appears in the novel, was not Zola's original conception of Claude's first important effort, for the *Dossier* reveals that he composed three versions of his description of the painting before he found the one that satisfied him.

Claude's sketches from Provence are not described in sufficient detail to permit us to identify them:

> The walls of the studio were . . . covered by a series of sketches made down there (i.e., in Plassans) by the painter during a recent trip. It was as though the two friends had around them the old horizons, the ardent blue sky over the reddish landscape. There, a plain stretched, with successive waves of little grayish olive trees, up to the pink, lacy outline of the distant hills. Here, between two scorched hills, the color of rust, the low water of the Viorne was drying up under the arch of an old bridge, flour-white with dust, with no other verdure than some bushes dying of thirst. Further off, the gorge of the Infernets opened its gaping cut, in the midst of landslides of blasted rock, an immense chaos, a savage desert, rolling its waves of stone out to infinity. Then, all kinds of familiar spots: the valley of Repentance, so narrow, so shadowy, with the freshness of a copse among the burned fields; the woods of Trois-Bons-Dieux, whose pines, a harsh, varnished green, wept their resin under the full sun; the Jas de Bouffan, white as a mosque in its vast lands, like seas of blood; others, still others, bits of blinding roads which curved away, ravines where the heat seemed to make bubbles rise to the burned skin of the stones, thirsting tongues of sand, drinking the stream drop by drop, mole hills, goat paths, peaks in the blue.[53]

These paintings certainly seem to have some relationship with the general type of painting which Cézanne did after his final departure for the Midi, but there is not enough said of the treatment of the matter, style, perspective, and arrangement to allow any certain identification. It is possible that they represent something like Zola's synthesis of his friend's Aix manner, though in general they are wilder in conception and less geometrical than the works of Cézanne's mature period. The best probability, given the tone of the works, is that they are reflections of Zola's own strong visual memories of the environs of Aix.

L'Oeuvre contains no other references to paintings from Claude's early period, save a brief description of some sketches, so vague and general that it again permits no identification:

> With the tip of his brush he pointed to a painted study hanging on the wall near the door. It was superb, carried off with the ease of a master; and beside it there were other admirable bits, the feet of a little girl, exquisite in their delicate exactness, a woman's belly especially, satin flesh, quivering, living with the blood which coursed beneath the skin.[54]

Quite obviously, these sketches could have come from any brush, Courbet's or Cézanne's or Renoir's.

Claude's paintings from the Bennecourt episode may symbolize Cézanne's manner of the Auvers period, though again sufficient details for anything like a certain comparison are lacking:

> He worked in the garden, at first out of boredom, made a sketch of the line of apricot trees, drew some giant rose bushes, composed still lifes, four apples, a bottle and a stoneware pot, on a napkin. Then he warmed to his work, the idea of painting a clothed figure in full sunlight came to haunt him; and from that time his wife was his victim. . . . He painted her twenty times over, dressed in white, dressed in red amid the foliage, standing or walking, half stretched out in the grass, wearing a wide garden hat, bareheaded under a parasol, whose cerise silk bathed her face in a pink light.[55]

Of these paintings, only one, the still life, "four apples, a bottle and a stoneware pot, on a napkin," has much resemblance to Cézanne's work of the years he spent with Pissarro, but there is no denying that this still life does seem to bear a remarkable, though general, resemblance to the marvelously simple creations of the mature Cézanne.

After the Bennecourt episode Claude attains maturity of outlook and undergoes a sharp change in manner, largely under the impulsion of his desire to be accepted by the Salon while not abandoning completely his revolutionary intentions. The three paintings of this period of maturity described in *L'Oeuvre* reveal Claude as something of an Impressionist, but unfortunately they do not aid us in identifying the model, if any, on whom Zola called:

> To begin with, the first year he planted himself four hours a day during the December snows behind the Butte Montmartre, at the corner of a vacant lot, where he painted a background of misery, low hovels dominated by factory chimneys; and in the foreground he had put in the snow a little girl and a guttersnipe in rags, devouring stolen apples. . . .
>
> The second year, he sought a contrast. He chose one end of the Square des Batignolles, in May; big chestnut trees casting their shadow, a glimpse of turf, seven-story houses in the background, while in the foreground, on a bench of a harsh green color, sat maids and tradespeople of the quarter, watching three children making sand pies.
>
> So the third year he spent his rage on a work of revolt. He wanted full sunlight, that Parisian sunlight which some days heats the pavement white in the dazzling reflection of the façades. . . . The subject that he chose was a bit of the Place du Carrousel, at one o'clock, when the sun beats straight down. A cab jolted by, with a somnolent coachman, a horse dripping sweat, head down, vague in the shimmering heat, some pedestrians seemed drunk with heat, while alone a young lady, pink and fresh under her parasol, walked at her ease with a royal step, as if in the element of flame where she must live. But what made this painting especially terrible was the new study of light, that "decomposition," very exactly observed and going counter to all the habits of the eye by accentuating blues, yellows, reds where no one was accustomed to seeing them. The Tuileries, in the background, disappeared in a cloud of gold; the pavement bled, the pedestrians were only barely indicated, dark spots eaten up by the too vivid light.[56]

It is evident from the subject matter alone that these three paintings have little or nothing to do with the art of Cézanne, who was not a painter of Paris and not a "realist" and who rarely if ever hazarded himself in subjects of the kind described here. The *Dossier* indicates, moreover, that they may be creations of Zola's own mind, based on his observations of Paris, for in the first plan of Chapter VIII, where these paintings are described, he says: "Paris can give me a series of tableaux swiftly brushed in, pictorial, interesting, without my insisting too much on them."[57]

Toward the end of Claude's career, he is driven by financial necessity to enter the artist's special hell:

> . . . Claude had had to resign himself to commercial work, so revolted, so desperate at having fallen into this hell-hole where

> he swore he would never descend, that he would have preferred to die, had it not been for the two poor beings who were agonizing with him. He came to know stations of the cross slapped up at a discount, saints by the gross, blinds decorated according to stereotypes, all the low jobs that debase art into a stupid game of picture-making that is not even naive. He even knew the shame of having twenty-five-franc portraits refused because he did not catch the resemblance; and he arrived at the lowest degree of misery, he worked "by the number"; tiny dealers who sold on the bridges and shipped pictures to savages, bought from him at so much a canvas, two francs, three francs, according to the standard dimension.[58]

A bit later he finds another source of income, little paintings of flowers for England. Obviously, nothing here recalls Cézanne, who, so far as we know, was never forced into this kind of torture; the episode may, however, be a reflection of Zola's memories of some of the bitter realities of the lives of Monet or Renoir.

Only two more paintings from Claude's career are described in *L'Oeuvre,* the painting of the dead child which is accepted by the Salon because of Fagerolles' "charité" and the vast painting of the Seine on which Claude's ambitions finally founder. The first of these may have been inspired by a painting of the little-known Dubois-Pillet,[59] though its idea may also have been suggested to Zola by an incident in Monet's career:

> Ah! the "Dead Child," miserable little cadaver, which at this distance was nothing more than a confused mass of flesh, the stranded carcass of some formless beast. Was it a skull, was it a belly, that phenomenal head, swollen and white? and those poor hands twisted on the coverlet, like the retracted feet of a bird killed by the cold! and the bed itself, that paleness of the sheets beneath the paleness of the members, all that sad white, that disappearance of color, the end of all! Then, one could distinguish pale, fixed eyes, one could recognize a child's head, a case of some illness of the brain, profoundly and frightfully pitiful.[60]

Claude's final painting, unnamed but called by Ebin the "Apotheosis of Paris," must either be a creation of Zola's own or a reminiscence of some other painter than Cézanne. It begins as a "naturalistic" study of Paris, with the customary sociological overtones; this is how Claude describes its original conception:

> Look! I place myself under the bridge, in the foreground I have the Port Saint-Nicolas, with its crane, its barges being un-

loaded, its crowd of longshoremen. Eh? you understand, this is Paris, working, this is! stout fellows showing their bare chests and arms. Then, on the other side, I have the swimming pool, Paris enjoying itself, and a boat there, probably, to occupy the center of the composition; but I don't know about that yet, I've got to search. Naturally, the Seine in the middle, wide, immense. . . .

Finally, I have the background, the two arms of the river, with the quays, the triumphant Cité between them, rising toward the sky. Ah! that background, what a miracle! We see it every day, we pass in front of it without stopping; but it gets into you, admiration builds up and one afternoon it appears to you. Nothing in the world is greater, it is Paris itself, glorious beneath the sun. . . . And, you remember, there is a spot of shadow on this side, the sun here shines straight down, the towers are over there, the spire of the Sainte-Chapelle tapers upward, fine as a needle in the sky.[61]

This first sketch culminates in a finished canvas, not described, which like the works of Claude's period of comparative calm and maturity is rejected by the Salon. It is this last rejection which drives him to mania and insanity and finally suicide. Immediately after the rejection the painting begins to lose its generally "naturalistic" appearance and to evolve in the direction of sexual symbolism:

The background, the quays, the Seine, from which rose the triumphant prow of the Cité, were there at the stage of a sketch, but a masterly sketch, as if the painter had been afraid to spoil the Paris of his dream by finishing it further. To the left there was also an excellent group, longshoremen who were carrying off sacks of plaster, well-marked bits, those, of a fine, powerful workmanship. Only, the boatload of women in the center opened up the picture with a flame of flesh which was not in its place; and the great nude figure especially, painted in a kind of fever, had the splendor, the dimension of a hallucination and a strange and disconcerting falseness in the midst of the neighboring realities.[62]

Finally this new tendency completely destroys the original conception and Claude ends in hallucination:

He would never finish this painting, that was certain now. The more he struggled at it, the more its incoherence grew, with heavy, thick colors, a gross and shifty drawing. Even the background, the group of longshoremen especially, once so solid, were being spoiled; and that was where he came a cropper, for he had

> wanted to finish everything before repainting the central figure, the nude who remained the fear and the desire of his working hours . . . her thighs were gilded like the columns of a tabernacle, her belly became a sun, dazzling with pure yellows and reds, splendid and outside of life. Such a strange nudity, like a monstrance, where precious stones seemed to shine for some religious rite, drove her (i.e., Christine) at last to anger.[63]

There are several possibilities for an original for this painting in the work of contemporary artists, none of them particularly good. It might be based on a large tableau by the cartoonist André Gill,[64] or it may be based on Monet's "Argenteuil: les Déchargeurs de charbon" or on Gervex' "Le Bassin de la Villette," exhibited at the Salon of 1882.[65] It may be, however, that the painting was elaborated in Zola's mind as a result of his own observations. At all events, the site of the painting is described in his notes in considerable detail,[66] and the possibility of his having borrowed the idea for the "Apotheosis of Paris" from anyone else is remote. Curiously enough, the phrases "Paris qui travaille" and "Paris qui s'amuse" were coined by Zola some years before the composition of *L'Oeuvre*. They appear in his article in *Le Voltaire* for August 19, 1879; their presence in the description of Claude's painting seems to be another bit of evidence pointing to origins that are literary and "naturalistic." The best possibility, then, is that Cézanne provided nothing in the way of ideas for this last painting of the fictional hero and that Zola meant it to represent certain ideas of his own on Paris and perhaps further intended it to symbolize some of his own literary and psychic tendencies.[67]

It seems obvious that this final failure of Lantier's can have had nothing to do, in Zola's mind, with Cézanne's painting, even the fiercely erotic painting of the period of "L'Enlèvement." Quite clearly, the great project in which Lantier comes finally to realize the limitations of his genius is the culmination of his whole psychic evolution; as such it cannot be based on the work of the man who perhaps more than any other painter of his time relied on the simple lessons of nature as his best guide and model.

So far as we see it in the book, Claude's career is a long and profound evolution. He moves from pure scenes of nature, absolutely devoid of idea or literature to scenes of modern Paris, the last of which is clearly literary in character. Bennecourt gives way to Les Halles, Les Halles themselves give way to the dream, to the ideal, and that is the tragedy of this artist who cannot find his way. His difficulty is plain: he is torn between his desire to be an objective realist, painting representational scenes of modern life, and an original artist, offering a new view of man and nature, giving the fullest expression to his personality, and so departing, by the very terms of his originality, from the objective and the representational. This was not only Claude's difficulty; it might well be argued that it was Zola's too and that the dilemma posed by the double intention of the writer is responsible in no small measure for both his shortcomings and his achievements.

But Claude did not have the redeeming power of his creator, so his life is spent in a long and fruitless search for the formula which he hopes will allow him to solve his dilemma and permit him to reconcile the realism of his conscious mind with the romanticism of his spirit and to force into a single synthesis the true and the ideal, the real and the dream. The formula is unfindable, and its pursuit leads Claude to madness and death.

But with all his "lesion" and his incompleteness, with all his inability to find the saving formula, Claude remains a man of genius. His paintings, those of the mature period, are intensely modern in subject and wildly opposed to the accepted matter and manner of the Salons and the Louvre; but more than that, they introduce a whole new notation of color, air, and light which revolutionizes the technique of painting of a whole generation and will leave an indelible mark on all French art of modern times. The Salon des Refusés is mocked by the crowd, but Claude and a few of the elect, among them Fagerolles himself, are not deceived by the public laughter, for they see in these incomplete and groping works the promise of a new era and the sign of a new vision. So, in his failure, Claude triumphs and becomes with time a kind of legend, the absent head of a school with which he has lost contact. Other men borrow their "sensation" from his work, Fagerolles and the rest, by softening his violence and attenuating the integrity of his vision, accomplish the revolution, while Claude, in silence and in torture, ruins his life over the last, impossible conception of his deviated genius. But the revolution is his, no one else's, and the wanderer of Bennecourt, of the banlieue and of Paris, this outcast, this bohemian, rejected even by the group of the Baudequin which he had inspired to ultimate victory, is the final conqueror, failure, madness, suicide, and all.

How then, can the artistic career of Lantier, taken as a whole, be interpreted as a representation of Zola's opinion of Cézanne's evolution? Lantier moves in a direction exactly opposite from that taken by Cézanne, from revolutionary realism of the early plein air type to the most exaggerated symbolism, from almost purely decorative painting to a gross form of neo-romanticism, from pure painting to literary, from nature to the false and tormented vision of the inner eye. Whatever the limitations of his critical method and perception, could Zola possibly have believed that Cézanne by 1885 had evolved in this manner, when he had before his eyes precisely contrary evidence in the form of the canvases executed by Cézanne in the Ile-de-France during his numerous trips north? If he could have believed this, then indeed he was as blind as some of his critics believe.

It is undeniable that the opinion that Zola never did, never could, understand Cézanne's painting is very widespread. Many of the critics who have addressed themselves to the relationship between the painter and the novelist have flatly concluded that Zola was as biased and uncompromising as the worst of the traditionalist critics of the 1870's and 1880's, and although their judgment is usually expressed without benefit of supporting evidence, it has had wide acceptance. Nearly all of them claim that Zola considered Cézanne a complete failure, a victim of radical impotence,[68] and they back their claim by pointing out Zola's repeated failures even to mention Cézanne seriously during his long career as critic and journalist. True, he defended him somewhat lukewarmly in a letter to the *Figaro* in 1867,[69] but in no case, at least so far as known, did he ever come openly and frankly to the support of the mature Cézanne. It is possible, of course, that a newspaper article by Zola or a letter from him might some day provide evidence in the matter, but that possibility seems less than likely.

It is difficult to explain why Zola did not attempt to aid his friend's career when he certainly had the opportunity to do so, given his long years as an influential journalist. Most of his writings on art were reviews of the official Salons, and since Cézanne never exhibited in these, save in 1882, Zola could hardly mention him in his articles, but it is still arguable that he might have drawn his name into some discussion had he cared to. It is also possible that Zola's editors would not allow mention of the "madman" and even that Cézanne might not have wished any publicity, though this possibility seems remote, given Cézanne's desire to succeed in official circles. The fact remains that Zola could have materially aided his friend's career by some kind of favorable notice, but that he did not. Why? The answer most frequently given and which seems to have the force of logic to support it is that he did not regard Cézanne's work highly enough to wish to talk about it publicly.

The positive considerations are equally hard to argue away. They consist of Zola's early remarks to and about Cézanne in the letters of his early career, his refusal to give Théodore Duret, when he asked for it, in 1870, Cézanne's name,[70] his statement in the *Figaro* article of 1896 that Cézanne was "a great painter aborted," and his declaration to Gustave Geffroy during his exile in England that he was disappointed in the achievements of Manet, Monet, the Impressionists in general, and Cézanne because of a lack of finish and composition.[71] A small piece of circumstantial evidence also seems to support the hypothesis that Zola saw Cézanne as a failure. In a letter written to Zola in June 1875, Paul Alexis, complaining of his lack of accomplishment, declared that he did not want to be another Valabrègue or another Cézanne or another Dethez.[72] If Alexis thought of Cézanne in such terms, so may Zola.

It is beyond doubt that Zola, if he did not consider Cézanne as precisely a flat failure, had very serious reservations about his accomplishment. Everything he wrote about him was lukewarm, at best, every time he had a chance to defend him publicly he failed to do so, never, either at the beginning or the end of his career, did he indicate that he thought Cézanne had succeeded.

But with respect to *L'Oeuvre,* how much do such considerations weigh? The letters in which Zola most discusses Cézanne's talent and achievement are all from the very early part of his career, and after about the middle of the 1860's references to Cézanne become ever more rare. Zola's correspondence, as we have it today, gives little or no indication of what he thought about Cézanne in the 1870's and 1880's. Again, all the really unfavorable remarks he made publicly about his friend came toward the end of Zola's life, long after the two had broken—and after the Dreyfus case, it might be added—and they too give no idea of what Zola's opinion might have been at the time he composed *L'Oeuvre.* That period remains a blank, and it is very likely that whatever information is discovered it will remain essentially a blank.

But one thing is certain: *L'Oeuvre* cannot be used as effective evidence to prove that Zola thought Cézanne a failure. Claude Lantier is not Cézanne, he is a fictional figure, partly composed on the model of several men, among them Cézanne, but essentially a creature of Zola's imagination. He possesses important traits from Zola's old friend, some of his first paintings seem to resemble Cézanne's at least in subject, and his position in the art world as outcast and Jonah recalls Cézanne's. But to infer that Lantier represents Zola's intimate opinion of his friend or contains any kind of final judgment on his art and genius is to presume on the facts. In this debate the facts have never been very important.

VI

Lantier—Manet

Cézanne's principal rival for the doubtful honor of being Zola's model for Claude Lantier has always been Édouard Manet. There is a great deal of evidence in the novel and in extraliterary sources to back the belief that he was one of the chief figures if not *the* chief figure on whom Zola called for details of his fictional artist, and from the first appearance of *L'Oeuvre* a large group of critics have held that Lantier is Manet and not Cézanne.[1]

It will be recalled that in the *Ébauche Zola* refers to Claude as "A Manet, a dramatized Cézanne,"[1a] and though he adds "closer to Cézanne," it is clear that he was first thinking of Manet. One or two other details in the *Ébauche* likewise seem to indicate that he had Manet in mind. In the *Liste des personnages* he refers to Berthou, one of Claude's teachers, as Thomas Couture, who was Manet's master for a time,[2] and in the *Ébauche* he recalls "Manet's duel" as one of the events he wishes to portray.[3] It may be too that when he refers to Claude's work, in the *Ébauche,* as "very light painting" he was thinking of Manet, to whose work the phrase seems more applicable than to the work of any other painter Zola might have known.

There is much other evidence to back the position that Manet was Zola's model, though it must be said from the outset that there is little possibility of establishing a relationship between Claude Lantier the man (as distinguished from the artist) with Manet, for the character of the fictional painter seems very different from that of Zola's friend. Manet was, if we can believe the testimony of those who knew him, including Zola, very different in temperament from the artist we see in the pages of *L'Oeuvre,* much less dramatic, with none of Lantier's traits of aggressiveness or monomania. It is not apparent that Manet suffered from anything like the manic depressive tendencies, with swift and wide alternations between hope and despair, which are

Claude's, and there is little evidence in Manet's biographies that he was anything but what the layman would call psychologically normal. There are indications that he suffered from something like the artistic torment which harasses Claude, illustrated by the anecdote which has him tear up his portrait of Gambetta when it will not turn out right and exclaim "Another one whose portrait will be painted by Bonnat!" but it can be assumed that most artists, at least those of integrity and professional honesty, suffer from much the same torments, and Zola had no reason to call specifically on Manet for this aspect of his hero. And so far as the bulk of the evidence goes, Manet did not suffer very often or very long from this torment, nowhere near so badly as Claude does in his pursuit of the ideal. It is also true that Manet was often disturbed by what was said of him by both critics and artists, and he was distressed by the reaction of the crowd to his work—as who would not have been?—but the picture which emerges from his biographies is of a man who worked consistently, steadied by a continuing hope that his work would eventually be accepted and that he would finally attain the position which he knew his gifts should give him. His quite considerable production in a comparatively short career seems to indicate that he did not spend a great deal of time brooding over his shortcomings or the reaction of others to his painting. It should be observed, though, that the incessant evolution in his work which Zola noted in his preface to the Manet catalogue[4] may be a sign of the same kind of self-doubt which tortures Claude; but if Manet did suffer from this particular torment, there is a vast difference in intensity between what we see in Claude Lantier and what we can assume of Manet. If Zola took this trait of his hero from Manet, then it is clear that he romanced it fairly extensively.

There are also indications that Manet suffered from something like Claude's timidity and its resulting brutality of manner and expression. Antonin Proust, Manet's friend and biographer, notes this trait and adds that after 1865, when Manet had become disgusted with the crowd and the critics because of the uproar over "Olympia," a change came over him, making him more somber, caustic, and solitary.[5] But there is no hint that this timidity was carried to the sickly lengths which we find in Lantier, and above all there is no sign that it made Manet distrust and flee women or find solace and release in the painted flesh of his female figures. So far as we know, Manet was anything but an offender against Venus, and the chastity which brings Claude to destruction, if Zola found it in any artist he knew, almost certainly did not come from Manet. Nor is there much evidence to indicate that Manet could have provided Zola with the idea of making his hero a

Romantic, for if the painter of "Le Bon Bock" was a sufferer from Lantier's "romantic gangrene," Zola did not seem to see the malady in him; had he believed Manet to be so cursed, he surely would have mentioned it somewhere in the pages he wrote on him.

Above all, there is no evidence to indicate that Zola, or any other critic, saw in Manet the kind of impotence—the famous "lesion"—which keeps Claude from self-realization. It is true that Zola came to see Manet as incomplete, but nowhere in his discussions of this aspect of his friend does he attribute what he regards as Manet's principal shortcomings in art to anything like the terrible hereditary psychophysiological tare which is Claude's curse. It may be possible, however, that Claude's "lesion" represents in dramatized form the inability Zola noted in Manet to make his hand render what his eye saw and to formulate a clear philosophy which would enable him to determine in advance the direction each new canvas would take, instead of yielding always to impulse and inspiration. But if the "lesion" represents these things, then Zola is exaggerating badly in the novel. Nor is there any good evidence that Manet was given to the fits of anger which characterize all of Claude's career or to his propensity to quarrel. Manet was, certainly, sensitive and stubborn, as Claude appears in the novel, but no biographer shows these traits in Manet as developed to anything like the extent they attain in Lantier's temperament. Again, there is no reliable indication that Manet hated the bourgeoisie with Claude's fine passion. Manet was a man of the world, something of a boulevardier, with connections in good society and an interest in people of his own social class—the easy bourgeoisie—and he shows nothing of Claude's violent rejection of the Parisian social world. Indeed, in writing about Manet Zola stresses his worldliness, his love of elegance and refinement, which makes him so different from the crude and brutal Lantier. Nor, so far as we know, did Manet have Claude's feverish desire to move ahead before the work in hand was finished; Manet was somewhat impatient in manner, but Zola's accounts indicate that he was usually able to dominate his nerves and carry on a task to the point where it satisfied him.

It is clear, too, that Manet was not a bohemian in Claude's style, and in writing of him Zola does his best to make him out to be a settled, tranquil man, almost a good bourgeois. But it is significant that Zola should do so, for this indicates beyond any doubt that Manet had a reputation among the critics and with the general public for being a revolutionary in manner—the worst kind of nineteenth-century beatnik. On several occasions in his pages on Manet, Zola refers to the legend of a mocking and shiftless bohemian,[6] so it is possible that

Zola gave Claude his bohemian characteristics on the basis of this widespread public belief, not on the basis of the truth about Manet or, for that matter, about Cézanne.

Not much can be concluded from Zola's other remarks on Manet's personality and attitude toward the world. He saw him as deeply devoted to his art,[7] but what great artist is not? Like Claude, Manet had a considerable reputation as a madman—Baudelaire, for instance, refers to him in a letter as "M. Manet, who is thought to be mad . . ."[8]—but as many painters of Manet's time had this reputation, as some do now, it is difficult to believe that Zola called on his friend's legendary role for this aspect of Lantier's life. Like Claude, Manet was charged with not knowing his craft;[9] but the same thing was said so often of the Impressionists that it is not possible to draw any conclusions from such a similarity. The same is true of the sincerity and integrity which Zola saw in Manet. Over and over again he stresses the honesty with which Manet approached his work, perhaps to counter the unfortunate reputation the painter had acquired with the uninitiate as a conscienceless and cynical mocker; but once more, Zola's observations of these qualities in Manet do not imply that he used them as a basis for the same traits in Lantier, for he could have observed them in many painters of his acquaintance—Monet, Pissarro, Cézanne, Renoir, and a half-dozen others.

It seems evident that Claude Lantier, the man, was not intended by Zola to represent the Manet he had known so long and had so long supported. If the personal aspect of the fictional artist had any model at all—and it is not essential that he should have had—it must have been the young Cézanne or some other painter of Zola's early circle, not Manet. In personality, Lantier is nearly as different from Manet as he is in physical appearance.

But, generalities of personality aside, there are details in the novel which surely were taken by Zola from the life of Manet and which indicate that he consciously used Manet as part of his model.

One of these is the incident near the beginning of *L'Oeuvre* where Dubuche naively protests at the inclusion of a fully clothed man in the group of female figures in "Plein-Air." His protest has scarcely crossed his lips when Sandoz and Lantier fall upon him with shouts of indignation, pointing out that in the Louvre there are a hundred canvases where the same kind of grouping is to be found.[10] This surely echoes a passage from *Édouard Manet*, where, in discussing "Le Déjeuner sur l'herbe," Zola says:

> That nude woman scandalized the public, which saw only her in the painting. Great Heavens! what indecency: a woman

> without the slightest veil, between two clothed men! That had never been seen before. And that belief was a gross error, for in the Louvre there are more than fifty pictures in which clothed characters are mingled with nudes. But no one is going to seek to be scandalized at the Louvre.[11]

Another close approximation of reality is provided by the portrait of Sandoz which Claude includes in "Plein-Air," described briefly but effectively.[12] Later, when Claude assesses the real value of his painting, as he sees it at the Salon des Refusés, he notes this detail: "Decidedly, the male figure in the velvet jacket was no good, fleshy and awkwardly seated; only the hand was beautiful."[13] That Zola was here thinking of his portrait by Manet seems to be indicated by the description he gives of the painting in *Mon Salon*, where he goes out of his way to describe the hand in the foreground and to call it "a marvel of execution"; if the whole portrait could have been finished as perfectly, the crowd would have called it a masterpiece.[14]

Again, Claude's relationship with his early teacher, Berthou, is certainly taken from Manet's experiences. In the *Ébauche* Zola refers to Berthou as Couture,[15] and in the text of the novel he describes him as the famous painter of "Néron au Cirque."[16] Couture was most famous for his "Romains de la décadence." Zola adds that Berthou had told Lantier on a score of occasions that he would never accomplish anything. In *Édouard Manet* Zola used almost exactly the same phrase when speaking of Manet's apprenticeship to Couture: "You will never do anything, said the schoolmaster. . . .[17]

A similar case seems to be Claude's project to illustrate Sandoz' book of short stories. As noted[18] Cézanne and Zola also had such a project in mind for a time, but the idea seems to have been carried a great deal further by Zola when he met Manet. He proposed it to the publisher Lacroix in 1867,[19] and though the second project was never carried out, it seems more probable that Zola was thinking of it rather than the earlier and vaguer plan with Cézanne.

Still another such detail is provided by the incident in *L'Oeuvre* in which Bongrand raises his voice in protest at the treatment given by the jury to Claude's "Enfant mort":

> . . . . Bongrand, silent up to that point, his cheeks flushed by the anger he was restraining, burst out suddenly, inappropriately, and uttered this cry of his revolted conscience:
>
> —But, for God's sake, there aren't four of us here capable of knocking out a piece like that![20]

Almost exactly the same thing seems to have been said by Cabanel, who was helping Manet get his "Portrait de Pertuiset" accepted by the jury and who was encountering the same kind of rough going as does Fagerolles when he tries to win the jury to acceptance of Claude's painting, for Antonin Proust declares that when Cabanel met opposition from the jury he cried: "There probably aren't four of us here capable of painting a piece like that."[21] Significantly, it was Henri Gervex who made possible the acceptance of the "Portrait de Pertuiset," for he persuaded Vollon and Neuville to vote as Cabanel wished; here the parallel becomes very close if Fagerolles is considered to be anything of a depiction of Gervex.[22]

It might also be pointed out that the epoch represented in *L'Oeuvre* is historically much more closely identified with the name of Édouard Manet than that of Paul Cézanne, as Ebin argues.[23] Zola obviously intended to depict the art world of the Second Empire, just as he intended to show his other worlds in the *Rougon-Macquart* series, and it is beyond argument that the period 1850-70 was Manet's and not Cézanne's. The years 1863-76 represented in the novel were just the time when Manet was fighting his great battles, while Cézanne and the Impressionists did not succeed in gaining even unfavorable public attention until after the time when the novel closes, their first exposition not taking place until 1874.

Moreover, it is not impossible that the friendship between Sandoz and Claude Lantier reflects the relationship between Zola and Manet, however much has been written on the bond uniting Zola and Cézanne. Zola was not a boyhood friend of Manet's, as he was of Cézanne's, and there is no sign that Zola's idea of presenting three young "inseparables" from Provence to Paris was based on anything but his own early experiences with Cézanne and Baille; but Zola had known Manet for more than fifteen years before the painter's death and had formed a certain attachment for him. It is notable, too, that a good part of the notoriety surrounding the young and struggling Lantier is created in the novel by Jory's noisy articles in *Le Tambour,* just as Zola contributed mightily by *Mon Salon* and *Édouard Manet* to the enormous publicity which Manet began to receive toward the end of the 1860's and the beginning of the 1870's.[24] Moreover, when Zola began *L'Oeuvre* Manet had been dead two years and had already passed into the domain of legend; Cézanne and most of the Impressionists were very much alive in 1885-86, and it seems far more likely that Zola would have written a retrospective novel than a novel whose key figure was a living friend. So perhaps Rewald is right in arguing that the "artistic friendship" linking Manet and Zola was stronger than the childhood friendship between Zola and Cézanne;[25] if he is, then it would appear that Manet must have been Zola's model, not the painter of Sainte-Victoire, whose public career had scarcely begun in 1886.

Another such detail, which may come from the life of either Cézanne or Manet, is provided by Lantier's general situation in the Baudequin group. He is shown, especially later in the novel when his failure has become established, as living apart from his old friends, alone, feared, even despised by his fellow artists.[26] Zola seems to have believed, perhaps with reason, that in the mid-1870's Manet found himself in much the same situation vis-à-vis his colleagues:

> He has always figured as an apple of discord. If his colleagues have treated him outrageously today, it is because they have never ceased seeing in him an enemy, a refractory fellow whom they would have been happy to crush. It was enough that one or two bigwigs risked an impertinent remark, after which the others hesitated for ten years. The desire to separate themselves from Manet has always existed, and it was enough to find someone rude enough to put the desire into action.[27]

That Zola was not greatly exaggerating Manet's ostracism by his fellow painters is evident from the testimony of other observers. Théodore Duret says, for instance, that when the Impressionists decided on a private exposition in 1874, Manet did not participate.[28] The situation in the novel is reversed, true enough—in actuality Manet was the successful one, the Impressionists the struggling outcasts, while in the text Claude is given their role—but the fact of a certain ostracism (perhaps the term is too strong) is there nonetheless. Mauclair makes the same point as Duret, but renders the parallel between Manet and Lantier even more evident. Manet, he claims, tried to persuade his fellow artists to continue his assault on the official Salon and to force acceptance of their ideas there, as he had, but the Impressionists, fearful of more public scandal, refused and left it to Manet to clear a path for them.[29] If Cézanne was a pariah for his fellow fighters, so indeed was Manet.

Along the same line, Claude Lantier, especially toward the beginning of the novel, is shown as a frequenter of the Café Baudequin, and this again seems to point to Manet rather than to Cézanne. Rewald notes that Manet (who was one of the oldest frequenters of the Café Guerbois, while Cézanne was one of the youngest) was clearly the leader of the group,[30] as Lantier surely is also, and further states that Cézanne came only rarely to the cafe.[31] Duret maintains that Manet provided the first bond among the early visitors to the Guerbois, for all the first group shared his ideas, and even when the meetings began to include a good many men of letters Manet remained the dominant figure.[32] Duret, who knew the Guerbois group at first hand, does not even mention Cézanne's presence there, so even if he was a pillar of the group, as seems doubtful, he certainly was not the central figure, and here again Zola seems to have called on Manet's role as inspiration for the acts of his hero.

A whole group of more specific details seems likewise to come from Manet's life, though possibly Zola took them—if he did not imagine them—from the career of Cézanne or some other painter.

One of these is the Bennecourt episode, which has been traditionally ascribed to Cézanne's experience, for it is known that he was there with Zola on at least one occasion.[33] It cannot be argued, of course, that Manet ever went to Bennecourt, for there is no evidence that he did, but it is not impossible that Zola was thinking of some similar experience of Manet's as he composed the Bennecourt episode, for in his preface to the Manet catalogue of 1884, he remarks: "Illness gripped him, but he kept his courage, went to spend his summers in the country, whence he brought back sketches, flowers, figures lying in the grass."[34] When these words are compared to Zola's description of Lantier's painting at Bennecourt, a certain similarity strikes the eye, for at Bennecourt he paints simple outdoor scenes and often sketches Christine lying in the grass.

Again, Claude Lantier is constantly shown as a wanderer in Paris, seeking the "motif" in all the corners of the great city, along all its boulevards and quais. There is little evidence that Cézanne was addicted to such random excursions as Lantier's, for he clearly preferred the suburbs, but Antonin Proust emphasizes that Manet, much more of a city dweller than the untamed Cézanne, had a deep interest in Paris as a source of subjects and that he, like Lantier, was a persistent stroller.[35] Moreover, it may well be that Zola took from one of Manet's subjects, itself perhaps stemming from his wanderings in the city, the idea of having Claude propose a huge series of epic paintings portraying Paris in all its aspects, railway stations, markets, city halls, the life of the rich and of the poor, at the race track and on the boulevards, in the populous quarters, all the trades, all the passions, all the beasts, all the workers.[36] There is no evidence that Cézanne ever had such a project, which seems foreign to his interests and his genius, but it is a matter of record that Manet once proposed a somewhat similar project and at a time when Zola might have known of it, might indeed have proposed it to him or encouraged him to suggest it. In a letter of 1879 to the prefect of Paris Manet offered to decorate one of the meeting rooms of the Hôtel de Ville so as to portray all the interests of modern Parisian life, "Paris-Halles, Paris-chemins de fer, Paris-bon port, Paris-souterrain, Paris-courses et jardins," along with portraits of those who had most contributed to the greatness and wealth of the capital.[37] It is entirely possible that Lantier's "confounded series of paintings" was only a symbolic rendition of Zola's own ideas for the *Rougon-Macquart* series, which certainly resembles the artist's project in some essential ways, but it is equally possible that Manet's idea was the germ of Lantier's ambitious dream.

And there are other details, like the duel which almost takes place between Jory and some unnamed antagonist because of one of Jory's articles. As noted[38] Zola mentions in the *Dossier* Manet's duel with Duranty, and it is possible that he was thinking of this rather bizarre encounter as he related the little event. Also, like Cézanne, Manet resembles Claude Lantier in that he marries his mistress after years of life together without benefit of clergy.[39] There is no evidence that Manet called on his mistress-wife, Suzanne Leenhoff, very frequently to model for him, as Claude calls on Christine (and Cézanne called on Hortense Fiquet), and although one of Manet's finest portraits shows his wife at the piano, it is not likely that this detail of *L'Oeuvre* came from Manet's life.

It is much more certain that the scene at the Salon des Refusés was based on Manet's life, not the life of Cézanne or any other painter. The great explosion of public mockery which greets "Plein Air" could hardly have been modeled on any other event of the art world of the 1860's and 1870's than the terrible reception given "Le Déjeuner sur l'herbe," for no other painting (except "Olympia") seems to have been treated with the same scorn, vituperation, and total lack of comprehension or even common good will and good sense. Zola had evidently been deeply impressed by the scene at the Refusés in 1863, for three years later, in *Mon Salon,* he spoke with considerable bitterness of the crowd's reaction to the great masterpiece of Manet's early career.[40] Another detail of the scene at the Salon des Refusés, in addition to the inept joy of the crowd, seems to have stuck in Zola's mind, to be reproduced when he wrote his chapter on Claude's sad experience at the Refusés. After he has finished his description of the crowd's hilarity, he adds: "He saw a critic who stopped without laughing, some famous painters, surprised, their faces serious, *père* Malgras, very dirty, going from painting to painting with his connoisseur's pout, stopping short before his, motionless, absorbed."[41] In *Édouard Manet*

(1867) he notes a similar detail, for Manet now has defenders, even admirers.[42]

Of course, Cézanne was the victim of public mockery—every Impressionist was—but no single canvas of his, at any single showing, ever created quite the scandal that "Le Déjeuner sur l'herbe" did in 1863; the explosion of criticism and laughter it caused was surely the outstanding evidence of public stupidity and professional jealousy in Zola's early experience in the art world, and it seems beyond question that the scene of the Refusés in *L'Oeuvre* is a somewhat romanticized and dramatized, yet basically true reminiscence of what Zola had seen and felt as the new art fought its first great battle for recognition.

All these details indicate that Zola took some ideas for his novel from Manet's career; they do not prove that the painter of "Olympia" was the model for Lantier. But when we compare Zola's writings on art with what he says through Lantier in the pages of *L'Oeuvre*, it seems almost beyond doubt that Manet was the principal model for the fictional artist—at least until the point where Claude is gripped by monomania and driven to suicide. For Lantier is clearly conceived by Zola as much the same kind of artist as Manet and is given a role in the art world of his fictional time much like that played by Manet from 1863 to his death.

The primary professional characteristic of both Lantier and Manet, as Zola describes them, seems to be their independence and complete rejection of the past, of tradition and of the influence of the Ecole des Beaux-Arts and all accepted convention. This—with his "lesion"—is the reason for Claude's failure with the public, this art, "so incomplete and so revolutionary, where the bewildered eye found none of the admired conventions."[43] If there is one note that keeps recurring in Zola's *Salons*, it is the idea that Manet was a revolutionary independent and pioneer. Nearly every time he discusses Manet's work, he insists on his rejection of the past, at least as guide for the art he wants to produce, and emphasizes Manet's fixed desire for a new technique and a new view of the universe which will be the expression of his own personality, not the personality of a master, and of his own conceptions of reality. His early remarks in the pages of *Édouard Manet* are typical of his whole belief about Manet's art and his intentions.[44]

Like Lantier, Manet, in Zola's mind, "refused all acquired knowledge, all the experience of the past, he wished to seize art at its beginnings, that is, at the exact observation of objects."[45] And it is interesting that Manet and Lantier agree in their appreciation of some of their immediate predecessors. Lantier speaks critically of the "dark" painting of Courbet and, after damning Ingres for his "glaireous" work, remarks that he is after all an amazing designer, a painter who could force the idiotic public to swallow his technique.[46] Antonin Proust noted that Manet had a deep admiration for Ingres and that he regarded the famous "Enterrement à Ornans" as decidedly "too dark."[47] Perhaps Manet had expressed some such idea to Zola in one of their discussions; certainly the parallel is significant.

But even more significant seems to be Zola's emphasis on Claude's situation as a successor to Courbet and Delacroix, which he himself recognizes when he cries out that he has Delacroix "in his eye" and that the hand he has just painted is straight out of Courbet.[48] Later, when he speculates on the possibilities of success of his huge painting of Paris, he takes hope from his very situation in time, coming as he does just after Delacroix and Courbet, neither of whom had left a school and whose art seems destined to be no more than a simple testimony of the taste of their time. In discussing Manet's role in the retrospective catalogue of 1884 Zola places Manet in exactly the same position vis-à-vis his predecessors.[48a] Zola could never have thought that the place of successor to the two great earlier figures might go to Cézanne, younger than Manet by nearly a decade and fated not to find success with critics or public until after Manet's death.

But it is in their theories of art, including the role of subject, manner, light and color, approach, intention, and so on, that Lantier and Manet, at least as Zola thought of him, draw close together. Claude is shown throughout the greater part of his career as independent seeker, realist, analyst of nature. Until his final failure, he paints constantly from nature, from some kind of model, inventing nothing, striving only to render his own individual and unique vision of reality. He avoids the picturesque, the historical, the imaginary, the anecdotal, and confines himself, until his "lesion" gets the upper hand, to a study of the real, the existent, the solid, and the here-and-now. Throwing off all influences, all conventions, he tries to give expression to what he sees and, through his brush, to the strong and daring personality within him. Perhaps his most significant single pronouncement on his approach to the problem of painting is the one which occurs early in *L'Oeuvre,* when these thoughts pass through his mind as he works on "Plein-Air":

> In art, was there anything else than giving what one had in his belly? didn't everything come down to putting a woman in front of one and rendering her according to one's sensation? wasn't a bunch of carrots, yes, a bunch of carrots! studied directly, painted naively, in the personal note in which one sees it, worth all the scraps of the academic tradition, that tobacco juice paint-

ing, shamefully cooked up according to the recipes? The day was coming when a single original carrot would contain a revolution.[49]

That Zola saw Manet as possessing almost exactly the same theory and the same approach is evident on more than one occasion in his pages on the painter. As early as 1867, in *Édouard Manet* he says:

> Feeling that he was getting nowhere by imitating the masters, painting nature seen through other personalities different from his own, he understood, one fine morning, that he still had to try to see nature as she is, without looking at her through the works and the opinions of others. As soon as that idea had come to him, he took an object of any kind, a being or a thing, placed it in a corner of his studio and began to reproduce it on canvas according to his faculties of vision and comprehension. He made an effort to forget everything he had learned, the painted works he had looked at. And thenceforth there was only an individual intelligence, served by organs endowed in a certain fashion, placed in face of nature and translating her in its own manner.[50]

A little later, in the *Salon* of 1868, he has Manet say:

> —No, I can do nothing without nature. I cannot invent. As long as I wished to paint according to the lessons I had learned, I produced nothing worth while. If I am worth something today, I owe it to exact interpretation and faithful analysis.[51]

And in his final pages on Manet, in the preface to the catalogue of 1884, Zola returns to the same idea:

> Manet's formula was quite naive: he placed himself in face of nature and for his sole ideal he tried to render her in her truth and her strength. Composition has disappeared.[52]

Francis Jourdain seems to be right when he argues that "Claude Lantier bases his work on an aesthetic, expresses desires and tastes (notably for certain specifically modern spectacles) which Zola knew better than anyone were Manet's and not Cézanne's."[53]

It is not only as theorist and philosopher of realism that Lantier resembles Manet, it is also as practicing artist. Zola emphasizes the "real" nature of Claude's paintings, their lack of "ideas" in the anecdotal sense. His earliest sketches from Provence betray his congenital realism, and when he has begun to paint in the "free studios" in Paris he produces strikingly lifelike studies. As he seeks his formula, during the creation of "Plein-Air," he demands a new kind of painting for the new world: "A light and young painting, things and beings as they act in real light—I can't say it, but *our* painting, the painting that our modern eyes should make and look upon."[54] As he and Sandoz discuss the whole tendency of modern art, literary and pictorial, he demands "all of modern life!"[55] A little later, when Mahoudeau tells him that his statue will be a bacchante, he indignantly cries out that there are no bacchantes in modern life, only women. Claude flatters himself that he cannot invent, that he must copy nature—there can be no doubt that he is a member of the new school of realists, for when Bongrand tells him and his group about the Salon des Refusés, he emphasizes that it is their realism which has shocked and alienated the crowd.[56]

After Bennecourt, when Claude returns to Paris, he sees subjects everywhere around him: "The whole city, with its streets, its squares, its bridges, its living horizons, unrolled in immense frescoes . . . and he came home trembling, his brain boiling with projects."[57] When he begins to paint, with his new technique and clearer eye, his canvases show a powerful and brutal realism. The Montmartre scene, the painting of the square des Batignolles, the light study of the Place du Carrousel are in the tradition of Zola's own novels, even the terrible little painting of Claude's dead son is realistic—or naturalistic in the Zola canon. Part of his tragedy is that he cannot sustain his realistic vision to the end, for his "lesion" and his romanticism corrupt his eye and shackle his hand and make him finally a kind of poet, an "idealist," as Zola would put it, doomed to failure by his inability to remain in the modern world.

Exactly the same notes of realism-naturalism, modernism, naiveté, and simplicity are struck time and again in Zola's pages on Manet. As early as *Mon Salon* he observes that "M. Manet's talent is made up of simplicity and exactness" and that "he has painted keenly each thing as he saw it."[58] In *Édouard Manet* he calls him a "simple analyst," and in 1868 Manet is a "naturalist," and if the "actualists" (Monet, Bazille, Renoir) are on the way to triumph, it is partly because Manet opened the path for them. In the "Russian" *Salon* of 1875, calling Manet a modern artist, a realist, a positivist, he declares that "he paints people as he sees them in life, in the street or at home, in their ordinary surroundings, dressed in our modern clothes, in short, as contemporaries."[59] Even in 1880, when his enthusiasm for Manet had somewhat waned, he praises him as one of the tireless workers of naturalism and speaks appreciatively of the naiveté which he always displays in the face of nature.[60]

Zola is especially careful to point out Manet's lack of "ideas" in painting. In *Édouard Manet* he protests against the filiation established by some critics between Manet's canvases and the poems of Baudelaire,[61] and a little later in the same text he remarks, with considerable perspicacity, given the times, that Manet must not be judged as moralist or as litterateur, but only as a painter.[62]

It is plain, far plainer than in the case of Cézanne, who never was a realist as Zola meant the term, that Claude Lantier was intended to be much the same kind of painter as Édouard Manet. That he cannot remain true to the realistic canon of observation, simplicity, and naiveté is of course no indication that Zola believed the same thing of Manet, for nowhere in his writings on art is there any hint that he ever thought the artist was on the point of forsaking realism; Manet was, for him, *toujours fidèle,* a realist, an analyst, a naturalist from the start of his career to its end. If he failed, at least partly, it was not, Zola thought, because of any philosophical failing, it was because of physical and temperamental deficiencies.

It is interesting that at least two of Lantier's paintings seem to resemble works of Manet. In spite of all the efforts to prove that Zola was inspired by some painting by Cézanne when he composed the description of "Plein-Air," or that he combined several reminiscences of Cézanne and Manet, it seems beyond all doubt that he was thinking of "Le Déjeuner sur l'herbe." In the first place the painting is shown publicly at the Salon des Refusés, and it was there in 1863 that Manet's first famous canvas was introduced; there is no good reason why Zola should not have employed the real painting, which caused a scandal, as his model, inasmuch as he was depicting a real situation, and it is difficult to imagine why he should have taken and rearranged a canvas by Cézanne as his model.[63] In the second place "Plein-Air" occupies in the career of Claude Lantier exactly the same position as "Le Déjeuner" did in Manet's. It is a first great work, employing a wholly new technique and manner, and a defiance cast in the teeth of a public happy only with the traditional, the banal, and the academic. There is no such work in Cézanne's career, nor is there any comparable work in the career of any other Impressionist whose work Zola might have known. In the third place the fictional painting clearly resembles "Le Déjeuner sur l'herbe," as Zola describes the latter in *Édouard Manet.* After the first description of "Plein-Air,"[64] Zola adds a second when the painting is nearly complete:

> The man in the velvet jacket was entirely sketched out; the hand, more complete than the rest, made a very interesting note in the

> grass, with a fine freshness of tone, and the dark spot made by his back stood out with such vigor that the little silhouettes in the background, the two women wrestling in the sun, seemed to have drawn back, in the luminous trembling of the clearing; while the main figure, the nude lying down, still barely indicated, floated like flesh in a dream, a desired Eve born of the earth, with her smiling face, eyelids closed.[65]

In *Édouard Manet,* "Le Dejeuner sur l'herbe" is presented thus:

> There is some foliage, some tree trunks, and, in the background, a stream in which a woman wearing a chemise is bathing; in the foreground, two young men are seated facing a second woman who has just come out of the water and who is drying herself in the open air . . . surely, the nude of the *Déjeuner* is there only to give the artist the opportunity to paint a little flesh. What we must see in this painting is not a luncheon on the grass, it is the entire landscape, with its vigor and its delicacy, with its wide and solid foreground and its delicate and light background; it is that firm flesh, shaped by great areas of light, those supple and strong fabrics, and especially that delightful female silhouette amidst the green; it is, finally, this vast ensemble full of air, this bit of nature rendered with such an exact simplicity, all this admirable page in which an artist has put the rare and individual elements which were within him.[66]

It is certainly possible that the figure of the woman in "Plein-Air" was suggested to Zola by "Olympia"—the pose would indicate this, as well as the sketch of the face, but the ensemble indicates that it was imitated (though not slavishly) from Manet's first great work. This is the opinion of Ima Ebin,[67] who also thinks that "Olympia" may be a secondary model, of Mitterand,[68] Martineau,[69] Vizetelly[70] and Fosca.[71]

It has also been suggested that the third painting of Claude's mature period, after the Bennecourt episode and before his attempt at synthesizing modern life in his final work, may be modeled on one of Manet's canvases.[72] It will be recalled that this painting treated "a corner of the Place du Carrousel, at one o'clock," with heavy emphasis on dazzling light effects surrounding some sketchy figures. It is possible that this painting may be a kind of reminiscence on Zola's part of Manet's "Le Jardin des Tuileries," often called "La Musique aux Tuileries." In *Édouard Manet* Zola describes the work in this fashion:

> . . . imagine, beneath the trees of the Tuileries, a whole crowd, a hundred persons perhaps, moving in the sun; each person is a

> simple spot, hardly outlined, in which the details become lines or black dots.[73]

There is a certain similarity here, to be sure, but it seems more likely that Lantier's painting is a creation of Zola's imagination, with perhaps some distant memory of Manet's work providing the fundamental scene.

But even if there are not many precise comparisons that can be made between Claude's work and Manet's, one generality is certain and significant: both of them are essentially painters of Paris, in love with the modern world the city represents, and realists again in their desire to break with the tradition of the "Greeks and the Romans" and to render the modern world in a modern way. After Claude finds his vision and his technique at Bennecourt, he devotes himself completely (with the exception of his portrait of his dead son) to scenes of Paris, and every canvas of his mature period is a scene of contemporary life in the great city. So also with Manet. Perhaps no other painter of what Zola would call the school of realists (or naturalists or actualists) ever executed so many canvases with Parisian subjects, and it was surely of Manet, not of Cézanne or of any Impressionist, that Zola was thinking when he caused Lantier to wander the boulevards and the quais in search of his "motif."

Another evidence of the similarity of the realism of the fictional painter and the painter of "Le Déjeuner sur l'herbe" is their attempt to create "real" light in their canvases. Both of them are, above all, colorists, and their principal goal is to render the objects of nature in simple outline, with no attempt at arrangement or picturesqueness, putting their emphasis instead on obtaining a certain "blond" color which will approximate the effect of sunlight. Both are, in considerable measure, "open air" painters (but not wholly so, for Lantier, like Manet, begins his most important large canvases outside and then tries to finish them in the studio), and the rendering of the effect of living light and air is the goal of their most persistent efforts and the secret of their originality. In the *Ébauche* Zola speaks of Lantier's work as being "very light,"[74] and in the novel he is careful to stress this aspect of the painter's canvases more than any other. When Zola writes of Manet, the same note recurs constantly. In *Édouard Manet,* for instance, he remarks:

> Edouard Manet ordinarily starts with a tone lighter than the tone existing in nature. His paintings are blond and luminous, with a solid and firm paleness. Light falls white and wide, illuminating objects in a gentle way. There is not the slightest forcing;

> the people and the landscapes bathe in a kind of light and gay clarity which fills the whole canvas.[75]

A little later, he observes that the general aspect of any of Manet's canvases is a "luminous blond"[76] and again, in the same essay, he repeats that "the new note that he brings is that blond note filling the canvas with light."[77]

More importantly, both Lantier and Manet are depicted as facing the realist's eternal dilemma, the reconciling of exact observation with originality of view, and both go through a constant evolution in search of an answer they cannot find. Both are realists, by and large, but neither, as Zola describes them, ever finds exactly the realistic path he would follow. For instance, in Lantier's work he progresses from sketches of nature and "académies" executed in the studio to the moderate realism of "Plein-Air" (which seems to be painted almost completely in the studio, in spite of its name), from there to the true open-air painting of fairly traditional subjects in the Bennecourt episode, then to the crude, brutal outdoor naturalism of the years when he seeks entrance to the Salon, and finally to the abandonment of the realistic canon almost completely with the introduction of the symbolic nude into the last canvas. He is a groper, a seeker, never content, always moving on, with no theory (save a general faith in the realistic approach) to sustain him permanently and no technique which he finds constantly adequate. He never finds "the" formula without which, in Zola's mind, there could be no true creation. His cry, "I am still seeking myself," uttered at the very time when his example is being more and more followed, his innovations more and more imitated, is typical of his whole career and, sadly, of his knowledge of himself.

Zola does not show Manet in the same kind of evolution as Lantier's, but no doubt he considered him to be something of a restless seeker, and there is evidence from other sources that he was not wrong in his assessment of his friend's career. Zola insists over and over that Manet is a realist, a naive and simple spectator of nature, a painter who cannot work without a model and who contents himself with rendering exactly what he sees, no more no less. But at the same time that he emphasizes Manet's realism, the word "originality" keeps recurring, and Zola is at almost as much pains to prove that Manet's vision is new as he is to prove it exact. And the dichotomy between the realistic urge and the drive for originality leads Manet, as Zola sees his career in retrospect, into a perpetual search, "a ceaseless evolution."[78] It is not mere chance that Zola's preface to the catalogue of the posthumous Manet exhibition in 1884 is in the nature of a study in change.

At all events Manet was never to find "the" technique, any more than Lantier did, at least as Zola envisioned it. Manet was to be a victim of what Zola called his "departure for the unknown" with every canvas he started,[79] and Zola's remark in the Manet catalogue that the artist was not always master of his hand as he painted and that he never had any real idea of how the work would turn out,[80] is entirely typical of the novelist's attitude toward him; it would be equally typical of his opinion of Claude Lantier as a practicing artist.

Perhaps Zola was also thinking of Manet when he portrayed Claude as an untiring worker. Again and again Claude passes through furious crises of effort; he is seized by a rage for work, he staggers away from his easel, half-dead with fatigue, he spends years of sixteen-hour days on his last, back-breaking effort—never has a fictional artist expended so much sweat and physical agony on his canvases.

In his writings on Manet, Zola portrays him—with a good deal less drama—as the same kind of whole-souled, dedicated artist, devoting all his time, all his energy, all his mind and body to his work. In an effort to counter the opinion, apparently widely held, that Manet was only an idler, a joker, he spoke of his conscientiousness, his sincerity, his love of work, and after Manet's death: "If he fell into error, it was not through lack of study, as was claimed, for no painter worked with as much restlessness."[81] There is little evidence of a similar tendency in Paul Cézanne, who was as likely to tear up a canvas which would not come out as he wished as he was simply to walk away and leave it, but there is a certain similarity between Manet's relentless efforts—which may betray a deep self-doubt—and Lantier's eternal retouching, eternal reconstruction, and the profound unsureness of himself which his perfectionism reveals.

As a painter, then, Lantier strongly resembles Édouard Manet, and it is clear that the resemblance is not coincidental.

But where the two, the real painter and the fictional artist, draw closest together is in their general situation in the world of art, for there is an amazing similarity in their positions, so close that the conclusion seems inescapable that here Zola was deliberately and consciously modeling the events of Lantier's career on what he had seen of Manet's.

To begin, both artists are convinced that they must "conquer" the Salon and the critical and public acceptance it represents. Almost all of Lantier's career is concerned with getting his work admitted to the yearly exposition, for after "Plein-Air" he sends five paintings to the jury, and to the very end of his life the Salon remains his constant goal, his "fugientem italiam." Success for him is not only artistic success, the perfect rendition of his vision in paint and canvas, it is success with the critics and public; he is no pure artist, wanting to produce solely for the sake of producing, he is an ambitious man whose real goal is the imposition of his view and his technique on a reluctant public. When he has been rejected the first time in his attempt to storm the citadel of academic art after his stay in Bennecourt, he recovers from his disappointment and chagrin and evolves the philosophy which will guide him henceforth: an artist must, each year, send a work to the Salon if only to put it in the wrong, and he must use it as the only possible means of revealing his talent quickly and dramatically. And, with all the blows he receives, all the failures which gradually erode his early reputation he never forsakes the dream of triumph. When "L'Enfant mort" is at last accepted, near the end of his career, he has a moment of unhappiness, wanting only to take the painting and hide it, but this soon passes and he awaits the opening of the Salon with the impatience of a beginner. Even the great, impossible final painting is destined for the Salon, and only at the last moment, when he realizes its deficiencies, does he refuse to carry out his intention.

Zola was clearly aware that Manet's career was also oriented in the same direction and that he likewise could not believe that success was truly success without the esteem of the critics and the public. The pages which he devoted to Manet are full of references to the innumerable struggles the painter had to endure even to the end of his career to obtain any kind of acceptance, either from his colleagues or from the public in general, and Zola is fond of remarking on the capricious way in which the jury accepted a work of his one year and then rejected an equally valid work the next. Over and over again he stresses Manet's courage in perpetually returning to the attack, over and over he associates Manet's struggle for public acceptance with his idea of success, and when he looks back at his friend's career, in the catalogue of the posthumous Manet exposition, he notes that this rebellious painter had always dreamed of success as Paris knows it: the compliments of women, a life of luxury, the adulation of the crowd.[82] So smitten was Manet with the idea of this kind of success, according to Zola, that he deliberately changed his manner at one time, with the idea of winning the public over by grace and charm.[83] He was, then, not merely stubborn: he would have liked to please. Camille Mauclair not only recognizes this tendency in Manet, he recognizes that it was not characteristic of any other painter of the revolutionary group of the 1860's and 1870's: Manet was convinced, he said, that the duty of an artist who had made an honest discovery was to offer himself courageously to the public.[84] Certainly, Mauclair is right: the Impressionists, either discouraged by their early rejection or contemptuous of the kind of official success the Salon promised, were not as a group much concerned with capturing the stronghold of academic art. Their victories were won at smaller exhibitions, and here at least, Manet was not one of them. It seems almost beyond question that Zola was thinking of him when he made Claude Lantier follow the same path to the same kind of deception.

For Lantier, again apparently in imitation of Zola's memories of Manet's career, brings on himself, by his persistence in offering his revolutionary art to a public which is not yet ready for it, nothing but the mockery of the crowd and the contempt of his fellows in art. This popular reaction to his painting is one of the surest indications that Zola deliberately and consciously modeled the fictional career on the struggle and chagrin of Manet's career. Lantier makes only two public appearances, one in the Salon des Refusés of 1863, the other years later when his poor "Enfant mort" is accepted through Fagerolles' intervention; the reception accorded "Plein-Air" is something very much like the first climax of *L'Oeuvre,* the first really important event: it is an explosion of contemptuous and insulting laughter—Zola gives it epic proportions—never paralleled in the history of French art.

The same note of public mockery, of the outrageous and insulting contempt of the crowd for a superior creator, is one of Zola's most stressed pages on Manet. From first to last he mentions it, suffering in his own flesh from the terrible sting that Manet must have felt as the jeers of the crowd resounded in his ears at each attempt. Manet, for Zola, was always one of the persecuted, always scorned by his inferiors, always the object of the wounding mockery of men of lesser minds and lesser hearts. As early as *Mon Salon* Zola reveals his own hurt and anger at the stupidity of the public,[85] and in succeeding treatments of Manet's career he returns frequently to the theme.

Once again, it would seem almost beyond argument that when Zola made Claude Lantier the laughingstock of an ignorant public and the butt of the jokes of his fellow artists he was thinking of Manet's experiences and of no one else's. Surely none of the Impressionists was ever in a position to receive this kind of treatment from a large public, and none of them had the reception given Manet at the Salon des Refusés; above all, Cézanne, who for twenty years almost never appeared before the public after the Refusés of 1863—where he seems to have gone unnoticed—could hardly have provided Zola with the kind of bitter memories he dramatized here.

But not only does Lantier resemble Manet in being the scapegoat of an ignorant crowd, he is like him in suffering the unjust and dishonest opposition of the official painters of his time, the academicians, the success hunters, the traditionalists, and the tellers of neat anecdotes and the shapers of creamy mythological nudes. When Lantier, after suffering one refusal by the jury, deliberately softens his manner and blunts his technique, he and his friends are convinced that he will at last be accepted and that the Salon will be revolutionized by this new and marvelous art: their indignation and stupefaction at the news of his rejection are in proportion to their hopes in him. There can be no doubt, a cabal is systematically excluding him. The whole incident of "L'Enfant mort" is another illustration of the unfairness with which he is treated by those in high places in the world of art, an unfairness demonstrated by the scene in which Fagerolles argues with the members of the jury in the vain hope of persuading them to accept Lantier's canvas. The jurors reply to his pleas by calling "L'Enfant Mort" a "daub."

Zola was evidently convinced that Manet had been, at the start of his career at least, the victim of some such cabal, for in listing the members of the jury for 1866 he notes that the painter Dubufe, a member of the jury, had sworn that no such paintings as Manet's "Le Joueur de fifre" would ever be accepted.[86] Somewhat later in *Mon Salon,* and speaking of Manet, Zola addresses himself to the "artist whom a group of his colleagues have put out of the Salon," and refers to the creator whose works have been consciously excluded, who was not thought worthy of figuring among the two thousand eunuchs whose works were welcomed with open arms. Manet is a pariah to his fellow artists, barred like a leper from the painters' little world. Even if there was no cabal properly speaking, Manet was the victim of the indifference and lack of courage, so Zola argues in *Mon Salon,*[87] of many contemporary artists; and Camille Mauclair relates that when a group of rebellious young painters obtained a second medal for Manet in 1881, a group of more conservative artists successfully opposed their reelection to the jury.[88] Lantier's situation was no different.

Significant, too, is the attitude of the fictional painter and that of the real-life pioneer of Impressionism toward the way of winning success. Both are independent revolutionaries, determined to conquer the public by sheer force of talent and persistence of effort, but both desire success so keenly that for a moment each is ready to sacrifice some of his integrity and his violence for a chance to hang his work in the sanctum of traditional art. Claude, after he has found his manner at Bennecourt and after he has suffered his first rejection by the Salon, tries to soften his painting a little, to give it some of the "charm" that the official painters used so willingly to catch the public. Zola believed that Manet had done the same thing and for the same reasons, for in the Manet catalogue he declares openly that after Manet had moved to the rue Saint-Pétersbourg and opened his own salon in his studio, he was willing to make some concessions.[89] But what is more significant as a similarity is that neither of these revolutionaries can really make any important concessions to official and popular taste. Such is the force of their talent and their desire to paint the universe as they see it in their originality, that they must progress in their path at whatever cost in success or acclaim. Their concessions are the weakness of a moment, no more. After the great scandal of the Salon des Refusés, Claude is momentarily downcast, but then he regards his "Plein-Air" again and compares it to the other works on display, and he is buoyed up by faith in the gay courage of the young school, strengthened in his desire to attack the public head-on. An hour or so later, when he and the "band" are gathered before their *chopes,* he lays down the program of the new school:

> What? the public is laughing? We'll have to educate the public. . . . After all, it's a victory. Take away two hundred grotesque canvases and our Salon beats theirs. We have bravery and audacity, we are the future. . . . Yes, yes, they'll see later, we'll kill it, their Salon. We'll enter there like conquerors, by dint of our masterpieces. Laugh, laugh, great stupid Paris, until you fall at our knees.[90]

And when his effort at "softening" fails at the second Salon after the return from Bennecourt, he turns his anger toward the painting itself (the scene at the Square des Batignolles), calling it false, dishonest, execrable. His resolve is made: he will persist in his path, even though he should lose his artistic life in following his genius. Manet's temperament permitted him no more malleability, at least as Zola saw it. As early as *Mon Salon* Zola singles out this trait of stubbornness—or is it really the automatism of genius, which allows no softening?—and describes Manet as a convinced fighter, an unpopular man who did not tremble before the public, who did not seek to win it but to conquer it, to "impose his temperament" upon it. And as late as the posthumous Manet catalogue he was repeating the same observation: in spite of Manet's desire to water down his work a little in order to gain some acceptance, the force of his inner drive was too strong, he could make no real concession. So Claude persists, even to the great and grotesque nude of the final painting. Is there much doubt that he does so in the image and likeness of the career of Édouard Manet, who to the end of his short life remained ineluctably faithful to the vision that only he possessed?

As the two painters push forward in their independent paths, finding only failure and mockery, they become legends in the contemporary world of art, heads—rather, founders—of schools which will triumph when the tumult and the shouting of the battle have died. After Jory's explosive article on his talent (a reminiscence of *Mon Salon,* almost surely), Claude becomes the object of a certain amount of half-terrified attention, and the "band" appoints him its leader. After the Salon des Refusés, Bongrand congratulates the group on its courage and its accomplishment and then turns to Lantier and calls him head of the school. As time wears on and the plein air school fails to accomplish what it had hoped to do and finds it cannot win the success it feels is its due, the "band" turns more and more to him as their last, best hope; they scorn Fagerolles for his complaisances, for his compromises, for his concessions, and prostrate themselves before Lantier, the only one of them with the talent and the temperament to take advantage of the growing influence of the "open air" painters and to create a school.

But as he persists in his manner, as he meets failure after failure, as he consistently fails to impose his way and his view on the art of his time, a disturbing legend begins to form around his painting, so definitively excluded from the Salon, and gradually even his group becomes discouraged and turns from him, its hopes deceived; and as the group breaks up Claude becomes the guilty one, the Jonah. At Sandoz' last dinner for his friends, Jory, Mahoudeau, and Gagnière vent their spleen in the bitterest and most unjust terms. Lantier is finished, and so is the plein air school.

If Zola and other contemporaries are to be believed, Manet also enjoyed during the latter part of his life the situation of leader of his group. The pariah, the unpopular and grotesque painter, the "leper" of *Mon Salon,* the butt of all the jokes, the object of the insults and the irony of the crowd of *Édouard Manet* acquires, in the "Russian" Salon of 1875, the role of master in his domain, and the leader of a constantly growing band of artists to which the future manifestly belongs. By 1879, again in one of the "Russian" *Salons,* Zola sees Manet as having been "chief of the group of impressionist painters"[91]—it is not clear whether he believes that Manet's role as leader is now finished, or that he has been replaced by another artist—and in the posthumous catalogue of 1884 he describes his role: "In 1863, Manet aroused the public at the Salon des Refusés, and yet it was he who was the head of the movement. How many times, nowadays, does one stop before a 'light' canvas, with its frank tone, saying: 'Look! It's a Manet!' "[92] Gagnière, at the dinner where Claude is disparaged, had said almost the same thing: he is tired of having heard, for fifteen years, the same refrain: "It's a Lantier!"

Nowhere in Zola's writings on Manet does he refer to any difficulties the painter of "Olympia" may have had with the younger Impressionists, and nowhere does he establish that he suffered from the same kind of eventual rejection by his friends and fellow fighters as befalls Claude in the novel, nor does any other contemporary critic or historian see such a separation as Zola describes (though Manet is nearly always treated as a solitary, an independent, a man outside and above all schools). But Manet's role as one of the founders of the movement of Impressionism is beyond question, and here he occupies much the same situation as does Claude Lantier. Duret notes his dominant position in the Guerbois group,[93] which included some of the Impressionists (Fantin-Latour, Guillemet, Degas, Stevens), and Camille Mauclair, though denying that Manet was either the inventor of Impressionism or the real head of the school, describes him as the man who created a great movement[94] and concedes that though the reputation he enjoyed as leader of the Impressionists was inexact (since Manet was not truly an open-air painter), yet that reputation—he calls it a legend—did persist.

Actually, Claude is presented in *L'Oeuvre* less as the head of a school—or even its founder—than as a forerunner who makes possible the creation of a new movement by other men who will come after him and carry his work further. At the close of his career, when he has finally become convinced that he will never revolutionize the Salon and after he has seen his "Enfant mort" on the wall of the Palais, he recognizes his role as precursor. When Sandoz attempts to console him by pointing out that he has "created" all the new, young artists and that the art of tomorrow will belong to him, Claude replies.

> "What the hell difference does it make if I've made them, when I haven't made myself. . . . You see, it was too big for me and that's what chokes me."
>
> With a gesture he finished his thought, his inability to be the genius of the formula he brought, his torment to be a precursor who sows the idea without reaping the glory, his grief at seeing himself robbed, devoured by slap-up painters, a horde of slippery fellows, scattering their efforts, debasing the new art, before he or another could find the strength to establish the masterpiece which would mark the close of the century.[95]

It is clear from his *Salons* that Zola held much the same opinion of Manet, that he was not truly the leader of a viable school, the perfect and complete representative of a new art, but that he was a sower of seeds, a forerunner who could never quite bring to bear all the genius that the imposition of his new formula required, leader of the advance guard but not himself one of the kings of art. A note he keeps striking in his *Salons* is that Impressionism has never managed to work out a solid and durable formula and that no artist of this group exemplifies perfectly either the theory or the technique of the new art. In *Le Naturalisme au Salon,* of 1880, he argues that no single artist of the group has yet "realized," powerfully and definitively, the formula which is everywhere evident among them. They are all precursors, the man of genius has not come, and their struggle has not yet ended, may never end.[96] True enough, Zola is speaking of the Impressionists, not of Manet, but it is plain that he frequently, if not always, identified Manet with the group, and it is significant also that no contemporary artist, not even Manet, is exempted from the sweeping criticism he draws up here.

But the rejection of Manet by his contemporaries and the parallel failure of Claude Lantier to impose himself may not have been entirely unjust, in Zola's view, for it is obvious that he considered both the real painter of "Olympia" and the fictional creator of "Plein-Air" to be victims of a fundamental and destructive tare, incompleteness of talent. Neither ever imposes himself upon a reluctant public or on an equally unwilling professional group, artists and critics, and neither does so because he can never manage to create those perfect, finished works which are the only ones which can force the doors of success.

From the first, Zola clearly intended to depict Claude as incomplete, lacking in some essential of the true artistic makeup, for in the *Ébauche* he describes him as "the incomplete genius, without entire fulfillment, he lacks only a little, he is a little too much on this side (i. e., of genius) or a little too much on the other, by his physiology,"[97] and the idea is constantly recalled throughout the novel, especially after the failure of "Plein-Air" at the Salon des Refusés. When the laughter of the crowd has compelled him to look at his painting with something of an objective eye and when he has seen its qualities and its defects, Claude himself recognizes that he has not succeeded, for his canvas is incomplete. When the jury rejects his third painting after the Bennecourt stay, although he still flourishes a kind of brave obstinacy, his doubts about himself reappear; each rejected work seems incomplete to him, a proof of his impotence. His torture is never to be able to give himself entirely in the masterpiece of which he dreams. His work, so incomplete and so revolutionary, frightens prospective buyers, and as he sinks lower and lower into the abyss of failure he suffers the tortures of the damned by impotence. And when he has at last finished his career in failure and suicide, Sandoz delivers his epitaph: "No, he was not the man for the formula he brought, I mean that he did not have a clear enough genius to set it upright and force its acceptance by a definitive work."[98]

Nowhere in Zola's writings on Manet, of course, is there any such dramatization of a psychic situation—or physiological one—for never could Zola speak with such abandon about a known contemporary and friend and never could he publish in the columns of a newspaper, such emotionally charged prose as he devotes to Claude's agonies. But almost exactly the same idea is there, nonetheless, the idea of a mysterious incompleteness (never called a "tare" or a "lesion" of course), a strange and frustrating inability on Manet's part to express himself fully and to create the definitive work which his qualities seemed to promise. True enough, in his *Salon* of 1868 Zola took to task Arsène Houssaye for claiming that Manet would be "an exceptional artist if he had a 'hand' " and for arguing that it is not enough to have a thinking mind and a seeing eye, the artist must also have a hand that "speaks." To these charges Zola replied that Manet was worth a thousand of the mediocrities of the Salons. This was the note he was to strike frequently in all his early writings on Manet: the painter of "Olympia" is often crude, brusque, violent, but his qualities of force, originality and sincerity more than offset any lack of ability, in the current sense, that his work may display. Manet is "real," his talent has power, his paintings speak with directness and clarity, and if he is not as clever or as unscrupulous as some of his contemporaries that will be his title to eventual glory.

As time went on Zola clearly underwent a change of heart toward Manet and came to a new and much more critical appraisal of his accomplishment. Writing for his Russian public in 1879 he reveals a reservation about Manet's talent which he had never hinted at before: Manet encounters terrible difficulties in execution, his hand does not equal his eye. He has no solid technique and is never sure of adequately rendering the impressions of nature. When he is "right," he is excellent, when he is not his canvases are imperfect and uneven.

In the very next year he declared that he was not alone in holding a critical view of Manet's artistic equipment and that the young painters may talk all they want about Manet's incompleteness, may say all they want about his failure to keep his artistic promises, claim that the artist in him is not up to the formula he brought after Courbet, he is still the man who "made" them all. The similarity of his remarks here to what he had said in 1879 of course leaves it open to question if Zola was really quoting opinions he had heard or if he was simply putting in the mouths of some anonymous and perhaps nonexistent critics and fellow-artists what he himself felt about Manet's talent.

But there is no doubt who is speaking in the posthumous Manet catalogue: "The fingers did not always obey the eyes, which were marvelously 'right.' If he fell into error . . . it was simply by his nature. He did what he could and he could not do otherwise."[99] Perhaps Arsène Houssaye had been right twenty years before. If Adolphe Retté is to be believed, Zola had come completely around to Houssaye's point of view by the late 1890's, had even gone a good deal beyond it, for he has Zola say, in reply to a compliment Retté paid Manet on the "Portrait of Zola," that although the portrait was not bad, Manet was not a great painter, he was at best an incomplete talent.[100]

At all events, Zola was certainly not the only one to hold this view of Manet, and it may be that he took it from some artist or critic who had expressed similar reservations. It is clear, for example, that he had read Edmond Duranty's pamphlet *La Nouvelle peinture* (1876) before he wrote his own *Salon* for the *Vyestnik Yevropy* of Saint Petersburg in the same year.[101] And in *La Nouvelle peinture,* Duranty had said of Manet that with all his courage, independence, and originality, he did not always have the means to give his creations body and reality.[102] Hemmings points out, in partial explanation of Zola's change of attitude toward Manet in the late 1870's, that it is very possible that Zola neither liked nor appreciated the path in which Manet's canvases were evolving after about 1867 and that it was his reservations on Manet's new manner which prompted the open criticism of 1879. But whatever the explanation, Zola came to see Manet as an incomplete talent, destined never to find the full expression of his vision and of his "formula," and it is not far from his written appreciations of the work of his old friend to the description of the torments and the failures of Claude Lantier. Perhaps it was Manet, not Cézanne, who was here dramatized.

There is another kind of evidence, equally cogent, that it was really Manet's career of which Zola was thinking as he caused Lantier to move through the Salons of his day; it is provided by the relationship between Lantier and Fagerolles, a relationship much like the one described on several occasions in Zola's writings on art between Manet and a group of younger artists, such as Gervex, Bastien-Lepage, and Carolus Duran. In his *Salons* Zola is much concerned that such men as these—and they are typified in *L'Oeuvre* by Fagerolles—are succeeding with the public to a degree which Manet never attains, largely because they are skillful enough and perhaps unscrupulous enough to soften

Manet's art, to bastardize it with the outworn but still popular technique of the Ecole des Beaux-Arts and so to adapt its vigor, its sincerity, and its originality to a vulgar and reactionary popular taste. In the novel Bongrand (like Zola in the *Salons*) sees what is happening between Fagerolles and Lantier, and when Jory attempts to defend the former for his success, he explodes:

> Give us a little peace, will you, with your Fagerolles! Do you think we're too stupid to live? . . . . Look, you see the great painter right here. Yes, this young gentleman before you. Well! the whole trick consists in stealing his originality and fixing it up in the sauce of the Ecole des Beaux-Arts. Exactly! you take something modern, you paint light, but you keep the commonplace and trite drawing, the agreeable composition used by everyone, in short the formula that they teach over there for the pleasure of the bourgeois. And they drown it in facility, oh! that hateful facility of the fingers, which might as well make sculptures out of coconuts, that flowing, pleasant facility which makes success and which ought to be punished by prison, do you understand![103]

Zola says almost the same things, less the exaggeration, on at least a half-dozen occasions in his *Salons,* and though he does not always name Manet as the victim of these subtle thefts, often referring only to the Impressionists as the source from which the slick artisans take their ideas and vision, he never explicitly names any painter other than Manet in this regard. Here, for example, is what he says of Carolus Duran in the "Russian" letter of 1875: he is adroit, he renders Manet comprehensible to the bourgeois, he follows him up to "proper" limits, seasoning Manet's discoveries to the public taste—and he has a great reputation.[104] A few years later, in *Le Naturalisme au Salon,* Zola is more explicit, more developed and forthright about the position of Manet vis-à-vis the other painters of the time:

> . . . today, his importance can be measured by the decisive role he has played for twenty years; it is enough to determine the amount of influence he has had on all the young painters who have come after him. And I say nothing of certain painters who have pillaged him thoroughly, with an incredible skill at assimilation while pretending to smile down upon him; these gentlemen have taken his blond color, his exactness of tone, his naturalistic method, not naively but by seasoning this painting to the public taste, so that they have had the crowd with them all the while it continued to scoff at M. Manet. . . . As for the young painters who have profited greatly from M. Manet's works, they form

> today a vast school, of which he ought to be the true chief; . . . he has been the ray of truth which opened their eyes when they were still groping their way, in the Ecole des Beaux-Arts. That is the true glory of M. Manet: his influence has touched the pupils of M. Cabanel and of M. Gerôme, passing through the impressionists, who are his direct descendants.[105]

When it is remembered that Fagerolles in the novel is a student of Mazel's, these words have point and cogency.

In Zola's final words on Manet in the catalogue of 1884 almost his final idea is the same:

> There is no painter whom they imitate more, without admitting it. But direct imitations are not the most characteristic ones. What must be observed carefully, is the action exercised by the artist on the clever men of the epoch. While his originality, without any possible concessions, caused him to be jeered at, all the clever operators were gleaning behind him, taking as much of his formula as the public would tolerate, seasoning open-air painting with bourgeois sauces. I shall name no one, but how many fortunes were made on his back, how many reputations were built with the best of his blood! He laughed about it sometimes a little bitterly, knowing full well he was incapable of those pretty little ways. They robbed him in order to give him out in tidbits to delighted amateurs, who would have shuddered at a real Manet, and who swooned before contraband Manets, fabricated by the gross, like fancy goods.[106]

If Fagerolles is Gervex, or Bastien-Lepage, or Guillemet, or Carolus Duran, or all of them—and there is good reason for thinking that he is—then Claude Lantier must be Manet, at least in his relationship to other artists and in the role he plays in the artistic evolution of his time. This impression is strengthened when we consider that in the novel Sandoz passes through exactly the same phases of appreciation of Lantier as artist as Zola did in the case of Manet, from early faith in his certain triumph, to doubt of his ability to "realize" himself, and to final conviction of grave and essential limitations. Sandoz is the one who brings Lantier his early notoriety by his noisy articles in *Le Tambour,* and his strong faith endures through all the vicissitudes of the artist's unsuccessful career until almost its close, when the novelist finally realizes that Lantier's great painting is not only a popular failure but, worse, an artistic fiasco. Only he, of all the "band" remains true to his original belief that Claude has an important message and the means to deliver it, and as Gagnière, Mahoudeau, and

Jory, not to mention the traitorous Fagerolles, drop away, he remains, *semper fidelis.* But, toward the end, even he begins to have doubts about the painter's ability to speak clearly, and when he takes the way to the rue Tourlaque and its dilapidated studio, he does so for human, not artistic, reasons, for he now sees the failure of a genius, a man in the torments of impotence. As he looks on the pitiful "Enfant mort" he reviews the past and his old friendship with the artist, his dreams of success for both of them, their hopes for the future:

> Ah! what disgust he felt at this wretched life! He suddenly lived their youth over again . . . and, later in their existence in common, he remembered their efforts, their certainty of glory, the sharp pang of limitless appetite which would swallow Paris at one gulp. At that period, how many times had he seen in Claude the great man, the man whose unbridled genius was to leave far behind the talent of the others. . . . It was an endless struggle, an effort of ten hours a day, the giving of his entire person. And then, what? after twenty years of this passion, to end at that, at that poor, sinister thing, little, unperceived, heart-breakingly melancholy in its leprous isolation. So many hopes, so many tortures, a life used up in the hard labor of birth. And that, and that, my God![107]

When Claude is about to enter the earth, to rejoin the "belle nature" he loved so well, Sandoz speaks his last word on him and his career: "A heroic worker, a passionate observer whose brain was crammed with knowledge, the temperament of a great painter, admirably endowed—and he leaves nothing."[108]

Zola's words in the *Salons* are of course not so strong, but the same evolution is clearly there. From the very first he proclaimed in the loudest of voices and the clearest of terms that Manet would some day be given the high place his talent deserved, and in *Mon Salon* he was willing to declare without reservations that future generations would stand in ecstasy before his works and added without qualification that in ten years Manet's canvases would sell for fifteen and twenty times what they then brought. It is of no moment that in 1879 Zola changed the challenging phrase "in ten years" to "in fifty years," or that he set the ultimate financial value of Manet's works much too low; what counts is the faith that these lines express, a faith that he almost alone was to feel for some time. True enough, *Mon Salon* was a book of combat if ever Zola wrote one, and such phrases as "M. Manet's place is marked at the Louvre, like Courbet's"[109] and "it is impossible—impossible, do you understand, that M. Manet will be denied his day of triumph and that he will not crush the timid mediocrities who surround him,"[110] might be explained away as evidences of Zola's overriding desire for notoriety for himself. But in *Edouard Manet* he returns to the attack, declaring without a shadow of hesitation that the "future is his," and adding:

> The eternal story of talents mocked at, then admired to the point of fanaticism, will be repeated for M. Manet. He will have the destiny of the masters, of Delacroix and Courbet, for instance. He is at the point where the storm of laughter is dying down, where the public's ribs are sore and where it asks nothing better than to be serious again. Tomorrow, if not today, he will be understood and accepted.[111]

In the very next year, 1868, Zola is already certain that Manet has actually won his battle with the public: the tumult is abating, the public is becoming accustomed to Manet's art, success is near. As late as 1875 he was willing to hazard that Cabanel's paintings will grow pale before twenty-five years have passed and that Manet's will live on with the eternal youth of original works.

Strangely, at the end of this same *Salon,* addressed to the public of St. Petersburg, the first note of doubt appears and sets the tone for much of what is to follow in Zola's criticism of Manet, for he declares that although Manet is continuing the victory of Courbet and Delacroix, the triumph of the new art is not foreseeable in the near future: "A painter of genius is needed, whose fist will be strong enough to force the triumph of realism."[112] It would seem that Manet was not this genius.

In the following years the doubt is still veiled, Zola is still not willing to name Manet openly as a disappointment to him and to call him a mere forerunner, but he does say, in tones that reflect the earlier criticism, that the French school will live on imitations until a talent arises which will bring with it the new formula for art. By 1879 —still speaking to the Russians—he is ready to say aloud what he has been thinking for some time, that Manet's hand does not equal his eye, that he has never been able to form a technique, that he sometimes wanders.[113]

One paragraph of this *Salon* attracted particular attention:

> Moreover, all the impressionist painters sin by technical insufficiency. . . . The impressionists are in my view pioneers, precisely. For a moment they put great faith in Manet, but the latter appears to be exhausted by hasty production; he is satisfied

with approximations, he does not study nature with the passion of the true creators. All those artists are too easily satisfied. They disdain, wrongly, the solidity of works long meditated; that is why it can be feared that they will only point the way to the great artist of the future whom the world awaits.[114]

On July 26, 1879, not long after the appearance of this statement in the St. Petersburg magazine, the *Revue politique et littéraire* ran this note:

> The latest letter sent by M. Emile Zola to the *European Messenger* (St. Petersburg) contains some judicious reflections on the importance of form in the arts. M. Zola has just spoken of the paintings of M. Manet, whose hand, he says, often betrays his thought.

Zola's words were then quoted as they appear above.

The little story made something of a sensation in Paris, as well it might, given Zola's friendship for Manet and his long defense of his work, and it was not long before a reporter for *Le Figaro,* Adolphe Racot, headlined his story of the affair: "M. Zola has just broken with Manet." Zola immediately wrote Manet as follows:

> My Dear Friend:
>
> I read with stupefaction the *Figaro*'s note announcing that I have broken with you, and I want very much to send you a warm clasp of the hand.
>
> The translation of the passage is not exact; moreover violence has been done to the meaning of the piece. I have spoken of you in Russia as I have spoken of you in France for thirteen years, with a solid affection for your talent and for your person.
>
> Emile Zola[115]

Thereupon Manet asked Racot to publish the letter and the reporter did so with good grace, insisting nonetheless on his role as simple intermediary.

The curious part of this small episode is that the Russian text of this *Salon* undeniably bears the name of Monet, not Manet, in the passage quoted, and this led Hemmings and Niess, in their edition of Zola's *Salons,* to change the usually accepted text of the *Salon* to read: "For a moment they had placed great hopes in Monet, but Monet seems exhausted by hasty production. . . ." But this text is apparently erroneous, and Zola must have intended to speak of Manet, no matter what the Russian *Salon* may have contained, for a letter from Paul Alexis to Zola, written on August 6, 1879, makes it clear—though not explicit—that Zola had meant to criticize Manet and not Monet:

> And poor Manet! have they ever shaken him up about you! I saw him the same day, in his studio. The fellow named Vigneau, who was there, was pouring salt in the wound. Later, your letter poured some balm on it. But . . . you should have lied boldly and said that it was a question of Monet. The Russians will probably lose by this; henceforth you'll be less frank.[116]

Apparently, two erroneous transliterations took place, one from Zola's manuscript into Russian, the other from the Russian into the French text published by the *Revue politique et littéraire;* it is also possible that someone on the staff of the *European Messenger* who had seen Zola's manuscript transmitted its true form to the French journal.

The reservations of Zola's "Russian" salons appear openly in *Le Naturalisme au Salon* of 1880, and in much the same terms as used in addressing his foreign audience. The Impressionists are all precursors, he says, the man of genius has not yet come, none of them has produced the masterpiece which "must impose the formula and make all heads bow"; they stammer, without being able to find "the word."[117] When he mentions Manet by name, it is as an artist who holds a capital place in the contemporary transitional era, a man who will be known in the history of painting as "the most acute, interesting, and personal" characteristic of his epoch; his real glory will not have been the creation of perfect pieces of beauty, the successful practice of his technique, and the ideal rendition of his vision, but his influence on even the students who learned under academic masters and his powerful aid in the artistic education of the Impressionists. This is faint praise: Manet's importance is not intrinsic, only historical.

If this is faint praise, the praise of the posthumous Manet catalogue is even fainter. The tone of the short piece is reluctant, a little dry and distant; Zola seems to be writing words he would rather leave unsaid. True, there is a reflection on his earlier prediction of Manet's success, which he had foreseen almost two decades before, but there is no real rejoicing in the late triumph, only a bitter comment on public stupidity and critical blindness. The best Zola can do, in all conscience, is to return to the idea that Manet's chief glory must reside in his influence. He concedes that this role of inspirer and model is a great one and that Manet had an all-important function in his time. Manet does not appear here as a master creator in his own right, only as "one of the most energetic instigators of 'light' painting," only as a "regenerator." Nowhere is there a claim that Manet ever fulfilled his promise, realized himself, created great paintings, great in their own right; he is a forerunner, not much more. His canvases are original, novel, but Zola does not call them beautiful or definitive; Manet had a splendid vision, but Zola thought he was never completely master of his hand; his genius was composed only of "unconsciousness and the natural gift of truth." Here is the substance of his thought:

> Forget all ideas of perfection and the absolute, do not believe that a thing is beautiful because it is perfect, according to certain physical and metaphysical conventions. A thing is beautiful because it is living, because it is human. And then you will taste delight at this painting of Manet's, which came at the hour when it had its word to speak, and which spoke it with penetrating originality. It is intelligent, witty, much more than the skilful creations with which they tried to bury it and which now sleep in the dust of attics. It could grow only in Paris, it has the slim grace of our women grown pale by gaslight, it is indeed the daughter of the obstinate artist who loved the world and who exhausted himself in conquering it.[118]

And the very last words are the knell of an old admiration:

> No further discussion is possible, we bow before the heroic effort of the master, before the considerable role he played. Even those who do not accept him entirely recognize the enormous position he occupies. Time will finish classing him among the great workers of this century, who gave their lives for the triumph of the truth.[119]

This certainly is no paean: Manet's effort is only "heroic," Zola does not say it is successful; his role in his time was only "considerable"; his real glory is that he was a worker for the truth, but Zola does not commit himself on the merit of his accomplishment. And when we add that Zola, who had cried that "Manet had his place marked at the Louvre," refused to subscribe to the fund which was to hang "Olympia" in the Luxembourg, we see that his attitude had evolved far from its original enthusiasm. And this change, occurring in the last five years or so of Manet's career, was the same—less the drama and the tears—as the change in Sandoz' view of Lantier. *L'Oeuvre,* it would seem, was not only the history of a moment in the history of art, it had the meaning of an autobiography.

Curiously, this conviction of something like failure, this deep reservation as to the intrinsic merit of Manet's creations, is accompanied in the *Salons* by a repeated statement of a kind of ultimate victory which is closely parallel to an important element of *L'Oeuvre*. Lantier is a failure, the most complete failure of his time perhaps, but he is the victor in his long struggle nevertheless, for his example, his technique, his new view of the world, and his philosophy of art finally manage to dominate the Salon completely and to change the whole tone and manner and matter of contemporary art from academicism to a sort of "realism," from the anecdotal to a rendition of true nature, from the dark, "bituminous" palette of the past to the brilliant light and color of plein air. During the terrible outburst of mockery which greets his first painting in the Salon des Refusés Claude turns to regard the other canvases, and in the midst of his disillusionment and hurt he has a moment of renewed courage and hope in the future, for he sees that the whole tone of the Salon has changed under the influence of the new painters. It is true, of course, that the Salon des Refusés does not take its inspiration and its tone from his work alone, for he is only one of many workers in the vineyard of the new art, but he is a leader, one of the most egregious revolutionaries and certainly the painter who attracts most public attention and creates the most outrageous scandal. He may not have caused the revolution and the tempest, they were in the air, but his name will be forever connected with them, both in the mind of the public and in the memory of the artists, as the chief of the open-air painters who brought about the change. Some years later, when he has returned from Bennecourt and is ready, with his new technique and practiced eye, to conquer Paris, he speculates on the art he sees around him, the rise of the young school and the decline of the academic: art has become enamored of the sun, it is "blonde," a revolution has taken place. And at the very moment when he fails most humiliatingly, with "L'Enfant mort," Sandoz confirms his triumph:

> ". . . . Look! You should be proud, for you are the real victor at the Salon this year. It is not only Fagerolles who imitates you, all now imitate you. You have revolutionized them since your *Plein-Air*, which they laughed at so. Look, look! there is another *Plein-Air*, and another, and here, and over there, all of them, all of them!"
>
> With his hand, through the halls, he pointed out the paintings. In fact, the ray of lightness introduced little by little into contemporary painting, finally was bursting forth, the old dark Salon, steeped in bitumen, had given way to a sun-filled Salon, gay as spring. It was the dawn, the new day which appeared first at the Salon des Refusés, and which now swelled, revivified the paintings

with a fine, diffuse light, decomposed into infinite nuances. Everywhere the bluish tone could be found, even in portraits and genre scenes, raised to the dimensions and to the seriousness of history. They too, the old academic subjects, had disappeared, with the warmed-up juices of tradition, as if the condemned doctrines were bearing off their shadow people; imaginative subjects were becoming rare, the cadaverous nudities of mythology and of Catholicism, the legends without faith, the anecdotes without life, the bric-à-brac of the traditional school, worn out by generations of clever fellows or idiots; and, among the last defenders of the ancient recipes, even among the aging masters, the influence was clear, the ray of sunlight had passed that way. From afar, at every step, one could see a picture pierce the wall, open a window on the world outside; soon the walls would fall, great nature would enter, for the breach was wide, the assault had swept away routine in this gay battle of audacity and youth.

"Ah; your share is still a fine one, old fellow!" Sandoz continued. "Tomorrow's art will be yours, you have made them all."[120]

The same idea, almost to the very words, is everywhere in Zola's later writings on art. In his Russian letter of 1876 he comments on the undeniable appearance of a new school in art, Impressionism, and predicts that in a score of years its revolutionary ferment will transform the whole aspect of the Salon, from which these innovators are now excluded. Manet gave the example, and now a dozen painters have joined in his assault on the sacred rules; other artists are now even copying the new school. The movement of triumph has begun.[121] In *Le Naturalisme au Salon* Zola confirms his belief that the new art is gaining ground rapidly and demonstrates Manet's influence in the evolution by pointing out the decisive role he has played for twenty years: not only has he become a source of inspiration, of technical ideas and of philosophy for all the young painters, his juniors, but he has been robbed right and left by the glories of the Academy themselves. For the young, Manet has been "the ray of light which has opened their eyes"; his sons are the Impressionists, who are near triumph, and he has even contaminated the children of the antique muse, the students of Cabanel and Gérome.

In the Manet catalogue especially, this idea is hammered home: Manet himself might not have kept all the promises of his early career and might even have failed to realize his genius completely, but he triumphs nonetheless because of his originality, his force, his audacity, and his truth to nature. Manet, Zola implies, may not himself have attained the fullness of creative power, but his real importance lies elsewhere:

> . . . one would have to write the history of our school of painting for these past twenty years to show the all-powerful role that Manet played. He was one of the most energetic instigators of "light" painting, studied in nature, taken in the full light of the contemporary milieu, which little by little has drawn our Salons out of their dark, bituminous cookery, and has enlivened them with a ray of true sunlight. It is, then, in this task of regenerator that I wish to show him in these few short pages. . . .[122]

A little later, he cites Manet's "definitive formula, which was to have such a great influence on contemporary painting,"[123] and remarks that this formula finally became, in Manet's works, "so clear . . . that it is today the formula of all our successful painters."[124] He then establishes his idea in detail:

> . . . the influence is there, undeniable, becoming more pronounced at every Salon. Go back in thought twenty years, remember those black Salons, where nude studies themselves were dark, as though covered by dust. In their great frames, History and Mythology were coated with a layer of bitumen; not one opening on the real universe, living, bathed with sunlight; rarely, here and there, a landscape daring to include an opening of blue sky. And little by little, we have seen the Salons lighten. The Greeks and Romans in mahogany, the Nymphs in porcelain have vanished from year to year, while the flood of modern scenes, taken from everyday life, rose, invaded the walls, which they covered with sunlight. It was not only a new world, it was a new painting, the tendency toward open air, the law of values observed, each figure painted in the light, at its own level, and no longer treated ideally, according to traditional conventions. At this time, I repeat, the evolution is accomplished. You have only to compare this year's Salon to that of 1863, for instance, and you will understand the enormous step that has been taken in twenty years, you will feel the radical difference of the two periods.[125]

After remarking on the number of reputations made "on Manet's back" by the skillful cheats who took his method, his vision, and his technique, Zola adds the final word:

> Things even came to the point where the Ecole des Beaux-Arts was corrupted. The most intelligent pupils, affected by the contagion, broke with the recipes taught them, threw themselves also into the study of open air painting. At present, whether they admit it or not, the young artists who are at the head of our art,

> have all undergone the influence of Manet; and if they maintain that this is only a chance encounter, it is none the less evident that he was the first one to walk in the path, indicating the way to the others. His role as precursor can no longer be denied by anyone. After Courbet, he is the last real force to reveal itself, I mean by force a new expansion of the way of seeing and rendering.[126]

In his notorious article "Peinture," of 1896, Zola expresses almost exactly the same ideas: "So they are all Manets!" "These 'light' canvases, I know them, they are the Manets for which, in my youth, I almost got myself killed."[127] Manet, Lantier, they may not resemble each other very much in physiognomy, in personality, in achievement certainly, but as Zola saw them, they walked very near together down the road of art.

VII

Lantier—Zola

Paul Cézanne and Édouard Manet are by no means the only models suggested for the figure of Claude Lantier in *L'Oeuvre.* From the novel's first appearance in *Le Gil Blas* other names have been proposed, so that there is a good-sized gallery of more or less probable candidates from whom to pick. First and most important among them is Emile Zola himself; from the beginning some who knew him suggested that events of his own life, the traits of his own personality, and the details of his own career were material in the construction of his hero. As investigation into the book's origins has been carried on, a fairly wide agreement among the critics and biographers has been reached that Lantier is, in considerable measure, Zola himself.[1]

There is some evidence in the *Dossier* of the novel to support the belief in a Zola-Lantier relationship, but it is not conclusive, the more so since there is an obvious difference between what Zola proposed in the *Ébauche* and what he actually wrote in the novel. The *Ébauche* opens with what seems to be a declaration of an intent to write some kind of autobiography:

> With Claude Lantier I want to depict the struggle of the artist against nature, the effort of creation in the work of art, an effort of blood and tears to give his flesh, to create life, always in a battle with the truth and always conquered, the struggle against the angel. In a word, I shall recount in it *my intimate life of production, this perpetual, painful birthgiving;* but I shall enlarge the subject by drama, by Claude, who is never satisfied, who grows exasperated by his inability to make his genius produce, and who kills himself at the end before his unrealized work.[2]

This is the only passage of the *Dossier* which may reasonably be interpreted as expressing an intention on Zola's part to call upon his own life in the making of Claude Lantier, and it was obviously written before he had decided to embody his own career and ideas in the figure of Sandoz. But a good deal of evidence in *L'Oeuvre* itself supports the idea that Lantier is in some way an autobiographical figure.

We have, for instance, such facts as the name "Claude"; the painter's lack of a baccalauréat degree (Zola failed his examinations twice, while both Cézanne and Manet succeeded); the circumstance that the painter is born in Provence, moves to Paris with his family, returns to Provence at the age of nine, then goes back to Paris at sixteen, a series of moves which recalls but does not exactly reproduce Zola's own; Lantier's tendency to wander in Paris, not really attributable to Cézanne, but characteristic of Zola in his first years in the capital; his love of nature, reflected in the Bennecourt episode, reflecting the same sentiment expressed by Zola in numerous articles in his early journalistic career;[3] the cooling of Claude's friendship for Dubuche, perhaps a reminiscence of the separation between Zola and Baille; the painter's marriage at the age of about thirty after some years of life with his mistress, a circumstance which almost exactly parallels Zola's own experience. Claude's long stay at Bennecourt may be the most important element of this kind of evidence, for the episode (Chapter VI) surely seems to owe something to Zola's own residence there. Of course Cézanne was with Zola at Bennecourt during the latter's first stay in 1866, so it is impossible to know whether Zola was thinking only of his own experiences as he composed this chapter or whether he also had Cézanne in mind. In any case, Rodolphe Walter, who has studied the whole Bennecourt matter in detail, believes that Zola transposed some of his own experiences of 1866 and later into the experiences of Claude Lantier[4] and there is every reason to assume that he is right, the more so since we know absolutely nothing about the visits which Cézanne and other painters made to Bennecourt, save some approximate dates.

Whatever the importance of such evidence, it is undeniable that Zola gave something of his own situation in the world of art and letters to Lantier. He is the founder and, in a manner of speaking, the head of a new school of painting, originator of a style and an aesthetic doctrine, just as Zola was, and his relationship to the older Bongrand recalls Zola's relationship to Flaubert. In the course of his career he is fiercely attacked by the critics and jeered at by the public—and who was more attacked, more mocked, more scorned than the founder of Naturalism? His statement in *Le Figaro* in 1896 that for twenty years he swallowed a "toad" every morning as he read the newspapers[5] was only too true, and he had no need to borrow from the life of either Cézanne or Manet to know the tortures of the unpopular and misunderstood pioneer. Again, Claude is surrounded in the novel by men of little talent and no success, his "school," as a school is a failure, and yet gradually his style and aesthetic come to dominate the realm of contemporary art. Here Zola could have been thinking of the vicissitudes of his own career. Surrounded from the outset by men doomed to comparative obscurity—no writer in either the Aix group or the Médan group, save Maupassant and Huysmans, would be known today were it not for Zola's name, and Maupassant and Huysmans were birds of passage among the "little naturalists"—heading a band which got its only glory from his presence, he saw his "school" enjoying a half-success at best and yet, even in 1886, could sense clearly his victory in the world of literature. The novel of the years of 1880-90 was dominated by his name, as the late Salon of the close of *L'Oeuvre* is dominated by Lantier's and those lesser men who imitated him and made his violence palatable to the public have their reflection in Fagerolles in the novel—were not Maupassant and Bourget partial models for the "peintre à succès"? Once again, there was no need for him to call upon Manet here—Cézanne is out of the question—for he knew all there was to know of struggle and wounds and victory. Moreover, the circumstance that Claude finds himself at the center of a group whose origins came largely from Zola's friends—not Cézanne's or Manet's or anyone else's—certainly seems to indicate that Zola was thinking of himself a good deal of the time as he caused his painter to move in the fictional art world of *L'Oeuvre.*

Not only Claude Lantier's general position in the world of art, but his whole aesthetic theory and practice can reasonably be interpreted as a transposition into other terms of Zola's own, and once again there is no overwhelming reason why Zola should have turned to the ideas and the creations of either Manet or Cézanne to find material for his painter's career. The similarities between the writer and the painter leap to the eye, once it is admitted that Zola was under no obligation to follow any set scheme of circumstances or to copy the reality of any career. Both Zola and Claude are modernists, independents, and revolutionaries filled with disgust for the bourgeois tradition of the past, and Zola seems to have been as much opposed to the Académie as the painter was to the Institut.

Modernists both, then, the creator and his creature, but they were modernists in their own especial way. Modernism implies realism, for there is little point in depicting the contemporary scene if it is not shown realistically; if realism is not the ultimate goal, then any scene, any landscape will do. Claude Lantier evolves, in the middle of his career, into a true realist, leaving behind the tortured, "impressionistic" scenes of Provence and the attenuated realism of "Plein-Air" to become a reporter of the contemporary scene in the paintings which he unsuccessfully submits to the Salon each year until he arrives at the conception of his final canvas. He evolves a method, a style, an aesthetic in which an exact, "naive" rendition of the scenes of contemporary urban life becomes the end, a rendition which by its violence, power, and originality will give the sense of the modern world. But, troubled by the "lesion" of his eye and by the deep disequilibrium of his time of transition, he cannot quite complete his formula and because of the pressure of some mysterious force within him gradually evolves away from it, as he works ceaselessly on his final painting, and becomes a realist of strongly marked romantic tendencies, first manifested in the early violent canvases of Provence. The last painting begins as a realistic picture of Paris, but one with "meaning": on one side of the Seine is "Paris working," on the other, "Paris playing," and the sense of the work is obviously a kind of synthesis of modern life in a metropolis. But as the canvas progresses through endless retouchings and changes, it acquires a new figure, the huge nude which comes to dominate the whole composition and eventually to ruin it. Realism is Claude's goal, but he cannot hold himself to realism and so dies without ever having completely elaborated the formula which his time requires of its art.

Here, it goes without saying, there is more than a reminiscence of Zola's own work. Realist he was and aimed to be, and a great portion of the bitter criticism which greeted him each morning in the books and articles of the intellectual gendarmes of the time bore specifically on that aspect of his work. But no one was really deceived by the externals of this art, with all its technical details, with all its careful settings, its precise lexicon of industry and commerce, for from the beginning it was clear that if what Zola wrote was realism, then what Flaubert and Maupassant wrote was not, because his work contained an element which true realism cannot stomach, the "epic" element, "black poetry," exaggeration, imagination, which makes its presence visible in a half-dozen ways, in the vitalism and animism which the novels show on every page, in the colossal movement of crowds, in the enormity and brutality of the acts, in the exceptional and diseased men and women who dominate, in the whole tone of violence and energy and passion which suffuses the books. In him is something of the same evolution as in Claude Lantier: moving from the sketches of his youthful career, he too elaborates a theory of realism based on direct observation, conceives a kind of art which will render his time with accuracy, yet one which will transcend questions of mere accuracy in its search for profound meaning and hidden law. No more than Claude, could Zola hold to the canon of realism—the invention of the term naturalism testifies to his restlessness—and like his own creature he moves from plain realism to the epic, to grandeur, to imagination—to romantic realism.[6]

Moreover, there is Claude's situation in time. He comes, as Zola emphasizes, in a period when a clear originality of artistic theory and an absolutely personal expression are nearly impossible, for he finds himself at the confluence of two main artistic currents, romanticism stemming from Delacroix, realism from Courbet. He is a product of their union, too close to them to deny either completely, yet rebelling against their force and their "corruption" of his eye. Zola's situation was almost exactly the same, for he arrived at artistic maturity at precisely the same moment, at the confluence of Balzac and Hugo. The same influences, romantic on the one hand, realistic on the other, which formed Lantier's incomplete genius were the ones, transposed to a different art, which made Zola the poet of realism. The same heredity is there, the same pressures, the same reminiscences, and the same vain search for complete liberty. And perhaps it was the poetry of modern life as exemplified in Paris which made both creator and creature turn so often to the city as the chief well-spring of their inspiration. As his career advances, Claude becomes more and more a painter of Paris; leaving behind the violent landscapes of Provence, the Barbizon setting of "Plein-Air," the flowers and vases of Bennecourt, he turns more and more frequently to the great city and in the middle and end of his career paints almost nothing but scenes of urban life. So also with Zola: moving from the *Contes à Ninon* and from the suburban sketches of his early newspaper career, he feels himself, quite obviously, more and more completely captured by the metropolis: of the novels of the *Rougon-Macquart* series, twelve are set almost completely in Paris and nearly all of the remaining eight have incidents there; of the thirteen novels of the series which appeared before *L'Oeuvre,* eight had Paris as their setting; *Thérèse Raquin, Madeleine Férat, La Confession de Claude* are all or nearly all completely Parisian in locale. The city was a magnet for Zola, as a half-hundred of his little *chroniques* and *causeries* in the newspapers testify—if the novels are not enough—to the fascination the metropolis held for him. Thus, the similarity of artistic intention between Claude Lantier and Zola takes on more force as "confession": what is the "confounded series of paintings" if not a transposition of the fundamental idea of the

Rougon-Macquart series? When Zola says early in the *Ébauche* that he will give Lantier "the dream of immense pages of decoration, a fresco summing up the epoch,"[7] could he really have been thinking of any painter? It sufficed him to return in memory to his own first elaboration of the idea for his series, one of the first and most viable ideas he was ever to hold, an idea already almost two decades old in his mind and one with antecedents reaching back to the "universal" poem of his youth. Certainly, Lantier's painting of Les Halles could have stemmed from no other source than Zola's own concept of the beauty of modern Parisian life, and though it is true that it does not appear, except in a brief mention, in *L'Oeuvre,* it is a clear indication nonetheless that Zola had no need to depend on anyone else for the artistic inclination of his painter. More than Manet, certainly far more than Cézanne, Zola felt himself called to render the life of the great, teeming capital, and just as this is one of his profoundest originalities, so is it the originality of subject matter which makes Lantier's bitter work of his middle career so repulsive to the jury of the Salon.

Even the extreme violence and energy of his art, his refusal to make concessions to popular taste, to soften his picture of the contemporary world, or to attenuate the harsh lessons of reality which he tries to force upon the jury are evidences of his close filiation to his creator. In spite of the obvious truth that Zola's descriptions of Lantier's paintings may well betray a reminiscence on his part of Cézanne's early work, they seem much more applicable to Zola's novels and short stories, terrifying in themselves, full of "superb violence" and pulsing with colors from the whole spectrum of contemporary industrial existence. Force and originality are the painter's great contributions to the artistic revolution which he heads; a hundred pages from Zola's *Salons,* from his dramatic and novelistic criticism, from his newspaper essays testify that he had the same contempt for popular success sought through compromise, the same admiration for power, the same belief that only in the strength stemming from a strong personality can salvation be found in art, as Claude demonstrates throughout the pages of *L'Oeuvre.* Zola's words on the Michel-Angelo of the Sistine Chapel contained in *Mes Voyages* testify that Claude's adoration of force and strength and power was in actuality his own adoration.[8]

But perhaps the last, unfinished painting offers the best evidence that Claude is another Zola, imperfect but purer. The painting begins by emphasizing the specifically modern, industrial, and social aspects of Paris in the manner of *L'Assommoir* and *La Curée,* but as it evolves under the force of Lantier's automatism it takes on different aspects, becomes a kind of second *Nana.* As it does so, it acquires the familiar dominating, devouring quality of Zola's great symbols, the mine in *Germinal,* the bed in *Nana,* the still in *L'Assommoir,* the department store in *Au Bonheur des dames,* the Halles in *Le Ventre de Paris,* the apartment building in *Pot-bouille,* "le Paradou" in *La Faute de l'Abbé Mouret.* And it becomes above all a literary painting, symbolic in the manner which Zola had already made his own in a half-dozen major novels. If any more evidence were needed that Claude is a kind of Zola *manqué,* the painting, so obviously inspired in the manner and structure of the *Rougon-Macquart* novels, would surely provide it.[9]

Since as painter, Claude clearly resembles Zola as novelist, there can be no denying some kind of close bond. Now, is he in any important measure a reflection of his creator as a man, as a living individual? Does he reflect Zola's personality and outlook on life? Is *L'Oeuvre* a confession?

On the basis of what we know directly of Zola's intimate life, that is, what we know by his own admission in letters, private remarks in the notes to his novels, and so on, there can be no certainty. But if the testimony of those who knew him and, perhaps more importantly, the testimony of his own creative works are worth anything at all, it seems beyond doubt that Zola consciously or unconsciously created the painter partly in his own image.

One of the basic themes of *L'Oeuvre* is the conflict between art and life, between intellectual creation and physical creation, and from the inception of the novel's planning, as the *Dossier* shows, Zola intended to write a work in which what he conceived to be the essentially sexual nature of all creation should become evident. The list of possible titles which he drew up for the novel is most revealing: "To Make a Child," "To Make Life," "Creation-Create-Procreate," "To Fertilize Nature," "Birthgiving," "Accouchement," "Parturition," "Conception," "To Give Birth," "Fecundation," "Blood," "Living Flesh," "Our Flesh," "The Unappeased," "The Anguish of Creating," "This Is My Flesh," "The Century in Childbirth." Titles of this general tenor heavily outweigh such intellectualized possibilities as "The Struggle with the Angel," "Defeat," or "Genius."[10] Throughout the *Dossier* the same idea recurs.[11]

The novel itself is full of the same spirit, which finds its final expression in the jeweled nude of the last painting. When Sandoz sees her for the first time he remonstrates with Lantier, pleading that the logic of the scene demands her elimination, and arguing that a modern painter, priding himself on depicting only realities, has no business introducing such phantasmagoria when it is easy to select subjects in which nudity is appropriate:

> But Claude grew stubborn, gave weak and violent explanations, for he did not want to admit the real reason, an idea of his, so vague that he could not have recounted it clearly, the torment of a secret symbolism, that old renewal of romanticism which made him incarnate in that nudity the very flesh of Paris, the naked and passionate city, resplendent with a woman's beauty. And he put in it his own passion, his love of beautiful bellies, of thighs and fertile breasts, like the ones he burned to create for the continual birthgiving of his art.[12]

So the theme of the struggle between art and life is rendered by another struggle, this one in symbolic terms, the struggle between the powerful sexuality of the artist and his repressions, because if the nude of the final painting has any significance at all it is as a kind of sublimation of Claude's deep, unsatisfied desires, for as he elaborates her he grows more and more detached from Christine, to the point where they become almost complete strangers sexually. Claude's vital force is expended in vain pursuit of a sexual ideal that no living woman can long incarnate.

If one note recurs with such frequency as to be fundamental to the understanding of Claude's character, it is the energy of his sexual drive. From the very beginning of *L'Oeuvre* to almost its end, Zola emphasizes over and over that Claude's violent painting is only a manifestation of his strongly sensual nature. The *Dossier* does not make it clear that Zola's original intention was to endow the painter with such a powerful sexual drive, for the only reference which could reasonably support such a view is contained in the *Ébauche:* "What must animate all this novel is *passion.* Claude is a passionate man who will set fire to the whole book. I must have a great human passion in the book."[13] Does this mean that Claude Lantier is to be a victim of sexual or artistic passion, or both? Whatever its sense, it is plain enough that when Zola proceeded to the writing of the novel, he interpreted his own intentions in a violently sexual sense—thereby perhaps rendering a secret reality of his own life. Certainly, one phrase of the *Dossier* confirms this assumption: when Zola has finished his description of the last painting and of the symbolism of the nude, he adds: "A chaste man, with the love of flesh in his painting; these are my ideas."[14]

But almost as well marked a characteristic is his unusual timidity toward women, the concomitant of his strong sexual urge and the reason for his repression. This note is struck fairly often in the *Dossier*, leaving no doubt that from the first Zola meant to shape his artist in the form which he finally takes in the novel. As he ruminates his ideas for the work, he says of Claude, after noting that he is to be a passionate man, that he is to be gauche, timid, and a virgin, like Christine, at the beginning of the book.[15] In the novel, the note of timidity and fearful chastity comes back again and again, and it is significant that although Claude and Christine meet in July, they do not become lovers until the following spring, after the disaster of the Salon des Refusés—and the delay is in no way due to lack of willingness on Christine's part. And it is the timidity, the misplaced chastity, which, coupled with Claude's overwhelming passion for the nude of his dreams, eventually destroys their marriage and leads to the suicide of the incomplete genius.

This combination of overpowering sexuality striking against a puritanical repression and obsessive timidity seems to be the very essence of Zola's temperament, and it is entirely possible that as he shaped the figure of Claude Lantier, he was, consciously rather than unconsciously, calling upon the profoundest elements of his own life to provide his material.

His novels themselves would give testimony, if we lacked other documents, to the powerful sexuality that moved him, to something like an obsession with female flesh and the act of love: *Thérèse Raquin, Madeleine Férat. La Confession de Claude, La Curée, Le Ventre de Paris, La Faute de l'Abbé Mouret, Son Excellence Eugène Rougon, L'Assommoir, Nana, Pot-bouille, Au Bonheur des dames, La Joie de vivre, Germinal*—to mention only some of the works which preceded *L'Oeuvre*—testify to the potency of his desires, at least if the large place he gave to sex in his scheme of things is any indication. Sexual symbolism fills these books—one has only to think of Le Paradou in *La Faute de l'Abbé Mouret,* or of Les Halles in *Le Ventre de Paris*—and their plots turn so frequently on the good or evil consequences of sexual desires and sexual acts as to justify the belief that Zola was the creator of a new genre, the epic of the flesh. The critics of the time said or implied on a hundred occasions that such a content of sex in his works was either the evidence of an illness of Zola's—thus the writers of the "Manifeste des Cinq"—or of an ignoble desire for publicity and sales through scandal and pornography; but it may have been rather that when Zola wrote of sex and love and woman and did so in the violently voluptuous manner of *Nana* or *La Curée,* he was simply expressing an instinct so strong that it had to find outlet in his prose and that his interest in the act of love had nothing to do with pornography or scandal but came directly from what F. W. J. Hemmings calls his "sex-ridden imagination."

Strongly sexual, then, but was he the gauche, timid, chaste man of *L'Oeuvre*? Was his sexuality thwarted in its urge for expression? The novels themselves answer: he would not, of course, dwell so much on woman and love if he had not suffered from something like Claude's complex, and his plots would not have turned so often on sexual acts and desires if he had lived what is called a normal sexual life. Had the force of his drives been dissipated in normal relationships, he would not have been the creator he was, and the decline of his talent after the establishment of a satisfactory relationship with Jeanne Rozerot is testimony that can scarcely be denied.

But the novels are not all, for there is evidence, some from Zola's own lips, that he himself knew the torments of chastity amid the tempests of desire. The old legend of a "bon bourgeois," apparently untroubled by the call of the flesh, serenely composing four pages a day, oblivious to women and love, disappears in the light of what he told Dr. Edouard Toulouse, who, after hearing Zola's reminiscences of his youth, concluded that the sexual instinct was frustrated by timidity, as often happens with neurotics, whose ideas often inhibit sexual expression.[16] For Toulouse, as for some of his modern followers, the shock of a powerful system of desires against the wall of inhibition was one of the sources of what the physician describes as a neurosis; it was this condition that caused the sexual force to have such a great resonance in Zola's psychological life. Claude Lantier does not seem much different.

It is interesting to speculate that Zola may have moved Lantier by the same motive, idealism, which seems to have been at the source of his own timidity toward women and his persistent monogamy long after he had become disaffected from his wife. It will be recalled that in the *Ébauche* Zola had first proposed including an ideal woman in Claude's life, a woman whom he sees but cannot reach and who, finally, in a burst of generosity, satisfies his passion; in the novel, this ideal woman apparently became the nudes of Claude's two large paintings, but even in her form as a painted being she effectively inserts herself between Claude and Christine and eventually makes any real union between them impossible. An ideal of somewhat the same kind may have influenced Zola's early life, if we can believe the words of Jules Hoche, who in 1887 published an account of "Le Premier roman d'Émile Zola," the story of the "little red hat" which he evidently got from Zola himself. According to Hoche, Zola saw a young girl, Jeanne, when he was about nine or ten and contracted for her a childish passion which the impossibility of reaching her—she came from a good bourgeoise family of Aix—only intensified. For years her vision remained intact in his mind; finally it faded, only to be revived in 1879, when by chance he witnessed her funeral cortege passing in a street of Aix.[17]

A dozen passages from Zola's early letters and from the *Contes à Ninon* betray the same idealism in love, the same hope of a perfect union; and Zola's long, puritanical attack in both novels and articles on the moral looseness of the Second Empire indicates how deeply idealism had penetrated his mind and heart—and how difficult it had made satisfactory human relationships for him.[18]

If this evidence has a meaning, it is that Claude Lantier is in a real sense a direct, conscious reflection of his creator. The struggle between Christine and art is not a struggle between woman and art at all, but a battle between a living woman and the chimera of a mind driven to disease by its preoccupation with a sexual ideal. And that struggle would seem to symbolize the struggle in Zola's own mind between the ideal woman whom he conceived early in his life, perhaps under the influence of Michelet and Musset, and whom he incarnated in L'Aérienne, in Ninon, in Miette, in Albine, in Pauline, in Christine, and the eternal Delilah, the mysteriously attractive destroyer which his imagination elaborated during his youth and middle years and which gave rise to such figures as Nana and Séverine and Clorinde Balbi. The first nude of "Plein-Air," simple, fresh, pure, becomes, with the years, the terrible figure of jewels and gold of the final painting—just as Ninon became, with the years, Nana.[19]

Perhaps this aspect of the work accounts, in a slightly different sense than mere sublimation or release, for the existence of *L'Oeuvre* itself, perhaps it is a hidden record of Zola's own disaffection from Alexandrine in the years just preceding his liaison with Jeanne Rozerot. It is curious that Claude's detachment from Christine is mentioned no less than three times in the *Dossier*, the first time as early as the very first page, where Zola sets out to determine what direction the novel will take.[20] Such a frequent recurrence of the detail makes it seem that it had unusual importance for Zola, and this impression is borne out by the careful and effective treatment Zola gives to the scene of the wedding night. Claude Lantier and Christine are married after some seven years of life together, and Zola makes it clear that Claude agrees to the ceremony only out of a kind of pity for his mistress. The scene after the belated event (which Claude almost misses in his anxiety to help Mahoudeau, whose huge statue has just collapsed) is heart-breaking in its brutality, and though it may be argued that the scene and its implications are necessary for the development of the theme of rivalry between the woman of flesh and blood and the woman of the painting who inserts herself between Claude and Christine, it is still possible that Zola here was rendering, in fictional form, a reality of his own existence. There is some evidence from Edmond de Goncourt that from fairly early in his marriage Zola was slipping away from Alexandrine[21] and there may be a reflection of this state of affairs and its consequences in *L'Oeuvre,* for Zola's disabused remarks on marriage in an article of 1881 appear to be more than a statement of general views, they surely contain a fairly strong element of personal confession.[22]

No solid evidence supports this contention, but it seems to be true that Zola's feelings for his wife never went beyond the kind of staid attachment which Sandoz shows for his wife in *L'Oeuvre*—he says of her that in effect she was only another comrade. It is true, though, that we have no other evidence of a growing estrangement between Zola and Alexandrine, but the fact that he took a mistress not long after the publication of *L'Oeuvre* certainly seems to indicate that all was not well in the ménage in 1885-86. It is sometimes argued that Zola contracted his liaison with Jeanne Rozerot because his wife could not give him children, but Alexandrine told Louis de Robert in 1925 that Zola had not wanted children while she was still young enough to bear them. The explanation of the whole matter is probably not a simple one: Zola undoubtedly wanted children, at least after he had established himself in the literary world, but it is also possible that he was not deeply in love with his wife, that he felt himself growing steadily away from her with the years, that he was sexually unappeased, and that he wanted, in his adoration for life, one more chance to live it fully. If this is so, if the affair with Jeanne Rozerot was not simply the result of a kind of accident, if it was the product of a long disaffection, then *L'Oeuvre* is more than a record of Zola's life in the art world, it is a record of his innermost evolution.

There are other kinds of evidence in *L'Oeuvre* to back the claim that Zola consciously used elements of his own psyche as part of the foundation for the character of Claude Lantier. An important one of these is that Claude displays exactly the same kind of psychic conflict present in Zola and of which Zola, a trained observer and an honest man, was surely aware. This is the struggle within the painter's mind between his unending desire to dominate, to impose his ideas, to conquer the Salon and Paris, and the eternal self-doubt which makes him a retoucher, a perfectionist, a hesitant on the path to perfection. In the *Ébauche* Zola remarks that he will include his memories of his youth in Aix, his friends, their long walks, their readings, then: "Paris to be conquered."[23] It seems clear from the expression that he is thinking of himself at least as much as of the others. Certainly, the note is frequently stressed in the novel; as Claude looks from the Palais toward the Arc de Triomphe he cries: "Ah! Paris, it's ours, all we have to do is take it!" After his scandalous failure at the Salon des Refusés he declares that Paris may laugh all it wants, some day it will fall at the feet of the "little band." Even as his career gives signs of ending in failure, Claude does not abandon his hopes: as his comrades proclaim that the open-air school is on the way to victory, that all it needs is the man of genius to incarnate the new formula in masterpieces, Claude listens and speculates: "What a place to take! Dominate the crowd, open a new century, create an art!" Again and again Zola returns to the idea, to Claude's ambition to "conquer everything" and his desperate effort, year by year, to win acceptance by the jury testifies to his ambition and to his belief that the creation of pure art is not enough, that popular and official success must put the seal on the career of the true master.

But even in his faith in himself and in his originality, there is always the self-doubt that poisons his hopes and ambitions. As his career progresses, the moments of hope and enthusiasm become fewer, and finally he is driven to admit to himself that his talent is incomplete, that he is impotent, that he will never be able to give himself completely. This sense of incompleteness makes Claude into the perfectionist he is, the constant retoucher unable to find satisfaction in what he does and constantly driven to new work before he has finished the business in hand. But from the depths of his conviction that the forces of heredity and environment have condemned him, Claude bravely seeks his "formula" in a constant evolution of style and subject and philosophy. The path from the first sketches to the symbolism of the last canvas is a long one; it leads only to a grave in the cemetery on Montmartre.

Can it be demonstrated that this conflict in Claude's mind between the ambition to conquer, the perpetual hope of success, and the gnawing doubt that drives him to perfectionism and failure are in any real sense a reflection of Zola's personality? In a measure it can, with the reservation that the forms of malady seen in the novel are a great deal more intense and more dramatic than anything which Zola apparently experienced.

Zola, like his creation, was an ambitious man, full of the desire to dominate, combative and aggressive to a degree in his search for the victory of his ideas and of his literature—Angus Wilson, indeed, calls his ambition and will to power "almost the most important elements in his genius."[24] Nearly everyone who knew him remarked on this aspect of his character, sometimes with a grain of irony or hostility, sometimes in admiration for the spirit of this quiet bourgeois, who was not so quiet as he seemed. Adolphe Brisson, for instance, says that Zola's first publisher, Albert Lacroix, told him that the comparatively minor success of *Thérèse Raquin* displeased Zola deeply: a resounding failure would have been better for his combative spirit. How could he unleash the salutary tempest which overnight would take him out of the shadows where he was languishing?[25] Zola knew how. He wrote *Mon Salon, Édouard Manet, Mes Haines,* and a score of articles castigating the official glories of the Second Empire and a score of others in which he chastised the leaders of the Third Republic; he wrote *Une Campagne, Nouvelle campagne,* the *Salons, Le Roman expérimental, Nos Auteurs dramatiques, Le Naturalisme au théâtre, Les Romanciers naturalistes, Documents littéraires,* he tried a dozen times for election to the Académie, he worked ceaselessly and often aggressively for the triumph of naturalism—and of Émile Zola. A half dozen commentators of his life and career—Edmond de Goncourt, Paul Alexis, Edmond Lepelletier, Dr. Toulouse, Jules Vallès, Ernest Seillière, F. W. J. Hemmings, Jean Vinchon—see in him a real "libido dominandi," a spirit of ambition and power perhaps unmatched among the writers of his time.[26]

The testimony is solid then: Zola was a man who wanted success and official recognition, who desired the ribbon and the Académie, just as Claude wanted to force the jury and the Salon and to impose his ideas in art on a reluctant public. And it is possible that when Claude, in the depths of his despair, makes some small concessions to popular taste in his effort to win over the jury, he is reflecting in slightly different terms a concession that Zola himself seems to have made on one or two occasions, witness *Le Rêve* and *Une Page d'amour.* The whole example of his career, from *Mes Haines* to the Dreyfus case and even beyond, proves his combativeness, his faith in himself and in his ideas, his hope to change the world in his own image; not for him the silent joys of the unknown artist glorying in the perfection of his effort—what he wanted was fame, notoriety, power, money. And he gave words to his desires as he fashioned the figure of Claude.

But what about the other side of the coin, the side of self-doubt and hesitation and fear? The testimony is equally ample and solid, and from it arises the picture of a different Zola, as different from the fighting Zola as the hesitant perfectionist in Lantier is different from the leader who dreams of beating down the doors of the Salon each spring until death stops his brush and his search for the formula.

The Goncourt *Journal* is full of reflections of this side of Zola's psyche. On a half-dozen occasions Goncourt cites Zola's doubts, his fears, his hesitations and difficulties, his complaints, his suspicions of himself, and of his own powers. Alexis finds the same attitudes. When the young Zola, timid, reserved, became a man he was seized by a nervous, sickly sensibility predisposing him to hypochondria; his ardent faith in himself and in his worth supported him only during his hours of work, and immediately he ceased working he began doubting himself.[27] Alexis believed that Zola's psychic difficulties, his self-doubt and hesitation, came largely from his highly developed critical sense, which led him to a perpetual feeling of the imperfection of his faculties and the nothingness of man; he often heard Zola say that he felt like a beginner, forgetting the twenty volumes he had already written and wondering what would be the fate of his next novel.[28] Like Claude, the Zola of Alexis' pages is tormented by the desire for an absolute, whose lack of realization turns him to black pessimism, and he has to make some effort to remember his successes. He is a pessimist, inclined to see the dark side, he believes that he has accomplished nothing, that all goes from bad to worse for him, that he is the most unfortunate of men.[29] This perpetual beginner, nervous, impressionable, cannot know tranquility; all he can do is work.

But here, it goes without saying, he differs from his creature. Unlike Claude, Zola was, in Alexis' words, a "reasonable rebel," a desperate but resigned man, a monomaniac who knew his own evil and got the most out of it.[30] And so, of course, is Sandoz.

Zola's own well-known letter-preface to Dr. Toulouse' study of him confirms Alexis' observations; protesting at the legend that makes of him a stupid beast of burden doing his task only in the hope of gain, he cries:

> Ah! the poor flayed man that I am, shivering, suffering at the slightest breath of air, sitting down each morning to his daily task in the continual combat of his will with his doubt! How he has made me laugh and weep sometimes, the famous plough-ox![31]

Dr. Toulouse, in fact, found in Zola a certain nervous instability, an exaggerated emotivity, and a cluster of morbid ideas, one of which was the idea of doubt: Zola was really constantly afraid that he could not do his work, that he could not finish a book. He never reread his novels, fearful of making disappointing discoveries about himself, and he showed no confidence in himself in either the large or the small concerns of life.[32]

Zola's own words, uttered publicly, give more proof of his self-doubt and self-detestation. At the end of December 1878, he confessed in the columns of *Le Voltaire* that he wept with rage over his manuscripts, called himself an idiot twenty times a day, and never published a book without thinking it inferior to his others.[33] And when Edmondo de Amicis talked to him in 1881 Zola spoke of his continual doubt, saying that he almost killed himself working and never succeeded in doing what he wanted. Everything he had done, he declared, was "horrible," he cannot look back, cannot reread his works: when he rereads something he has written, he is so disgusted with himself that he almost weeps.[34]

It is remarkable how, in a way, Claude's life parallels Zola's own. Surrounded in youth by a band of kindred souls, in love, wandering the streets of Paris and glorying in its sights and sounds, full of hope and ambition to conquer the great city, he becomes, as his life wears on, morose, solitary, abandoned by everyone, no longer in love, doubting himself and his art, seized completely by the demands of his work, so completely that he ceases to live at all and becomes the puppet of his overriding complex. Did Zola not pass through somewhat the same experiences? Did he not also see his "little band" slip away from him, did he not also cease to love, at least in the old, fine manner, did he not become more and more solitary, holed up in Médan most of the year, more and more difficult of character, more and more alone as his work swallowed his existence and made him a kind of relentless copy-machine? Claude's life seems to be a melancholy reflection on his own, and it seems certain that Zola quite consciously incarnated in Claude the quality which he felt did as much as any to make life difficult and complicated for him, his persistent and unreasoning romanticism, the quality which above all makes life in the modern world impossible. No doubt Zola intended Claude to be a modern representative of the spirit of 1830, for in the *Ébauche* he says that he is thinking of giving Claude another love than Christine, a love which will be "ideal, a higher love," a woman he will glimpse from his window, perhaps, and whom he will never be able to reach. Then he adds of Claude: "The romantic substance that persists, the earthworm in love with a queen."[35] A little later in the *Ébauche* he says that Claude will be "a romantic at bottom."[36] When he came to write the novel, the idea continued to hold a fairly important place: not only does Claude carry with him into his art the ideal love that he can never reach, not only does he spoil his own realism by his love for an intruder from the past, but he is conscious that his romanticism makes it impossible, along with his inherent "lesion," to find the formula he seeks. As he struggles with "Plein-Air," he cries out his agony at the "gangrene of romanticism" he feels within him and somewhat later, when he is caught almost in spite of himself by the spectacle of the picturesque rue Vieille-du-Temple he becomes furious with the romanticism which surges up in him in spite of all his lessons in realism and logic. Sandoz, himself a victim of romanticism, recognizes its appearance in Claude and as he talks to Bongrand at the funeral he discloses that he, like the painter, saw the "gangrene" as the painter's curse; but Sandoz has the wisdom or the luck to combat his disease with the sound lessons of nature.

There is abundant evidence that Zola saw his generation as ineluctably romantic, ineffaceably marked, and that try as he would, he could not wash the stain from his own spirit. His novels are proof of the bond that the old temptation had laid on him, from the *Mystères de Marseille* to *Fécondité,* and his own words testify not only that he saw himself as a romantic, but that he deplored the influence which romanticism exerted on him as he struggled toward realism and objectivity and documentation. His famous phrase "I am of it (i. e., romanticism), and I rage to be of it," of *Le Roman expérimental,* is paralleled by a dozen passages of *Nos Auteurs dramatiques* and *Les Romanciers naturalistes,* by statements in a half-dozen articles, in letters, by enough confessions of his own, in short, to leave no doubt that he felt himself cursed by his birth at a time when romanticism still held the youth of France in sway.[37]

But to say that Zola deliberately created Claude Lantier as a romantic, partly in imitation of himself and partly as a representation of his own generation, is not to say much that is concrete. What kind of romantic did he make Claude out to be? What kind of romantic did he think himself to be, for that matter?

The answer may lie in the contrast, parallel to the hope-doubt contrast, in Claude's desire to seize all of nature in his art, his faith in and love of the created world–his adoration of life, in a word–and the opposing pessimism which eventually corrupts his happiness in his work. As Zola first sees Claude, in the *Ébauche,* he is "a creator, with too wide an ambition, wanting to put all nature on canvas,"[38] and when Claude appears in the novel he brings with him this same wide ambition, exemplified both in his theories ("Ah! to see everything and paint everything!") and in his attempt toward the end of his career to synthesize all of Paris–"Paris working," "Paris playing"–and to render its whole meaning in a single work. It is he, not Sandoz, who pronounces this hymn to existence:

> —Ah! life, life, to feel it and render it in its reality, to love it for itself, to see in it the only true beauty, eternal and changing, not to have the stupid idea of ennobling it by castrating it, to understand that its supposed uglinesses are only the protrusions of character, and to give life, and to create men, the only way of being God![39]

Nearly all through his life this adoration of the totality of created things sustains Claude Lantier in his struggle for self-realization and success, but as he sinks into failure and as it becomes clear to him and to everyone else that he will never discover the formula, he loses some of the assurance of his youth, some of the hope in the future which has buoyed him for so long, some of his love of life. When Sandoz, after the last bitter visit to Bennecourt, delivers a lecture on the fallacy of any belief in artistic immortality and then characteristically concludes on a note of hope in the future, Claude contradicts him bluntly and rudely—"our works won't add an atom to the world's dust."[40]

Does this descent from hope to despair, this loss of faith in life and its beauty, reflect anything like a reality of Zola's own life? The problem is most difficult, and the question of Zola-optimist-Zola-pessimist must exercise anyone who studies the *Rougon-Macquart* series and the subsequent writings. There can be no firm answer, for Zola's work shows abundant evidence of both tendencies, particularly in the novels of his middle career. While it is true that the *Quatre Evangiles* demonstrate that optimism finally conquered pessimism in his psyche, for many years, from at least 1880 to the end of the *Rougon-Macquart* series, the struggle characterized his inner evolution. The series itself testifies to his deep interest in life, in all of creation, his acceptance of all forms of existence as legitimate subject matter for art; it is his "confounded series of painting," and its very presence is proof that at bottom Zola was not a pessimist, at least if we mean by pessimism a sterilizing and paralyzing malady of the mind and will. No one glorified life and creation so much as he; and the emphasis on man's sexual forces, both in *L'Oeuvre* and in his other novels, proves his deep attachment to this world. In *Le Naturalisme au théâtre* he says: "To live, morality is there only, in its necessity, in its grandeur. And outside of life, outside the continuous labor of humanity, there is nothing but metaphysical folly, dupery and misery." Guy Robert makes love of life and attachment to the world one of Zola's main characteristics,[41] and he argues that Zola's adoration of the forces of life, hidden or open, gradually won a battle in his mind with the forces of death; he situates the turning point, when optimism began finally to triumph, about

1883.[42] It is difficult to gainsay Robert's opinion, for victory does come eventually to the "forces of life," but *L'Oeuvre* seems to represent a moment of the struggle when Zola's courage failed and when he succumbed to the call of the forces of death. *L'Oeuvre* came at a low point of Zola's life, and not long after its publication he established a new center for his existence; it represents one of the fluctuations of hope and doubt, of faith and rejection, which characterized his mature existence.

When all is said and done, perhaps the best indication that Zola intended Claude Lantier to reflect his own romantic nature comes from the fact that the painter, like the novelist, kept always before him the figure of an ideal woman, who was the center of his existence no matter what form she might take. It is she whom he perceives behind the flesh and blood of Christine, whom he paints in "Plein-Air," with whom he lives for years as he works on his final painting, who finally appears, in gold and jewels, as the goddess of Paris and of creation. Did Zola not know her at first hand, this Aérienne, who becomes with the years Nana, this Ninon who evolves into Clorinde, this Miette changed into Renée? In giving to Claude his same automatism, his same recurrent vision, Zola must have consciously made him in his own likeness.

VIII

Lantier and the Others

A HALF-SCORE of other figures in addition to Cézanne, Manet, and Zola himself have been suggested as complete or partial models for Claude Lantier. Of these, the two most frequently discussed, and for good reason, are the caricaturist André Gill and the leader of the school of Impressionism himself, Claude Monet.

Gill, on the basis of the evidence and the logic of the total situation, seems to be the likelier choice, for numerous details of his life and career appear to coincide with those of Lantier's fictional life; nowhere, though, does Zola mention Gill as a possible model for his painter, and all the evidence that supports the connection is circumstantial.

But there is a good deal of it and some of it seems fairly convincing. Guy Robert does not hesitate to claim that it is probable that the plot of *L'Oeuvre* owes a good deal to some articles in *Le Figaro* (May 11, 1882, and May 2, 1885) concerning Gill's lack of success at the Salon and his death,[1] and Patrick Brady believes that Claude's madness may have its prototype in the life of Gill.[2] These views seem well founded. Gill, who was almost exactly Zola's age and hence about the right age to serve as a model for the fictional painter, studied in Parisian ateliers, then turned to architecture briefly, but lost interest in it when he failed in the *concours* of 1858.[3] In 1859 he joined the staff of the *Journal amusant*, but rarely appeared in its pages, and from this early period dates his almost constant poverty, which was frequently close to outright misery, and his gaudy bohemianism. Eventually, he attracted the attention of the publisher Polo, and his work began to appear in several of the latter's comic papers, *La Lune*, *L'Éclipse*, and *Le Hanneton;* soon he became very successful and attained something resembling real—albeit temporary—fame in the widely circulated *Charivari* and in *La Lune rousse*.

In addition to his work as a caricaturist, Gill had ambitions to be a serious painter and as early as 1865 had taken advantage of a cholera epidemic to profit by his brush, making portraits of the dead for their families.[4] Between 1875 and 1882 his work appeared in the Salon every year, but he apparently received no official awards of any kind, a circumstance which did a great deal, apparently, to heighten the melancholy which appeared early in his personality. The failure of one of his favorite projects, a diorama, contributed materially to his loss of confidence in himself and to his sense of failure. The diorama, which he conceived of as the crowning point of his career as journalist and caricaturist, was to assemble in a huge panorama portraits of many of the leading personalities of the time; it was displayed on the Place Vendôme in January 1881, but Gill could find no buyer for it, and the whole enterprise turned out to be a disaster for him.

Gill was also interested in literature, producing some three plays, writing verse, mostly light but occasionally serious, and frequenting literary as well as artistic circles. But nothing he did here either obtained much success, and in the 1870's his popularity even as caricaturist began to decline, and he slipped further and further into disillusionment and bitterness. His son died in infancy, he was very poor, the many comic papers on which he collaborated were short-lived, he drifted into nearly complete solitude toward the end of the decade, and in 1881 clear signs of insanity (he suffered from paresis) began to appear. He was first confined to the insane hospital at Charenton in October 1881, but was released, apparently cured, in January 1882. Immediately, he set to work on a painting, "Le Fou," which he hoped would win success at the Salon; according to reports he was driven mad again by disappointment at the placing of the canvas, but in any case he suffered a relapse and died at Charenton on the night of May 1-2, 1885.

Zola was very much aware of Gill's existence. He apparently met the caricaturist at the offices of Jules Vallès' *La Rue* in 1867, and from that time on an intermittent relationship between the two continued until Gill's death. The latter parodied Manet's portrait of Zola in *La Parodie* for June 9, 1868—*Le Salon pour rire* called it "the best portrait in the Salon"—and from that time on Gill caricatured Zola fairly frequently for many years—in *L'Éclipse* of 1875, *Les Hommes d'aujourd'hui* in 1878, twice in *La Lune rousse* in 1879, and so on—and also illustrated several of his novels in editions by Marpon and Marpon et Flammarion: *L'Assommoir, Nana, Le Ventre de Paris.* He also published separate drawings based on scenes from Zola's novels. During the first part of 1880 Gill and Zola were both on the staff of *Le Voltaire,* and one of the last drawings to be completed by the caricaturist before his death was a portrait of Zola published in *Le Monde illustré* of May 9, 1885.

The relationship between novelist and caricaturist was apparently not always easy, for Zola was difficult at times, according to the testimony of nearly all those who knew him, and the timid and hypersensitive Gill could also display inordinate pride and some arrogance; moreover, after 1882, he suffered from hallucinations and showed marked signs of "la folie des grandeurs," which often took the form of exaggerated ambition. Alphonse Daudet, his firm friend, remarked after Gill's death that he used to sketch "enormous paintings for giant frames, which his dreams exceeded even then." He had, according to Daudet, the ambition to become a great painter and to find his place "between Vollon and Courbet."[5]

Zola, then, must have known Gill well, and the newspaper articles on his death, as well as the publication of some of his letters in *Le Figaro* a few days later, both of which coincided almost exactly with the beginning of work on *L'Oeuvre,* must have recalled the memories of a relationship two decades old and the physiognomy of a man who still figures as one of the most striking personalities of his era. It is obvious that Gill's life and career—even his appearance, for his portraits (two of them by Zola's friend Fernand Desmoulin) show him to have been dark haired, mustached, and with strongly marked facial bones, like Claude—could have given him considerable material for *L'Oeuvre.* The probability is that they did, but it is no more than a probability.[6]

Claude Monet's name, like Manet's, was mentioned in connection with Claude Lantier very soon after the appearance of *L'Oeuvre.* Philippe Gille saw in the painter "a little of Monet,"[7] and since his time other critics and biographers of Zola have made the same observation. Hélène and Jean Adhémar think that the central figure of *L'Oeuvre* is "sometimes" Cézanne but also Monet,[8] and John Rewald declared that in Lantier's paintings details could be found which might have come from works of Cézanne, Manet, Monet, and others.[9] Patrick Brady also suggests Monet as a model, declaring that his life resembles Lantier's more closely than does Manet's and citing certain similarities of detail in the biographies and the careers of the real painter and the fictional artist.[10] Sven Lövgren also sees Monet in Lantier, but gives no evidence to support his position.[11] It is not impossible that Monet believed that he recognized himself in the traits of Claude for on April 5, 1886, he wrote Zola a letter indicating that he was troubled by possible interpretations of the novel which might be damaging to Manet's name or to "ours."[12] Lionello Venturi interprets the "ours," perhaps rightly, as an indication that Monet thought Zola was aiming at the Impressionists and at him specifically, and he adds that it was rumored that a duel between the novelist and the painter almost resulted.[13]

If Monet did recognize himself, at least partly, in the character of Claude Lantier, there seems to have been some reason. He and Zola had known each other for more than a decade and a half in 1885 (they both appear in a painting by Frédéric Bazille of 1869), and Hélène and Jean Adhémar remark on the close relationship which Zola and Monet enjoyed during the 1870's;[14] the novelist was clearly in a position to know some of the more intimate details of the painter's life. There is no proof that he used any of them, but certain aspects of Monet's biography make it seem quite possible that he did. Brady notes that Monet took a mistress in 1865 (Lantier's liaison with Christine begins in 1863), that he had a son by her in 1867 (Lantier's son is born in 1864), and that he married her in 1870 (Claude's marriage takes place toward the end of 1869). Brady also points out that Monet was unquestionably the leader of the Impressionist school, as Lantier was of the plein-air school, and that Monet attempted suicide in 1868.[15] He might have added that not only was Monet the head of a school but that the school took its name from one of his paintings, just as the plein-air school gets its name from Claude's first major effort. The circumstances surrounding the baptism of the "little band" seem to recall those surrounding the christening of Impressionism; after the explosion of laughter at the Salon des Refusés, where his "Plein-Air" has been the chief source of merriment, Claude cries: "Open air—that amuses them . . . all right, then, since they want open air, the open air school. . . . Eh? it was just among us, yesterday, it didn't exist outside of a few painters. And now that they've uttered the word, they've founded the school . . . Oh, *I'm* willing. The open air school it is!"[16] The real circumstances were not far different: after the first "independent" exhibition the reporter Louis Leroy of *Le Charivari,* referred to the painters represented as "Impressionnistes," using as his basis Monet's painting "Impression-soleil levant." The "independent" painters accepted the name, as the "little band" does in *L'Oeuvre,* and it endured, as plein air does in the novel.

Several other details could be added which may constitute something like evidence that Monet partly served as a model for Lantier. Claude as an adolescent in *Le Ventre de Paris* demonstrates a precocious talent which brings attention from those around him and which causes an enthusiast to support him in his early studies in painting. Monet, by his own declaration, was similarly gifted,[17] and like Claude he also found an enthusiast, a M. Gaudibert of Le Havre, who was willing to help him financially so that he could embark on a course of formal instruction. It is possible the Claude's early studies were in imitation of Monet's at the Atelier Gleyre, which he attended in 1862 with Bazille, Sisley, and Renoir, for Monet was surrounded from the first by young men of his own age, a "little band," while Cézanne, at the Atelier Suisse in 1861, had the older Pissarro as his chief companion, with Guillaumin and Oller, with whom Cézanne does not appear to have been intimate. Monet's physical appearance may have inspired Zola's portrait of Lantier, for Renoir's portrait of Monet, reproduced in the first volume of Venturi's *Archives de l'Impressionnisme,* makes him look about as Zola would have us imagine the fictional painter. Monet's awful and almost permanent poverty may also have been a source for Zola's depiction of Claude's last years, when his capital is exhausted and when he is living from hand to mouth by all kinds of tasks in the scullery of the art world. On several occasions Monet was in such tight circumstances that he could not even buy oils to continue his work, and his letters to various correspondents, including Zola, reveal a constant, pressing need for money.[18] Given his generally morose and pessimistic disposition, this harassing financial situation, worse apparently than that of any other Impressionist—which is saying a great deal, since poverty was endemic among them—might well have driven Monet to attempt suicide and might well have provided Zola with an important detail for the depiction of his Claude.

One curious event in Monet's life—his painting of his dead wife—may have been Zola's inspiration for making Claude paint his dead son. In 1875 Camille Monet fell fatally ill, but neither her illness nor the constant harassment of his landlord kept Monet from working hard, and, swept along by his inspiration (or rather, by the automatism of a life of effort), he could not help painting her. Monet's description of the incident, quoted by Georges Clemenceau, has a number of details in common with Zola's account of Claude's painting of his dead son.[19]

Many other details, all discovered by Rodolphe Walter, seem to point to a connection between Monet and Claude Lantier. For instance, "La Rivière," one of Monet's first impressionistic paintings, was executed at Gloton (near Bennecourt) in 1868; Zola and Cézanne were frequent visitors to Gloton. Moreover, Zola referred to a group of Monet's works as a "series" as early as 1868; Monet began to frequent the Café Guerbois in 1869; Christine Hallegrain, in the novel, seems to owe a good deal to Camille Monet, a bourgeois girl who gave up a secure existence to live with her painter; Monet and his mistress had one son; Monet spent three summers and four winters at Vétheuil, exactly the same length of time Claude spends at Bennecourt; Monet painted Camille scores of times and also painted his son; like Claude, Monet painted gardens, river banks, and snow.[20]

Temperamentally, Lantier shows marked resemblances to Claude Monet, at least in the incomplete way in which we know the latter. One of Lantier's chief traits is discouragement and pessimism about his talent, indeed, about the whole business of art and his aptitude for its practice. Monet was troubled by such doubts, and Gustave Geffroy's book on him contains a most significant letter from Octave Mirbeau to Monet in which reflections of Monet's inquietude, anxiety, self-doubt, and exaggerated perfectionism are to be seen in the reproaches Mirbeau addresses to him for the mental state to which he has allowed himself to descend, which led him to destroy a good many canvases. Mirbeau told him that he was "stricken by a malady, a madness, the malady of the 'always better.' "[21] Monet in his letters, some of them quoted by Geffroy, complains continually of his discouragement, his impotence, his inability to render what his eye perceives.[22] These letters all date from the 1890's, and Mirbeau's letter was probably written between 1885 and 1890, but there is no reason to think that this black and moody temperament was not the same in the years when Monet and Zola were close friends. If it was, it may have given Zola ideas for his painter. It is perhaps not without significance also that Monet was a constant researcher in the technique of art, forever seeking a "formula," as Lantier does, and not ceasing his inquiry into the nature of painting until death stopped his efforts.

But if Monet was often discouraged, often depressed and on the point of abandoning his art, he also possessed notable combative qualities and many of the traits of the leader—he had to have such qualities to make himself the recognized chief of any such band of difficult individualists as the Impressionists and to impose his vision and his techniques on a mocking public. Lionello Venturi says of him that he was endowed with a magnificent nature for a fighter, sincere, honest, and convinced that his path was the only right one. His strength, Venturi claims, arose from his power to "go to the very end, to sacrifice everything to the success of his ideal."[23] Like Lantier, Monet, in spite of his difficulties, remained "superbly indifferent to success and, notwithstanding his ambitions, showed himself preoccupied solely with his art."[24] Of all the true Impressionists, Monet seems to have yielded the least to popular taste, and here again he may have been a model for Lantier's intransigence. True, he did not share

Lantier's (and Manet's) belief that really to conquer one must conquer in the Salon, and no painter was more stoutly contemptuous of official honors than he, whereas Lantier seeks them all his life. But that detail aside, Monet could have been the source for the general attitude which Claude displays toward success and popularity, integrity and courage.

Some attempts have been made to link one or another of Monet's paintings to those of Lantier. Walter believes that the final "Apotheosis of Paris" owes something to Monet, and he sees the other works, save for "Plein-Air," as reflections of Monet's canvases, though he does not have much evidence to back his claim.[25] Hélène and Jean Adhémar claim that Lantier's painting of the Place du Carrousel is based on Monet's "Les Tuileries,"[26] while Marc Elder thinks it may be an imitation of Monet's "Le Boulevard des Capucines" of 1874.[27] Walter believes that the "Square des Batignolles" resembles Monet's studies of the Parc Monceau.[28] It might also be suggested that Monet's "Argenteuil—Les Déchargeurs de charbon" could be the source of one of the details of Lantier's last painting, longshoremen unloading plaster from a barge,[29] and the whole idea of this painting as a view of the Seine might have come from Monet's "Vue prise du Louvre." Brady advances the idea that Monet's preoccupation with rendering the color of the object according to the light of the moment finds an echo in Lantier's hesitancy before the "twenty different Cités" which he perceives,[30] but given Zola's devotion to Parisian scenes, it seems more likely that he was merely rendering the essence of a familiar experience of his own.

It is difficult to establish any close connection between the actual painting of Claude Monet and the fictional canvases of Claude Lantier, but Zola's *Salons* provide some fairly solid evidence that Monet may have been a model even though Zola may not have represented any of his canvases in the paintings of his hero. The very first note he strikes in first mentioning Monet in *Mon Salon* of 1866 is the note of force and realism; Monet is a "temperament" among the eunuchs of conventional, academic art; he is a realist, his painting opens a window on nature.[31] His canvases make no concessions to popular taste or to the conventional rendition of reality; it is tempting, Zola says, to make pretty colors with water, sky, and sun, and we must thank any painter who "consents to deprive himself of a certain success by painting waves as he has seen them, glaucous and dirty, and by putting on them a big rascal of a ship, dark, solidly built, coming out of the yards of the port."[32] The tone might be that of *L'Oeuvre* itself when Zola describes Claude's efforts to render the truth of nature as he sees it.

But more than simply a realist, Monet is a modernist,[33] and even more than a modernist, he is a painter of contemporary Paris, and his "Parisianism" takes forms which recall the paintings of Lantier's middle period: "Last year, they refused a painting of figures, ladies in light summer dresses, picking flowers in the paths of a garden; the sun fell straight down on the dazzling white skirts; the warm shade of a tree outlined on the paths, on the sun-drenched dresses, a wide gray sheet."[34]

Painter of Paris, modernist, realist—even a "naturalist," for Zola says he is that too[35]—Claude Monet is above all a revolutionary, like Claude Lantier. In 1876 Zola sees him in this role, and in 1880 he classes him among the "true revolutionaries in form."[36] But not only in form, for Monet's revolution operates mainly in the domain of light, as Claude Lantier's does also; in the "Russian" letter of 1876 Zola declares that "his brush is distinguished by an extraordinary brilliance,"[37] and in his final article on art, "Peinture" of 1896, he says that Monet and Pissarro were the first to study "these reflections and this decomposition of light" which he now sees all around him in the Salon.[38] Monet's revolutionary tendencies and originality make him the unquestioned leader of his school, just as the same qualities make Claude Lantier the founder and leader of the school of plein-air, and on two occasions, in 1876 and in 1880, Zola places Monet at the head of the movement of Impressionism.[39] But this leader remains obscure, as Claude Lantier remained unknown, and in 1880 Zola could say, as he might have said of Lantier, that it is astonishing that such a painter as Monet can still struggle obscurely after having exhibited at the Salon paintings which were so much discussed.[40] So obscure is he that Zola believes his canvases must have been received out of pure charity, as was Lantier's only successful attempt to force the Salon.[41]

Perhaps the most telling evidence that Zola might have fashioned his painter in the likeness of Monet comes in the evolution of Zola's own view of him, which closely parallels the change of his opinion regarding Manet and which recalls Sandoz' eventual change of attitude toward Lantier as he increasingly reveals a radical impotence. In his early and middle writings on art Zola had a very considerable faith in Monet's talent: endowed with a fine eye and a marvelous hand, Monet could not fail in his attempt to conquer.[42] Constantly in his later discussions of Monet there is assurance that such a talent cannot go unnoticed forever, that he will have his place alongside the modern masters. But as time passes, Zola grows less sure, and by 1880 he speaks quite openly to his Parisian public of his reservations regarding Monet: Monet's error lies in yielding too readily to the temptation of facile production, too many simple sketches have come out of his studio, and he is losing the taste for long and painful effort. He must work harder, study longer, and pay less attention to quick success.[43] True enough, the reproach is exactly the opposite of the reproach of impotence which could be brought against Claude Lantier—and it is not impossible that Zola imagined his situation as an opposite reflection of Monet's—but what is important is the disillusionment following on the early faith and the early prophecies of success and fame. With Monet, as with Manet, Zola passed through exactly the same phases as Sandoz does with Lantier; perhaps he is only a type-figure, a composite representing a disappointment close to Zola's heart.

Disillusioned or not Zola recognized that Monet, like Manet, was ultimately the victor in his struggle with the public and the critics, and in "Peinture," he said of him much of what he said of Manet and, in the novel, of Lantier: defeat but triumph, obscurity but influence, mockery but final domination.[44]

The evidence for Monet as a model, then, is good—not so good as that for Manet and even Zola, but still solid and fairly plentiful. It does not seem that Monet could have been Zola's chief source for the character of Claude Lantier (if he had a source at all); rather, his example contributed details, and the essential physiognomy of the fictional painter owes him little. Lantier, if not completely fictional, must be a composite figure, representing all the struggling artists Zola had known from the middle 1860's to about 1880; if he is a composite, Monet's contribution to his temperament, art theories, and career was only that of one of a large group. If we knew more of Monet's intimate life and had more details of his career, his early theories, his artistic likes and dislikes, we might be able to make a better case for him, but he is in somewhat the same position as Cézanne—too shadowy, too elusive, to provide much that is certain and solid.

No other figure, artistic or literary, offers real possibilities as a general model for Claude Lantier, but many others have been cited as possible models for individual details of his personality or of his life and artistic career. One of these is the painter Jules Holtzapfel, first cited by Rewald[45] and later by Niess.[46] Rewald suggested that Zola in describing Lantier's suicide was recalling an incident in the spring of 1866—a visit he made to the studio of a painter who killed himself because the Salon had refused his painting. Zola had discussed Holtzapfel's death in a short piece entitled "A Suicide," in *L'Événement* for April 19, 1866, and had put a good deal of blame on the jury, which had rejected one of his paintings, for the painter's death.

La Petite revue for May 10-12, 1866, included a supposed letter from Holzapfel which contained the phrases: "The members of the jury did not know me. I had neither friends nor enemies among them; they reject me, hence I have no talent. I must die." This letter was a forgery, according to Holtzapfel's friend Jules Ravel, who published a denial of its authenticity in *L'Événement* for May 6, 1866. Ravel explained the reasons for the painter's suicide and criticized the chroniclers for their use of it, claiming that they did so only as a means of attacking the jury, without taking into consideration the merit and the honorable reputation of its members. Ravel's letter and the details of Holtzapfel's death made Patrick Brady believe that the connection between Zola's article and Claude's suicide is much smaller than Niess made it seem; for him the only resemblance was that a painter kills himself before his unfinished work.[47]

But the resemblance is not a minor one, and Holtzapfel's death may well have been the incident which led Zola to bring Claude Lantier to such a tragic end. Holtzapfel's death stirred up a storm which Zola would not have been likely to forget, even twenty years later, when he composed *L'Oeuvre*. The jury of the Salon of 1866 had apparently been very harsh in its rejections, and when the news of the suicide was published in the newspapers it added to the fury of the artists, who proceeded to a fierce attack on the members of the jury, using their friends among the newspaper reporters and columnists and even enlisting a senator, the eccentric Marquis de Boissy, who published a diatribe against the "jury of assassins" and carried the matter to the floor of the senate, where he demanded a new Salon des Refusés. Brady maintains that the disclaimer by Ravel, Holtzapfel's friend, was directed especially at Zola, but this is not certain, for Ravel never mentioned Zola, and there is a fair chance that Ravel had someone quite different in mind—Édouard Manet himself. A. Tabarant reported that Manet was accused in some quarters of having instigated the articles on Holtzapfel's death out of pure rancor for having been rejected by the jury of 1866.[48] Whether this is true or not, the Holtzapfel incident made a tremendous stir in the newspapers in 1866, just at the time when Zola was most active in art criticism, and the strong possibility exists that he recalled the event as he described Claude's tragic end before his apotheosis of the Seine and sex.

Of course, Zola had no need to depend on Holtzapfel's suicide as inspiration for the closing scenes of *L'Oeuvre*, for a good many artists might well have served him here. The history of art in the nineteenth century records a considerable number of suicides, any of which Zola might have known about through newspapers, word of mouth accounts, or his own activities as a reporter. He could have had in mind, for instance, the nearly anonymous young Alexandre, who had been a *rapin* in Édouard Manet's studio and who had posed for his "Le Gamin aux cerises." Alexandre—biographical details are almost entirely lacking—was, according to Ernest Vizetelly, who first suggested him as a model, a moody young fellow with artistic ambitions, who, when he saw that they were to remain unsatisfied, hanged himself.[49] Georges Bataille believes that the suicide resulted from a reprimand which Alexandre received from Manet,[50] but whatever the circumstances of his death Zola could have known about them either through Manet or from Baudelaire's story "La Corde," where Alexandre's death is recounted in semifictional form. Baudelaire's tale appeared in *Le Figaro* for February 7, 1864, then in *L'Artiste,* and finally in *Le Spleen de Paris.* There is no way of examining the probability of Alexandre's role as model for Lantier's suicide, for he is completely lost in obscurity, and we have no word from Zola that he even knew of the case. But Vizetelly had excellent sources of information and his suggestion is not to be taken lightly.

Another possibility from Zola's past is the painter Charles Marchal, who killed himself in the spring of 1877 and whose death was the subject of one of Zola's "Notes parisiennes" in *Le Sémaphore de Marseille* (April 4, 1877). Marchal had been a fairly well-known artist in Paris and his death caused general surprise, for he had the reputation of a bon vivant, and he had been fairly treated by the newspapers. Zola's account of his suicide does not contain many details which link it with Lantier's death. But Zola had no need to look far for examples of suicides. The years just before 1885 were apparently extremely difficult for nearly all artists save the accepted, patented, and conventional painters and sculptors of the Beaux-Arts tendency, and the art chronicle of the time is full of accounts of deep poverty, misery, near-starvation, and general hopelessness. The record of the Impressionists' sufferings is striking—nearly all of them had the greatest difficulty in keeping body and soul together—and their difficulties seem characteristic of the hardship that many obscure painters endured for years before the new tendencies were accepted by the public. Suicides in the 1880's were fairly frequent, perhaps because of a crisis in the art market (mentioned by Zola in his correspondence in *Le Sémaphore de Marseille* after 1877 and also toward the end of *L'Oeuvre*) brought on in part by the crash of the huge Union Générale in 1882 and the resulting near-catastrophe in French economic life. Furthermore, a tax levied by the American Congress on art imports in 1881 had serious effects in France; in 1885 *Le Courrier de l'art* reported that French art exports had declined from more than nine million francs in 1882 to less than three and one-half million in 1884.[51] Perhaps Zola, in causing

Claude to die by his own hand, was rendering not so much the fact of a single life but a tendency which he saw in the art world around him. He had before him, for instance, two striking examples from the year 1884 alone, and it is quite possible that Claude's death is in effect a copy of one of these. In May 1884 the *Chronique des arts et de la curiosité* reported the death of the sculptor Pierre Richard, who had hanged himself after being rejected by the Salon.[52] The circumstances are not so far from those of the death of Claude Lantier to make it impossible that Zola should think of Richard's suicide, but there is no evidence beyond the death itself to link it with the novel.

Another sculptor, Frédéric Combarieu, also might have provided Zola with the idea for Lantier's suicide. Combarieu, who was born in 1834, had competed unsuccessfully for the Prix de Rome in 1864 and, after an undistinguished career, had apparently pinned his hopes for fame on the final version of a statue of Juvenal which received an honorable mention when it was shown in plaster in 1878. When he showed it in final form in 1884 he did not get the medal which he had anticipated, and in despair and chagrin killed himself in his studio in July 1884.[53] But as with the others who have been cited as possible sources of Lantier's suicide before his unfinished canvas, there is no proof that Zola called on the final events of Combarieu's life for the climactic scene of his novel and no evidence that he even knew of them. It remains possible, though, that he did and that they gave him the idea for unraveling his plot in the most tragic way possible.

Another detail of the novel, Claude's painting of his dead son, has been the subject of speculation and has led some critics to believe that a real portrait might have been Zola's point of departure. As has been said, it is not impossible that Claude Monet's painting of the dead Camille was the source here, but another possibility is a canvas by the comparatively unknown painter Albert Dubois-Pillet. An army officer by profession, he was born in 1845 and died in 1890 at Le Puy, where he had been stationed and where he carried on his avocation of painting. A kind of guerrilla fighter for Impressionism and one of the founders of the Société des artistes indépendants, Dubois-Pillet, who was largely self-taught, like Claude Lantier, but who had studied with Couture, had shown several paintings, some of them of Parisian scenes, like his "Quai de Bercy à Paris," in the expositions of the Artistes indépendants before his transfer to Le Puy. Among these works was a painting of a dead child apparently done in 1881 and shown at the Indépendant exposition in the Tuileries gardens in 1884. The portrait, which now hangs in the Musée Crozatier at Le Puy and which is reproduced in Sven Lövgren's *The Genesis of Modernism,* displays a treatment which is, in Lövgren's words, "unsentimental and realistic, with a pronounced emphasis on the material, like a still-life by Manet."[54] It is exactly, as Lövgren points out, the kind of painting which may well have aroused Zola's "fantasy" and satisfied his "demand for epic naturalism."[55] The possibility is certainly strong that Zola knew this work or had heard of it, but again there is nothing but a curious parallel of circumstances to justify us in believing in a filiation between reality and fiction.

It is nearly certain, however, that another scene of *L'Oeuvre*, Claude Lantier's lonely funeral, was based on a real incident from Zola's own experience, the exhumation of Edmond Duranty's remains and their interment in the cemetery of Père Lachaise. Maurice LeBlond, in the notes to his edition of *L'Oeuvre*, declares[56] that Zola had called upon his memories of Duranty's funeral in 1880 for details of the scene of his fictional painter's funeral, but Tabary points out that a numerous group was in attendance then, in contrast to the pitifully small cortege of Claude's friends, that the funeral expenses were met by the Société des Gens de Lettres, that three speeches were given over Duranty's grave, and that Duranty was buried at St. Ouen cemetery in April, while Claude is buried in November, details which would make it seem impossible that Zola had this particular event in mind. Tabary thinks, apparently correctly, that Zola's memory goes back to the exhumation of Duranty's remains and their transfer to the cemetery of Père Lachaise, December 16, 1885.[57] Brady points out, to further the connection with Claude Lantier, that Zola did not believe that Duranty had found his "formula" any more than Claude had and that Christine's unhappy fate after Claude's death seems to reflect the reality of the situation in which Duranty's mistress found herself when her protector died. All in all, it seems almost beyond doubt that Duranty's figure did contribute something to the formation of Claude's character and career, and it certainly seems true that his life did provide one striking scene for the novel, though it would be difficult in the extreme to define his place in the gallery of possible models.

Still another detail may come from reality, though there is no indication whatsoever that Zola was aware of the incident in question. Sven Lövgren points out that the painter Louis Anquetin passed through a phase which resembles Claude's elaboration of his final painting: in 1884 Anquetin was working on a genre painting, "Intérieur de chez Bruant," when Édouard Dujardin persuaded him to introduce a symbolic figure into his otherwise realistic canvas. Anquetin, like Claude, was unable to reconcile realism and symbolism and at last cut up the "cartons" and put away the sketches. Certainly, the detail seems likely as a starting point for Claude's struggles, but whether or not Zola knew of it is not susceptible of investigation for documents are completely lacking.[58]

Nearly a dozen other figures from the art world have been proposed, more or less seriously, as whole or partial models for Lantier, but none seems to offer enough similarities, either personally or intellectually, with Zola's fictional painter to permit anything like valid conclusions. Among the better-known Impressionists, Renoir and Pissarro have been cited, sometimes with no supporting evidence; then there are some less illustrious figures, Frédéric Bazille, Cézanne's friend Emperaire, Jongkind, Marcellin Desboutin, Emile Bellot, Léon Robert, François-Germain-Léopold Tabar, and one or two rank "outsiders" such as J. M. W. Turner and Diderot's friend Mme Therbouche. It is difficult to believe that any of them could have been a general model for Claude Lantier, but it is not impossible that the life and career of one or more of them may have given Zola ideas for his novel and that he might have incorporated some of their theories on art in the philosophy which he attributes to Claude.

Renoir seems only a dim possibility as a model for Lantier, though Lövgren thinks it "obvious" that Zola borrowed traits from him for his fictional artist. Only one or two details from his life might have been the source of details in the life of Lantier, his painting of blinds in order to maintain himself, his deep poverty for some years, his early admiration for Delacroix, his numerous unfinished canvases; and there is little evidence that his personality could have been interpreted by Zola in such a way as to give rise to the personality of Claude, for Renoir appears to have been quite different, temperamentally, from the manic-depressive fictional figure, although it is true that when he was a young man he displayed a very fantastic, uncertain, and contradictory nature. Nor does Zola say enough about Renoir in his *Salons* to permit us to draw any real conclusions as to his feelings about his art or his theories. He does remark on Renoir's modernism[59] and on his "range of light tones,"[60] but nowhere in the *Salons* is there any extended discussion of Renoir as either painter or theorist. But in *Le Naturalisme au Salon,* of 1880, Zola does say one or two things about Renoir which might indicate that he borrowed at least one detail of Claude's career from Renoir's experience, his persistence in attempting to force the official Salon as the only forum where a true conquest could be established. Speaking of the Impressionists' independent exhibitions of the late 1870's and early 1880's, he comments on the reasons which brought them about—the persistent refusal of the jury to accept them, except occasionally, the bad faith of the administration which caused their works to be hung disadvantageously —and then on the gradual breakup of these expositions because of the differing theories of the individual Impressionists and their realization that independent showings were not advancing their cause. He adds that Renoir was the first to realize that no paintings would be sold at the independent expositions, so he decided to send his works to the Salon, an act which made the Impressionists call him a renegade, but which Zola finds entirely reasonable.[61] It was not necessary for Zola to remember this detail of Renoir's career to create Claude's continuing desire to triumph officially, for he might have gotten it from Manet or from his own desire for entrance into the Académie. But perhaps it was Renoir's example which inspired this detail of Claude's life after all, and if this is so, then Renoir's contribution to the formation of the fictional artist is not a small one.

There is another kind of evidence, this one less certain, which may also support some kind of a connection between Renoir and Lantier. It is provided in an article "L'Art décoratif contemporain," published in *L'Impressionniste* on April 28, 1877. The article, signed "Un Peintre," is attributed to Renoir by Lionello Venturi, and though there is no indication that Zola knew of it, its contents make it seem possible that it inspired him with some of the artistic theories which Claude Lantier expresses in the course of the novel. Generally, the article advances the thesis that modernism is the only hope in the world of art and the author finds that the influence of the dead past, in the form of the teachings of the Ecole des Beaux-Arts, has corrupted all the arts. The painter's praise of the Halles as the only really modern, functional building in Paris and his belief that the arts must move forward together on a broad front also appear at one time or another in *L'Oeuvre,* and it is possible, though perhaps not probable, that Zola had read and remembered them or that he had some copies of *L'Impressionniste*[62] in his study which he consulted for ideas for his novel. Add to this that Renoir considered himself to be at least partly a product of the double influence of Courbet and Delacroix, that his art education was not academic (he developed fairly freely in Gleyre's studio), that he changed his manner radically in the early 1880's, and that he was seemingly as obsessed with female flesh as Claude himself, and it is apparent that more than a fair case can be made for Renoir as one of Claude's originals. But at the very best Renoir was surely not *the* model for Lantier; he may have figured in Zola's memories, on which he obviously constructed the painter, but it was probably only as a background figure, a typical suffering painter of the 1860's and 1870's.[63]

Much the same could be said of Camille Pissarro. Philippe Gille, who knew Pissarro, as he did most of the Impressionists and Zola too, believed that he saw "a little" of "Pizarro" in Lantier, along with "a little" of Cézanne and Monet, but no other critic or historian mentions him as a possibility. Nevertheless, a kind of case can be made for him, as it can for Renoir, because numerous details from his life and career resemble those from Claude Lantier's. One is struck particularly by Pissarro's fearful poverty, which dogged him most of his life and which recalls the misery into which Claude and Christine sink as their capital dwindles and Claude finds only failure. Nearly all the Impressionists were poor at some period or other of their careers, but Pissarro seems to have suffered more than any of them save Monet. To Pissarro's poverty and long struggle for success might be added that he was driven, like Renoir and Lantier, to paint blinds for a living at one point in his career, that he spent his life searching for a satisfactory "formula," that he changed his style radically in midcareer, that he painted many scenes of Paris, that he was a terrible revolutionary and a fearsome enemy of the bourgeoisie (actually, Pissarro had tendencies toward political anarchism, which may be rendered in attenuated form by Claude's strongly antisocial tendencies). It is possible, too, that Zola had Pissarro, not Manet or Monet, in mind when he made Lantier the founder and chief aesthetician of the school of plein-air. Monet was something of an "official" leader of Impressionism for a time before the breakup of the school, but his leadership was probably based on his personal qualities of energy and combativeness and on his talent in carrying out the Impressionist theory, not on his abilities as aesthetician. It is quite possible that Pissarro was the man of ideas in the group and the artist who really elaborated the Impressionist theory, for there is no question that he taught Cézanne the true fundamentals of his art in the early 1870's and that Cézanne always regarded his artistic principles as the very principles of Impressionism itself.[64] The difficulty is, of course, that we know too little of Pissarro's life—he is even more elusive and shadowy than Monet or Renoir—and almost nothing of his theories as he elaborated them in the 1870's, when he was Cézanne's mentor and companion.

Zola's *Salons* do not give much testimony which might serve in establishing a case for Pissarro as model for Lantier. Zola knew him well,[65] and what he said of him in his writings on art bears the mark of friendship and of sincere admiration, but nonetheless there is little in the way of solid evidence. The references to him in the *Salons* contain indications that Zola saw Pissarro in the same light as he saw the other revolutionary Impressionists—and Lantier also—but their content is not very conclusive.

Clearly enough, some of the things Zola said of Pissarro could apply to Claude Lantier, but too many elements in his career preclude a real filiation. He was not a modernist as Zola understood the term; he was chiefly a landscape artist and not a true urban "naturalist"; he did not become a "symbolist" and was never the leader of the group in which he found himself, though indeed he might have been its best aesthetician and its real pioneer. It does not seem that he was anything like a general model, and it is significant that he did not see himself as represented in the novel and did not believe that it would do the Impressionists any harm, as Monet feared it might. *L'Oeuvre* was for him, according to a letter he wrote Monet, "a not very successful novel by the author of *L'Assommoir* and *Germinal,* that's all."[66]

Edgar Degas offers somewhat the same case. His name has not been suggested in the search for Lantier's original, but it is not impossible that Zola had him in mind as he gave Claude certain attributes. Degas was the most independent of men, it appears, a true solitary and so determined to maintain his individuality that he was thought of, toward the beginning and middle of the 1880's, as something of a troublemaker, just as Claude is regarded as he fails to fulfill the promise of his youth. Degas was a painter who liked to work from memory, as Lantier finally does in elaborating his final painting, an extreme perfectionist and an absolutely tireless worker. Like Lantier too he was of somewhat morose disposition, at least in his middle and later years, and about the time of *L'Oeuvre* was given to deep crises of despair and self-doubt, many of which are reflected in his letters.[67] But of course fits of depression must have been common enough among the painters whom Zola knew, given their general lack of success until about the time of *L'Oeuvre,* and there was no especial reason why Zola should have turned to Degas for an example of this kind of despair and self-denigration. But there is one aspect of Degas' character which does not seem to have a parallel in any other painter Zola knew and which may have provided him with one of the most effective details of Lantier's personality and outlook—the kind of misogyny which makes him regard Christine's nude body as not much more than an interesting arrangement of planes and lights. As Claude grows older and takes his mistress-wife more and more for granted, his love for female flesh in a kind of abstract, completely painterly sense becomes more and more pronounced, and as she poses for him he tends more and more to ignore the woman in her and to see her only as an object. Some of his comments to her as she poses are filled with such a ferocious objectivity and such a cold detachment that the posing sessions become a torture, as she receives from his own lips the final proof that his love is dead. It is not improbable that Degas provided Zola with this aspect of his character, for it is known that the crusty bachelor reacted to his nude models in almost the same way as Lantier does to Christine, once all passion was spent. Nearly everyone who has treated Degas at length mentions that he took a wry pleasure in arranging his nudes in anything but dignified positions and situations—in tubs, stooping, squatting, and so on—and that his contemptuous treatment of the young girls who posed for him gratified a kind of rancor he seemed to feel against the whole feminine sex. Claude's detached observation of Christine stems essentially from his devotion to the ideal woman he carries within his mind, but it still is not impossible that Degas' contempt and scorn for the weak creatures he saw before him gave Zola the idea for Claude's trait.

Zola's *Salons* offer almost nothing which could be used as evidence that he ever thought of Degas as a general model for Lantier. The probability seems to be that Degas may have figured in Zola's memories of the art world as he planned *L'Oeuvre,* but the painter's style, subject matter, and scope completely disqualify him as anything like a general model for the rough, crude Lantier, the romantic realist. Zola's remark to Huysmans that Degas was only a "constipé du plus joli talent" sums up his attitude toward the artist who lived at the ballet and in the dressing rooms of the ballerinas; no one of Degas' leanings could have inspired him to create Claude Lantier.

Ambroise Vollard, the prolific and unreliable biographer of the Impressionists, suggests that Claude Lantier is "drawn in part from Cézanne, and in part from another of the group of Impressionist painters, Bazille, who was killed in the Franco-Prussian war."[68] As usual, Vollard gives no evidence to support this contention, and none seems to be available. Bazille was one of Zola's early friends in Paris,[69] but there is absolutely nothing in their relationship, so far as it is known, or in Bazille's character, in the few details which have come down to us, to justify the claim that he had anything to do with the construction of the figure of Claude Lantier. Bazille may figure as a model in *L'Oeuvre,* but it is surely not as model for the failure; if he is present at all, it is in the figure of Gagnière.

Another such suggestion, wholly beyond proof as matters stand, is the idea advanced by E. A. Vizetelly that Claude was a kind of copy of the obscure painter François-Germain-Léopold Tabar. Vizetelly thinks it likely that Zola met Tabar at about the time he met Manet and describes him as "a born colourist, whom Delacroix had favored and helped." Tabar, he says, produced one "striking and almost perfect painting," a "Saint Sebastian," but then spent the rest of his life in ineffectual efforts to repeat his success. He was an admirable sketcher, Vizetelly says, but could never properly finish a canvas; looked upon for years as the coming great man, he spent much of his time dreaming of producing one colossal work until, finally, having accomplished nothing, he died in misery. "So much of his story corresponds with that of Zola's novel, *L'Oeuvre*, that it seems certain the author must have met the unfortunate painter, and have blended his life with that of Cézanne and others when preparing his study on the art world of Paris."[70] Armand Lanoux agrees with Vizetelly that Tabar was a partial model for Zola's painter, but like his predecessor he gives nothing but circumstantial evidence to back the claim.[71]

The difficulty is that Tabar, about whom some anecdotes must have circulated at the time of his death in 1869 (he was born in 1818) and which Zola may have heard, was too little known to have left anything in the way of a complete record either of his life or career. Tabar was an admirer and apparently something of a disciple of Courbet,[72] but nothing else of any consequence can be added which might establish him as a model. In spite of the vagueness of our knowledge of him, he remains a real possibility—Vizetelly is a powerful guarantor, with his direct access to Zola—which some of the other men suggested do not, and if more biographical information on him could be discovered, or if any connection between him and Zola could be found, an interesting case could be made.

Another figure of the same type is Émile Bellot, also proposed by Vizetelly, who does not actually name him but who says that "the lives of Cézanne and Manet, as well as that of a certain dissolute engraver, who sat for the latter's famous picture "Le Bon Bock," suggested to M. Zola the novel which he has called *L'Oeuvre*."[73] Vizetelly also believes that Christine Hallegrain was modeled on Bellot's wife, but gives no details to support the contention. So little is known of Bellot that it is impossible to establish any case for him as a model.

Jean Vinchon proposes Marcellin Desboutin, and with some reason.[74] Desboutin, who sat for Manet's "L'Artiste" and who was, according to Huysmans, "mercilessly rejected" by each succeeding Salon jury,[75] offers real possibilities, though some elements of his biography make it seem unlikely that Zola took anything more than details from his life and career. He was born in 1823 and died in the same year as did Zola, studied with Couture, became almost the type of the bohemian painter, imprudently wasting his patrimony and, finally, painting to keep alive. Desboutin lived in the rue Breda, "where he camped at the end of a court on the first floor. This lodging was low, dark, sad; a single room served as bedroom and studio, with a kitchen in a closet."[76] Desboutin, who was a frequenter of Montmartre cafes and a "pillar" of La Nouvelle Athènes, was not recognized for many years, but the "indépendants" began to perceive the value of his work and gradually sought out his engravings until toward the end of his life he enjoyed some success. Georges Lafenestre, official chronicler of the Salons, says of him that in manners and dress he was "one of the last and most aggressive romantics."[77] Desboutin, who sat for Degas as well as for Manet, executed two portraits of Zola. One of these may be the origin of Claude's portrait of Sandoz in "Plein-Air," for it shows Zola turned to the right, with his head leaning on his left hand, which is very much in evidence. It will be recalled that the hand of the man in "Plein-Air" is emphasized by Zola as being especially well executed. Zola apparently knew Desboutin well—in 1879 Desboutin referred to himself as "your old friend"[78]—and admired his work, for he wrote a preface to the *Catalogue de l'oeuvre gravé de Marcellin Desboutin* (Durand-Ruel, 1889), but we have nothing more than these details to establish a relation. It is true that the details are numerous and certainly more significant than in the case of some of the other originals suggested.

Emile Solari, son of Zola's close friend and himself Zola's godson, declares that the painter Léon Robert, with Cézanne, Guillemet, Manet, his own father, Philippe Solari, "have fragments of themselves in the pages of this book."[79] He almost certainly means that Cézanne and Manet were models for Lantier, that Guillemet was part of the model for Fagerolles, and that Philippe Solari was at least part of the original on whom the fictional sculptor Mahoudeau was based. But he does not describe the role of Léon Robert, whom he calls "an obscure painter and very much of an artist." Possibly, he intended that we should understand that Robert also figured as a partial model for Claude. It is impossible to trace this suggestion; there was a genre painter named Léon Robert and a landscape artist also, both contemporaries of Zola, and there is no way of telling which one Solari means.

Another possibility, though not a very likely one, is Cézanne's strange friend Achille Emperaire. It is not impossible that it was from the bizarre and erotic work of Emperaire that Zola got the idea for the strongly marked sensual aspects of Claude's paintings, for Emperaire, a dwarf, created paintings which were characterized by an inordinate emphasis on the sexual aspects of feminine beauty. According to Henri Perruchot, Emperaire had only one love, beauty, and especially beauty in the form of feminine flesh.[80] Emperaire, an impecunious idealist somewhat like Claude, could, however, have provided no more than a trait for the fictional painter, albeit a most important one. But Zola had no need to turn to Emperaire or to the young Cézanne for the idea of self-liberation in art—he knew it only too well at first hand.

Equally possible, although equally difficult to establish with any certainty, is Hemmings' suggestion that Johan-Barthold Jongkind may have also been one of the gallery of painters on whom Zola called as he constructed his imaginary artist. Zola met Jongkind through Philippe Solari, who wrote him in 1871, suggesting that he visit the painter and write an article on him in which he might mention Solari's just finished statue of Jongkind. Zola, who had written on Jongkind in his *Salon* of 1868, obliged Solari, and the article on Jongkind's work appeared in *La Cloche* for January 24, 1872 (it is in the volume of *Mélanges* of Zola's *Oeuvres complètes*). On his visit to Jongkind, Zola was especially struck by the numerous Parisian scenes in oils, water colors, and sketches which the painter had created, and he evidently saw in him something like a kindred spirit, another "naturalist" and modernist, and it is possible that the Parisian and modernist philosophy of *L'Oeuvre* had its origin in Jongkind's theories and works.

Certainly, the details of Jongkind's career seem to justify some such conclusion. Like Claude, he had considerable difficulty in liberating himself from the influence of his masters; like Claude, he came to paint largely from memory, without theory, guided by instinct only; like him, he painted many scenes of Paris; and just as Claude was the darling of the dealer Malgras, Jongkind was an early favorite of *père* Martin. But his early career was a long struggle against academic conventionalism, and the result of his new researches was that he was constantly and ruthlessly rejected by the Salon and could make his only notable public appearance at the Salon des Refusés. So rigorous was the jury toward him, indeed, that after 1872 he stopped sending canvases to the Salon, and found no recognition at all until the Impressionists, who saw in him a precursor and a fellow spirit of Turner's, laid the foundation for his later reputation. Jongkind was always very poor, living in constant and terrible difficulties, and the strain of poverty, along with efforts for recognition, brought him to a nervous breakdown in 1860; he apparently never completely recovered, suffering for years from various kinds of mental troubles, so that those who knew him sometimes thought him completely mad. After 1880 Jongkind left Paris and spent many years living in isolation in the country among the peasants. Is he Claude? The chances are that somewhere in Zola's mind, as he thought of his artist, the figure of Jongkind kept reappearing.

And still the list is not exhausted. Edmond de Goncourt declares that Claude's delirium and madness were imitated by Zola from the last years of Turner,[81] but there is so little evidence to support such a claim as to make it appear that Goncourt was only trying to back his contention that *L'Oeuvre* was a poor pastiche of *Manette Salomon,* in which the final phase of Coriolis' career seems to recall Turner's late evolution. And what of the claim by the journalist Robert Charvay that Claude Lantier is "astonishingly" like the real silhouette of Diderot's Mme Therbouche? In an article of May 6, 1886, Charvay, while discussing the connections between Diderot's aesthetic and Zola's as expressed in *L'Oeuvre,* had occasion to comment at some length on the possibility that the eighteenth-century eccentric was indeed Zola's source; he stresses the similarities of incomplete genius, the same horror of any concession, the same failure to "execute" properly, the same enthusiasm and the same despair, the same suicide.[82]

But perhaps the original of Claude Lantier was none of the men or women, real or fictional, who have been suggested or whose personalities, artistic accomplishments, or careers make it seem likely or possible that Zola called on them for the original idea for his fictional painter. Perhaps Claude is a literary portrait, much embellished, of someone of whom we have never heard and shall never hear, perhaps he was a composite of many artists, writers, and sculptors, perhaps he was almost wholly imaginary. The possibilities are legion, and a solution to the problem will never be found until we have some word from Zola's pen itself, some lost letter, some page of notes. Until that word appears we may speculate, we shall never know.

But it might not be useless to recall that Claude Lantier is, after all, a member of the *Rougon-Macquart* family, that he is a literary figure, a fictional figure, and that as such he may well have arisen from Zola's imagination unaided and unfathered.

IX

The Novel—Its Genesis and Development

Like the other novels of the *Rougon-Macquart* series, *L'Oeuvre* was the result of an elaborate preparation. The complete *Dossier* of the novel, now in the Bibliothèque Nationale (Département des Manuscrits, Nouvelles acquisitions françaises, 10316), includes the manucript of the work itself, a brief plan by chapters, two sets of more detailed plans by chapters, a series of *Personnages,* that is, more or less developed character sketches of the personae of the novel, a long *Ébauche,* or first draft, and a voluminous collection of notes of various kinds. All the pages of the *Dossier,* except for a letter addressed to Zola, are in Zola's own hand.

Though the various elements of the *Dossier* appear in the above order and are numbered in Zola's hand in that order, it is not certain that they were so composed. The notes seem to have been Zola's first order of business, probably followed by the *Personnages* and then the *Ébauche,* for the latter contains page references and other references to both notes and *Personnages.* After completing the *Ébauche* Zola composed the short plans by chapter, which were followed by the detailed plans (which appear in the *Dossier* in inverted order, the plans appearing first having been composed last). From these detailed plans and the notes he composed the novel.[1]

The *Ébauche,* comprising feuillets 261-318, is in some ways the most interesting and important part of the whole *Dossier,* for it represents the first conception of the novel as novel, as distinct from mere project. It is quite clear that Zola was "thinking aloud" as he composed the *Ébauche,* noting down ideas as they came to him *currente calamo,* creating incidents, details, characters, seeking a philosophy and themes for the work, groping, contradicting himself, revising, and refining. Apparently, he was not in the habit of using the *Ébauche* for the actual purposes of composition, so its connection with the final text is not always close, though sometimes it is very close indeed. But so varying is Zola's practice in this regard that it is impossible to draw any general conclusions about the relationship of the *Ébauche* to his final text save these: the *Ébauche* contains no major incident, scene, or character which does not appear in the novel, in one form or another, but some events, scenes, and characters of the novel do not appear in the *Ébauche*. These are the product of the *Personnages* and of the notes.

In the *Ébauche* Zola put most of his effort to creating the fundamentals of the main characters who were to animate his novel; all the chief figures of the book are here, though sometimes in different form than in the novel itself, and certainly the principal interest of the *Ébauche* lies in the people it presents, not in the events it sketches. It is notable that at this early stage of composition, all the characters who appear are considered as types, each representing some main tendency of humanity or, more frequently, some main aspect of the art world of the 1870's and 1880's, and only three of them, Claude, Bongrand, and Gagnière, appear with the names used in *L'Oeuvre*. Zola himself is there, though not yet named Sandoz and not identified exactly as to profession (journalist and novelist are his choices here) and with his role left very vague; it is clear almost from the outset of the *Ébauche* that some kind of autobiographical intention was basic in Zola's earliest conception of the novel. Claude, equally vague and rudimentary, is depicted as unstable, a failure, and, eventually, a suicide, but throughout the *Ébauche*—and he appears very frequently—he seems to be conceived as a fairly classic case of an artist caught in a struggle between a human love and a professional passion; nowhere is there any hint that he will actually fall in love with his painted creature, nowhere is there any indication that *L'Oeuvre* is to become a "naturalistic" version of the Pygmalion legend. Not only is there no real description of his personality, but we see little here of his ideas and theories in art and little of his situation in the art world of the time, save an indication that he is to be an Impressionist. Zola is not even clear as to the source of his failure, citing a half-dozen causes, some of them contradicting the others. Christine's (she is not yet named in the *Ébauche*) evolution is the most interesting single aspect of this first draft; she evolves, it will be remembered,[2] from an original and very vague figure which Zola conceived at the start of his preliminary work; her gradual emergence and separation from the "temptress" figure, later Irma Bécot, and from the "ideal" figure, who later appears as the central nude of each of Claude's two large canvases, is an enlightening glimpse into Zola's creative methods and, much more importantly, into his psyche in the middle years of his productive life.

In addition to these primordial figures, Zola began his work on *L'Oeuvre* with two type figures in mind, Valabrègue, who apparently seemed to him to symbolize radical failure in art, not the flawed genius of Claude, and whom he eventually employed as a source for both Mahoudeau and Chaîne, though in each of these cases he also called on other models, Solari and Chaillan, both named in the *Ébauche;* and Gervex, symbol of the false and dishonest artist, giving rise, of course, to the figure of Fagerolles in the novel. These two men, both of them Zola's acquaintances, were as fundamental to the development of the novel as Claude or Sandoz. But almost immediately after posing these two original type figures for his "band," Zola added two more, Alexis, whose role is almost wholly undefined here and who appears as not much more than a shadow, and Baille, whose role is sketched in considerable detail and who appears with the same physiognomy and passes through the same vicissitudes as he does in *L'Oeuvre.* Only two fictional figures appear at any length, Bongrand, who is less dignified here than in his finished form and whose role seems to have been planned as more important than it actually turned out to be, and Gagnière, conceived from the beginning in the vague terms which prevail in the novel and already cast in his role as painter musician. But there is no real appearance of a good many of the minor characters, Mathilde Jabouille, for instance, or Sandoz' wife, or any of the art dealers; all these supernumeraries were evidently not part of the original conception and owe their existence to the *Personnages,* where Zola really set about creating a full cast.

Nor does the *Ébauche* contain anything like an attempt at plot construction. True enough, the idea of Claude's failure and suicide is there, doubled by the idea of the rivalry of woman and art—even the detail of the dead child sketched by Claude is present—but there is no connection between the episodes, which evidently presented themselves to Zola in haphazard fashion. The very first pages of the *Ébauche* make it seem that the original germ of the novel contained only the idea of Claude's failure in art, but it is true that the second plot, the rivalry of woman and art, is also introduced very early, largely perhaps because of Zola's insistence that Claude be a man of passion; he was to "set fire to the whole book," so Zola thought physical passion necessary alongside the artistic passion; and then too he obviously needed some dramatic events for the novel and could not find enough of them in the artist's attempts to master his medium, so turned to woman and her conflict with the creations of Claude's spirit.

Many of the important scenes of the novel are either not present at all in the *Ébauche* or are barely indicated, with no hint of their later value. The long and crucial Bennecourt episode is only suggested, as are the Salon scenes and the dinners at Sandoz' various houses. Nothing is said about two of the best scenes in the novel, the collapse of Mahoudeau's statue and the *nuit de charrette* of the young architects, and there is nothing save the slightest hint of the jury scene, where acceptance of Claude's painting is taken as Fagerolles' benevolence. But on the other hand, another of the best and most striking scenes, Claude's encounter with Christine in the first chapter, is present in some detail and in something very much like the form it was to take in the novel.

About the same is true of the minor details: some are present in the *Ébauche,* some are not, and there is no knowing why in either case. Zola refers to the old man who finances Claude's art education (almost certainly because he had already figured in *Le Ventre de Paris*), to a duel, and to some other equally unimportant matters, but says nothing, for instance, of Sandoz' family and background, which are fairly developed in the novel. Nor is there any real indication of Claude's general situation in the art world. Zola does show him, quite early in the *Ébauche,* as head of a small school, but he gives almost no details of what Claude's career as a painter will be, no hint of his evolution, nothing about the nudes which come to obsess him, and nothing of the symbolism which eventually ruins his realistic attempts. There is no hint of "Plein-Air," nothing about the Provençal paintings or any others before the climactic effort which costs Claude his life; in the *Ébauche* this last one is based, like the final painting in *L'Oeuvre,* on a scene at the Port Saint-Nicolas, but in its preliminary form the work seems to have been conceived only as a piece of straight realism, with none of the social and sexual overtones which Claude introduces into it in its long elaboration in the novel.

Some details of the *Ébauche* seem to indicate that *L'Oeuvre* was to differ from most of the other novels of the *Rougon-Macquart* series in that it was not to deal entirely with the period of the Second Empire. It would seem that Zola first conceived it as a novel dealing with a transitional phase of French life, the period between the close of the Franco-Prussian War and the beginning of the twentieth century; it was to be, at least partly, some kind of forecast of our time. Certainly, this deliberate violation of the framework of the series must have been due to Zola's acquaintance with the Impressionists, whose victory was won after 1870; since they constituted the only school he knew well, it would be natural that he should deal with their time and with their dissolution as a group. In any case, *L'Oeuvre* itself goes beyond 1870 to 1876 and treats Claude as a transitional figure, which partly justifies the impression that *L'Oeuvre* is not really one of the *Rougon-Macquart* novels, or at least that it is ill-assorted with the other novels of the series.

As to the tone and atmosphere and philosophy of the work, Zola insists in the *Ébauche* on passion and gaiety. On the very first feuillet, he wrote this:

> *Passion, goodheartedness, gaiety.*
> *Genesis of the work of art, nature embraced and never conquered.*
> *Struggle of woman against the work of art, birth of the work of art against the birth of the real flesh.*
> *A whole group of artists.*

Of the general intentions indicated here, it is undeniable that Zola carried out most of them, but it is highly doubtful that *L'Oeuvre* could be said to be a novel of "passion, goodheartedness, gaiety," and here it is clear how far the *Ébauche* was from the finished work. Passion perhaps, if we take a great deal of dogged effort and some inflated rhetoric as signs of passion, but certainly no impression of real comradeship or real joy emerges from the pages of the novel, and when, at the end of the *Ébauche,* Zola says that he wants Valabrègue, Chaillan, and Alexis to be gay, even comic, when he says in closing, "I would like gay characters," he reckoned without the force of his subject, human and artistic failure, and most of all, he reckoned without the force of his own dark temperament and the pressure of his personal circumstances. It might be added, too, that the *Ébauche* contains some hints, not many, of a kind of optimism on Zola's part, but certainly these brief and fleeting indications produced no fruit in the work itself, for there is perhaps no volume of the *Rougon-Macquart* series in which the pessimistic and defeatist aspects of Zola's psyche found freer expression.

But if the *Ébauche* is far from the novel in tone and temper, it is remarkably close in another way, in the fashion in which it foreshadows Zola's somewhat curious dependence on contrast and antithesis. From the beginning, character is matched with character—Claude with Gervex, Bongrand with someone like Hugo (later Chambouvard)—emotion is matched with emotion (love of women and love of art), age is mated with youth (Bongrand and Claude), and so on. It may be supposed that such simplism of conception was dictated to Zola by his conscious or unconscious realization that his subject, the failure of an artist, lacked dramatic appeal; antithesis, drama in little, was doubtless part of his answer to the problem.

Be that as it may, the *Ébauche* gives little idea of what *L'Oeuvre* really is as a novel—Zola's hardest work was yet to be done: the translation of the scattered ideas, unconnected incidents, "type" characters, and vague philosophy into the stuff of novelistic reality.

The notes are arranged in six major areas of interest: the Salon, the general business of art (theory, technique, sales, dealers, models), architects and architecture, music, Paris, and the cemetery where the final scene of *L'Oeuvre* is laid. These notes, very extensive and detailed and almost all of Zola's hand, fill feuillets 321-475 of the *Dossier*. The first of them, Le Salon (feuillets 321-41), providing material for chapters V and X, consists largely of impressions gathered at first hand during a visit by Zola to a recent Salon, perhaps that of 1885. The second group, entitled "Marchands de tableaux, amateurs, peintres, sculpteurs, le jury, élections, les opérations" (feuillets 342-87), is mostly composed of notes which Zola got from the painter Antoine Guillemet. It also contains a long letter on Impressionist technique from another painter, Léo Gausson, and a brief note on the scholarships awarded to art students by the city of Aix. Material from this section of the notes is scattered all through the novel, and here Zola got most of the technical "color" which he used so liberally to give the illusion of observed reality, anecdotes (such as the story of Mahoudeau's collapsing statue and Fagerolles' benevolence), painters' techniques and tools, the role of the École des Beaux-Arts, dealers' tricks and publicity devices, models' names, and so on.

The third section, entitled "Architectes" (feuillets 389-401) is attributed to Zola's friend, Frantz Jourdain, though again the actual notes are in Zola's own hand. It contains material on current architectural education (relating to Dubuche), a short description of the "nuit de charrette" and some indications of new tendencies in architecture, used by Zola in his description of the relationship between Dubuche and Margaillan. A fourth section, "Musique" (feuillets 404-13), is a collection of clichés on Beethoven, Haydn, Mozart, Spontini, Weber, Rossini, Meyerbeer, Wagner, Berlioz, Schumann, and Chopin; it contains, additionally, the program of a Pasdeloup concert and of an unidentified concert. These notes came to Zola from Henry Céard, though there is no indication of his name and the notes are in Zola's own hand. They were used, of course, in conjunction with Gagnière's monologues and conversations with Mathilde Jabouille after the latter gains respectability by becoming Jory's wife. The fifth section, "Paris" (feuillets 415-64), is one of the most interesting and valuable. Evidently compiled by Zola himself from direct observation, these notes appear throughout *L'Oeuvre* and account for the generally impressionistic tone of the work. These are sketches, some of them extremely effective, of the quais and the Seine, the Cité (the "heart of Paris"), the rue Vieille-du-Temple, the rue du Cherche-Midi, Montmartre, the Place de la Concorde (and glimpses of the Champs-Elysées), and bridges and panoramas near the river; the last part, "Paris qui s'allume," is one of the best, a small work of art in its own right, but it appears only partly in the text. This section on Paris is accompanied by a large photograph taken from a roof or balloon, looking eastward and slightly southeastward toward the "heart of Paris." The last section, "le Cimetière" (feuillets 467-75), is a straightforward, almost reportorial description of the new cemetery of Saint-Ouen; it contains a pen-and-ink sketch of the cemetery and of some aspects of the neighborhood. These notes were used—transcribed is a better word, for they appear almost verbatim—in the final chapter of the book.

This large mass of notes resembles the *Ébauche* in that it is impossible to make valid generalizations about Zola's procedure. Some of the notes appear in the text almost unchanged, some are changed slightly, some a good deal, but some of them do not appear at all, and it is difficult if not impossible to discover any controlling principle which dictated Zola's practice. The only explanation must be in his perception of artistic necessity, his sense of proportion and appropriateness, his desire for accuracy of impression, and his need to render the circumstances of the time he is describing. But though no principles are observable, Zola's handling of his material, his transposition of observation to art, is in itself interesting and significant of his tendencies as constructor and of his personality as artist.

The notes most used in the text of the novel and where the transposition into novelistic form was the most direct were, naturally enough, in areas in which Zola had the least specific or recent knowledge. Generally speaking, the notes dealing with art dealers, models, the jury system of selecting paintings for the Salon, architecture and architects, music, sculpture and painting technique (brushes, oils, the preparation of the canvas, and so on) fall into this group, as do the notes on the cemetery of Saint-Ouen. In these areas Zola often transcribed almost literally, including the same details, turns of phrase, and order of incidents or particulars, and he used very nearly all of his material, leaving aside only the most minor portions and the least important details. Moreover, these notes provided him with practically all his material on the subjects concerned;

L'Oeuvre contains almost nothing of importance in these matters which is not found in some form or other in the notes. Here he invented little, contenting himself with observation, either his own or that of others. Examples of his practice with respect to these areas of the notes are legion in *L'Oeuvre,* and scores of pages could be cited to prove that his raw material often found its way into the finished pages of the novel almost without change.

Zola's practice throughout his use of these areas of his notes is the same: he clings very closely to both the essential and the detail, squeezing from them everything he can in the way of color and interest, but he also almost always lengthens and develops, adding the personal and dramatic element, and especially giving the passage a touch of his "epic" tone by aggrandizing and multiplying. No better example of his latter tendencies can be found, perhaps, than in the little scene of the "nuit de charrette," where the young architects bring their work at the last possible minute to the École des Beaux-Arts for judgment; the notes are much shorter than the passage in the novel, but the essence of the passage is there nonetheless.

One or two other areas of the notes were used a little differently. Zola left out of *L'Oeuvre* a considerable amount of material he had gathered on "Les Amateurs," apparently considering the latter as not so important as he had first thought, and he did the same with art theory. He possessed a long letter from Léo Gausson, setting forth in considerable detail certain aspects of Impressionist theory and relating it to the scientific discoveries of Chevreul. He could have introduced a good many discussions of the subject into the novel if he had wished, for Gausson's letter provided him with an ample stock of ideas and examples, but he apparently chose not to stress the matter in order not to identify Claude too closely with any school. Whatever the reason there is only one extended treatment of art theory in *L'Oeuvre,*[3] a passage which appears to have been dragged in to give credibility to Claude as artist; it is fairly close to a passage of Gausson's letter, though it does not reproduce his words textually.[4]

The two sections of the novel which offer the most interest from the point of view of their reliance on notes are the Salon scenes of Chapters V and X and the descriptions of Paris. The Salon scenes offer a contrast in method which has a certain interest for the study of Zola's processes of composition. The first Salon scene (Chapter V) treats the Salon des Refusés of 1863; it is highly unlikely that Zola had any notes at hand on that distant event, more than twenty years old (the notes in the *Dossier* include nothing from that time), so the chapter is probably an amalgam of memory, imagination, and direct observation transposed from the Salon of 1885. So far as the present notes in the *Dossier* are concerned, they seem to have provided Zola with material for only three portions of this chapter: the physical setting (the Palais de l'Industrie, its stairways, curtains, garden of statuary, windows, chairs, and so on), the architecture hall, where Dubuche shows his design, and the buffet where the "little band" retires after Claude's scandalous failure. But the essence of the chapter, and it is far from being the least effective or least authentic in tone and detail, came from the processes of memory and imagination.

Here is an example of how the notes of 1885, if that was the time when Zola visited the Salon for purposes of this novel, were adapted in Chapter V: Claude and Sandoz arrive at the Palais to see the fate of "Plein-Air":

> When they entered Claude shivered slightly in the gigantic vestibule, cool as a cellar, where the humid pavement rang beneath the feet like the flagstones of a church. He looked at the two monumental staircases at right and left and asked scornfully:
>
> "Tell me, are we going to go through their filthy Salon?"
>
> "No, confound it," replied Sandoz. "Let's go through the garden. Over there is the West staircase that leads to the Refusés."
>
> And they passed disdainfully among the little tables of the catalogue sales girls. In the opening of some immense red velvet curtains, the glassed-in garden appeared beyond a shadowed porch.
>
> At that moment of the day, the garden was almost empty, the only people were at the buffet, beneath the clock, the crowd lunching there. The rest of the crowd was on the second floor, in the exhibition halls; and, solitary, the white statues bordered the walks of yellow sand, which cut boldly into the green design of the turf. The statues formed a motionless people of marble, bathed in the diffused light which came down like powder from the high windows. On the south side, heavy linen drapes blocked off half the hall, blonde beneath the sun, marked at either end by the brilliant reds and blues of the stained glass windows. Some visitors, already tired, occupied the brand new chairs and benches, gleaming with fresh paint; while the flights of sparrows who lived above in the forest of steel beams, swooped down with shrill hunting cries, fearless and pecking in the sand.[5]

The source of this passage is, a little exceptionally, an amalgam of notes; Zola usually followed his notes in almost linear fashion, repeating details in his text about as they appear in the notes, but here he varied the practice. The first details, for instance, may come from feuillet 323 of the notes: "Differences in the hàlls, the vestibule finally, with its high ceiling, its garden glimpsed at the rear, its catalogues, its cellar-like coolness, the sand one walks on, the monumental staircases." Or they may originate in the notes of feuillet 326: "Downstairs, the vestibule has a flagstone floor. The entrance to the garden, red draperies, and, at the rear, the garden half glimpsed, with white statues. Cloakrooms, catalogues." But the major part of the description undoubtedly comes from feuillets 334-35:

> The garden seen from above.—The gallery around it, where architecture and sketches are shown. Shimmering of the window panes, spots of water color. The infrequent visitors who file by. Those who go that way in order to avoid the crowd and go from one hall to another. A red banquette against the ramp.—Below, the green design of the turf, shrubbery and flower beds, surrounded by marble or plaster statues. The yellow sand, with the black spots of the passersby, foreshortened.—Around, brown serge drapes below the windows. Opposite, the dark opening of the buffet, with the diners. The clock above.—The swarming of the crowd. People standing, those who walk. The ladies seated. The benches very green, old; the chairs very yellow, brand new. Isolated marbles and bronzes; white or dark spots.—The skylight above, round, supported by a steel structure. One half of the windows, to the south, furnished with blinds of gray linen. At the two ends, stained glass windows, personages against a blue background, a harsh sky; and the marks on the draperies, red, violet, yellow.—Cries, noises of the sparrows in the beams; they came in through broken panes, probably.—Below, the gay sound of the crowd, a distant and vague rumble, voices, feet. The muffled sound of the distant halls, the clock, black dial, gilded numbers.—Workers arranging the pedestals; noise of a saw. The sudden coolness of the garden. A great mass of palm trees in the center.

A good many details of the notes are not present in the text, at least in the pages quoted; but some of them appear later in the chapter, or in Chapter X, and moreover it is to be observed that in the Salon scenes, especially this first one, Zola omitted from his text a fair amount of the material he had gathered for background purposes, perhaps to keep the chapter short, more probably because he wanted to conserve his space for Claude's human drama as his "Plein-Air" becomes the joke of the Refusés.

The striking aspect of Chapter V is that the portions of it which were apparently the result of memory and imagination, without aid from any kind of recent observation, give the same impression of accuracy and precise detail as do those based on immediate observation and documentation. This seems to be the residual impression left with Zola, after a score of years, of the total effect of the Salon des Refusés—at least, there is nothing in the notes to indicate that it is anything but memory:

> Then all five of them wandered about, noses in the air, cut off from one another by a surge of the crowd, joined together again by another, swept along by the current. An abominable painting of Chaîne's stopped them, Christ forgiving an adulterous woman, harsh figures carved in wood with a bony structure that made the skin look violet, and painted in mud. But beside it they admired a very beautiful study of a woman seen from behind, buttocks outthrust, head turned. Along the walls there was a mixture of the best and the worst, all the types of painting pell-mell, the dotards of the historical school side by side with the young madmen of realism, the simply stupid in the heap with the showoffs of originality, a dead Jezebel who seemed to have rotted in the cellars of the Ecole des Beaux-Arts, near the "Lady in White," a very strange vision of the eye of a great artist, an immense "Shepherd" looking at the sea, a whole story in himself, facing a little canvas, some Spaniards playing pelota, a spot of light of splendid intensity. Nothing execrable was missing, military paintings with tin soldiers, pallid antiquity, the Middle Ages slashed with bitumen. But out of this incoherent collection, landscapes especially, almost all of them sincere and exact, portraits also, most of them very interesting in technique, there arose a good smell of youth, bravery and passion. If there were fewer bad paintings in the official Salon, the average there was surely more banal and mediocre. One felt as though he were in a battle, a gay battle, entered upon with verve, when daybreak comes, the bugles sound and when one marches on the enemy certain to defeat him before sunset.[6]

The other Salon scene, Chapter X, differs in origin in that Zola leans heavily on his notes. Most of the details included—details of setting, of the crowd, of the artists, the models, the types of spectators—are present in the notes, and he often transposes almost verbatim and uses practically all of his documentary material. No chapter of the book is so closely documented as this one, in contrast to the earlier Salon scene; in the later chapter he had no such dramatic focus as Claude's notorious failure, for this is a scene of quiet defeat, and consequently most of his effort went to creating a scene of great verisimilitude and accuracy, where a host of details would mask the lack of personal drama. Here is a typical example of Zola's reliance on documentation in this chapter (Claude is searching for his portrait of his dead son):

> . . . in his anger at his vain search, he was astonished at the vulgarity of the faces, seen like that in masses, at the disparate quality of the ladies' clothes, few elegant ones among many common ones, at the lack of nobility of this people, so much so that the fear with which he had trembled gave way to scorn. Were these the people, then, who were going to judge his painting again, if they could find it? Two little reporters were finishing up a list of names to cite. A critic affected to take notes on the margins of his catalogue; another was lecturing in the midst of a group of beginners; another, his hands behind him, remained fixed, overwhelming every canvas with an august impassibility. And what struck him the most was the rush of the crowd, its mass curiosity, without youth or passion, the harshness of the voices, the fatigue of the faces, an air of ill-tempered suffering. Already envy was at work: the man who says witty things before the ladies; the one who, without a word, gives a terrible shrug of the shoulders, then goes his way; the two who stand for a quarter of an hour, elbow to elbow, leaning on the guardrail, faces down over a little canvas, whispering very low, with the twisted glance of conspirators.[7]

The source is briefer, but the details are there:

> The reporters, the critics take notes.—The group of actresses. The slanderers: the one who jests, talking very loud. The two somber slanderers who stop before little canvases, with their elbows on the guardrail, and who talk, with the twisted glance of conspirators, whispering in each other's ear. The silent slanderer who shrugs his shoulders. The man who says witty things before the ladies. The critic who lectures in the midst of a group of very young men.[8]

And so it is throughout almost the whole of this chapter (save for the middle portion, where the reliance on notes becomes a little less pronounced, while still remaining considerable): at this stage of his career Zola's eye was so practiced and his notation so skillful that in effect he could write large sections of his novel as he stood observing his material.

But perhaps the most interesting case of all in the use of documentation in *L'Oeuvre* comes in the descriptions of Paris, numerous and highly effective. Again, the documentation is entirely Zola's, for he had no need to seek the opinions or the knowledge of others in order to supply himself with vivid and striking material. Here Zola, while still depending heavily on the documentation he had gathered, manifests more independence with regard to the notes. It is not easy to find any extended passage of description which reproduces detail with the fidelity displayed with respect to the notes on art dealers or models or the cemetery of Saint-Ouen, and it is obvious that Zola's powerful imagination and equally formidable powers of recall entered more into play than was the case where he felt less at home. His practice with regard to the notes on Paris seems to indicate that he intended the descriptive passages to be the stylistic high points of his work, worthy of close attention and of considerably more care than the passages of what might be called local color. Certainly, there is a far greater emphasis here on selection of detail than elsewhere, for Zola eliminates large portions of what he had originally noted down and also adds considerably to the original stock of notations; in effect, a good deal of the novel's descriptive element is not in the notes and a good many of the details recorded in the notes are not in the novel, but it is still true that no major descriptive passage was written entirely without notes. And it is also true that Zola apparently felt no such obligation to follow the order of his notes as he did in other areas; the descriptive parts of the novel are more nearly amalgams of notes than are any other parts. Above all, Zola's effort seems to have been directed at producing descriptive passages which would give the maximum amount of "impressionism," that is, would evoke—insofar as this is possible in literature—the same kind of emotion, the same kind of visual images, the same total effect as Impressionist painting.

The focal point of *L'Oeuvre,* physically, is the Cité and its surroundings, "the heart of Paris," as Zola calls it and as Claude sees it. Zola returns to it again and again, but perhaps never so effectively as in Chapter IX, where Claude begins serious work on his last painting. This is how the Cité appears to him as he returns day after day to catch its multiple aspects, its ever-changing physiognomies:

> At all hours, in all weather, the Cité rose before him, between the two channels of the river. Under a belated fall of snow, he saw it clothed in ermine, above the mud-colored water, standing out against a light slate-colored sky. He saw it, at the first sun of spring, wipe winter off itself, recover its childhood, with the green shoots of the tall trees of the terrace. He saw it, one day in a fine fog, retreating, evaporating, light and trembling as a dream palace. Then it was the beating rain that submerged it, hid it behind the immense curtain drawn down from the sky to the earth; storms whose lightning strokes showed it tawny, in the suspect light of a

> thieves' alley, half-destroyed by the crumbling of the great copper-hued clouds; winds that lashed it with tempest strokes, sharpening the angles, outlining it starkly, naked and flagellated, in the pale blue of the air. Other times again, when the sun broke up in powder among the vapors of the Seine, it bathed in the depths of this diffused clarity, without a shadow, lighted equally everywhere, with the charming delicacy of a trinket carved out of fine gold. He wanted to see it beneath the rising sun, freeing itself from the morning mists, when the quai de la Horloge grows red and the quai des Orfèvres remains heavy with shadow, living already in the pink sky by the dazzling awakening of its towers and spires, while, slowly, night descends from the buildings like a falling mantle. He wanted to see it at noon, under the sun beating straight down, as though consumed by raw light, discolored and silent like a dead town, having no life now but the life of heat, the trembling that stirred the distant roofs. He wanted to see it under the declining sun, letting itself be taken again by the night rising little by little from the river, keeping at the angles of its monuments the fringes of fire of a coal about to die, with final upsurges of flame which kindled in the windows, sudden flames from the glass which shot flakes of fire and pierced the façades. But before these twenty different Cités, whatever the hour, whatever the weather, he always returned to the Cité he had seen the first time, toward four o'clock, one fine September afternoon: that Cité, serene in the light wind, that heart of Paris beating in the transparency of the air, as though increased by the immense sky, traversed by a flight of little clouds.[9]

The whole long passage of the notes which Zola entitled "Le Coeur de Paris" (feuillets 436-48) contributes some details to this series of views, but the essential is contained in this section:

> The oblong block, the ship that is the Cité, between the two very wide channels of the river. Immense blue sky, where little clouds float. Rolling of waves under the Saints-Pères bridge. *He will always return to this first vision.*
>
> This, then, is the heart of Paris, in all weather. A very light spring evening, with much sharpness of detail, gaiety, transparency, cool shadows, immense sky with a trail of little white clouds that make it ever larger. A light wind, the soul of Paris diffused around its cradle; make this soul appear in the teeming life of the quays and bridges, in the living trembling of the painting. (Open air painting, beneath the setting sun, three or four hours.)—In the morning the sun rises, the Cité is doubtless different in the light, the shadows are displaced.—A time of light fog, which makes of it

a dream city, which pushes back and blurs everything, still visible, dusk on a gray day, the sun in a light vapor. Another view, tragic, in a storm, a yellow and pallid city, crushed under a dramatic sky, an avalanche of heavy, black clouds, with tawny lightning.—Then, in the cutting wind, in the cold of winter that stops the traffic, in the snow, perhaps in a beating rain which drowns everything, which buries everything behind a curtain.—At night finally, one to be selected.

The view of the river and the quays must follow these different views, which I will pass in review when Claude is on the point of painting his picture. I would like to have only the description with the painting, which makes it difficult to get the other views in the story.—All the other quays and finally the arrival at the Saints-Pères bridge, where the picture will be sketched.[10]

There is perhaps no better example in *L'Oeuvre* of Zola's ability to transform brute matter, hardly more than the details of an *aide-mémoire,* into the finished work of art. The notes here were a point of departure, no more.

And indeed, that is what they frequently were in these descriptions of Paris, raw material, sometimes not even that. Zola's reworking of his primary notations gives the best kind of testimony to his organizing eye, his "colored" imagination, his sense of progression and drama.

With his first sketch written, his characters established, and his notes collected, Zola was ready to begin writing his novel. His first step, as the methodical workman he had trained himself to be, was to draw up the plans which would guide him as he wrote. Before attempting to form detailed plans for the chapters, he drew up a very short plan, or better, a sort of stage direction to himself, in which he set down the kind of chapter he wanted in each case. Feuillets 2 and 3 of the manuscript contain this preliminary plan:

1. (July. In action.) The mistress with Claude. Studio. Both of them characterized. Sketch of the bosom. Request for a pose. Everything up to the departure.

2. (July. In narrative.) Claude, I, then the architect. The painting characterized. All our friendship at Plassans. All my ideas established. The three poses, Plassans and Paris. I pose. All my theories. Art, history and the point we have reached.

3. (July. In action.) A chapter to establish the secondary char-

acters. An evening at my home. Walks in Paris. The old boy in decline. Irma Bécot with the Gervex. Discussions. The band, the school.

4. (July to May, in narrative.) The mistress reappears. A comrade in Claude's studio. The duel perhaps. See about a general framework. I would like a dramatic act. The painting completed.

5. (May. In action.) The Salon des Refusés. Great discussions with me. All the friends reappear. The god passes by in the background. At the end of the chapter, Claude weeping and sleeping with the mistress, the Baille with Irma.

6. (Two years.) The passion of the mistress and Claude, how they live. In the country probably. Living at Bennecourt (or some other). Pregnant. Up to Claude's return (i. e., to Paris) Friends (I'll see). Irma Bécot brought by the Alexis. The future property of the Baille.

7. (A year.) Return to Paris. Another studio. All the friends reappear. Another dinner at my home, or an evening. The old boy in decline. Irma Bécot more chic. The Baille is going to marry.

8. (Three years go by.) The first idea of the painting. Life in Paris. Claude drifts away from the mistress, who struggles and slips further down each day. The marriage. I would like a scene there. The marriage must be the framework. The big painting put off from Salon to Salon.

9. (Seven years.) Deep poverty. The mistress (not a mother) working, forgotten. Irma Bécot tolerated by her. Another studio, more wretched. The child dead and painted. Christine's struggle, violence and a scene of struggle. The painting put off from Salon to Salon, the others refused. The pose.

10. (May.) The Salon, all return, very brilliant, the Gervex, the old boy, the god passes by again. Claude departs alone, no discussion with me. A word about the mistress, who has come alone with me. Very sad ending. How he goes back home, or rather his mistress waits for him, but no tears. Establish the suicide already, a visit to the theme (i. e., of the painting).

11. (May.) A chapter with me, the last of the Thursdays, all of them ruined and disbanded. Visit to the Baille and his children. The old boy in decline. Claude returns to the country where he was happy. (The three chapters follow each other in the same movement.)

12. (May.) All the drama of the mistress with Claude. She feels death and struggles. Great misery. He escapes from her, goes back to the theme and hangs himself in front of the painting.—The burial, conversation between the old boy and me. The mistress has become a maid.

These brief indications are in consonance with the finished text, but Zola did make some slight changes in time and in detail. There is no duel in Chapter IV, though Jory almost engages in one; the time, originally set as July to May, becomes late August to February, and the dramatic event which Zola wants here becomes Christine's nude pose in Claude's studio. In Chapter VI Zola intends to have two years elapse, but three and one half years pass, and the episode of the appearance of Irma with Alexis is omitted, as is the visit to Dubuche's property. The ending of Chapter X becomes different from what Zola intended at first, and Chapter XI contains no extensive treatment of Bongrand. Last, Chapter XII, as finally written, contains the dramatic episode of the night of love preceding Claude's suicide, an episode which does not figure in the original plan. But on the whole Zola was to follow these first indications fairly closely, developing and expanding constantly, adding many details and some episodes, but nevertheless pushing ahead much as his first instinct told him to do.

Once these brief indications were finished, Zola was ready to begin the detailed construction of his novel. To this end he composed a long plan for each chapter, listing each event, giving some snatches of conversation and indicating locales to be described. These plans did not satisfy him, apparently, for he made a second set, which was definitive. The changes from the first set of plans to the second are very numerous and interesting, for they shed a good deal of light on Zola's manner of composition, his sense of appropriateness, and the hold that literary logic had upon him.

These plans, and its clear that Zola used both of them as he wrote *L'Oeuvre*, contain many references to the *Ébauche*, which they replaced as a guide to the actual creation of the novel and to the notes. They were the final step before the completion of the book as we know it today; it was in them that the novel found its form.

After completing the plans Zola was ready to write, and he set about the task, if not with enthusiasm, at least with his usual doggedness, writing 719 feuillets from May 12, 1885, to February 22, 1886. This period comprises about 240 working days, at six working days a week, from which perhaps fifty days must be deducted for the vacation that Zola and his wife took at Mont-Dore in the summer of 1885; thus,

Zola had about 190 days for serious writing, and so he averaged for *L'Oeuvre* what he seems to have averaged for most of his novels, about four feuillets a day. The manuscript is in the Bibliothèque Nationale (Département des Manuscrits, Nouvelles acquisitions françaises, 10314-10315). It consists of sheets of good quality, unlined white paper, 20 cm. long by 15.5 cm. wide, written on one side only. As a literary document, the manuscript of *L'Oeuvre* is not of very great interest. It contains a large number of changes, but the majority of them are of single words; longer changes are nearly all in the direction of condensation and suppression, and scarcely any additions of importance are to be found. It is quite apparent that what look like changes at first glance are only evidences of false starts on Zola's part, for his pen often seems to have run away with him, like the pens of lesser writers. There is little evidence of extensive rewriting, perhaps because the plans had been so thoroughly made that they left little room for groping, and it is also clear that almost all the changes, whatever their nature, were made on the spot—the manuscript shows little evidence of later polishing.

Most of the changes in single words or short locutions are simple substitutions for rhythm or emphasis or to make the expression stronger or more violent. *Ridicule* becomes *imbécile*, for instance, *très longue* is replaced by *énorme* and so on. The more extensive changes are not really very much more complex than this, they are simply longer. An example of Zola's practice might well be his description of Christine's face in Chapter I (the words in parentheses were eliminated):

> . . . . [Claude] went on to the sketch (of the face) of the visage, studying it carefully. All the upper part showed a great goodness, a great gentleness (exquisite), the forehead limpid, smooth as a clear mirror, the nose small, with fine, sensitive nostrils (of a child-like delicacy); and one could sense the smile beneath the eyelids, a smile which should (illegible) illuminate the whole face (illegible). Only, the lower part spoiled (a little) this radiance of tenderness, the lower jaw projecting (slightly), the lips, too heavy, were blood red, showing solid (big) and white teeth. It was something like a surge of passion (illegible), puberty rumbling and yet ignorant of itself, in these traits which were suffused with a childlike delicacy.[11]

Passages of the manuscript in which Zola seems to have had considerable difficulty in finding the suitable expression for his intention include the description of "Plein-Air" in Chapter II,[12] Christine's recognition of herself in "Plein-Air" (Chapter III), the little incident where

Christine and Claude meet Sandoz and Dubuche on a walk along the Seine before their marriage, the fine scene where Christine undresses to provide Claude with his model for "Plein-Air" just before the Salon, the opening of Chapter V, the close of Chapter VII, generally in Chapter VIII (including the incident of the collapsing statue), the symbolism of the nude of the "Apotheosis" in Chapter IX (generally, like VIII, a difficult chapter for Zola), the last pages of Chapter XI, and the opening of Chapter XII. Not surprisingly, the Bennecourt episode of Chapter VI seems to have caused little difficulty—Zola had already written about Bennecourt-Gloton a half-dozen times in various newspaper articles and stories—and Chapter X likewise produced no stumbling blocks, perhaps because Zola had visited the Salon not very long before writing the chapter.

On the whole the manuscript changes are not important enough to interest us deeply, as a Balzac manuscript might; they reveal that while Zola was a conscientious and careful workman, he was not profoundly concerned by matters of style and preferred to put his attention on ideas, characters, and structure rather than on the pure technique of expression.

Once the manuscript was well started, Zola began its publication in *Le Gil Blas* and by steady work managed to keep ahead of the typesetter until the novel was completed. Before *L'Oeuvre* appeared in volume form, he made more changes in the *feuilleton* version,[13] none of them very important, and the work was offered to the public, which received it with less enthusiasm than it had some of the earlier novels of the *Rougon-Macquart* series, but still with a readiness which Zola must have found gratifying if not heady.

The elaboration of *L'Oeuvre* from germinal idea to finished form offers the portrait of a serious, hard-working Zola, master of a technique of assembly and transposition, concerned with structure rather than with style, solid, businesslike—but not inspired. Was his technique beginning to overwhelm his creative ability at this point of his career? Was he devoting too much attention to range of information, inclusiveness of form, and solidity of framework, to the detriment of more purely aesthetic considerations? Had the observer, the researcher, the "scientist" crowded out the poet? Not completely, surely, but in the struggle for Zola's mind the man of fact was clearly winning out over the man of vision. And that is perhaps why the novel is the novel it is, instead of the novel it might have been.

X

The Novel as Fiction

In all the controversy surrounding Claude Lantier and Zola's competence as an art critic and historian, the critics have scarcely discussed *L'Oeuvre* as a work of fiction, an imaginary action of imaginary people. True enough, most of the opinions expressed on *L'Oeuvre* since its publication have included some general statements, but with very few exceptions those who have written on the work have avoided anything like an extended or serious commentary on the book's qualities and faults.

But *L'Oeuvre* is a novel and must be judged as a novel, without regard to its origins among Zola's friends or to the philosophical and aesthetic ideas it expresses, and it seems that the public has so judged it over the years, giving it the place it seems to merit, below the best of Zola's novels and well above the weakest. *L'Oeuvre* is certainly not as good as Aurélien Scholl proclaimed it to be when he called it Zola's most beautiful novel[1] and not by any means so bad as George Moore made it out to be when he sneered that *L'Oeuvre,* "spun out for a franc a line in the *Gil Blas,*" did not contain a "single new or even exact observation."[2] The history of its public reception is an interesting chapter of Zola's career.

Critical comment at the time of the novel's appearance was fairly well divided and by no means so generally hostile as with some of the earlier books of the *Rougon-Macquart* series. The reviewer Vincent said of it that it was marvelously composed, often picturesque, with a calm and haughty audacity.[3] Albert Dethez' opinion was perhaps not aesthetically motivated, but it was highly favorable: he saw it as a superb book of protest and rebellion, but also a book full of pity, deeply good and human;[4] Hugues Le Roux, praising the novel's sincerity of observation and its precision and abundance of details, placed it very high: it is a magnificent novel, which if not superior to

Germinal, shows no decline in Zola's talent.[5] The anonymous critic of *Le Livre,* in a most favorable review, called it a powerful book and praised its sincerity and truth,[6] and Fernand Henry, declaring that no novel had ever gripped him so much, spoke feelingly of its power and force. Henry praises several scenes—the opening chapter, Christine's first pose, the closing episode—and declares that though Christine is mediocre, the "little band" is a living group and though some traits in the tableau may have already aged and others may be poorly observed, the ensemble is exact enough. Zola's descriptive technique is for him better than Flaubert's or Daudet's or Gautier's, he has the gift of expressing life, like Tolstoi. *L'Oeuvre* may not add to Zola's reputation, he concedes, but it is certainly stronger than some of his earlier novels.[7]

Zola's friends Philippe Gille and Gustave Geffroy were understandably favorable. The first spoke of the marvelous fidelity and exactness of the details, praised several scenes for their delicacy, remarked on the emotional effect of the novel, defying the most hardened not to be saddened by the story of Claude's failures, and concluded that *L'Oeuvre* appears to be one of the master's best books.[8] Geffroy, objective and disinterested as always, was somewhat less enthusiastic, but still could say that everything in the book is masterfully expressed and that none of life's abominations is attenuated.[9]

Some later critics have been equally favorable, on the whole. Edmond Lepelletier thought that Zola's vigor had given new life to the old theme of artistic disillusionment and that he had demonstrated his psychological virtuosity in this "cruel and gentle" fantasy;[10] Camille Mauclair called *L'Oeuvre* a "poignant and cruelly beautiful" book;[11] and Marcel Girard, in his excellent "Situation d'Emile Zola"[12] leaves a strongly favorable impression. Henri Guillemin, calling it a "fine book," praises several scenes and writes enthusiastically of Zola's "lucky choices of words" and of his brief character sketches.[13]

But by no means all the reactions have been so pleasant for Zola. Two of the principal official critics of the nineteenth century, Jules Lemaître and Armand de Pontmartin, had the most serious reservations and said so without amenity. For Lemaître the very manner of the book was wrong, it should have been a completely psychological study; Pierre Sandoz goes through the novel preaching sermons, there is pedantry everywhere in the discourses on art and life, Sandoz' cry that "who speaks the word 'psychologist' says 'traitor to the truth' " is the view of an innocent. Zola's claim to truth is nowhere more clearly false, for in none of his novels does his temperament more profoundly transform his observation. The artists of *L'Oeuvre* are, for Lemaître, animals of a forgotten species, as far from the present as the bearded Romantics of 1830; they curse, they cry, they have a false simplicity, a false coarseness, their tone is about like that of the workers in *L'Assommoir*. These ungentlemanly fellows are characters out of some new kind of historical novel. Nor does the book contain much real psychology or direct observation—and Lemaître is moved to speculate on what such a subject as that of *L'Oeuvre* might have become in the hands of "M. Paul Bourget." Yet Lemaître finds in *L'Oeuvre* Zola's peculiar genius, the gift of the concrete and yet vast vision, the gift of expressive exaggeration, and the gift of rendering the abominable sadness of things. And this is why everything in the novel tends to be materialized and aggrandized, why all the characters adopt poses like damned figures of Michelangelo, why the effort of artistic production becomes the struggle of Jacob and the Angel at a neighborhood fair. It is Zola's inevitable tendency to the grandiose, the unbelievable, which makes him create Claude as "the Failure, the Impotent, the No-Luck," as a monster whom we are delighted to see kill himself, this "Arpin-Prométhée" of Impressionist painting. The secondary figures are sharply sculptured, some pages are almost graceful, but these virtues are small in a work in which we find on every page a frightful sadness and a crushing hyperbolic violence of vision.[14]

Pontmartin was even more severe. While praising details of certain scenes, he found the work as a whole prodigiously boring and lacking in any wide appeal to the educated classes who form the bulk of the reading public, the characters untypical of any artistic movement he had ever known, the depiction of the art world one-sided and false, the action as repetitive and dull as the progress of an old horse drawing water from a well. The language is typical of drunkards and cab-drivers, he thinks, and the characters all resemble each other in their deadly monotony; worst of all, perhaps, is the "erotic and pornographic" note, the precise details, the varieties of nudity—the word *ventre* had appeared forty-five times when he stopped counting. Add to that the contempt expressed by the young revolutionaries for religion and the clergy, the awful fact that Christine is only a body for Claude, the vulgar tone of it all, and we can see why Zola is such a monster for the right-thinking classes.[15]

Edmond de Goncourt was more critical, though not publicly. Convinced that *L'Oeuvre* could be nothing more than a weak pastiche of *Manette Salomon*, in his *Journal*, on various occasions, he accused Zola of plagiarism, of a complete lack of knowledge of the art world, of writing à la Restif de la Bretonne, of vulgarity and commonness of expression (for him, the characters all talk like carpenters), until, finally, when the novel appeared in April 1886 (he had read parts of it in *Le Gil Blas*) he could restrain himself no longer and set down a long commentary, not all of which is devoid of point. He finds the novel well constructed in an old-fashioned way and Christine's love well handled, though it begins and ends with situations untrue to life. He accuses Zola of sentimentality and bad taste in selecting the course of Claude's conduct. Are there any real artists in the novel? Or are they all carpenters and masons? He is equally hard on the ideas in the book, finding them all in some way imitations of ideas expressed better by other authors, including himself. Zola at bottom is nothing but a "retreader" in literature; now that he has finished reworking *Manette Salomon*, he is about to begin the same operation on Balzac's *Les Paysans*.[16]

Zola's critics are clearly wrong in many of their charges, but nonetheless it would be difficult to argue that *L'Oeuvre* is a wholly successful work of art—no one pretends that it ranks with the best novels of the nineteenth century—and few would deny that part of the reason for its lack of absolute success is a certain absence of universality, of broad, general appeal and comprehensibility which its origin as a new treatment of the Pygmalion legend might have seemed to guarantee it.[17] The subject ought to be of wide and consuming interest, a man's attempt to play god and his weakness in his role, for this is a common enough human phenomenon; but somehow, in Zola's treatment, it lacks both the antique charm of Ovid's story and the engaging humanity of Shaw's play. *L'Oeuvre* is a novel for creators and for intellectuals who know something of creation; their name is not legion. Zola gave it too much locale, too much "color," too much of the here-and-now, he located it too firmly in time and place, and in consequence he took from it the possibility of the universal comprehension offered by a *Madame Bovary* or of the universal sympathy demanded by a *Germinal*.

But that is not all; the greatest reason that *L'Oeuvre* is not a wholly successful work lies in the contradiction between the apparent needs of the subject and the treatment which Zola decided to give it. Claude Lantier's struggles with art, with himself, with love, seem to call for some kind of compressed, intense psychological development, with no distractions, no byroads, something in the manner of Balzac treating the failures of Balthasar Claës or of Mauriac spinning the web of fatality around one of his *bordelais*. *L'Oeuvre* is in a certain measure a psychological novel—much more of a psychological novel than the theorist of "physiological man" might have been willing to admit—but it is not wholly one, and that is the origin of its greatest flaw.

L'Oeuvre is a novel of the *Rougon-Macquart* series, however far from the other novels of the series it may seem to be, and it shares their nature and rests on their theory. This is to say that its nature is really double: it contains a plot (actually, two plots fairly well interwoven) and what might be called a panorama, a study of a moment in French history, with full accompanying detail. But not only does it have a plot and a panorama, an extensive background, like *L'Assommoir* or *La Terre* or *Au Bonheur des dames,* it possesses a strong autobiographical element not wholly related to the plot, and moreover it shows clear signs of being devised at least in part as a vehicle for certain philosophical and aesthetic ideas of its creator. The worst of it is that the plot is not completely integrated with the panorama—what has Claude's inner world really to do with the world of painters and sculptors and writers around him?—and neither the autobiographical element nor the ideological content adds anything to either the plot or the panorama. It would seem that Zola never completely decided what his novel should be and that it suffered from the first from a certain lack of definition; it is a kind of catch-all, a portmanteau novel, and the reader sometimes has the sensation that Zola swept up all he knew of the world of art and creation and put it all, without much selection or distinction, into these pages.

But why should he have chosen a double form not in keeping with the internal needs of his subject? The answer lies surely in his fidelity to the theory of the *Rougon-Macquart* series. If this is a "natural and social history" of a family, he must have felt obliged to make *L'Oeuvre* conform to the pattern, that is, to make Claude's failure stem from two nearly equal causes, the hereditary and the social. The first was easy, of course: all Zola had to do was posit from the first that Claude came of a family suffering from mental disease; his evolution from sanity to suicide would follow of itself. But the external cause, the social cause, was harder to find. How does an author make a convincing case for an artistic failure generated, at least partly, by the times? Zola chose to answer the difficult question by selecting a period of transition and evolution, when romanticism was not yet dead and when modernism had not yet emerged with its formula, and by presenting this era with a full panoply of characters, movements, schools, and theories. The idea behind the novel seems to be that Claude fails because of his mental tare, but that the direction of his failure—symbolism, neo-romanticism—is determined by his environment.

It is also true that the theory of the *Rougon-Macquart* series demanded that Zola, while presenting the drama of one of the members of the family, offer a broad tableau of some aspect of modern life, as he had done in the novels preceding *L'Oeuvre* and as he was to do in those which followed. If environment was to be part of the cause of Claude's failure, then that environment should do double duty by representing the wide social panorama which the theory required.

So the other novel in *L'Oeuvre,* the account of the doings of Fagerolles and Bongrand and Mahoudeau and Dubuche and the others, the account of the contemporary movement in art, literature, sculpture, architecture, art education, and art politics, of models, dealers, collectors, sales practices, of the jury and the Salon, of the techniques of painting and sculpture and architecture, has a strong theoretical justification and indeed considerable intrinsic interest. Now and again one of Zola's opponents will make the remark, apropos of *L'Oeuvre,* that nothing in this whole panorama is accurate or typical, but the fact remains that *L'Oeuvre* is a most valuable book for knowledge of the art world between 1863 and 1885, and its documentary basis gives it real significance as an inside history of the times. It is by all odds the most complete novelistic treatment of the art world of the Impressionistic period—even its names are in part chosen from reality[18]—and its close reliance on the notes Zola gathered from practicing artists guarantees something like authenticity, at least so far as possible in such a work.[19]

The panorama is justifiable in the novel, theoretically at least, but its aesthetic justification is far more difficult to establish. However interesting and valuable the background of the art world may be as history, it is undeniably no more than tangential to the principal story line, for it is quite possible to imagine a novel about an attempt and a failure such as Claude's with none of this material included. The very size of the background, the very detail—even its very intrinsic interest—have the effect of lengthening the novel unduly, of slowing and complicating the progress of the action, and most of all of diluting the interest of the central problem, which is indubitably a psychological problem with little relation to the external world of art. Again and again in *L'Oeuvre* Zola returns to Claude after an expedition into the life of Mahoudeau or Fagerolles or Dubuche, obviously groping for the thread of his story, straining to find some adequate transition from the external world to the internal world of Claude's suffering, and usually ending by falling back on some happy coincidence which brings the principal actor back to the center of the stage. The two universes, the universe of Claude and Christine and the nudes and the universe of the jury and the Salon and the dealers, simply do not have much to do with each other, and the inclusion of too much material—Zola's besetting sin—renders the novel much weaker than the primordial subject promised to make it, that is, the struggle of man and creation and of woman and art. Zola himself was aware of the error he was committing as he composed the book, for during its composition he wrote to Henry Céard as early as August 1885 that he feared a yawn of boredom from his readers and again, a few months later, that the book had taken on an unexpected length, which apparently tired him a good deal, for he said frankly that he was happy to be relieved of the burden.[20]

And not all of the panorama is good, by any means, for it accounts for some of the novel's worst pages, the phrases on music uttered by Gagnière and Mathilde for instance,[21] or Sandoz' eternal philosophizing, and is responsible for some of Zola's most inexcusable distractions, the passages dealing with the youth of the three "inseparables" in Plassans—good enough pages in themselves, but without much significance in this novel—the episodes revealing the married life of Dubuche, the scenes of Sandoz' home life, and one or two more. By and large, if the panorama were not there, if the story were a classically controlled study of artistic failure and of the rivalry of woman with art, *L'Oeuvre* would have been a tighter novel, more intense, more dramatic, more touching, and perhaps more interesting. But the series was there, the theory was there, and Zola could no more forget them than he could forget the scenes of his ardent and combative youth.

But it would be wrong to lay the incomplete success of *L'Oeuvre* entirely to the presence of the background and to its real lack of integration to the plot line. There are other factors, perhaps even more telling.

First of all, there are the characters themselves, the essence of the novel. Except for Claude and perhaps Christine, all of them are flat, possessing the good outline and posture that this thwarted dramatist always knew how to confer on his fictional beings, but with little depth or complexity. They do not speak much, it will be observed, they thus very rarely characterize themselves, and they almost never characterize each other; their physiognomies are clear and sharp (and it is curious to see how much Zola depends on physiognomy to imply character), but they do not reveal much about their inner lives. It is Zola and almost he alone who does the revealing. He handles his figures as a director might, he manages them, and though some of them evolve very widely, almost incredibly, a little à la Proust, they do not seem to evolve freely, as a function of their beings. When Jory, from a conscienceless woman chaser becomes the meekest of husbands, when

Mathilde, from a vicious libertine becomes a paragon of bourgeois virtue, we have the impression that they do so not because of anything already posed in their characters, but simply because they were made to do so by their creator for ironic effect.

But it would be asking too much to expect them to move and act freely, for the secondary people of the novel, almost without exception, were devised as old-fashioned type characters, created to fill certain roles in the panorama. Bongrand is the great man in decline, Fagerolles is the cynical arriviste, Gagnière is the artist in whom one art is killed by another, Jory is the parasite, Dubuche is the man who mistakes his vocation, Irma is the Parisienne, Chambouvard is the artist without critical sense, even Claude and Christine have set roles in the pattern. They are, by and large, artificial and one-dimensional, and their raison d'être in the action of the novel is not often apparent.[22] While they are sharp, clear, often engaging, they are in effect not much more than figures in a complex frieze, and their sometimes unbelievable changes of attitude as the book progresses are no more than the steps of their controlled progress toward a destiny which Zola fixed for them in advance of their birth.

But all this is not so true of the two main living figures of the novel, Claude and Christine. Type figures they surely are, at least to a certain extent—Claude is the incomplete artist, possessed by an ambition exceeding his talent, Christine is "modestly sensual" and the self-sacrificing saint—but both are well executed psychologically, both have some complexity, give some impression of depth, and both are, up to a point, believable.

Claude Lantier, who is not the hero of the novel, for there is none, nor the central figure, for that is either the nude of the "Apotheosis of Paris," or Paris itself, remains somewhat dim in spite of his position in the foreground. He is seen at some distance, and though Zola fairly frequently employs "interior monologue" in his characterization, he does not quite succeed in allowing us to penetrate completely the psyche of the flawed artist, and we watch him progress into madness almost entirely from without. Lantier is more complex than the minor characters, but he is not a very interesting figure, and the impression grows as the book wears on that Zola grew tired of him, a little impatient perhaps, and finally lost sympathy with him, as we do when he mistreats and neglects Christine and turns into a maniacal egoist. We feel, as someone remarked, a certain relief at his suicide, and it is possible that Zola did also. But interesting or not, Claude is a carefully and logically built figure; his major characteristics are posed early, and he remains true to them.

It is not without significance that when Claude first sees Christine lying half nude and asleep, his first instinct is to paint her, not to touch her. So from the beginning we see him as he is to be throughout the book, gentle and brutal, harsh and timid, moved to some kind of sexual expression but fearful and distrustful of women; Ovid's Pygmalion suffers from the same fear and dislike; these are the traits on which his whole life will depend and one of Zola's successes in his portrait is the skillful way in which he makes one aspect of Claude's being gradually dominate the other, leaving him one-sided and open to madness. Claude is a highly interesting case of sexual ambivalence in whom we see the struggle between the masculine and the feminine principles of a diseased psyche. Did Zola intend him to be a crypto-homosexual?[23] Or is he another Hippolytus, a chaste huntsman of the ideal who dies because he affronted Venus? Zola's attraction to the Phaedra legend was already old by this time in his career, and it is not impossible that consciously or unconsciously he designed this modern pursuer of "a joy that does not exist" in the likeness of the figure portrayed by Euripides and Racine. Perhaps not, perhaps he meant him only as a modern Sisyphus.

Claude's progress toward madness seems well and discreetly handled, there is nothing excessive and his gradual loss of gentleness as his relationship with Christine cools shows that Zola was capable of accurate and subtle observation in the field of abnormal psychology. It is true that the mystic attraction of "the heart of Paris" for Claude never receives much explanation, perhaps for the very reason that it is a mystic attraction; it is simply "given" in the novel and no more explicable than the attraction he feels in his madness for the painted flesh his brush creates.

But his main flaw as a character—and his incomplete realization by Zola is symbolic of the incomplete realization of the novel as a whole—is a certain dimness, a certain blurring of outline. He is pale and distant alongside some of the minor figures who lack his complexity and solidity of construction—Jory, for instance, or Fagerolles or Irma. He does not speak enough to allow us to know him well, and, with an increased degree of depth and humanity, he allows the same impression to arise as in the case of the secondary characters, the impression of being handled and managed by Zola, of evolving on order, so to speak. His confused outline may stem from Zola's unfortunate tendency to shift point of view with him, to speak from within his mind in one sentence and externally in the next.

But it is possible that Zola never clearly made up his mind about what he wanted to do with Claude Lantier—the *Ébauche* shows a groping for some certainty of motivation and role—and never properly decided just how he should construct his artist, whether from imagination or from the observed reality of multiple models. Nor, it would seem, could he establish clearly whether he wanted Claude to be an individual of sharply marked physiognomy and angular personality or a type, a kind of caryatid to carry part of the burden of the vast panorama which lies so heavily on the novel. At all events, Claude leaves us with the sense of imprisonment, the impression of a man trapped by his heredity and by his environment, of one who could not be free, most of all, of a man whose dark motivations are never completely seen. And perhaps that is exactly the impression which Zola the determinist and the pathologist of society wanted him to leave. Claude is in one sense a true scion of the Rougons and the Macquarts, in his dominating passion and his ambition to "conquer" Paris by his talent; and it may be because of this that he is so drawn to "the heart of Paris." *L'Oeuvre* may not be very closely connected with the other novels of the series, but here, at least, the bond is strong.

Christine Hallegrain, the only personage of the novel who might be called "heroic," first appears as something of a stock character of Zola's, the symbol of lucid acceptance of life and courageous resignation to a pitiable fate. She recalls such successful figures as Pauline Quenu and Madame Caroline, but her nature is a little different from theirs, for like Claude she reflects the existence of two warring principles in her psyche, modesty and passion—her face, with its delicate brow and clear eyes and its sensual lips and heavy jaw, typifies her nature, just as Claude's fierce beard and brows are contradicted by his childlike eyes, the sign of his feminine timidity. Almost throughout *L'Oeuvre* she appears as she does in the first scene, reserved, shy, the very model of a Victorian girl of good upbringing. But near the end the same kind of change takes place in her as had taken place in Claude somewhat earlier, the triumph of one principle over its opposite, and she seeks revenge—sexual revenge—for the great sin the artist had committed against her, forcing her to contribute to the creation of the terrible rival who is to conquer her, draining her of her beauty so that her enemy may be more beautiful.

But this is to anticipate. Throughout nearly the whole book, Christine remains what she was at the opening, passive and a little uninteresting but always sympathetic; indeed, it is obvious that Zola was more drawn to her than to Claude or any other character save Sandoz, perhaps because as he created her he was incarnating some kind of unattained ideal of feminine beauty and charm. But Christine's passivity, lack of aggressiveness, and total absence of maternal love, while depriving her of personality, serve to intensify the cruel fact that her only weapons in her long struggle against the invading nudes of Claude's paintings are passion and sex. When these fail, as they ultimately do, her defeat is doubly harsh, for their failure implies woman's worst defeat and leaves her, after Claude's death, absolutely alone and defenseless. Perhaps Zola meant the lesson of her life to be the inverse of Claude's: if the painter dies for having scorned Venus, Christine suffers for not heeding Minerva.

Be that as it may, her treatment in the novel is delicate and perceptive. The growth of her love for Claude—a highly romantic and somewhat incredible love, a fatal passion which is to survive all brutality and all neglect—is especially noteworthy as an example of Zola's skill with "soft" characters; so brilliantly accomplished is it, indeed, that even Edmond de Goncourt gave it more than faint praise.[24] Like Claude, she is constructed and handled logically and like him, until his madness becomes the master, she remains constantly faithful to the characteristics posed from her first appearance, faithful, that is, until the sexual principle overcomes the social principle in her spirit. There are a good many examples of sound and subtle feminine psychology in her presentation: her slightly scornful surprise—she is still a virgin—that Claude does not even try to touch her in the first scenes; her eventual willingness to pose nude—still a virgin—for Claude when she discovers that her image has faded from "Plein-Air" and has been replaced by the face of his ideal woman; her determination to employ her nudity at any time and in any circumstances to combat Irma and eventually the jeweled nude of the "Apotheosis"; her refusal to become unduly concerned about Claude's brief intimacy with Irma, knowing that Irma is not her real rival; her reaction to Claude's brutal words as he details the parts of her body and compares her mature state with the freshness of the girl of "Plein-Air."

But at the end, when Claude has offended her once too often in her sexual pride, Christine becomes a different woman, just as Claude becomes a different man when his obsession is on him. In a great outburst of passion, this modestly sensual woman, this Eve, loses all her modesty and becomes purely sensual, lustful, a Lilith, and forces Claude (in a scene reminiscent of one of the great scenes of *Nana*) to fulfill her sexual demands like a slave. The scene mounts steadily in passion and frenzy, rising to a peak of lust not equaled in any other of Zola's novels.[25] And this is the woman whose modesty was so great that she refused, at Bennecourt during their honeymoon, to externalize even the most innocent details of her intimate life and thereby brought about the first catastrophic rift in their love. Is this plausible? Did

Zola yield to a taste for melodrama, or simply give exaggerated expression to some desires of his own? Can we believe that the modestly sensual woman of the early scenes could become the femme fatale, the destroying temptress of the last—her development parallels the evolution of the painted nudes—and could become more sexually aggressive than the artist?[26] Is Christine's early willingness to pose nude for Claude sufficient preparation for this scene of sexual abandonment? It would not seem so: there appears to be no really good reason why this well-sexed Victorian should become a maenad, and if Zola relied on the old belief that "hell hath no fury like a woman scorned" as sufficient motivation, he made a curious error, for a woman scorned would not be likely to act as Christine does on Claude's last night of life.

And there is a further question. Why, when most of Zola's "good" women find some kind of peace, some kind of consolation in their self-sacrifice and resignation,[27] is Christine made to suffer? Can it be that this woman, who in so many ways epitomizes health and the life urge, who is the complete opposite of the destroying woman of the paintings, is made to expiate the sin of coldness toward her child? It would seem that Zola, in spite of his obvious sympathy for her in most of the novel, could not let her go unpunished for neglecting little Jacques, for being first a mistress, then a mother. This was a sin against life, against the life cycle so dear to Zola, and Christine's fate is, for a man of his beliefs, only too well deserved.

The other principal figure of the novel, Pierre Sandoz, has little claim to attention. Immobile and unbearable, he has no real physiognomy at all. He is not much more than a spokesman, with no role in the novel save as a reflection of Claude; he is far too often a priggish sermonizer. This good fellow, who cannot invite Christine to dinner because she is not married to Claude, is aptly described by Jules Lemaître's quip that he gets drunk on big words like an illiterate at a political meeting.[28] As the novel progresses, as Claude's difficulties multiply, and as his own success broadens, Sandoz becomes more and more a philosophical vehicle, less and less a human being. Of all the characters he is the least living and the least attractive. Better Jory's vices, Fagerolles' unscrupulousness, and Irma's amoralism than this eternal rightness.

The minor figures, in spite of lacking depth and being stereotypes, are by no means wanting in interest. Paul Jory, for instance, attracts a certain sympathy, at least at first; he may not be as comic as Zola intended him to be, but he is engaging and amusing, and he indicates that Zola may have been better equipped to handle minor characters than major ones, that is, tightly controlled, brief, sharp portraits of no great complexity but of considerable precision and vigor. Zola's success with Jory is paralleled in the character of Fagerolles, a well-rendered portrait of intelligent cynicism and easy grace, Claude's opposite in nearly every way, including the sharpness of outline and clearness of physiognomy he displays. This Parisian, etched where Claude is brushed in, is evidence, along with Jory and Irma and the art dealer Naudet, of Zola's fascination with a certain kind of vicious personage, amoral, shrewd, winning, a little canaille, urban in origin, and urban in psychology. Not only is he fascinated with such people, he creates them with extraordinary facility and authenticity, as Irma Bécot demonstrates. An outgrowth of the original conception of the central female figure, Irma appears to have steadily lost importance in the intrigue, as Zola developed it, but far from losing interest, she may have gained it by slipping to the middle background. Zola was obviously intrigued by her—she must have represented one of those wicked women his bourgeois heart yearned to encounter—and gave her such attention that she occupies a very prominent place in the gallery of distinguished tarts that the *Rougon-Macquart* series offers. Like Fagerolles, Irma radiates intelligence of a particularly Parisian kind and emanates a brittle charm acquired in her hard youth; she has vitality and, more than that, some little depth and complexity, and just as Fagerolles is sharper than Claude, she is sharper than Christine, and a good deal more amusing to boot.

These four, Jory, Fagerolles, Irma, and Naudet—an especially effective portrait-vignette, barely present but highly amusing—represent the kind of vice Zola must have found most interesting, perhaps because it was so foreign to his nature. He treats them with a certain indulgence, as a fond father might treat his rascally sons and light-headed daughter. But when he treats vice that is only vice, unrelieved by intelligence or wit or charm, then his touch deserts him. Mathilde Jabouille is a case in point. He intended her to be evil, but his imagination—she is one of the few characters of purely imaginary origin, not supported by social observation—played him false, in the direction of exaggeration, which is where it only too often led him. Mathilde has no element of human credibility; of all the stereotypes the book contains, she is the worst, for she is there only as an ironic foil to the pure and suffering Christine. Her success at the end of the novel, parallel to the success of Homais, is too obviously contrived to stir any feeling of protest at the ways of the world.

Achille Bongrand, another obvious favorite of Zola's, shows many indications of careful treatment, but he is, paradoxically, not really very interesting. Perhaps his case is too special for the generality of readers, certainly his expression of his own situation is too exaggerated to attract much sympathy. The art dealer Malgras, like Naudet, offers another fine vignette of humanity. He has color, charm, and originality, and it is regrettable that his role is so small. The other figures are almost nonexistent. Mahoudeau and Chaîne have no real physiognomies, Dubuche does not live at all, Chambouvard is only glimpsed—but glimpsed very clearly—Henriette is a piece of the decor, Gagnière could have been interesting but is spoiled by his ridiculous mouthings. These are all part of the frieze, nothing more.

All the characters except Claude and Christine are episodic in the real sense of the word; they appear when summoned, to demonstrate a point about the art life of the time, but they have no true connection with the essential action of the novel. The females are more successfully drawn than are the men; on the whole they are more sharply individualized from each other in speech and appearance, and all of them are more aggressive and more dominating than the masculine figures. It is curious that all of the women except Henriette Sandoz are in some measure "devouring" women, exerting enormous force over the men, using the power of sex and vice to attain their ends, and, save only Christine, emerging successful from the novel's vicissitudes to a degree that the men, all of whom are failures in one way or another, cannot match.

Perhaps because the characters are episodic the action of the novel is episodic. *L'Oeuvre* consists, in effect, of a series of good dramatic scenes alternating with long, arid stretches of narration or philosophizing; it does not advance freely, and, like the people who populate its pages, it is obviously managed by Zola, the omniscient narrator who never abandons his anonymity for an intrusion into his book.[29] But it is also true that *L'Oeuvre* contains a really unusual number of excellent short scenes, from the romantic opening[30] to the melancholy close. All of the first chapter, delicate and skillful,[31] Christine's first nude pose, the idea of which may have come to Zola from George Moore,[32] the Salon des Refusés, best by far of all the chapters in its organization and impact,[33] the "*nuit de charrette,*" the collapse of Mahoudeau's statue,[34] the jury scene, Claude's criticism of Christine's body as she poses for him toward the end of his career,[35] the second Salon,[36] the hallucinatory scene of Claude's painting just before his suicide, his burial—these are all notable for vigor, life, and controlled force. In these scenes Zola generates real emotion—his choice and handling of situation and especially his strong dramatic sense more than compensate for the deficiencies of his fictional people. Most of them are really small dramas, set pieces in the Flaubertian manner, and like good dramas, most of them have highly effective openings and closings. The ending of Chapter V, the Salon des Refusés, where Christine at last gives herself to Claude, is typical of Zola's strength here:

> They adored each other, their comradeship had to end in this love, on this divan, in the adventure of the painting which little by little had united them. The dusk enveloped them, they remained in each other's arms, prostrate, in tears beneath this first joy of love. Near them, in the center of the table, the lilacs which she had sent that morning perfumed the night; the scattered bits of gold, falling from the frame, alone gleamed with the vestiges of daylight, like a host of stars.[37]

Another terminates the sad little scene of the collapsing statue:

> Emotion had seized Claude, whose eyes also moistened in his sense of artistic fraternity. He hastened up, but the sculptor, after having called for his aid, wanted to be the only one to pick up the pieces of the statue, as if he feared they would suffer from the brutality of any other man. Slowly he dragged himself on his knees, took the pieces one by one, laid them on a plank, brought them together. Soon, the face was restored, like one of those girls who commit suicide for love by jumping off the top of some monument, and who are put together again, comic and lamentable, to be carried to the morgue. Falling back into a sitting position before her, he did not take his eyes off her and forgot himself in heartbroken contemplation. But his sobs grew calmer, he said finally, with a great sigh:
>
> "I'll sculpt her lying down, what do you think of that! . . . Ah! my poor girl, I had so much trouble setting her upright and I thought her so great!"[38]

But not all of Zola's closings are so effective as these, and it goes almost without saying that not all of the set pieces are successful. A fairly large number of key scenes are comparatively weak and lacking in dramatic power, human interest, and even sometimes relevancy. The three dinner scenes at Sandoz' house, obviously meant to be focal points of the action when all the dramatis personae are drawn together, are contrived, nearly all the episodes where Dubuche figures are uninteresting and undramatic (their role, of course, is only to intensify the sense of melancholy and to drive home the terrible punishment of the man who sells his soul for a mess of pottage), the wildly melodramatic scene of sexual struggle near the end of the book is badly exaggerated and unbelievable, leaving the impression that Zola included it only as a means of "shedding his sickness." Some of the other episodes are similarly lacking in drama and interest, but nevertheless weak scenes are clearly outweighed by good ones, and the loose construction of the novel is partly redeemed by the vigor and tightness of the successful vignettes, episodes, and chapters.

Zola's use of compositional devices in *L'Oeuvre* is neither new nor startling. He employs, for instance, a good bit of the traditional kind of foreshadowing—the storm in the opening scene, boding no good to the love of Claude and Christine; Christine's refusal to allow Claude to finish his first sketch of her, a hint of his later frustrations; the rainstorm during the couple's installation at Bennecourt; the conception of little Jacques on the very day when Claude meets his great defeat at the Salon des Refusés; the collapse of Mahoudeau's statue on Christine's wedding day. These and many other devices bespeak Zola's reliance on a technique already worn thin by the romantics and their immediate followers in the school of realism. But the incidence of such guideposts to the later development of the characters and the turn of the action is as nothing when compared with the almost unbelievable number of coincidences which mark the progress of the novel. The very first scene is a chance meeting in the purest sense of the term, and all through the book just such encounters open the scenes and episodes which constitute the action. When the connections between scenes are examined carefully, it becomes evident that Zola made no attempt to work out an integrated plot which would bring the various characters together according to a logical pattern. Instead, he allows them to meet by the merest chance, in cafes, at the Salon, on the street; they visit each other a little aimlessly, they reappear in one another's lives by a kind of destiny, but there is no force which raises their meetings to the level of pattern. These chance encounters—one has only to think of Bongrand or Chambouvard or Naudet to realize how frequent they are—demonstrate Zola's inability or unwillingness to integrate plot and panorama; episodic characters make for episodic and loose action, and most of the characters are episodic by the very definition of their being.

As a consequence of this reliance on chance, hazard, fate, Zola allowed himself to incorporate perhaps a larger number of improbabilities in the action of *L'Oeuvre* than a realistic work ought properly to contain. A good many scenes simply have no logical raison d'être at all. The visit of Jory and Irma to Claude's studio when Christine is there—possible enough, but surely not probable—is only one small example. Irma's brief intimacy with Claude is another, but these are minor when compared to the two basic improbabilities of the book, the fact that Claude creates a revolution in painting with one canvas alone, "Plein-Air," a canvas which is the scandal of the Salon and which is never seen again, and Claude's enormous, endless, intolerable labor on the "Apotheosis of Paris," a labor so long and so exhausting that no questioning mind can accept it. Human endurance and patience could never have stood such a test—*L'Oeuvre* is based on the wildest of improbabilities.

A number of other devices strengthen the impression that, here at least, Zola composed like a romantic. There is the pathetic fallacy, for instance; nature is constantly in harmony with Claude's moods, the light effects change markedly as his hope declines, the color of Paris evolves from gold, rose, blue, white, yellow, sometimes red, to gray and black. The cottage at Bennecourt is all white and rose and pastel at first, when love is new, all gray and grim and dark when love has died. And so everywhere. Then there is the device of antithesis, so widespread that it seems that the novel might have been inspired in Victor Hugo—certainly it reflects Taine's advice to Zola to use antitheses of all kinds,[39] and perhaps goes beyond what the old critic might have intended. Antitheses are everywhere, contrast is the soul of the work. There are contrasts of characters: Claude (flawed genius, never content) and Sandoz (imperfect also, but resigned), Claude (integrity) and Fagerolles (unscrupulousness), Bongrand (the artist with a critical spirit) and Chambouvard (blinding ego), Christine (virtue in sex) and Irma (sex). There are contrasts within characters—Claude is timid and brutal, Christine is modest and passionate, Irma is vicious but intelligent, and so on. There are innumerable contrasts in concept between woman and art, painted flesh and real flesh, the new painting and the academic, realism and symbolism, hope and doubt, enthusiasm and despair. Even Claude's paintings contain antitheses: "Plein-Air" presents nudes and clothed figures, the "Apotheosis of Paris" has Paris enjoying itself and Paris working. And Claude's whole life is a long antithesis: his philosophy of art and existence is a philosophy of creation, his career is a tremendous struggle to create, to produce, to give birth—and it all ends in a cemetery. All these examples testify as nothing else can to the dramatic simplism of Zola's mind.[40]

But among all these romantic techniques, there is one which is more specifically realistic, that is, one which is more closely identified with literary realism than the others described here, the technique of ironic reprise, much used by the realists for their pessimistic effects. Reprise lies at the basis of many of the antitheses in *L'Oeuvre* and plays a major role in creating the atmosphere of defeat and melancholy which, it seems, was Zola's aim in this novel, for it accounts for most of the duplicated scenes. The most notable repetition is the one linking the two Salons. In the first, recounted in Chapter V, Claude is a kind of hero to the other *refusés,* and though an outburst of derision and mockery greets "Plein-Air," he still is at the forefront of the new movement, with hope of eventual victory over the very public which mocks him in defeat. But in the second Salon, described in Chapter X, not one of the thousands of spectators even stops to glance at his miserable portrait of "L'Enfant mort," received, ironically, through the benevolence of Fagerolles, his imitator, before whose canvas, an attenuated version of Claude's "Plein-Air" of a dozen years earlier, a vast and enthusiastic crowd gathers. The two Bennecourt episodes, while not quite so striking, offer another example of reprise. In the first, all is happiness, love, calm for Claude and Christine. They have a son, nature reflects their joy, the world lies before them waiting to be conquered. But in the second, which comes near the end of the novel, the tone changes radically. Nothing is left of the old life, the little house has changed, the roses are dead, the Seine is gray, despair and desolation are everywhere. And so also with the three dinners given by Sandoz: the first (Chapter III) shows Claude surrounded by the "little band," full of enthusiasm and hope and the spirit of solidarity; the second (Chapter VII) shows the beginnings of the breakup of the group, the first intimation of the doubt of Claude's talent which will turn all his comrades against him; the third (Chapter XI), a sumptuous affair, brings the breakup before our very eyes, here all is jealousy, gossip, rivalry, bitterness, and the tone of petty rancor is in the sharpest contrast to the elegance of the table, just as the tone of hope and enthusiasm of the first dinner was in contrast to the simplicity of the fare. There are others: the two scenes at the Café Baudequin, representing respectively the solidarity and the dissolution of the group; Christine's two nude poses, before the Refusés and later, when Claude criticizes her body; the scene in the restaurant after the Refusés and the scene in the buffet after the second Salon.

All these devices unquestionably contribute to the sense of a kind of geometry in *L'Oeuvre,* and they bring about a certain impression of artificiality quite at odds with Zola's insistence on realism. They form a curious contradiction to his various pronouncements in the essays which constitute *Le Roman expérimental* that plot and "arrangement" of life are an unimportant part of the novel.[41]

What we really have in *L'Oeuvre* is the contrary of what Zola preaches here, not life itself, but an arrangement of life, a structure of devices which contribute powerfully to the impression of drama and of pessimism which Zola must have wanted but which do not succeed in rendering the spirit of human freedom or the sense of human events.

Stylistically, *L'Oeuvre* does not offer exceptional interest. Zola's expression is generally adequate and sometimes excellent, but it does not reach the level of *L'Assommoir, Germinal, La Terre,* or even of such lesser works as *La Bête humaine* or *Pot-bouille.* The style is the familiar one of the realists, the "nominal" or impressionistic style, with strong emphasis on nouns, especially in combination with neuter verbs. In Zola's hands, the nominal style, as is not unusual, is sometimes a little gauche and heavy; the inordinately large number of nouns gives the impression of weight and density and produces a solid impression of the "chose vue," but Zola's preference for the nominal construction (learned in part from Goncourt and Flaubert) made him pay a high price in length, faulty rhythm and awkwardness. The substantives, like the verbs, are generally of a strongly active and violent nature and include many substantized adjectives. These usages contribute heavily to the total "phenomenological" effect Zola must have wanted to produce in this novel of the art world.

The rhythmical patterns which Zola establishes in *L'Oeuvre* show no significant differences from his usual manner. The pace is generally slow, a little ponderous (because of so many nouns, perhaps), giving the impression of a kind of inexorability which is not without effect. Zola likes above all a ternary construction which gives a good sense of completeness and solidity but which also slows the rhythm and produces a certain sense of heaviness. Given the generally "military" nature of the rhythm which Zola elected to use in this novel, it would be surprising to find many inversions of verb and subject, which always have the effect of disturbing the stylistic progress. In fact, there are very few inversions in *L'Oeuvre,* not more than half a dozen or so, aside from those required by standard grammar, and none of them seems very daring. Likewise, verbless sentences are uncommon, the whole novel containing less than a dozen and a half; many of these are concentrated in the formless mouthings of Gagnière and Mme Jabouille on music. Asyndeton, the avoidance of connectives, is fairly frequent. It is rarely used to speed the pace of the narrative, as it often is by Maupassant, and is almost never designed in this novel to produce the effect of breathlessness or disorder. Rather, it is one more device which contributes to the total effect of denseness and heaviness that this prose creates. Rhythmically, *L'Oeuvre* offers little that is new or different; here Zola is as conservative as he was revolutionary in *L'Assommoir.*

Tenses and the general handling of time in *L'Oeuvre* likewise offer nothing new or revolutionary or even very interesting. The narrative is conducted in the past tenses, with almost no evidence of the narrative present, and Zola's practice here might be called standard realist. It might be remarked, though, that the book is a kind of opposite of *Nana* in one sense, for where Nana went through enough adventures in three years to fill several ordinary lives, not many events of moment happen in the existence of Claude and Christine in the fourteen years of their relationship. This is why *L'Oeuvre* seems to drag from time to time; if Zola had been less interested in his panorama and more interested in the psychological drama, he might well have shortened his chronological time and so given greater impact to his novel.

The metaphorical elements of *L'Oeuvre* are not unimpressive. There is no complex or large structure of metaphors, but frequent short metaphors are generally successful, full of strength and color. Long metaphors are rare, and there is no pattern evident in their use, save that there are more metaphors using water comparisons and battle or military comparisons than any other kind. These categories are well chosen, given the note of conflict and struggle that the novel carries and especially given its emphasis on the theme of death and departure.

Of the other classical rhetorical devices favored by the realists and naturalists, not much can be said. Synecdoche appears infrequently but effectively in *L'Oeuvre,* the particular sharpness of detail which this figure implies apparently suiting Zola well; synesthesia scarcely appears at all, though Zola does like to introduce two sensations of different order closely juxtaposed; personification is rare, inexplicably, for this is precisely the kind of subject in which personification might have played a large role. It is true that the nudes of the two important paintings are indeed personified, but aside from them, examples are hard to find. Hyperbole, of course, is not missing in the novel, for Zola "saw large," as Victor Hugo did, and rendered large too, and examples of epic aggrandizement are moderately frequent, as for example in the scene of the "nuit de charrette."

The "style indirect libre," or "interior monologue," the form which contributed so much to the success of *L'Assommoir,* plays a fairly important role in *L'Oeuvre.* There are about 150 examples, or about one every three pages, on the average; the great majority of these examples are very short, a sentence or two, and they are usually so well fused into the true indirect discourse or narration that it is difficult to ascertain whether it is Zola or one of the characters who speaks.

But they are colorful, lifelike, and spirited, and they almost always avoid the error which is the main shortcoming of this form of composition, the tendency to make the characters feel or think or say what is clearly beyond them. The interior monologue, although not stressed in *L'Oeuvre,* helps fill a need created by the lack of good dialogue in the novel. The people do not speak enough, we do not hear them clearly, and when we do hear them they do not always succeed in differentiating themselves as living people do. When the artists speak, and they do most of the speaking, they use a kind of undifferentiated roughness which is nothing more than a literary convention. *L'Assommoir,* of a decade earlier, had employed dialogue and interior monologue very freely and had found its success in these techniques; *L'Oeuvre* has little of the drama or of the human flavor of *L'Assommoir* and the lack is a pity, for Zola proves from time to time—as in the excellent jury scene—that he knows as well as any author of the century how to recapture the rhythms, the tones, and the effects of the human voice. The worst of it is that there is a good deal of speech, but not much good dialogue. There are long, tedious sermons on art and life, discourses on man's fate, detailed exposés of pantheism and pessimism, but too few believable conversations. Their rarity is the novel's greatest deficiency.

But if there is not enough good human speech in the book, that defect is balanced by an undeniable quality, the unusual amount of excellent description which the novel contains. The best writing in *L'Oeuvre,* taken on the whole, is in the scenes of Paris, which are surprisingly numerous and effective. These varied scenes produce a fine illusion of exactness and include a good range of poetic and realistic effects; Paris is, without a doubt, the best realized character of the work, for in the rendition of her multiple aspects Zola shows as clearly as anywhere in his whole vast work the proper alliance of poetry and "science," the alliance which he could not always achieve but which, once achieved, raised him from the level of novelist to the rank of artist. The best pages of *L'Oeuvre* are pages of description, and the best elements of those pages are provided by Zola's skill in the rendition of light and its effects. This is a novel about painters written by a man who was a painter himself.

Although the connection between *L'Oeuvre* and other novels by Zola, especially those of the *Rougon-Macquart* series, often seems slight, there are numerous ways in which it resembles them. Certain themes, scenes, and details, constituting what might be called Zola's idiosyncrasies, keep reappearing and become, given their repetition, guides to Zola's psychology, view of the nature of the novel, and outlook on life. It would be nearly impossible to draw every line of connection between *L'Oeuvre* and the other novels and stories, but certain elements show such a clear link that it would be hard to ignore them. Christine, for instance, is an orphan and a "good" character, as is Henriette Sandoz, and "good" orphan girls are fairly frequent in Zola's fiction, perhaps as reflections of the orphaned Alexandrine Meley. Christine abandons Claude, at least momentarily, to Irma Bécot just as another lay saint, Pauline Quenu of *La Joie de vivre,* abandons her suitor to her rival. She is involved, as numerous Zola heroines are, in a triangle situation, though her rival is not a woman but a painted nude.[42] Claude is dependent on the more worldly and able Sandoz, as other Zola heroes depend on stronger men;[43] he lives a life of struggle against established power, as several other figures of the *Rougon-Macquart* family do,[44] and he is driven into a nearly complete solitude as his life wears on, losing first his friends and admirers of the "little band" and then Christine, and this situation is common to Zola's figures, who become more and more isolated from society under the pressure of their driving ambitions.[45] Little Jacques, a distant cousin of the neglected and abused Lalie of *L'Assommoir,* dies as a kind of retribution to his heedless parents, as Hélène Grandjean's daughter dies in *Une Page d'amour.*[46] The love-death juxtaposition is present, as in *Thérèse Raquin, La Fortune des Rougon, Germinal, L'Inondation,* and *Rome.* The river is a suicide theme, as it is in several other novels,[47] and deaths occur with great frequency—there are no less than fourteen of them in *L'Oeuvre*—as they do everywhere in Zola's fiction. The figure of the intruder—the painted nude who comes between Claude and Christine—is here too, as it is in *Thérèse Raquin* and *La Joie de vivre,* as well as in a good many other novels, in various forms and ways. The novel centers on one great symbol, the painting, just as most of the novels of the *Rougon-Macquart* series do—in *Germinal* the mine, in *La Terre* the earth, in *Nana* the bed, in *Au Bonheur des dames* the department store, and so on.

Lapp has pointed out a number of similarities between *L'Oeuvre* and *Thérèse Raquin*—resemblances between Claude and Laurent (not always absolutely valid because Lapp takes it for granted that Claude represents Cézanne), the attempted destruction of the painting, the theme of the river, a kind of automatism which makes the same figure reappear constantly in their paintings—and there are other similarities with other works. The Bennecourt episode, for example, has reflections in "Une Farce, ou bohèmes en villégiature" and "Aux Champs; la rivière," of *Contes et nouvelles,* in *La Confession de Claude, Madeleine Férat,* and *Le Voeu d'une morte;* and the youth of Sandoz and Claude, seen in retrospect in Chapter II of *L'Oeuvre,* is paralleled by similar recollections in "Alfred de Musset," of *Documents littéraires,* "Victor Hugo," of *Nos Auteurs dramatiques,* and "Aux Champs: le bois," of *Contes et nouvelles.*

Add to these the sleeping girl scene, which may reflect similar scenes in *La Confession de Claude* and *Madeleine Férat,*[48] the cemetery theme, observable in a good many of Zola's early writings,[49] autumn as a setting for death, as in *Thérèse Raquin,*[50] the lunch scene during Claude and Christine's first visit to Bennecourt, perhaps an echo of a similar event in *La Confession de Claude,*[51] the scene of sexual humiliation, in which Christine forces Claude to abjure painting and to act as her puppet, surely a reminiscence of the great scene in *Nana* where Muffat is made to play the fool. It is likely that a close examination of Zola's other novels and stories would yield many more parallels. But these suffice to show that *L'Oeuvre* sprang from the same background and the same psychology as did many of Zola's other creations, and they point to the identity of world view which subtended his long evolution.

XI

Theses and Messages

THE QUESTION MUST ARISE with any novel by Emile Zola: is the work solely a fiction, with purely aesthetic aims and intentions, or does it contain some kind of thesis or message, a meaning? All the novels of the *Rougon-Macquart* series have a kind of thesis implicit in their economy, the heredity-environment thesis suggested by the phrase "a natural and social history of a family under the Second Empire," and many of them unquestionably carry an additional message. *Germinal,* for instance, conveys a thesis about the role of capital in modern industry, *Au Bonheur des dames* advances the theory that large enterprise must swallow small enterprise, *Nana* gives a lesson on vice and its necessary punishment, *L'Assommoir* can be read as a kind of tract on the effects of poverty in a great city. Does *L'Oeuvre* do the same thing in some way? The answer is almost certainly that Zola did intend some judgments to arise from his novel, but unfortunately not all of them are clear.

The first of these theses or messages seems to concern the Impressionist movement in painting. Several critics and art historians have addressed themselves specifically to the question whether or not Zola intended *L'Oeuvre* to be a condemnation of the group which he had done so much to encourage in his early career. All of them ask, in one way or another, the same questions: was Claude Lantier intended to be an Impressionist and does his failure have symbolic meaning for Impressionism in general? Does he represent in microcosm a whole movement, and does his sad career symbolize Zola's opinion of the artistic movement of his time?

Some critics reply in the affirmative. Ima Ebin, for instance, after linking Claude Lantier with Manet, says:

> The later stage of Lantier's art is, however, a diluted or theoretical form of Impressionism, not related either to Manet or

> Cézanne. Claude's "Apotheosis of Paris" with its enormous nude is a definite step backward. . . . But this distortion of Lantier's art is not only . . . due to the fact that Zola impregnated the works of Claude with his own literary spirit but that he failed to understand the essence of Impressionism. If Lantier never achieved a great masterpiece, it is because Zola, disappointed in Manet, no longer saw the possibility of a great work's being produced by any modern artist. The whole problem of the relation of Lantier to the new school of art, is but a reflection of the relation of Manet to Impressionism as seen through the eyes of Zola. . . .
>
> . . . Zola's own success gradually led him to doubt the greatness of Impressionism. He considered its scientific analysis of color and light and realistic subject matter as naturalism in painting. Yet the public which accepted Zola's naturalism in literature was still hissing at the new art. Thus, Zola arrived at the conclusion that it was the Impressionist technique, which he now accused of lack of form, that was standing between the spectator and the innovator. Sandoz says: "ils en restent tous aux ébauches, aux impressions hâtives." Zola probably expected Manet to find a more formal expression of realism; hence he made Lantier an adherer to Impressionism, but basically a romantic, a constructivist.[1]

Robert Ricatte is even more direct, calling *L'Oeuvre* a novel written against the Impressionists.[2] Georges Charensol, by implication at least, agrees with the thesis of Bazin and Ebin, and though he does not go as far as Ricatte it is clear that he thinks of Lantier as a kind of Impressionist.[3]

Those who disagree argue that the evidence does not support any claim that Zola used his novel to condemn the spirit of Impressionism. John Rewald offered this view in his first book on the Zola-Cézanne relationship. He declares that Claude Lantier is not an Impressionist—indeed, he is not an artist at all, but "the son of a novelist"[4]—and that Zola wanted to create an artist who should belong to no school, who should be a real innovator. And though Zola did give Claude, as the *Ébauche* indicates he would, some theories of the Impressionists, he did not have him paint a single Impressionist canvas, largely because Claude's paintings are in reality literary works. Of the "Apotheosis" he asks: "What Impressionist would have dared offer this academic and even banal composition?" and of Claude's other paintings he declares that all they prove is Zola's lack of understanding of Impressionism. After describing two paintings of Claude's middle period, before the beginning of the "Apotheosis," he says:

If Zola did not speak, à propos of these paintings, of the "new study of light," it would be difficult to believe that he wanted to depict in Claude Lantier an artist linked with the Impressionists. Now, as he himself had said, it is not the subject which determines the character of a work; but it is not uniquely that new study of light that makes an Impressionist painting either. It often makes only that "softened Impressionism" against which Claude Lantier rebelled and which, nevertheless, he practiced himself, because what he lacked was the Impressionist eye.

That Claude Lantier should be a failure was doubtless a necessity imposed by the history of the *Rougon-Macquart*, but that he should be a painter steeped in the literary spirit and even in the academic tradition, that was not a willed effort, it was—how doubt it?—an involuntary deformation.[5]

Brady takes a different tack. He believes that Zola intended Lantier to be exactly what he is sometimes called in the *Dossier*, a "naturalist," that is, a "scientific" observer of truth and reality: Lantier will adopt, as Zola intended him to, some theories of the Impressionists —light tonality, open air painting and "decomposed" light—but will remain "essentially a naturalist."[6] Brady thinks that Claude was not intended to be an Impressionist, not a pure Impressionist, at least—he could not have been, for Zola says in the *Dossier* that he "rises up against their hasty work." He does not agree with Rewald that some of Claude's pieces represent Impressionist tendencies, for to him they do not seem to be representative of Impressionism either as they are described in the *Dossier* or in the novel itself. Likewise, he denies that Claude's works are literary or academic, as Rewald had charged them with being; for him, they are naturalistic and arise from a naturalistic aesthetic. To support his claim Brady analyzes some of the paintings described in the novel and concludes from his analysis (and it might be noted in passing that nearly all his attributions had previously been proposed by other critics, who are not always mentioned) that nothing as to whether or not Lantier was intended to be an Impressionist is proved save that Claude's paintings and those of his comrades *could* be based on paintings by contemporary artists. He also notes that of all the possible sources, only three are by an Impressionist, Monet, and even his "Déchargeurs de charbon" was an exception in his work. Rejecting the charges of academicism, banality, and literariness advanced by Rewald, Brady concludes:

L'Oeuvre does not prove that Claude was a painter steeped in the literary spirit and even in the academic tradition; and as

> for demonstrating "how little Zola had grasped the new elements of Impressionistic art," it does not do that either, nor, a fortiori, that Zola "understood nothing of painting."
>
> That is Claude Lantier's tragedy: they begin by accusing him of being an Impressionist, which is not accurate, and then they reproach him for not painting impressionist pictures.[7]

The position taken by Rewald and Brady does not seem completely sound. Rewald's argument of literariness is not valid, for of all Claude's paintings, only one, the "Apotheosis," is really literary in theme, and this painting is conceived in the decline of his talent. The paintings of his middle period, after his return from Bennecourt and before the "Apotheosis," surely seem anything but literary in their direct presentation of unarranged reality and in their lack of "intention." Moreover, though Rewald is right in arguing that the "new study of light" is not enough in itself to make a painting Impressionistic, it is nevertheless true that such a study of light is an essential of Impressionism and that when Zola spoke of Impressionism and the Impressionists, it was this new treatment of light effects that he most often mentioned. Indeed, Zola in Part II of *Le Naturalisme au Salon* mentioned that it is the study of light "in its innumerable decompositions and recompositions" that has been called, more or less correctly, Impressionism (p. 240). If he mentioned a "new study of light" at all in reference to Claude's works, that is in itself a kind of proof that he thought of him at least partly as an Impressionist.

As for Brady, his argument is really a play on words and actually supports the thesis that Claude is some kind of Impressionist. He argues that Claude is a naturalist, an observer of reality and hence not an Impressionist, but it is undeniable, as Brady must have known, that for Zola naturalism and Impressionism were one and the same thing. Again and again in his *Salons* Zola called the Impressionists realists or naturalists, making it clear that he thought little of the term Impressionist and that he regarded the painters of the new school as workers in his own vineyard of exact observation and direct rendition of reality. Occasionally, he is specific: "For me, the group of artists in question (he has been speaking of the Impressionists) is simply a group of naturalistic artists, that is, of conscientious artists who have returned to the direct study of nature."[8] Again: "The group, moreover, is formed of the most diverse and opposite temperaments, a fact which excludes any idea of a school. Their only bond is a need for truth, that need which is making itself felt so vigorously today in all the arts."[9] And still again: "I think that we must understand by 'Impressionist' artists, artists who paint reality."[10] Moreover, Brady makes a point of quoting Zola's declaration in the *Ébauche* that Claude will rise up against the Impressionists' hasty methods, but he does not tell us that nowhere in the novel does Claude do such a thing; it is Sandoz-Zola who utters this criticism.

A good deal of evidence does exist to indicate that Zola had the Impressionists in mind as he composed *L'Oeuvre,* and it is quite certain that Claude has something of an Impressionist in him. Admittedly, it is impossible to make a solid, air-tight case for this thesis, but with all the difficulties it still seems possible to demonstrate that Claude Lantier was intended to be, for at least part of his career, an Impressionist. It should be said at the outset that Claude is a composite character, something of an abstraction or "type," and that he probably does not represent any single artist living or dead. It is unthinkable that Zola could have constructed such a figure with no thought of the Impressionists, the artists he knew best and the artists with whom he was publicly identified. To expect him to create a fictional artist who would have no connection with Impressionism would be like expecting Simone de Beauvoir to write the intellectual history of the 1930's and 1940's in France without regard to the group of Existentialists then coming into being.

The *Dossier* makes it clear that Zola did intend to introduce some aspects of Impressionism in the novel and that he thought of Claude Lantier from almost the very start as a representative of the school. In the *Ébauche* he states this intention clearly: "Now, I have to arrange my Claude. I make of him, of course, a naturalist. . . . I take him, in the history of painting, after Ingres, Delacroix, Courbet. . . . He would like more nature, more open air, more light. Decomposition of light."[11] A little later he adds:

> Let's see what the impressionists can give me for my band. I am under the Empire, I can scarcely include their independent exhibitions. . . . For Claude, I could take some theories of the impressionists, open air, decomposed light, all that new painting which needs a genius to be accomplished. That is Claude's effort; he fails in it, but another may succeed. Transition, progress.—I can also indicate the impressionists at their beginnings, turbulent, with their exhibitions born of the difficulty of getting into the official Salon. . . . But I return to the impressionists: Claude will rise up against their hasty works, the painting completed in two hours, the sketch that satisfies, Monet's hasty sales, the "very good!" the whole bad side of the band, with the rivalries. And yet the undeniable role, the Salons changed by this current. *Claude's*

> *departure from the movement,* the vulgarization by the Gervex, the invasion by the clever fellows of the School.[12]

The text of the novel contains numerous indications that Zola's intentions to make his "band" a group of Impressionists and to make Claude their leader and hence an Impressionist, too, was carried into execution. One of Claude's earliest pronouncements of aesthetic position seems clearly to indicate that his point of view is essentially that of the Impressionists: "Do you understand, we need the sun, we need the open air, a light and young painting, things and beings as they act in real light. . . ."[13] These are exactly the qualities of Impressionism of which Zola most often speaks in his *Salons*—sun, open air, a "light" palette, realism.[14] A little later, Bongrand, speaking to Claude of the impression made upon him by the Salon des Refusés, refers to the "frightful realists" who form Claude's group;[15] "realist" for Zola was "impressionist." Once more, when Christine objects to a "lilac terrain" or a "blue tree" or a "poplar washed with azure" in Claude's paintings, he shows her that such surprises do exist in nature; here Zola is giving fictional form to an idea which he had quoted from Théodore Duret in his *Salon* of 1878:

> The sky is cloudy, the impressionist paints water as glaucous and heavy. The sky is brilliant, he paints water as azure and scintillating. The sun sets, he puts yellow and red on his canvas. Then the public begins to laugh. Winter has come, the impressionist paints snow. He sees that in the sun, shadows on the snow have blue glints, and he paints blue shadows. Then the public really laughs. Certain clay soils of the countryside take on lilac shades, the impressionist paints lilac landscapes. Then the public begins to become indignant. In the summer sun, in the reflections of green foliage, skin and clothing take on a violet tint, the impressionist paints lilac people. Then the public breaks out, no mistake, the critics shake their fists at the painter and call him a scoundrel.[16]

One of the best pieces of evidence that Claude was intended to be at least partly an Impressionist comes in a series of close parallels between what Zola says in his *Salons* about Impressionism as a movement and what he says about Claude's plein-air school. The most frequently recurring generalization which the *Salons* contain about Impressionism, taken as a whole and without reference to individual artists, is a paradoxical combination of rejoicing at the school's spreading influence and a pessimistic reservation that it has not yet found a real master to "impose its formula," to use Zola's phrase. This is the same paradox as is to be found in Zola's treatment of both Monet and Manet. Zola's first references to the school as a school, in *Mon Salon* of 1868, reflect his hope that Impressionism will eventually triumph and will arrive at the dominating role in French art which it deserves;[17] in the Russian *Salons* of 1875, 1876, and 1879 the same note is struck.[18] But gradually this hope is replaced in the *Salons* by the observation that Impressionism is already on its way to victory, or at least is deeply influencing the art of all the men who exhibit in the yearly Salon. As early as 1878 Zola could tell his Russian audience that a dozen painters have joined Manet, the pioneer, in the assault on the sacred rules and that a few painters are daring to copy the new art. By 1879 Zola sees the Impressionists as the "true inspirers of the official Salon, whence they are driven out,"[19] and a group of talented imitators—Bastien-Lepage, Gervex, Carolus Duran—are already adapting the Impressionists' discoveries to bourgeois taste. But it is in *Le Naturalisme au Salon,* of 1880, that Zola makes a formal declaration of the Impressionists' victory. Their influence is already enormous, they are the "true workers of the century," from their little galleries they are imposing their formula, they are at the head of the whole art movement of the epoch. "Naturalism, impressionism, modernism, whatever one may call it," he says, "is today master of the official Salons. We are going to see shortly that success lies here, even with the crowd."[20] It is on this same victorious note that this *Salon,* perhaps the most important one Zola ever wrote, ends.[21]

But at the very time Zola is proclaiming Impressionism's victory, he also makes a curious reservation on the movement as a whole. Victory, he tells the Russians, is not to be seen in the immediate future, for a painter of genius is still necessary to "impose its formula,"[22] which is to say, of course, that he sees no painter of genius among the Impressionists.

Nor will he ever; for as often as he predicts the ultimate domination of modern art by Impressionism he makes the same reservation about the school. In 1878 he expresses the hope that the new art will find in its ranks "one or several painters well enough endowed to fortify the new formula by their masterpieces,"[23] and he is sure that the French school will drag out a miserable existence, living on imitations, until the arrival of an "original talent which will bring with it the new artistic formula."[24] The Impressionist movement is an excellent thing, but we must still wait for the genius who will "realize" the new formula.[25] By the next year, he is willing to be more specific: if there is no leader, no genius, this is because the Impressionists all suffer from technical insufficiency and from a neglect of such considerations as solidity of form and perfection of finish; because they are too easily satisfied with their own efforts they can be nothing but pioneers and transitional figures.[26] In 1880, in *Le Naturalisme au Salon,* Zola is more specific and even harsher: no artist of the group has fully exploited the formula, the man of genius is not born, they have produced no masterpieces; they are all inferior to the task they have chosen.[27] At the very end of his career as art critic, in *Peinture,* Zola repeats these charges almost word for word: Impressionism has conquered the art world, yet no master was there to give it true existence.

L'Oeuvre contains passages which are almost textual duplications of these two contentions of Zola's. When Claude returns from Bennecourt he is received by Mahoudeau and Gagnière with cries of joy, for it was time that their movement find again someone strong enough and vital enough to be the recognized chief. The open air school is growing, its influence is undeniably spreading, but the efforts are scattered, the new recruits are only sketchers, the man of genius must put order in the house and compel the victory of the movement by his genial creations.[28] And when Claude establishes his new studio in Paris he finds the moment propitious: Delacroix and Courbet have left no followers of consequence, their own masterpieces have joined the art of the museums, the new formula's success is easy to predict. The palette is growing lighter, the Salons are becoming "blond," even the Ecole des Beaux-Arts is being won over:

> And what a stroke it would be if, in the midst of all those unconscious copies by the impotent, in the midst of those fearful, sly attempts by the clever fellows, a master was revealed, carrying the formula into effect with the audacity of his strength, sparing no one, setting the formula afoot as it should be set up, solid and complete, to be the truth of this close of the century![29]

Certainly, the most significant of these statements in *L'Oeuvre* occurs at the final Salon, where Claude exhibits his "Enfant Mort." The painting is a failure, of course, but Sandoz demonstrates to him how much he is the victor in the very debacle of his hopes and ambitions: the whole color of the Salon has changed, imitations of him are everywhere, the sun lightens every canvas, all the old mythology and bric-à-brac are gone, the assault of the new school on the old theories has swept away routine, and the new school has established its victory.[30] Seen in the context of what Zola had said a half-dozen times in his *Salons,* it must be the triumph of Impressionism that he is depicting here—the fall of the academic school, the triumph of truth, of nature, of realism, the "fine, diffuse, decomposed light," the "bluish" color, the "ray of sunlight." And all of the change stems from "Plein-Air." Claude is not only an Impressionist, he is the founder of the school.

Almost at the close of *L'Oeuvre* Zola returns to the thesis of the *Salons*—that no master has yet appeared. Sandoz is aware that in spite of the triumph of a tendency there is no one yet who has succeeded in "imposing the formula";[31] and when his words are compared to the judgments of *Peinture,* an article undeniably directed at the influence of the Impressionists—who are named—then it becomes evident that Claude can have been, in Zola's mind, nothing but an Impressionist, for this passage is so close in idea and even in expression to certain pages of *Peinture* that it is nothing less than a first draft of the article which contained Zola's final stand on Impressionism.

And there is a good deal more evidence to back the case for Claude as an Impressionist. The epoch is the Impressionist epoch, for though the novel ends in 1876 it is clear by Zola's constant references to the "end of the century" that he intended it to be far more than a historical account of the years between the Salon des Refusés and the beginnings of Impressionism. Over and over again he makes it clear that the movements he describes in the novel—movements not only in painting but in literature, and notably the rise of music as a primary source of inspiration for artists of all kinds—are contemporary to the writing of *L'Oeuvre* and that he is depicting contemporary time, not the preceding generation. Moreover, Zola's insistence that Claude is not an academic painter either by training, temperament, or technique seems to mean that he intended him to be an Impressionist, for the *Salons* demonstrate that he saw the art movement of the years 1863-85 as a contest between academicism and Impressionism, called variously naturalism or realism or modernism. The presence of Fagerolles is another bit of evidence: he is clearly designed to represent a familiar figure for Zola, the slick operator who steals from Manet and the Impressionists and popularizes their technique and subject matter; the existence of such an artist as Fagerolles is, indeed, almost certain proof that Zola was thinking of Claude and his "band" in exactly the same terms as he thought of the Impressionists, for Fagerolles is the sign of Claude's victory even as Gervex and Bastien-Lepage and Carolus Duran were proofs of the "rightness" of the Impressionist effort. So are the light theories advanced by Claude and taken by Zola from Léo Gausson's letter, based itself on the writings of Chevreul, who provided the Impressionists and Postimpressionists with some of their ideas on color. So is Claude's struggle to storm the Salon, a struggle described by Zola a dozen times when he speaks of Manet and the Impressionists, perhaps the most significant artistic campaign of the century. So is the reaction to *L'Oeuvre* of Claude Monet himself, who seemed to Zola for a time to be the leader of the school; if Monet saw Impressionists behind the figures of the novel, if he saw Impressionism in Claude's paintings, it was very probably because they were there. The whole atmosphere of the book, all its details, confirm that it is the era of Impressionism which is depicted, and it would be unthinkable that Zola could have so completely re-created the era of struggle and victory which the Impressionists had lived without including them in his fiction.

But this is not to say that throughout his career Claude Lantier is portrayed as an Impressionist. Rather, *L'Oeuvre* is a study of an evolution toward Impressionism and then, at the end, of an evolution away from it toward symbolism and what Zola often calls "idealism." Claude's earliest sketches, made in Provence, do not seem to fit the formula of any school; they are wild, personal impressions, showing evidences of a mind and eye which when more mature and more educated will become truly Impressionist. Even "Plein-Air" is not wholly an Impressionist painting, any more than is Manet's "Le Déjeuner sur l'herbe," for while it contains a new notation of light effects, it is still a studio painting and does not contain some of the identifying marks of an Impressionist canvas, the use of the "tache" for instance. Nor are the paintings of the Bennecourt period wholly Impressionistic, insofar as we can see them; they probably represent Claude's gropings toward a mature technique and so are described in only the most summary fashion. But the paintings of the middle period of Claude's career, from the end of the Bennecourt stay to the conception of the "Apotheosis," clearly seem to represent Zola's idea of what the typical Impressionist canvas might be. The paintings of this period, again insofar as we see them, are all open-air paintings, they emphasize light effects and give lesser importance to design, they are modern in theme and realistic in subject, in short they possess all the qualities which Zola saw, rightly or wrongly, as characteristic of the new school.

After the middle period, when Claude fails to win the acclaim he had expected by use of the new technique brought back from Bennecourt and perfected in the following years, he slips away from Impressionism and, driven by madness, lapses almost entirely into a bizarre kind of symbolism, where the realism of the primary conception—itself Impressionistic enough, if we look only at the subject—gives way to a sickly dream. Claude appears to be an Impressionist really only during the period of the maturity of his powers; but it seems beyond all argument that in that time he did represent for Zola the main tendencies of the school.

Unfortunately, although many paintings are mentioned in the pages of *L'Oeuvre,* not many are described in detail and rarely does Zola go beyond a short indication of subject and a line or two about technique or light effect. To demonstrate that Claude was intended to be an Impressionist and was, in Zola's mind, the founder and chief theorist of the school, is therefore nearly impossible, for there is little direct evidence, only a good many circumstantial indications. But can Zola have meant Claude to be anything but an Impressionist when he speaks of his canvases as "works of such a personal notation, where for the first time nature bathed in real light, beneath the play of reflections and the continual decomposition of colors?"

Then does Claude's failure symbolize the failure that Zola saw in the whole Impressionist movement? Scarcely, for Claude does not end his career as an Impressionist but as a kind of "symbolist" or "idealist." But his inability to find *the* formula, *the* technique which will adequately render his vision seems to exemplify the inherent flaw of Impressionism as Zola saw it, the final lack of a theory which would have guaranteed the school immortality. Claude is a transitional figure, as the Impressionists were for Zola; he occupies exactly their situation in the evolution of art. But this is an observation, a "message," not a thesis proper.

On one point there can be no debate: *L'Oeuvre* was clearly intended to exemplify in prose the practice of the Impressionist school. Literally dozens of passages betray Zola's intention to render in words the effects which he believed the Impressionists sought by the medium of light and color. Light effects are everywhere, and they are Impressionist light effects; here Zola quite evidently set out to be an Impressionist of the pen, just as in *Le Ventre de Paris* he set out to be a "Dutch master," just as in *Germinal* he set out to be the Delacroix of the nether world. A score of brief glimpses like these testify to his aim: "with her elbows lifted, she rolled and pulled the ribbons without hurrying, her face in the golden reflection of the sun"; "the beautiful day was ending in a powder of sunlight"; "you would have called it a dog wearing a hat, a rain of short blond hair over a delicate nose, a wide, laughing mouth in a pink muzzle"; "everything was blazing, the tight lines of carriages, the new foliage in the trees, the fountains in the basins, which sprang up and scattered in a golden dust"; "the women walked easily, stopped in profile; and his painter's eye was especially drawn by the flowers on their hats, very intense in tone, among the dark waves of the high black silk hats." Sometimes the glance is longer, the painting more detailed: "suddenly the sun, which had already disappeared, pierced the rampart with such a powder of light that shafts of sparks rose up, going from one side of the sky to the other, visible like a flight of golden arrows." Or again: "they saw Paris passing in a cloud of glory, carriages with wheels shining like suns, the great yellow busses more gilded than triumphal chariots, horsemen whose mounts seemed to throw sparks, pedestrians who were transfigured and glowed in the light." In all the full-scale paintings of Paris and the Seine which *L'Oeuvre* contains, the same qualities are always present: diffusion of light, depiction of masses and only the most significant details, a general lightness of tone, the use of color to indicate transient light effects. They demonstrate that though Zola might have been reluctant to disclose openly that he intended his painter to be an Impressionist and so refrained from describing much of his work in detail, he did intend the novel to give the sense of Impressionism. Like Claude Lantier, he is here an Impressionist.[32]

But *L'Oeuvre* is considerably more than a fictional depiction of some aspects of Impressionism and Claude Lantier is much more than a symbolic representation of the Impressionist painter. *L'Oeuvre* is, implicitly at least, a prophecy and a defense.

A prophecy, surely, of the coming of what Zola called "idealism," the complex of interests and antipathies which we mean when we say symbolism, the flight from realism and the realist ethos, the escape from the gray modern industrial world into dream and fantasy and exoticism, the passion for the unconscious and the instinctual, the conviction of the "bankruptcy of science," the flight to religion, the enthusiasm for intuitional and antirationalistic philosophies, the interest in the primitive, the deviant, the "mystic," the almost incredible love of music and of Wagnerism in particular, and all the other symptoms of the syndrome. When Claude introduces the colossal nude into his realistic painting of the Seine he begins to worship at the altar of these new gods, for the nude has no realistic raison d'être; when his aberration, his "lesion," makes him decorate her like a pagan idol, when he enlarges her and causes her to dwarf and conquer the longshoremen around her in the canvas, when he makes her the incarnation of sex and desire, he symbolizes the movement of art and letters toward domains that Zola could not understand and which he could only condemn. When Gagnière allows music to invade his life, to paralyze and finally atomize his painting, he typifies the whole direction of the art world, a direction which Zola could not but hold in scepticism and finally in contempt, but which he could not deny in 1885 and 1886. When Claude fails in his mad enterprise Zola seems to be prophesying that all such mystic enterprises are doomed to failure, that salvation in art can be found only in truth to nature, that verity is the absolute canon of art, and that when the aberrant forces of personality so far overwhelm rationality as they do in Claude in his last years, then the nonrational as a source of valid subjects for art is condemned by its inherent unintelligibility. This is the real sense of Claude's failure: it is a sign of what Zola considered the fate of art when it fell into the morass of symbolism, when it abandoned reality, positivism, the "truth." Impressionism may have been a failure, Claude's expressionism is a catastrophe.

Of all the artists who appear in the novel, the only ones to succeed artistically are Bongrand, defender of truth in art, and Sandoz-Zola, who unflinchingly practices his role of naturalist observer and recorder of the external world. Sandoz' steady faith in the "documentary" method, his belief in the observable as the only valid source of inspiration, his enthusiasm for the modern world, where there are no miracles and no nude symbols, and his love of nature make of him the exact opposite of the late Claude Lantier; his success, countering the painter's failure, is not so much the success of a personality as of a system. In 1885-86 realism and naturalism were entering a period of stress, and Zola, with his amazing intuitional grasp of contemporary forces and movements, knew it: their long domination of French art was about to be challenged by the rising forces of mysticism, intuitionism, and irrationalism. *L'Oeuvre* is Zola's manifesto, his proclamation that though the world of art might change around him, he was still faithful to the doctrine of Médan. In the contest between the forces of "science" and the forces of "personality" within him, "science" clearly wins.

In reality, *L'Oeuvre*—at least at its end—is not so much a novel about Impressionism as a novel about the coming decades: it does not end in 1876 or even in 1886, it ends in 1896, for in his *Peinture* of that year Zola explicitly and eloquently condemns the tendency that brought Claude to his catastrophe:

> . . . this is a lamentable outpouring of mysticism. . . . What barely formulated stammering, what a chaos of the most irritating pretentions! English aestheticism has come and has completed the derailment of our clear and solid French genius. All kinds of influences, which it would be too long to describe here, have united and massed themselves to cast down our school into this scorn of nature, this hatred of the flesh and of the sun. . . .
>
> I know very well all that can be said in explanation, and this movement, which I shall call idealist in order to give it a name,

> has had its raison d'être, as a natural protest against the triumphant realism of the preceding period. It has also manifested itself in literature, it is a result of the law of evolution in which any action calls for a reaction. And we must admit the fact that young artists cannot remain forever faithful to existing formulas; they must seek the new, even when it is extravagant. And I am far from saying that there have not been strange attempts, interesting discoveries in this return to dreams and legends. . . .
>
> But let us have no painting of souls! Nothing is as irritating as painting based on ideas. Let an artist put an idea into a skull, but let the skull be there, solidly painted and strongly enough built to scorn the centuries. Life alone speaks of life, truth and beauty arise only from living nature.[33]

So *L'Oeuvre* is prophetic, wrongly perhaps, but nonetheless it is important as one more example of Zola's perception of the forces around him. He may not have seen symbolism steadily or rightly, but at least he saw it at its very birth and realized its implications for his own art and his own outlook on the world. He was as "modern" as J.-K. Huysmans himself, which in 1885 it was not given to every observer to be.

But possibly *L'Oeuvre*'s greatest importance and interest lie not in its depiction of Impressionism and not in its prophecy of the coming of symbolism and not in its implicit defense of realism, but in its revelation of the state of Zola's soul in 1885 and 1886. Of all the self-portraits he left, the portrait created by Lantier and Sandoz, the two halves of the creator's personality, is by far the most intimate and the most honest. Lantier's career is a disclosure, not of an Impressionist's failure, but of the novelist's own sense of his lack of perfect achievement, his disappointment with himself and with his art. Sandoz' long confession in Chapter IX, in which he protests the bonds that work has laid upon him and proclaims his growing dissatisfaction with his own accomplishment, in which he rises up against the torture of intellectual life—this long confession is his clearest and frankest declaration of the torments of the suffering "beast of burden" who seemed to his compatriots not much more than a bourgeois prose-machine or a cheap publicity seeker or a dangerous corruptor. In Lantier and Sandoz we find the true Zola, romantic, agonizing, the Zola before Jeanne Rozerot, the dark poet of misery and revolution, the pessimistic prophet of the Catastrophe, the prophet who had not yet known paternity.

For this is a pessimistic book, if the nineteenth century ever produced one, a major document in the history of pessimism in France, as worthy an example of the fin-de-siècle spirit as any poem by Leconte de Lisle or any essay by Paul Bourget.[34] In its pages nearly everyone fails, and those who succeed, like Sandoz, find only disillusionment, or, like Fagerolles, face the certainty of eventual unmasking. Those who are faithful are paid in base coin indeed: Claude destroys himself, Christine ends her life in misery, Sandoz has the reward of carrying his friend's body to the grave. Nearly every act is useless, vain, pointless; honesty and integrity bring only derision; love dies and with it all possibility of beauty. Nothing is left at the end, not even faith; *tout passe.* And failure is not the product of man's sins or omissions; it is everywhere, endemic, it is fate. Even the last hope of man, posterity, and the future, give no assurance that the pains and failures of this life will not have been in vain.

The last pages of *L'Oeuvre* contain a curious debate between the forces of life and the forces of death, between hope and despair in Sandoz' soul. Zola was debating within himself in these years of stress and torment before he found satisfaction in love and fatherhood. As Sandoz and Bongrand meditate on the meaning of Claude's life they give form to the opposing forces of the epoch and reveal something of the torment of Zola's own life:

> "Bah! the man of genius will be born, nothing is lost, light must be."
>
> "Who knows? not always," said Bongrand. "Life also aborts. You know, I'm listening to you, but I am a despairing man. I'm dying of sadness, and I feel everything else dying too. Yes, the air of the period is bad, this close of the century full of demolitions, with its gutted monuments, with its soil turned over a hundred times, all giving off a stink of death! Can one be a well man in this atmosphere? Our nerves are failing, the universal neurosis is taking a hand in it, art itself is troubled; this is the final upsetting, anarchy, the madness of the personality driven to the wall. Never have we quarreled so much and never have we seen so dimly as since the day when we claimed to know everything."
>
> Sandoz, pale, watched the great reddish clouds of smoke rolling in the wind.
>
> It was inevitable, he thought, half-aloud, this excess of activity and of pride in knowledge had to bring us back to doubt; this century, which has made so much light, had to finish in the threat of a new flood of shadows. . . . Yes, our uneasiness comes from that. We promised too much, hoped too much, we expected the conquest and the explanation of everything; and now our im-

> patience is grumbling. What! We don't move any faster? science has not given us, in these hundred years, absolute certainty, perfect happiness? Then, what good is it to continue, since we'll never know everything and since our bread will always be as bitter? This is the failure of the century, pessimism is twisting our guts, mysticism befogging our minds; for in vain we drive out the phantoms with the great shafts of light given by analysis, the supernatural has taken up the battle again, the spirit of the legends has risen up in rebellion and wants to reconquer us, in this moment of fatigue and anguish. . . . Ah, certainly, I can't affirm anything, I myself am torn. Only, it seems to me that this last convulsion of the old religious terror was to be foreseen. We are not an end, but a transition, a beginning of something else. It calms me, it does me good to think that we are marching toward reason and the solidity of science.
>
> His voice had changed, in deep emotion, and he added:
>
> Unless madness upsets us in the darkness and unless we all depart, strangled by the ideal, like the old comrade who is sleeping there, in his four planks.[35]

The voice of pessimism has the last word—how could Zola have ended on any other note when his whole tale is a tale of failure?

And the last line of the book, "Let's get to work" (Zola had originally written "Let's get to work—we've got to hope all the same") is the best proof that Zola meant *L'Oeuvre* to be a document in the history of pessimism. For what value does work have when its products are hopelessly flawed and when they can reach no future life and when oblivion is man's only reward? "Let's get to work"—there is no hope in that, only habit, resignation, stoicism. The words are the sign of the triumph, momentary perhaps, of the forces of death in Zola's soul; the spleen was on him, and he would not lose it until the great victory of his last decade.

Create a world, found a school, revive art, conquer Paris, these are Claude's dreams, as they were Zola's. And Claude does come at last to dominate Paris, but it is from within the pine boards of his coffin on the hill of Montmartre. In the sad irony of the symbol is the whole meaning of *L'Oeuvre.* It may render Zola's profoundest judgment of himself.

Notes

CHAPTER I

1. Léon Deffoux, "Emile Zola et ses éditions depuis 1902," *Le Figaro,* Oct. 1, 1927, says that *L'Oeuvre* had sold approximately 60,000 copies by 1902, but only about 85,000 by 1927, one of the smallest percentages of increase of all of Zola's works. Its total sales were then greater only than those of *La Fortune des Rougon, La Curée, Le Ventre de Paris, La Conquête de Plassans, Son Excellence Eugène Rougon, La Joie de vivre* and *Vérité.*
2. Henri Massis, *Comment Zola composait ses romans* (Paris: Charpentier, 1906), p. 71. Massis points out à propos of Claude's family name that in this first plan of the *Rougon-Macquart* series all Gervaise's children were by the same father. Dulac was also called Duval in the sketch.
3. Maurice LeBlond, in the "Notes et commentaire" to *L'Oeuvre,* claims that the work was completed on Feb. 22, 1886. *L'Oeuvre, Oeuvres complètes d'Emile Zola,* XVIII (Paris: Bernouard, 1928), p. 401. It is difficult to understand how LeBlond could have made this small error, since Zola was careful to date his manuscripts clearly.
4. Emile Zola, *Correspondance, 1872-1902, Oeuvres complètes,* XLIX, pp. 655-66.
5. Letter to Céard, Aug. 23, 1885. *Ibid.,* p. 644. Zola in this same letter indicates that he had also negotiated with *Le Figaro* for publication of *L'Oeuvre,* but had been fearful that *Le Figaro*'s readers would yawn with boredom at this book of "pure artistic and passional physiology." *Ibid.*
6. Other reviews were by M. Français (*L'Autorité,* Apr. 5), P. d'Aramon (*La France libre,* Apr. 16 and 24), A. Dethez (*Le Siècle,* Apr. 17), M. Fouquier (*La France,* May 2), R. Charvay (*L'Evénement,* May 6), De Larivière (*Revue générale,* May 15), C. Bigot (*Gagne-petit,* Apr. 5), R. Bernier (*Revue moderne,* May), Vincent (*Le XIX*e *Siècle,* Apr. 17), and H. Le Roux (*La République française,* Apr. 28). Anonymous

reviews appeared in *L'Echo de Paris* (Apr. 6), *La Gazette anecdotique* (Apr. 30), *Le Français* (May 21), *Le Livre* (May 10), and *Le Moniteur universel* (Aug. 30). Some of the dates and authors given by LeBlond in the "Notes et commentaire" to *L'Oeuvre,* pp. 425-36, are erroneous. LeBlond does not cite the favorable article of Fernand Henry, now contained in his *Critique au jour le jour* (Paris: Savine, 1887), pp. 87-102. More recent commentaries on the novel include those by Edmond Lepelletier in *Emile Zola, sa vie, son oeuvre* (Paris: Mercure de France, 1908), pp. 372 sqq., Camille Mauclair, "Le Crépuscule de l'art pictural," *La Revue des revues,* Apr. 1, 1930, and Marcel Girard, "Situation d'Emile Zola," *Revue des sciences humaines,* new series, no. 65, Jan.-Mar. 1952, pp. 137-56.

7. In his *Souvenirs de Paris et de Londres* (Paris: Hachette, 1880). I have been unable to consult this volume, but in its English translation, *Studies of Paris,* translated by W. W. Cady (New York and London: G. P. Putnam's Sons, 1886), there is this passage: "Then another novel, *The Struggle of Genius Making a Way for Itself in the World,* a band of young men who go to Paris to seek their fortunes, the life of journalism, literary life, art, criticism, poverty in decent dress, the efforts, desperations and triumphs of young men of genius who are devoured by ambition and hunger—a history in which he will pour out all the blood which issued from the wounds of his heart when he was twenty." (Pp. 239-40)
8. Fernand Xau, *Emile Zola* (Paris: Marpon et Flammarion, 1880), p. 49.
9. Paul Alexis, *Emile Zola, notes d'un ami* (Paris: Charpentier, 1882), pp. 121-22.
10. Louis Desprez, *L'Evolution naturaliste* (Paris: Tresse, 1884), p. 213.
11. Quoted in Guy Robert, *La Terre d'Emile Zola, étude historique et critique* (Paris: Société d'Edition les Belles Lettres, 1952), p. 127.
12. Chincholle had written Zola asking information for his article and received a reply indicating that Roybet would not be the hero of the novel. Zola went on to say that toward the end of his novel he would say a word or two about the present generation of artists, rich and successful, as opposed to the poor and passionate artists of his work; but that would be only a "note," he added, for the real interest of his book would lie in the struggle of an incomplete genius with nature and in the struggle of a woman against the call of art. *Correspondance, 1872-1902,* letter of June 6, 1885, p. 640.
13. Unpublished letter, Bibliothèque nationale, Département des manuscrits, NAF no. 24545, p. 165.
14. *Emile Zola's Letters to J. Van Santen Kolff,* edited by Robert J. Niess (St. Louis: Washington University Press, 1940), p. 7.
15. *Ibid.,* letter of July 26, 1885, p. 8.
16. See note 5. An unpublished letter from Paul Ginisty, Bibliothèque nationale, Département des manuscrits, NAF no. 24519, p. 96, dated

Feb. 24, 1886, indicates that *La Vie populaire* purchased serial rights to the novel for 3000 francs after the conclusion of the *Gil Blas* serialization.

17. Robert J. Niess, "Nine Letters from Emile Zola to Frans Netscher," *Publications of the Modern Language Association*, LVI (1941), p. 263.
18. *Correspondance, 1872-1902*, letter of Dec. 15, 1885, p. 650. In an unpublished letter to Zola (Bibliothèque nationale, Département des manuscrits, NAF no. 24516), p. 178, dated Dec. 14, 1885, Céard indicates that *Le Gil Blas* had advanced the date of publication.
19. *Emile Zola's Letters to J. Van Santen Kolff*, p. 9.
20. See note 5.
21. For an excellent, though overly systematic, discussion of this nineteenth- and twentieth-century literary tradition, see Theodore R. Bowie, *The Painter in French Fiction* (Chapel Hill: University of North Carolina Press), 1950.
22. *Le Chef-d'oeuvre inconnu*, in *Etudes philosophiques*, II, *Oeuvres complètes de Balzac*, ed. Bouteron et Longnon (Paris: Conard, 1925), p. 31.
23. *L'Oeuvre*, édition intégrale publiée sous la direction d'Armand Lanoux, études, notes et variantes par Henri Mitterand (Paris: NRF-Bibliothèque de la Pléiade, 1966), IV, p. 342. All citations of *L'Oeuvre* are from this edition. Mitterand discusses *Le Chef-d'oeuvre inconnu* as a source, p. 1351.
24. *Le Chef-d'oeuvre inconnu*, pp. 25-26.
25. *L'Oeuvre*, p. 346.
26. *Le Chef-d'oeuvre inconnu*, p. 33.
27. *L'Oeuvre*, p. 345.
28. *Le Chef-d'oeuvre inconnu*, p. 33.
29. *L'Oeuvre*, p. 363.
30. Armand Lanoux seems to believe that Zola based his story on Balzac's, but adds that Zola found his title by merely shortening the one Balzac had invented; this claim is not borne out by Zola's notes. *Bonjour, Monsieur Zola* (Paris: Amiot-Dupont, 1954), p. 202. For detailed discussions of the relationship between *L'Oeuvre* and *Le Chef-d'oeuvre inconnu*, see R. J. Niess, "Another View of Zola's L'Oeuvre," *Romanic Review*, XXXIX (1948), pp. 282-300, and Patrick Brady, "Les Sources littéraires de l'*Oeuvre* de Zola," *Revue de l'université de Bruxelles*, new series XVI (Aug.-Sept., 1964). In the notes to the Pléiade edition of *L'Oeuvre*, Henri Mitterand discusses this question, p. 1351.
31. James admits his debt—in a perfectly Jamesian fashion—when he has one of the painters in the tale remark that if the painter Theobald's unknown masterpiece is ever seen, it will doubtless turn out to be no more than the painting in "that terrible little tale of Balzac's."
32. "The Madonna of the Future" first appeared in the *Atlantic Monthly* for Mar. 1873.

33. James was in France from the fall of 1875 to almost the end of 1876, and in a letter of May 28, 1876, he mentions meeting Zola. It is quite possible that during the course of their conversation he called Zola's attention to the fact that he had had a piece accepted by the *Revue des deux mondes.* See the *Letters of Henry James,* edited by Percy Lubbock (New York: Scribner's, 1920), II, pp. 47-50, for his reference to Zola.
34. Henry James, "The Madonna of the Future," in *Stories of Writers and Artists,* edited by F. O. Matthiessen (New York: New Directions, n. d. [1944]), p. 47.
35. In the first family tree of the Rougon-Macquarts, published in *Une Page d'amour,* in 1878, there is no mention of a child of Claude Lantier's; the child appears only in the definitive tree published in *Le Docteur Pascal.*
36. "La Madone de l'avenir," *Revue des deux mondes,* Apr. 1, 1875, *passim.*
37. Charles Baudelaire, *Nouvelles histoires extraordinaires* (Paris: Quantin, 1884), p. 276. Since Zola's command of English was weak, it is not likely that he had read Poe in the original, but it is entirely possible that he knew Baudelaire's version of Poe's tale and hence I cite Baudelaire's work.
38. *Ibid.,* p. 277.
39. Bowie, *op. cit.,* pp. 5-6.
40. *Ibid.,* p. 25.
41. *Ibid.,* p. 28. Bowie also adds, in this respect: "When Lantier paints "L'Enfant mort," a subject presented to him by the circumstances of his son's death, this fact is of the utmost psychological importance. The tragedy has affected Lantier as an artist as well as a human being; since the two are not separable, any and all experiences are transmutable into art, and there can never be any consideration given to sentimental objections based on sorrow, propriety or modesty. Indeed, for the artist the only way to obtain release from private grief is precisely to translate it by the means at his disposal. It is interesting to see the Naturalist Zola thus harking back to Romantic practice, best exemplified perhaps in Musset's *Nuits.*" (pp. 28-29)
42. *Ibid.,* p. 30. Bowie seems to be in error in declaring here that Zola and the Goncourts are in opposition to Balzac, who, he appears to believe, approves the philosophic tendency in Frenhofer. But it is not "perhaps irrelevant" that Frenhofer's meditation leads to disaster, it is the essence of his failure that he speculates too much and does not paint enough.
43. *Ibid.,* pp. 30-31.
44. *Ibid.,* p. 44.
45. Edmond and Jules de Goncourt, *Manette Salomon* (Paris: Flammarion-Fasquelle, n. d. [1926]). Edition définitive publiée sous la direction de l'Académie Goncourt, postface de Lucien Descaves, pp. 457-58.
46. *Ibid.,* p. 459.

47. Robert Ricatte, *La Création romanesque chez les Goncourt, 1851-1870* (Paris: Armand Colin, 1953), Chap. VII.
48. *Ibid.*, p. 376.
49. François Fosca (Georges de Traz), *Edmond et Jules de Goncourt* (Paris: Albin Michel, 1941), p. 242.
50. There is a curious little passage in *Manette Salomon* in which Zola himself may figure. When Coriolis has been ruined by Manette, and when she has forced him to sell his two best canvases, which illustrate his theories of modern beauty, the sale attracts great attention. A literary beginner, brilliant and already in the public eye, wanting to make a further name for himself and seeking a personality on whom he can hang his own novel ideas, sees "his man" in Coriolis. He writes three noisy articles full of enthusiasm for the painter in the most widely read of the small newspapers of the time. The parallel with Zola's relationship to Manet is of course clear (see *Manette Salomon*, pp. 439-40). For the sake of completeness, it might also be noted that there is a small similarity of detail between *L'Oeuvre* and *Manette Salomon*, the description by both Zola and the Goncourts of the names and addresses of models written on the studio walls. Needless to say, this may be a product of similar observation by both parties and does not constitute real evidence of borrowing on Zola's part. For a detailed study of the relationship between *L'Oeuvre* and *Manette Salomon*, see Brady, *op. cit.*
51. Edmond et Jules de Goncourt, *Les Hommes de lettres* (Paris: Dentu, 1860), p. 183.
52. *Ibid.*, p. 177.
53. Suggested also by Ricatte, *op. cit.*, p. 350, note 110.
54. Philippe Burty, *Grave imprudence, La Nouvelle revue*, V (1880), pp. 583-609, 806-30; VI (1880), pp. 154-87. Mitterand, *op. cit.*, also discusses *Grave imprudence*, p. 1352.
55. *Grave imprudence, La Nouvelle revue*, V, p. 601.
56. *Ibid.*, p. 601-2.
57. Édouard Rod, "La Nuit vendue," in *Les Allemands à Paris* (Paris: Derveaux, 1880), p. 166.
58. Édouard Rod, *La Femme d'Henri Vanneau* (Paris: Plon-Nourrit, 1884), p. 54.
59. Joris-Karl Huysmans, *En Ménage, Oeuvres complètes* (Paris: Crès), vol. IV.
60. *Ibid.*, pp. 129-30.
61. Georges Duval, *Le Quartier Pigalle* (Paris: Marpon et Flammarion, n. d.).
62. Alexandre Dumas *fils, Affaire Clémenceau* (Paris: Calmann Lévy, n. d.).
63. Unpublished letter, Bibliothèque nationale, Département des manuscrits, NAF no. 24533, pp. 356 *et bis*.
64. George Moore, *A Modern Lover* (London: Tinsley Brothers, 1883), I, pp. 45-46.

65. For a more extended treatment of this episode, see my article, "George Moore and Emile Zola Again," *Symposium,* Spring, 1966, pp. 43-49.
66. See p. 174.
67. Brady, *op. cit.,* discusses *L'Éucation sentimentale* as a source for *L'Oeuvre,* as does Mitterand, p. 1351.
68. Charles Beuchat, *Histoire du naturalisme français* (Paris: Corrêa, 1949), I, p. 233.
69. The apparatus of sketches, notes and so on, which Zola compiled while planning the composition of *L'Oeuvre* will be referred to henceforth as the *Dossier.* This reference occurs p. 348.

CHAPTER II

1. It is possible that in this rivalry between woman and art for mastery of Claude's soul Zola was reflecting the drama of his own menage, though to date there has been no evidence that his wife was ever so jealous of his efforts as Christine is in the novel. It may be that Sandoz's bitter words in Chapter IX on the extent to which work has captured him and destroyed his family life are an echo of words he had heard at home.
2. Zola declared in a letter to Ludovic Halévy that he intended the terminal date to be 1876 and seemed surprised that Halévy had been confused. See John C. Lapp, *Zola Before the Rougon-Macquart Series* (Toronto: University of Toronto Press, 1964), p. 114.
3. P. 122.
4. *Le Voltaire,* May 2, 1886. Zola had already made a much more direct pronouncement than this, but not publicly. In a letter of July 6, 1885, to J. Van Santen Kolff, his Dutch admirer and commentator, he declared flatly: "I have begun my next novel and this novel, in fact, has as its milieu the literary and artistic world. I have taken up again my Claude Lantier of *Le Ventre de Paris.* I shall recount my whole youth, I have put my friends, I have put myself in it." *Emile Zola's Letters to J. Van Santen Kolff,* p. 7.
5. Emile Solari, "Circonstances dans lesquelles Zola composa ses oeuvres," *Grande revue,* CXIV (June, 1924), p. 615. See also Philippe Gille, *La Bataille littéraire, troisième série* (1883-1886) (Paris: Harvard, 1890) pp. 113-14; Ernest A Vizetelly, preface to the first English edition of *L'Oeuvre, His Masterpiece* (London: Chatto and Windus), p. viii; Beuchat, *op. cit.,* II, p. 69; John Rewald, *Cézanne, sa vie, son oeuvre, son amitié pour Zola* (Paris: Albin Michel, 1939), pp. 302-3 and 311-12, and *Paul Cézanne, a Biography* (New York: Simon and Schuster, 1948), p. 143; Hélène and Jean Adhémar, "Zola et la peinture," *Arts,* Dec. 12-18, 1952; Bibliothèque nationale, *Emile Zola,* exposition organisée pour le cinquantième anniversaire de sa mort (Paris, 1952), p. 53.

6. Fernand Doucet: *L'Esthétique d'Emile Zola et son application à la critique* (The Hague: De Nederlandsche Boek- en Steendruckerij, n. d.), pp. 132-37. See also Armand Lanoux, *op. cit.*, p. 203. François Fosca, *op. cit.*, p. 240, identifies all the major characters with specific individuals (sometimes incorrectly) and then adds: "It seems to me that the word 'caddishness' is even too weak to describe such a lack of feeling and delicacy." Gerstle Mack, in *Paul Cézanne* (New York: Knopf, 1935), says this: "Was Zola guilty of treachery, or at least of a breach of good taste, in thus making use of his friends to bring to life the characters of a novel? He has been accused of both; but I cannot see that either charge is tenable. It is inevitable that a novelist—especially a realistic novelist like Zola—should use the people he knows and understands as the raw material from which his characters are fashioned. As long as there is no petty malice, no taint of personal spite in such derivations, they are a legitimate component of the novelist's stock in trade. And there is no evidence whatever that Zola was malicious in the treatment of his old friends, however unpleasant some of the characters he created out of the ingredients they supplied may have turned out. His book required such characters, and to build them up he appropriated from life a trait here, an incident there; but there was no animus behind his borrowing." (Pp. 295-96). For still another treatment of the question, see Bernard Dorival, *Cézanne* (Paris: Pierre Tisné, 1948), p. 76.
7. Joachim Gasquet, *Cézanne* (Paris: Les Editions Bernheim-Jeune, new edition, 1926), p. 21, note 1.
7a. Maurice LeBlond, "Notes et commentaire" to *L'Oeuvre, p.* 402.
8. Beuchat, *op. cit.*, p. 69, also identifies Madame Sandoz *mère* as Madame François Zola.
9. *L'Oeuvre,* p. 205. Manet's portrait of Madame Alexandrine Zola resembles her fictional description closely.
10. Beuchat, *loc. cit.*, shares this opinion, as do Lanoux, *op. cit.*, p. 107; Marcel Batilliat, *Emile Zola* (Paris: Rieder, 1931), p. 40; and F. W. J. Hemmings, *Emile Zola* (Oxford: Clarendon Press, second edition, 1966), p. 213.
11. Rewald, *Paul Cézanne*, p. 146, and *Cézanne, sa vie, son oeuvre, son amitié pour Zola,* p. 308 (Paris: A Michel, 1939); Dorival, *op. cit.*, p. 11; Doucet, *op. cit.* p. 134; Fosca, *op. cit.* p. 240; LeBlond, "Notes et commentaire" to *L'Oeuvre,* p. 403; Patrick Brady, "Les Clefs de l'*Oeuvre* de Zola," *Australian Journal of French Studies,* Sept.-Dec. 1964, pp. 266-67; Mitterand, *op. cit.*, pp. 1365-66, all agree on this identification.
12. *Dossier*, pp. 292 and 299; see also pp. 272 and 311.
13. *Ibid.*, p. 313.
14. Only one specific detail seems to have survived, and that in changed form. It will be recalled that Dubuche installs a trapeze in the garden of

his home so that his sickly children may exercise a little and here Zola seems to be recalling a practice which Baille himself engaged in, at least if a letter of June 6, 1860, is a certain guide. Here Zola says: "I have always execrated gymnastic exercises; but since your accident, I am even more incensed against them. To injure oneself, to inflict on oneself a life-long suffering while climbing a trapeze!" *Correspondance, Lettres de jeunesse, Oeuvres complètes,* XIII, p. 83.

15. *Ibid.,* p. 100, letter of June 24, 1860. See also letters of July 4, 1860 (pp. 110-18); July 25, 1860 (pp. 122-33) and Sept. 21, 1860 (pp. 165-67).
16. Léon Deffoux and Emile Zavie, *Le Groupe de Médan* (Paris: Payot, 1920), p. 235, note.
17. Zola's only two references to Baille around the time of *L'Oeuvre* come in letters to Numa Coste (*Correspondance,* 1872-1902, p. 563, letter of Nov. 5, 1881; and p. 646, letter of Sept. 1, 1885). They reflect nothing resembling ill will on Zola's part. Both Baille and Solari were founding members of the Association Emile Zola in 1909.
18. Henri Perruchot provides the only documentation available on Chaillan: "This Chaillan, son of a peasant of Trets, was twenty-seven (i. e., in 1858). . . . One day that autumn he left his village and, dressed in a jacket and yellow nankin trousers, a stick in his hand, went on foot to Aix. What did he want? Quite simply, to become an 'artist.' Arriving at the Cours, he asked a policeman 'where the artists of Aix met?'—'My word, the artists,' the policeman replied, 'I don't know them; but look over there, at the Café des Deux Garçons; in the back room there are always people who make a lot of noise. Perhaps that's it.' The information was right. The 'artists' welcomed with a mocking indulgence this naive fellow. 'Did you study painting at the School of Fine Arts in Trets?' Numa Coste asked him mockingly. 'No, I haven't studied,' replied Chaillan haughtily. 'There is no need to study. What one man has done, another can do. Why shouldn't I do what Rembrandt or Van Dyck have done?' However—pure condescension—Chaillan was willing to accompany the 'artists' of Aix to Gibert's place." *La Vie de Cézanne* (Paris: Hachette, 1956), p. 59. Later, p. 291, Perruchot identifies Chaillan completely with Chaîne, as Brady seems to do in "Les Clefs de l'*Oeuvre* de Zola," p. 269, and as Mitterand does, *op. cit.,* p. 25.
19. LeBlond, "Notes et commentaire" to *L'Oeuvre,* p. 403; Doucet, *op. cit.,* p. 136; Beuchat, *op. cit.,* p. 25.
20. *Dossier,* p. 240 *(Personnages)* and p. 297. There are three other references to Chaillan in the *Dossier,* pp. 51, 315, and 316.
21. See letters of Jan. 16, 1860 (*Correspondance—Lettres de jeunesse,* pp. 29-31); Apr. 26, 1860 (pp. 60-64); May 14, 1860 (pp. 77-82); and two letters of July 1860 (pp. 118-22 and 128-29). An article of Zola's in *Le Voltaire* for Aug. 12, 1879, seems to forecast the character of Chaîne: "But the most typical students were sent to us by the neighbor-

ing *départements,* the Var and the Basses-Alpes. Each year there descended upon us a new band of big, rough-hewn fellows, wearing heavy steelshod boots and a loutish air. They were, for the most part, the sons of rich farmers or of merchants, living on some little business in a mountain village. The position of the family was unimportant, however, for the sons of lawyers and pharmacists showed on their arrival a mountaineer crudeness that never completely disappeared. Almost all of them had heads harder than the rocks on which they had grown up. . . ."

22. *Dossier,* p. 316.
23. P. 51, first plan of Chap. III.
24. Léon Deffoux, "Zola, Chaîne et l'huile d'olive," *Mercure de France,* Dec. 15, 1927, p. 739.
25. See Fosca, *op. cit.,* p. 240; Doucet, *op. cit.,* pp. 135 and 183; LeBlond, "Notes et commentaire" to *L'Oeuvre,* p. 403; Bowie, *op. cit.,* p. 19; Perruchot, *op. cit.,* p. 291; Mitterand, p. 1366. Brady, "Les Clefs de l'*Oeuvre* de Zola," p. 266. Brady believes that Albert Wolff was also a partial source for Jory.
26. *Dossier,* pp. 231-33, 272, 298, 311, and 315.
27. *Ibid.,* p. 272.
28. D. LeBlond-Zola, "Paul Alexis, ami des peintres, bohème et critique d'art," *Mercure de France,* Mar. 15, 1939, pp. 292-303.
29. Bibliothèque nationale, Département des manuscrits, NAF no. 24510, p. 138.
30. It is possible, though, that the origin of this little episode did come from Alexis's career, for in July, 1882, Alexis fell into very serious difficulties with Albert Wolff, Aurélien Scholl and Léopold Stapleaux, who challenged him singly and collectively for certain of his articles in *Le Henry IV.* Alexis rather ignominiously avoided combat and as a consequence lost his position on the newspaper. Céard, in a letter to Zola of July 12, 1882, says: "They want to make Alexis pay for all his ingratitude, his gossip." (Bibliothèque nationale, Dept. des manuscrits, NAF no. 24516, p. 168). Generally speaking, the letters addressed to Zola by his friends of the literary world seem to indicate that Alexis was widely disliked, as Jory is in *L'Oeuvre.* It should also be recalled that Alexis did fight a celebrated duel with the journalist A. Delpit.
31. *Dossier,* p. 118.
32. See especially Rewald, *Paul Cézanne,* p. 145, and *Paul Cézanne, sa vie, son oeuvre, son amitié pour Zola,* p. 307; Bibliothèque nationale catalogue of the Zola exposition, p. 53; and I. M. Ebin, "Manet and Zola," *Gazette des beaux-arts,* sixth series, XXVII (1945), p. 375.
33. In the *Dossier,* however, Zola seems to deny that Jory's articles are to resemble his own writings on Manet, for they are to be neither very independent nor very courageous.

34. See Chap. 1, note 10. In "Les Clefs de l'*Oeuvre* de Zola," Brady also suggests that Roybet may have been a model for Fagerolles.
35. Fosca, *op. cit.*, p. 240; Bowie, *op. cit.*, p. 52; Perruchot, *op. cit.*, p. 291; Doucet, *op. cit.*, p. 136; LeBlond, "Notes et commentaire" to *L'Oeuvre*, p. 403. In "Les Clefs de l'*Oeuvre* de Zola," Brady claims to see "un peu de Guillemet" in Fagerolles's character (pp. 264-65). The compilers of the Bibliothèque nationale catalogue of the Zola exposition also seem to see Guillemet as Fagerolles, and Mitterand, *op. cit.*, p. 1369 also mentions him as a model.
36. Letter to Zola, July 12, 1880, Bibliothèque nationale, Département des manuscrits, NAF no. 24516, p. 134.
37. *Dossier*, p. 386.
38. Camille Pissarro, *Letters to His Son Lucien*, edited with the assistance of Lucien Pissarro by John Rewald, translated by Lionel Abel (New York: Pantheon Books, 1945), p. 73. No trace has been found of Zola's letter, but Guillemet's contained this sharp phrase: "Provided, for heaven's sake, that the little band, as Madame Zola says, does not recognize itself in your uninteresting heroes, for they are evil on top of everything else." Quoted in *Emile Zola: Salons*, edited by F. W. J. Hemmings and R. J. Niess (Geneva: Droz, 1959), p. 36.
39. Bibliothèque nationale, Département des manuscrits, NAF no. 24519, p. 156.
40. *Op. cit.*, p. 121.
41. *Dossier*, p. 237. Brady, in "Les Clefs de l'*Oeuvre* de Zola," also cites Maupassant and Bourget.
42. *Dossier*, p. 289.
43. *Ibid.*, p. 237.
44. *Ibid.*, p. 353.
45. Only one critic, and an early one at that, had seen Gervex in Fagerolles; this was Ernest Vizetelly, who made the identification in his preface to the first English edition of *L'Oeuvre*, p. viii. Brady, *loc. cit.*, says that Fagerolles is "surtout le Gervex."
46. *Dossier*, p. 271.
47. *Ibid.*, p. 288.
48. *Ibid.*, pp. 235-37, 263, 265, 270, 279, 281, 289, 290, 296, 298, 301-2, and 311.
49. Camille Pissarro claims as much in the letter to his son cited in note 38. Pissarro said that after Guillemet wrote Zola his letter of complaint about *L'Oeuvre*, Zola reassured him by telling him that Gervex, not he, had served as the model for Fagerolles. If Zola did write such a letter, it has not been published. It is curious that nowhere in his *Souvenirs* does Gervex even mention *L'Oeuvre*. One detail of Fagerolles's life seems to come from Manet's, his affair with Irma Bécot. Méry Laurent used to signal Manet with her handkerchief when her "official" lover, Dr. Evans, was absent; Irma does the same with Fagerolles.

50. See also Henry Houssaye, *Revue des deux mondes,* June 1, 1882, p. 563; and Antonin Proust, *Gazette des beaux-arts,* June 1, 1882, p. 547.
51. *Emile Zola: Salons,* pp. 228-29, 248, 254. In the latter article Zola expresses exactly the same idea as J.-K. Huysmans was to enounce in *L'Art moderne,* where he accuses Gervex and Bastien-Lepage of being false modernists and imitators of the true masters.
52. *Emile Zola: Salons,* pp. 159, 209-11, 228, 230, 246-48, 252. Brady, *loc. cit.,* also sees Carolus Duran and Bastien-Lepage as sources for Fagerolles.
53. Curiously enough, works by two painters of this group, Gervex and Guillemet, may have given Zola ideas for Claude's last painting, called by Ima Ebin "The Apotheosis of Paris"—Zola never gives it a title in the novel. Gervex's "Le Bassin de la Villette," which was exhibited in the Salon of 1882, contained some coal handlers who resemble Claude's and also had some barges and other commercial vessels like those described in the fictional painting of the Seine. It is not known if Zola was acquainted with this painting, since he wrote no "Salon" in 1882. Two paintings of Guillemet's may have contributed to the original idea of the "Apotheosis." One of them, which Zola does not name but which was exhibited in the Salon of 1875, is described thus in his "Russian" letter of that year: "This year he sent a view of the Seine, but from the Quai des Tuileries; to the left, the Quai d'Orsay, with the Chamber of Deputies and the Palace of the Legion of Honor, then the bridges, under which flows the river dotted with boats, and in the background the Cité and the Cathedral of Notre-Dame standing out against a blue sky." (*Salons,* p. 167). Perhaps even more suggestive is Zola's description of Guillemet's "Le Vieux Quai de Bercy," exhibited in the Salon of 1880: "The Seine rolls on and loses itself; to right and left the quays string out the confusion of their construction work, sheds, workshops, restaurants; while in the background, behind the gray lines of the bridges, a distant quay in Paris lies white in the sun. Nothing more gay or more living than these innumerable details, this swarming suburb, this fall of sunlight on the great city, whose odor and noise one can almost sense. It stops one like a window suddenly opened on a familiar horizon." (*Ibid.,* p. 253). It is further possible that Gervex's "Une Séance du jury de peinture," shown in 1885, may have suggested the jury scene in *L'Oeuvre.*
54. Rewald, *Paul Cézanne,* p. 145, and *Cézanne, sa vie, son oeuvre, son amitié pour Zola,* p. 308; Marcel Provence, "Cézanne et ses amis: Numa Coste," *Mercure de France,* Apr. 1, 1926, p. 76; Bibliothèque nationale catalogue of the Zola exposition, p. 16; Vizetelly, *op. cit.,* p. viii; Fosca, *op. cit.,* p. 240; Angus Wilson, *Emile Zola* (New York: 1952), p. 11; LeBlond, "Notes et commentaire" to *L'Oeuvre,* p. 403. Brady, "Les Clefs de l'*Oeuvre* de Zola," pp. 268-69; Mitterand, *op. cit.,* p. 1368.

55. *Dossier*. p. 297.
56. *Ibid.*, p. 298.
57. Bibliothèque nationale, Département des manuscrits, NAF no. 24510, p. 138.
58. *Ibid.*, p. 156, letter of June 11.
59. Angus Wilson, *loc. cit.*, expresses the same idea in slightly different terms. In the only available study of any length of Valabrègue's career, there is little to indicate that he should have been a model for Mahoudeau. It is true that his friends, writing to him about his poems, stress his "grace," his "charm," the "lightness" and "fineness" of his verses, but little else points to him as Mahoudeau's original. Nevertheless, the author of the study, Maurice-Pierre Boyé, accepts the attribution of Mahoudeau to Valabrègue. See "Antony Valabrègue, poète et historien d'art," *Rolet*, Dec. 18, 1952, Jan. 1, 8, 15, and 22, 1953.
60. Unpublished letter of June 17, 1868, Bibliothèque nationale, Département des manuscrits, NAF no. 24523, p. 466.
61. *Op. cit.*, pp. 47-48.
62. It is notable that Zola wrote Valabrègue an extremely friendly letter on Oct. 8, 1885 (*Correspondance, 1872-1902*, pp. 646-47), while *L'Oeuvre* was already in progress, but that this is the last letter to him in the *Correspondance*.
63. *Op. cit.*, p. 54.
64. *Op. cit.*, p. 121.
65. *Op. cit.*, p. viii.
66. *Op. cit.*, pp. 136, 182. Brady, "Les Clefs de l'*Oeuvre* de Zola," pp. 269-70, cites Manet and Flaubert as sources, but also adds Courbet and hints that the careers of Delacroix and Daubigny could have contributed details.
67. *Dossier*, p. 289, cited in "Notes et commentaire" to *L'Oeuvre*, p. 403.
68. *L'Oeuvre*, p. 87.
69. *Dossier*, p. 45.
70. *Le Figaro littéraire*, Dec. 11, 1880.
71. *L'Oeuvre*, p. 180.
72. Bibliothèque nationale catalogue of the Zola exposition, p. 54.
73. *L'Oeuvre, ibid.*
74. *Ibid.*, p. 288.
75. "Mes Souvenirs sur Gustave Flaubert." F. W. J. Hemmings notes that Zola wrote an article on *L'Éducation sentimentale* in 1869 and another in 1879 and observes that in the first Zola sees Flaubert as epic poet, in the second as realist. In the first article, musical similes dominate, in the second, artistic; in the first, he stresses Flaubert's nerves and speaks of his "intense vie nerveuse" while in the second he speaks of the *Éducation* as "trop vrai"—Flaubert is no longer a poet. "Zola and the *Éducation sentimentale*," *Romanic Review*, L, 1 (Feb. 1959), pp. 35-40.

76. *L'Oeuvre,* p. 359, "La vie avorte elle aussi. . . ."
77. Unpublished letter of Mar. 26 (1886), Bibliothèque nationale, Département des manuscrits, NAF no. 24510, p. 173.
78. Although Flaubert is almost certainly the model for Bongrand, one detail of the latter's career seems to come from Courbet's life. Bongrand's last painting to appear in a Salon represents for Claude a kind of concession to popular taste, a last vain effort to regain his old position, and here Zola may have been recalling that in *Mon Salon* he had devoted a whole section to exactly the same kind of artistic compromise on Courbet's part. *Salons,* pp. 73-75. Both Hemmings, *op. cit.,* pp. 214-15, and Mitterand, *op. cit.,* pp. 1370-71, attribute much of Bongrand's character and personality to Zola himself. I do not share their view completely.
79. *Dossier,* p. 286.
80. *Ibid.,* p. 293.
81. Edmondo de Amicis, *Ritratti letterari,* French translation, *Le Figaro littéraire,* Sept. 24, 1881.
82. *Op. cit.,* p. viii.
83. Edmond et Jules de Goncourt, *Journal, mémoires de la vie littéraire,* Les Editions de l'Imprimerie Nationale de Monaco, 1956 et sqq., XII, pp. 159-60, entry of Mar. 9, 1882. Paul Alexis, writing at the same time, recounts the same scene in slightly different terms (*op. cit.,* p. 206).
84. *Dossier,* p. 258. Brady, "Les Clefs de l'*Oeuvre* de Zola," p. 217, also cites Martin and Aubourg as sources of Naudet. He also says that *père* Malgras's name recalls "le père Gras, vieux peintre de Louis Philippe." This last seems a bit far-fetched.
85. *Dossier,* p. 349.
86. *Op. cit.,* p. 53.
87. "Quelques Lettres de Manet et de Sisley," *Revue blanche,* XVIII (1899), pp. 433-37.
88. *Dossier,* p. 350.
89. *Ibid.,* pp. 351-52.
90. *Ibid.,* pp. 351-53.
91. *Ibid.,* p. 354.
92. *Ibid.,* pp. 356-57.
93. Unpublished letter to Zola, Bibliothèque nationale, Département des manuscrits, NAF no. 24510, p. 147.
94. *Emile Zola: Salons,* p. 195.
95. *L'Oeuvre,* p. 306.
96. *Op. cit.,* p. 136. Mitterand, *op. cit.,* pp. 1360 and 1369, also sees Béliard in Gagnière; he also suggests Théodore Duret and Ernest Hébert as possible models, p. 1369.
97. John Rewald, *The History of Impressionism* (New York: Museum of

Modern Art, 1946), p. 101. Doucet also thinks that Fantin-Latour was a partial model for Gagnière, *op. cit.*, p. 182.

98. Gaston Poulain, *Bazille et ses amis* (Paris: La Renaissance Du Livre, 1932), pp. 108-9, 140, 168.
99. *Ibid.*, p. 135.
100. Paul Alexis, "Trubl' au vert," *Le Cri du Peuple*, Sept. 2, 1887.
101. Baude de Maurcelay, "Un Salon disparu—souvenirs personnels," *Le Figaro littéraire*, Apr. 12, 1890; and Perruchot, *op. cit.*, p. 217.
102. Z., "Cabaner," *Le Figaro*, Aug. 7, 1881.
103. *Ibid.*
104. *Op. cit.*, p. 217.
105. Paul Cézanne, *Letters*, edited by John Rewald, translated by Marguerite Kay (London: Bruno Cassirer, 1941), letters of Apr. 12, May 7, May 20, 1881 (to Zola) and Apr. 16, 1881 (from Zola to Cézanne).
106. This aspect of Gagnière's career is especially stressed in the *Dossier*, where Zola makes it clear that he believes that landscape painting in France has sharply declined since the days of Corot and the Barbizon school.
107. *Dossier*, p. 194. Doucet, *op. cit.*, p. 136; Lanoux, *op. cit.*, p. 204; and the Bibliothèque nationale catalogue, p. 53, also identify Mazel with Cabanel.
108. Rewald, *Paul Cézanne*, p. 146; Bibliothèque nationale catalogue, *loc. cit.*; and Perruchot, *op. cit.*, p. 292. Brady in "Les Clefs de l'Oeuvre de Zola," says that M. Hue "may" represent Chocquet.
109. Bowie, *op. cit.*, p. 54. Brady, in "Les Clefs de l'*Oeuvre* de Zola," argues that the "Mare de Cagny" (*sic*), Courajod's most famous canvas, may have taken its name from Cagnes, Renoir's village, and Eragny, identified with Pissarro. It is difficult to accept this argument, since the text of the novel is clear: it is the "Mare de Gagny." Brady also cites Jongkind; quoted by Mitterand, *op. cit.*, p. 1465.
110. *L'Oeuvre*, p. 136.
111. Pp. 273, 297.

111a. Rodolphe Walter, cited by Mitterand, *op. cit.*, p. 1445, has identified Margaillan with an industrialist named Jules Michaux.

112. *Dossier*, p. 51. Brady, *op. cit.*, also sees Valtesse de la Bigne in Irma and hints that Sarah Bernhardt may have supplied some details; but the *Dossier* seems to indicate only that she might have served as a source for a single detail of one of the Salon scenes.
113. *Paul Cézanne*, p. 146.
114. *Op. cit.*, p. vi.
115. *Op. cit.*, p. 615.
116. *Dossier*, pp. 267-70, 284, 303, 305, 311, 317.
117. Mitterand, *op. cit.*, p. 1354, also expresses reservations about this critical opinion.

CHAPTER III

1. Philippe Gille, *La Bataille littéraire,* third series (1883-1886) (Paris: Havard, 1890), p. 113. Henry Céard, for years one of Zola's intimate friends, had no doubt that Sandoz was Zola; see his "Zola intime," *Revue illustrée,* III, 29 (Feb. 15, 1887), p. 42.
2. Denise LeBlond-Zola, *Zola raconté par sa fille* (Paris: Fasquelle, 1931), p. 140; see also "Notes et commentaire" to *L'Oeuvre,* pp. 401-3.
3. See for example: Armand de Pontmartin, *Souvenirs d'un vieux critique,* seventh series (Paris: Calmann Lévy, 1886), p. 375; Jules Lemaître, "M. Emile Zola—*L'Oeuvre,*" *Revue bleue,* XXIII, 16 (1886), p. 481; Fernand Henry, *op. cit.,* pp. 87-102; Robert Sherard, *Emile Zola, a Biographical and Critical Study* (London: Chatto and Windus, 1893), p. 76: Ernest A. Vizetelly, *Emile Zola, Novelist and Reformer* (London: John Lane, The Bodley Head, 1904), p. 224; Vizetelly, *His Masterpiece, loc. cit.*; Henri Martineau, *Le Roman scientifique d'Emile Zola* (Paris: J. B. Baillière et fils, 1907), p. 45; Ernest Seillière, *Emile Zola* (Paris: Grasset, 1923), pp. 17-18, 99; Fernand Doucet, *op. cit.,* pp. 133, 181-83; Alexandre Zévaès, *Zola* (Paris: Nouvelle revue critique, 1945), p. 128; Beuchat, *op. cit.,* II, p. 69; Marcel Girard, *op. cit.,* pp. 154-55; Angus Wilson, *Emile Zola, an Introductory Study of His Novels* (London: Secker and Warburg, 1952), p. 94; Bibliothèque nationale catalogue, p. 53; Jean Vinchon, "Un Psychiâtre relit Zola," in N. Angell, A. Artinian, et al., *Présence de Zola* (Paris: Fasquelle, 1953), p. 226; Lanoux, *op. cit.,* p. 107; Rewald, *Paul Cézanne,* p. 306; Bowie, *op. cit.,* p. 19; Fosca, *op. cit.,* p. 240; Dorival, *op. cit.,* p. 11; Ebin, *op. cit.,* p. 374; Lapp, *op. cit.,* p. 161: Brady, "Les Clefs de l'*Oeuvre* de Zola," pp. 259-60; Mitterand, *op. cit.,* pp. 1356, 1373; Hemmings, *op. cit.,* pp. 213-14.
4. *Dossier,* pp. 270, 287, 261, 263 ("Cézanne and I on our return"), p. 271 ("I'll use myself as a member of the band, a journalist, a novelist. . . ."), pp. 277-78, 294 ("I and the old boy"), p. 297 ("I born at Paris"), p. 300 ("See if the three receptions can't take place at my house. . . ."), and p. 316, where he gives a list of his memories to be included.
5. *Ibid.,* p. 2 ("Claude, I, then the architect"), p. 3 ("A reception at my house"), p. 5 ("great discussions with me"), p. 7 ("Another reception at my house"), pp. 10-11 ("A chapter with me, last of the Thursdays"), p. 12 ("conversation between the old boy and me").
6. *Ibid.,* pp. 97, 156.
7. *Ibid.,* pp. 5 and 263.
8. *Ibid.,* pp. 270-71.
9. *Ibid.,* p. 297.
10. *Ibid.,* p. 300.
11. *Ibid.,* p. 2.
12. *Ibid.,* p. 97.
13. *Ibid.,* p. 316: "My youth in school and in the fields—Baille, Cézanne—

All my school memories, teachers, coventry, friendship among the three of us.–Outdoors, hunting, swimming, hiking, reading, the families of my friends.

"In Paris. New friends. School. Arrival of Baille and Cézanne.–Our Thursday meetings. Paris to be conquered, walks, disdain. The museums. Pasdeloup.–My different lodgings . . . the cafés."

14. *Ibid.*, p. 226. The physical portrait of Sandoz corresponds almost exactly to the descriptions of Zola made by Emile Bergerat and Armand Silvestre. See Bergerat, *Souvenirs d'un enfant de Paris–Les Années de bohème* (Paris: Charpentier, 1911), p. 398; and Silvestre, *Au Pays des souvenirs* (Paris: Librairie Illustrée, n. d. [1892], p. 159.
15. In the novel, the apartment, located on the *quatrième,* consists of a dining room, a bedroom, and a tiny kitchen. Sandoz' mother has her room across the hall (p. 75). The apartment on the rue des Feuillantines had a dining room, salon (with "emplacement à côté pour la cuisine") and one bedroom. Léon Deffoux, "Zola à vingt-quatre ans. Deux documents inédits," *Mercure de France,* Oct. 15, 1927, pp. 509-11. Gille also believes that this fictional apartment was copied from the rue des Feuillantines, *op. cit.*, p. 120.
16. *Op. cit.*, p. 76.
17. *Loc. cit.*
18. *Emile Zola* (Paris: Quantin, 1883), p. 28.
19. *Journal* . . . XII, pp. 159-60, entry of Mar. 9, 1882.
20. *L'Oeuvre,* p. 35.
21. *Ibid.*
22. For a fictionalized account of the elder Madame Zola's difficulties with her daughter-in-law, see *La Joie de vivre, passim.*
22a. *L'Oeuvre,* p. 46.
23. *Ibid.*, p. 161.
24. *Ibid.*, p. 162.
25. *Ibid.*, pp. 161-62.
26. *Ibid.*, p. 190.
27. *Dossier,* pp. 27-28.
28. *L'Oeuvre,* p. 190.
29. *Ibid.* p. 324.
30. *Dossier,* p. 2.
31. *Ibid.*, pp. 277-78.
32. *L'Oeuvre,* p. 46.
33. *Ibid.*, p. 162.
34. *Ibid.*, p. 358.
35. *Ibid.*, p. 161.
36. But in an early page of the novel Zola speaks in a rather different way: "A suburb injustice exalted them, a willful ignorance of *the necessities of social life,* the *mad dream* of being only artists on this earth;" italics added.

37. *Dossier*, p. 300.
38. *L'Oeuvre*, pp. 337-38.
39. *Dossier*, p. 270.
40. *Ibid.*, p. 287.
41. *L'Oeuvre*, p. 191.
42. "Revue dramatique et littéraire," *Le Voltaire*, Dec. 31, 1878.
43. Edmondo de Amicis, *Ritratti letterari*, translated in *Le Figaro littéraire*, Sept. 24, 1881.
44. *Dossier*, p. 286.
45. *L'Oeuvre*, p. 363.
46. *Ibid.*
47. *Ibid.*, pp. 263-64.
48. *Ritratti letterari.*
49. Emile Zola, Preface to *Nouveaux contes à Ninon, Oeuvres complètes*, I, pp. 275-78.

CHAPTER IV

1. The first to mention Cézanne as a model was Zola's friend, Philippe Gille, in his review of the work on its appearance in book form, *op. cit.*, p. 119; the "legend" really begins, however, with an article by Arsène Alexandre, "Claude Lantier," which appeared in *Le Figaro* for Dec. 9, 1895. Other contemporaries who cite Cézanne are Georges Lecomte, "Paul Cézanne," *Revue d'art*, Dec. 9, 1899, p. 82; Camille Mauclair, *L'Impressionnisme, son esthétique, ses maîtres* (Paris: Librairie de l'Art Ancien et Moderne, 1904), p. 152; Ernest Vizetelly, *His Masterpiece*, p. vi, *Emile Zola*, p. 92 (Vizetelly's expression is most guarded and in the latter work he declares that Cézanne was not the principal model); Edmond Lepelletier, *op. cit.*, p. 73; Emile Bernard "Souvenirs sur Paul Cézanne," *Mercure de France*, LIX (1907), p. 393, and *Souvenirs sur Paul Cézanne* (Paris: Société des Trente, 1912), pp. 19-20 (highly suspect). For further discussions of the question see: Ambroise Vollard, *Souvenirs d'un marchand de tableaux* (Paris: Albin Michel, 1937), p. 321 (see also Vollard's *Cézanne*, 1914, and *Renoir*, 1925); Gustave Coquiot, *Paul Cézanne* (Paris: Ollendorff, n. d. [1919]), p. 84; Georges Rivière, *Renoir et ses amis* (Paris: Floury, 1921), p. 109, and *Le Maître Paul Cézanne* (Paris: Floury, 1923), p. 75; Joachim Gasquet, *Cézanne* (Paris: Les Editions Bernheim-Jeune, new edition, 1926), p. 23; Matthew Josephson, *Zola and His Time* (New York: Macaulay, 1928), p. 300; Denise LeBlond-Zola, *Zola raconté par sa fille*, p. 114; Henri Barbusse, *Zola*, tr. by Mary B. and Frederick C. Green (New York: Dutton, 1933), p. 199 (Barbusse expresses some reservations); Fernand Doucet, *op. cit., passim*; Lionello Venturi, *Cézanne, son art, son oeuvre* (Paris: Rosenberg, 1936), pp. 18-19; René Huyghe, *Cézanne* (Paris: Plon, 1936), p. 16;

François Fosca, *op. cit.*, p. 239; Alexandre Zévaès, *op. cit.*, p. 128; Hermann Kesten, preface to *The Masterpiece,* tr. by Katherine Woods (London: Howell Soskin, 1946), p. 10; Germain Bazin, *L'Epoque impressionniste* (Paris: Editions Pierre Tisné, 1947), p. 38 (Bazin says only that Lantier takes "some of his traits" from Cézanne, but he mentions no other model); Bernard Dorival, *op. cit.*, p. 11; Charles Beuchat, *op. cit.*, II, p. 30; Henri Perruchot, *op. cit.*, Pt. v. Chap. III. About the same attitude is expressed by Sven Lövgren, *The Genesis of Modernism* (Uppsala-Stockholm: Almqvist and Wiksell, n.d.), pp. 31-35; John Rewald, *Cézanne et Zola* (Paris: Sedrowski, 1936), pp. 1-2; *Cézanne, sa vie, son oeuvre, son amitié pour Zola, passim; The History of Impressionism,* p. 398. *Paul Cézanne, a Biography* (New York: Simon and Schuster, 1948), *passim*; Jean de Beucken, "Un Portrait de Cézanne," *Illustration, Supplément théâtral et littéraire,* Aug. 11, 1951, pp. 3-32, and Aug. 25, 1951, pp. 2-32; Martin Turnell, *The Art of French Fiction* (London: Hamish Hamilton, 1959), p. 111; Lanoux, *op. cit.* p. 203; Reginald Wilenski, *Modern French Painters* (London: Faber and Faber, 1954, third ed.), p. 90; Wilson, *op. cit.*, p. 102; Georges Charensol, "Zola et les peintres," *Présence de Zola,* p. 188; George H. Hamilton, *Manet and his Critics* (New Haven: Yale University Press, 1954), p. 267; Lapp, *op. cit.*, p. 101; Gerstle Mack, *Paul Cézanne* (New York: Knopf, 1935), pp. 293-94; Francis Jourdain, "A la Recherche de Cézanne," *Commune,* Apr. 1939, pp. 433-38, and *Cézanne* (Paris: Braun, 1950), pp. 6-7; R. J. Niess, "Another View of Zola's *L'Oeuvre,*" *Romanic Review,* XXXIX, 1948, pp. 282-300; Marcel Girard, "Situation d'Emile Zola," *Revue des sciences humaines,* new series, 65 (Jan.-Mar. 1952), pp. 137-56; Bibliothèque nationale catalogue, p. 53; H. and J. Adhémar, *op. cit.*; Brady, "Claude Lantier," *passim*; F. W. J. Hemmings, introduction to *Emile Zola: Salons,* p. 36 and *Emile Zola,* pp. 221-22; Mitterand, *op. cit.*, pp. 1353-54 and 1372 ff.

1a. Rewald, *Cézanne, sa vie, son oeuvre, son amitié pour Zola,* p. 327; *Paul Cézanne,* p. 155.

2. See Gasquet, *op. cit.*, pp. 78-79; Bernard, *op. cit.*, p. 393; Rivière, *Renoir et ses amis,* p. 109; Denise LeBlond-Zola, *Emile Zola raconté par sa fille,* pp. 142-50; Mme LeBlond-Zola repeats the same arguments in less developed form in her "Zola et Cézanne d'après une correspondance retrouvée," *Mercure de France,* CCXXV (1931), pp. 39-58. See also Barbusse, *op. cit.*, p. 200; Dorival, *op. cit.*, pp. 76-77; Lanoux, *op. cit.*, p. 109; Wilson, p. 11; Wilenski, *op. cit.*, pp. 114-15; Mack, *op. cit.*, pp. 216, 288-89.

3. *Cézanne et Zola,* p. 2.

4. *Op. cit.*, p. 129.

5. Quoted in "Notes et commentaire" to *L'Oeuvre,* p. 406; Cézanne uses the intimate "tu" form of the pronoun.

6. Rewald, *Paul Cézanne, sa vie, son oeuvre, son amitié pour Zola,* p. 328. Rewald advances the same arguments in *Paul Cézanne,* 1948, p. 56. Lanoux, *op. cit.,* p. 206, and Dorival, *op. cit.,* p. 76, agree with Rewald.
7. *Emile Zola raconté par sa fille,* p. 149. The same arguments are presented in her "Cézanne et Zola d'après une correspondance retrouvée," p. 57.
8. *Op. cit.,* p. 298.
9. *Emile Zola raconté par sa fille,* p. 150. Gasquet, *op. cit.,* pp. 23, 79, is in general agreement, as is Rewald, *Paul Cézanne, sa vie, son oeuvre . . . . ,* pp. 326-32. Jean Adhémar appears to agree that it was Mme Alexandrine Zola's hostility to Cézanne which kept the latter's paintings off the walls of the house at Médan. He also points out that at Zola's death, his estate included no fewer than thirteen canvases by Cézanne, a not inconsiderable number for a man so often reputed to have held Cézanne's work in contempt. "Le Cabinet de travail de Zola," *Gazette des beaux-arts,* sixth period, LVI (Nov. 1960), pp. 285-98.
10. Bibliothèque nationale, Département des manuscrits, NAF no. 24510, pp. 324-25.
11. Unpublished letter, Bibliothèque nationale, Département des manuscrits, NAF no. 24521, p. 137.
12. Camille Pissarro, *Letters to His Son Lucien,* p. 60.
13. See pp. 172-73.
14. *Dossier,* p. 163.
15. *Ibid.*
16. *Ibid.,* p. 302.
17. *Ibid.,* p. 316. This same reference is found on p. 33 in the first plan of Chap. II.
18. *Ibid.*
19. *Ibid.*
20. *Ibid.,* p. 28, second plan of Chap. II.
21. *Ibid.,* p. 104, second plan of Chap. VII.
22. *Ibid.,* p. 265.
23. *Ibid.,* p. 2, sketch of Chap. II.
24. *Ibid.,* p. 27.
25. *Ibid.,* p. 218.
26. *Ibid.*
27. *Ibid.,* p. 219.

CHAPTER V

1. *L'Oeuvre,* pp. 47-48.
2. *Ibid.,* p. 50.
3. *Ibid.,* p. 253.
4. For an excellent description of the difficulties of Cézanne's biography, see René Huyghe, *Cézanne* (Paris: Plon, 1936), p. 6.

5. Edmond Duranty, *Le Pays des arts* (Paris: Charpentier, 1881).
6. Lionello Venturi, *Les Archives de l'impressionnisme* (Paris-New York: Durand-Ruel, 1939), II, p. 297.
7. Alfred H. Barr, Jr., "Cézanne d'après les lettres de Marion à Morstatt," *Gazette des beaux-arts,* LXXIX (1939), p. 45.
8. *Ibid.,* p. 57.
9. Théodore Duret, *Histoire des peintres impressionnistes* (Paris, n. d., third edition), p. 147.
10. Unpublished letter, Bibliothèque nationale, Département des manuscrits, NAF no. 24518, p. 204 *bis.*
11. Paris: Quatre-Chemins-Editart, 1959.
12. *Ibid.,* pp. 11-12.
13. *Ibid.,* p. 13.
14. *Ibid.*
15. *Correspondance—Lettres de jeunesse,* p. 107.
16. *Ibid.,* pp. 118-22.
17. *Ibid.,* pp. 215-21.
18. *Ibid.,* p. 306.
19. *Ibid.,* p. 201.
20. *Ibid.,* p. 202.
21. *Ibid.*
22. *Cézanne et Zola,* p. 134.
23. Mack, *op. cit.,* p. 119, says ". . . . it is probable that the fictitious character of Lantier, hysterical and morbid as it is, bore some resemblance to Zola's inner conception of Cézanne; a much closer resemblance, in fact, than it had to the real Cézanne."
24. *L'Oeuvre,* p. 23.
25. *Ibid.,* p. 27.
26. See letters of July 26, 1866, to Coste, and Feb. 19, 1867, to Valabrègue, *Correspondance—Lettres de jeunesse,* pp. 285, 296.
27. *L'Oeuvre,* pp. 47-48.
28. *Emile Zola: Salons,* p. 242.
29. *Dossier,* p. 386.
30. Letter to Baille, Aug. 1861, *Correspondance—Lettres de jeunesse,* p. 18.
31. Letter of May 30, 1870, *ibid.,* pp. 357-58.
32. "Une Exposition—les peintres impressionnistes," *Le Sémaphore de Marseille,* Apr. 19, 1877.
33. *Emile Zola: Salons,* p. 242.
34. *Ibid.,* p. 266.
35. *Op. cit.,* p. 129.
36. Rewald, *Histoire de l'impressionnisme,* p. 358.
37. *Le Rappel,* Apr. 20, 1874; cited in *Les Archives de l'impressionnisme,* II, p. 297.
38. "L'Exposition des impressionnistes," *L'Impressionniste,* no. 2 (Apr. 14, 1877), cited *ibid.,* II, p. 315.

39. See p. 117.
40. *Ibid.*
41. *Dossier,* p. 27.
42. Gustave Geffroy, *Claude Monet, sa vie, son oeuvre* (Paris: Crès, 1924), II, p. 68.
43. *L'Oeuvre,* pp. 126 ff.
44. *Ibid.,* p. 64.
45. See pp. 138-39.
46. *L'Oeuvre,* p. 23.
47. *Ibid.,* p. 27.
48. *Ibid.,* p. 33.
49. *Cézanne et Zola,* p. 134.
50. *Cézanne, sa vie, son oeuvre, son amitié pour Zola,* p. 165.
51. Bibliothèque nationale catalogue, p. 53.
52. *Op. cit.,* p. 375. Mitterand, *op. cit.,* p. 1438, argues for "Le Déjeuner sur l'herbe" as the model.
53. *L'Oeuvre,* p. 41.
54. *Ibid.,* p. 44.
55. *Ibid.,* pp. 153-54.
56. *Ibid.,* pp. 180-82.
57. *Dossier,* p. 130.
58. *L'Oeuvre,* p. 249.
59. See pp. 181-82.
60. *L'Oeuvre,* p. 293.
61. *Ibid.,* p. 216.
62. *Ibid.,* pp. 281-82.
63. *Ibid.,* pp. 342-43.
64. See p. 171.
65. The description of this painting given by Henry Houssaye has a certain resemblance to Zola's description of Claude's painting. See "Le Salon de 1882," *Revue des deux mondes,* June 1, 1882, p. 568.
66. *Dossier,* pp. 282, 442-48.
67. See p. 161.
68. See Léo Larguier, *Le Dimanche avec Paul Cézanne,* pp. 67-68; G. Rivière, *Renoir et ses amis,* p. 109; Barbusse, *op. cit.,* p. 199; Mack, *op. cit.,* p. 82; Rewald, *Cézanne, sa vie, son oeuvre,* p. 296; Fosca, *op. cit.,* p. 241; Venturi, *op. cit.,* p. 13; Vollard, *Renoir,* p. 89; Huyghe, *op. cit.,* p. 16.
69. The letter was written to Francis Magnard, editor of *Le Figaro,* and is dated Apr. 12, 1867.
70. *Correspondance, 1872-1902,* pp. 357-58.
71. Geffroy, *op. cit.,* II, p. 80.
72. Bibliothèque nationale, Département des manuscrits NAF no. 24510, p. 408.

CHAPTER VI

1. Manet was identified almost immediately as the model, or one of the models for Claude Lantier. Van Gogh, according to Rewald, believed he was intended to portray Manet (*Cézanne, sa vie, son oeuvre*, p. 313) and Monet wrote a worried letter to Zola, in which he advanced the idea that the public might take Lantier for a portrait of Manet, or of one of the Impressionists. (Bibliothèque nationale, Département des manuscrits, NAF no. 24522, pp. 225-26). Edmond de Goncourt also thought Lantier was Manet, although he believed that the portrait was far off. (*Journal. . . .* vol. XIV, p. 109, entry of Apr. 5, 1886). The *Figaro* reporter "Charles" (Chincholle) also mentioned Manet as a possible model on June 9, 1885, and another *Figaro* reporter, "Parisis" (Emile Blavet), declared that Goncourt had told him that Lantier was Manet. (July 22, 1885). Emile Solari said flatly that Manet was one of the models (*op. cit.*, p. 615) and Philippe Gille saw "a little of Manet" in him (*op. cit.*, p. 119). Armand de Pontmartin was convinced that he saw Manet in the fictional painter (*op. cit.*, pp. 375-91) and Ernest Vizetelly saw a "close analogy" between Lantier's artistic theories and those of Manet (*op. cit.*, p. vii). Rewald, *Cézanne et Zola*, p. 133, and *Cézanne, sa vie, son oeuvre*, p. 303; Vinchon, *op. cit.*, p. 227; Jamot, Wildenstein, Bataille, *Manet* (Paris: Les Beaux-Arts, 1932), I, p. 10; Etienne Moreau-Nélaton, *Manet raconté par lui-même* (Paris: Henri Laurens, 1926), II, pp. 104-5; Brady, "Claude Lantier," *Les Cahiers naturalistes*, 17 (1961), pp. 11-13, and "Les Clefs de l'*Oeuvre* de *Zola*," p. 262; Mitterand, *op. cit.*, p. 1372, all discuss Manet as a model, as does Ebin, *op. cit.*, p. 356.

1a. *Dossier*, p. 266.
2. *Ibid.*, p. 217.
3. *Ibid.*, p. 316.
4. *Emile Zola: Salons*, p. 258.
5. "Edouard Manet—Souvenirs," *La Revue blanche*, XII, 1897, p. 174.
6. See *Emile Zola: Salons*, p. 65 especially; see also pp. 66, 86, 258.
7. *Ibid.*, p. 244.
8. *Manet raconté par lui-même et par ses amis*, p. 128.
9. *Emile Zola: Salons*, p. 125.
10. See *L'Oeuvre*, p. 48.
11. *Emile Zola: Salons*, p. 86.
12. *L'Oeuvre*, p. 33.
13. *Ibid.*, p. 127.
14. *Emile Zola: Salons*, p. 125.
15. *Dossier*, p. 217.
16. *L'Oeuvre*, p. 43.
17. *Emile Zola: Salons*, p. 87.
18. See p. 198.
19. *Correspondance—Lettres de jeunesse*, pp. 302-4, letter of May 8, 1867.

20. *L'Oeuvre,* p. 279.
21. *Op. cit.,* p. 413.
22. Théodore Duret, *Manet,* translated by J. E. Crawford Fletcher (New York: Crown Publishers, 1937), p. 106.
23. *Op. cit.,* p. 374.
24. In *L'Oeuvre,* p. 256, Jory "claimed to have made Fagerolles, as he formerly claimed to have made Claude"; in the *Dossier* Zola writes, "I made Claude." Certainly Zola had "made" Manet, if any journalist did, and the rapprochement seems significant.
25. *Paul Cézanne,* p. 72.
26. See, for example, *L'Oeuvre,* pp. 248-49.
27. *Emile Zola: Salons,* p. 191.
28. *Histoire des peintres impressionistes* (Paris: Floury, third ed., 1922), p. 14.
29. Camille Mauclair, *L'Impressionnisme, son histoire, son esthétique, ses maîtres* (Paris: Librairie de l'Art Ancien et Moderne, 1904), p. 58.
30. *The History of Impressionism,* p. 172.
31. *Cézanne et Zola,* p. 57.
32. *Op. cit.,* p. 8.
33. Rodolphe Walter, "Zola et ses amis à Bennecourt," *Les Cahiers naturalistes,* 17 (1961), pp. 19-32.
34. *Emile Zola: Salons,* p. 259. During one period of his career Manet painted scores of studies of Isabelle Lemonnier, Georges Charpentier's sister-in-law.
35. *Op. cit.,* p. 132.
36. *L'Oeuvre,* p. 46.
37. *Manet raconté par lui-même et par ses amis* (Vésenay-Geneva: P. Cailler), pp. 58-59.
38. See p. 36.
39. This matter has been treated by Brady in "Claude Lantier."
40. *Emile Zola: Salons,* pp. 65, 67.
41. *L'Oeuvre,* p. 130.
42. *Emile Zola: Salons,* p. 95.
43. *L'Oeuvre,* p. 210.
44. *Emile Zola: Salons,* pp. 83 ff.
45. *Ibid.,* p. 67.
46. *L'Oeuvre,* p. 46.
47. *Op. cit.,* p. 133.
48. *L'Oeuvre,* p. 47.
48a. *Emile Zola: Salons,* p. 261.
49. *L'Oeuvre,* p. 44.
50. *Emile Zola: Salons,* pp. 87-88; see also pp. 92, 101, 192.
51. *Ibid.,* p. 125.
52. *Ibid.,* p. 260.

53. Francis Jourdain, "A la Recherche de Cézanne," *Commune,* 68 (Apr. 1939), p. 435.
54. *L'Oeuvre,* p. 45.
55. *Ibid.,* p. 47.
56. *Ibid.,* p. 118. See also pp. 137-38 for Claude's ideas on modernism in architecture.
57. *Ibid.,* p. 203.
58. *Emile Zola: Salons,* p. 67.
59. *Ibid.,* p. 158.
60. *Ibid.,* p. 244.
61. *Ibid.,* p. 91.
62. *Ibid.,* p. 92.
63. Brady believes that it is "probably incorrect" to see "Plein-Air" as an echo of "Le Déjeuner sur l'herbe"; he bases his argument largely on the fact that the men in the painting are not turned toward the spectator. For him, "Plein-Air" is a literary rendition of Cézanne's "La Lutte de l'amour," with a fully-dressed man added. "La Peinture de Claude Lantier," *Revue des sciences humaines,* new series, fascicle 101 (Jan.-Nov., 1961), pp. 89-101. It should be pointed out that in both "Plein-Air" and "Le Déjeuner," it is the man's left hand which is most in evidence.
64. See p. 103.
65. *L'Oeuvre,* p. 47.
66. *Emile Zola: Salons,* p. 96.
67. *Op. cit.,* pp. 374-75.
68. *Op. cit.,* p. 1438.
69. *Op. cit.,* p. 61.
70. *Op. cit.,* p. vii.
71. *Op. cit.,* p. 239. Turnell, *op. cit.,* p. 111, also sees "Le Déjeuner" in "Plein-Air."
72. Bibliothèque nationale catalogue, p. 53.
73. *Emile Zola: Salons,* p. 95.
74. *Dossier,* p. 276.
75. *Emile Zola: Salons,* p. 90.
76. *Ibid.,* p. 91.
77. *Ibid.,* p. 92.
78. *Emile Zola: Salons,* p. 258.
79. *Ibid.,* p. 260. Georges Bataille says of Manet that "Behind the well-mannered façade of self-assurance . . . we glimpse a man vulnerable, temperamental, impulsive. . . . A little superficial, perhaps, but driven by inner forces that gave him no rest, Manet was possessed by something beyond his reach which he never fully understood and which left him forever tantalized and unsatisfied, on the brink of nervous exhaustion." *Manet,* tr. by Austryn Wainhouse and James Emmons (New York: Skira, 1955), p. 24.

80. *Emile Zola: Salons,* p. 259.
81. *Ibid.*, pp. 260-61. Paul Jamot, one of the authorities on Manet's career, agrees; see *Manet raconté par lui-même et par ses amis,* p. 210.
82. *Emile Zola: Salons,* p. 259.
83. *Ibid.*
84. *Op. cit.*, pp. 57-58.
85. *Emile Zola: Salons,* p. 66; see also pp. 65, 67-68, 83-84, 93-94, and the whole section of *Édouard Manet* entitled "Le Public." The same observation about Manet's career was made by Adolphe Tabarant, *Manet et ses oeuvres* (Paris: Gallimard, 1947), Chap V; and by Théodore Duret, *Histoire des peintres impressionnistes,* p. 4.
86. *Emile Zola: Salons,* p. 58.
87. *Ibid.*, pp. 64-65.
88. *Op. cit.*, p. 59.
89. *Emile Zola: Salons,* p. 259.
90. *L'Oeuvre,* p. 135.
91. *Emile Zola: Salons,* p. 227.
92. *Ibid.*, p. 262.
93. *Histoire des peintres impressionnistes,* p. 8.
94. *Op. cit.*, p. 63.
95. *L'Oeuvre,* p. 297.
96. *Emile Zola: Salons,* pp. 242-43. Camille Mauclair says almost the same thing, *op. cit.*, p. 61.
97. *Dossier,* p. 265.
98. *L'Oeuvre,* p. 359.
99. *Emile Zola: Salons,* pp. 260-61.
100. Adolphe Retté, *Le Symbolisme, anecdotes et souvenirs* (Paris: Messein, 1903), pp. 191-92.
101. *Emile Zola: Salons,* p. 31.
102. Quoted in *ibid.*, pp. 31-32. Such a talented critic as J.-K. Huysmans expressed much the same idea as Zola. See *L'Art moderne, Oeuvres complètes,* VI, pp. 177-78.
103. *L'Oeuvre,* p. 185.
104. *Emile Zola: Salons,* p. 159. Almost exactly the same attack, although more developed, is made on Carolus Duran in the *Salon* of 1880; Manet is not named here as Duran's master.
105. *Ibid.*, p. 244.
106. *Ibid.*, p. 262.
107. *L'Oeuvre,* pp. 295-96.
108. *Ibid.*, p. 356.
109. *Emile Zola: Salons,* p. 68.
110. *Ibid.*, p. 69.
111. *Ibid.*, p. 101.
112. *Ibid.*, p. 168.
113. *Ibid.*, pp. 220-21.

114. *Ibid.*, p. 227.
115. *Ibid.*, p. 29.
116. Bibliothèque nationale, Département des manuscrits, NAF no. 24510, pp. 104 *et bis*.
117. *Emile Zola: Salons*, p. 243.
118. *Ibid.*, p. 261.
119. *Ibid.*, p. 262.
120. *L'Oeuvre*, pp. 296-97.
121. *Emile Zola: Salons*, p. 193.
122. *Ibid.*, p. 257.
123. *Ibid.*, p. 258.
124. *Ibid.*, p. 260.
125. *Ibid.*, p. 261.
126. *Ibid.*, p. 262.
127. *Ibid.*, pp. 266, 269. Mauclair expresses the same idea, *op. cit.*, pp. 63-64, as does Perruchot, *Manet*, p. 280.

CHAPTER VII

1. Edmond de Goncourt recognized Zola behind Lantier from the first and openly confronted Zola with his conclusion, which Zola did not deny; see *Journal. . .*, XIV, p. 108 and p. 111. Others who saw Zola in the fictional painter were Geffroy, quoted in "Notes et commentaire" to *L'Oeuvre*, p. 436; Robert Charvay, "Zola et Diderot," *L'Evénement*, May 6, 1886; Denise LeBlond-Zola, *Emile Zola raconté par sa fille*, p. 141; Maurice LeBlond, "Notes et commentaire" to *L'Oeuvre*, p. 404. Among contemporary commentators who have seen Zola in Lantier are Hemmings, *op. cit.*, p. 203; M. Girard, *op. cit.*, p. 154; Wilson, *op. cit.*, p. 102; Lanoux, *op. cit.*, pp. 110, 204; Charles Lalo, "L'Art et la vie II–Le Complexe de Zola," *Revue des cours et des conférences*, first series XXXVII, 6 (Feb. 26, 1937), p. 510; Perruchot, *La vie de Cézanne*, pp. 293-94; Brady, "Les Clefs de l'*Oeuvre* de Zola," pp. 260-61, and "Claude Lantier," p. 18; Rewald, *Cézanne, sa vie, son oeuvre. . .*, pp. 303, 305, and *Cézanne et Zola*, p. 127. Numerous other critics have also discussed the question at greater or lesser length.
2. *Dossier*, pp. 261-63; italics added.
3. "Livres d'aujourd'hui et de demain," *L'Événement*, Mar. 24, 1866, for instance.
4. "Cézanne à Bennecourt," *Gazette des beaux-arts*, Feb. 1962, pp. 103-18; see also "Zola et ses amis à Bennecourt (1886)," *Les Cahiers naturalistes*, 17 (1961), p. 27.
5. "Le Crapaud," *Le Figaro*, Feb. 28, 1896.
6. Lepelletier, *op. cit.*, p. 231, discusses this question excellently.
7. *Dossier*, p. 262.

8. Emile Zola, *Mes Voyages–Lourdes–Rome,* journaux inédits présentés et annotés par René Ternois (Paris: Fasquelle, 1958), p. 214.
9. Fosca makes the same observation, but uses it to indicate how far Zola was from understanding Cézanne, whom he takes to be the only model for Claude Lantier. After pointing out that the painter evolved from realist to romantic–from Manet to a kind of Van Gogh–he notes that Cézanne's development was precisely the opposite, that under the influence of Pissarro he abandoned the early "truculence" and came to hold the ideal of creating art as solid and durable as the "art of the museums." "Zola erred completely in imagining for Lantier an evolution which is exactly the opposite of Cézanne's. But this passage from realism to romanticism, which is the evolution of the hero of *L'Oeuvre,* was accomplished by Zola, not by Cézanne." *Op. cit.,* pp. 241-42.
10. "Create", alone or in combination with other words, occurs four times in the list, as does "To give birth."
11. *Dossier,* pp. 261, 277-78.
12. *L'Oeuvre,* p. 236.
13. *Dossier,* p. 266; italics Zola's.
14. *Ibid.,* p. 444.
15. *Ibid.,* pp. 266, 309.
16. *Emile Zola* (Paris: Société d'Editions Scientifiques, 1896), p. 116. See also Goncourt, *Journal. . . . ,* XI, p. 14, p. 90 and p. 178; Alexis, *op. cit.,* p. 26, 30; Hemmings, *op. cit.,* pp. 138-39, 148-49; Wilson, *op. cit.,* p. 45; Lalo, *op. cit.,* pp. 512-13, 520; J. H. Matthews, *Les Deux Zola* (Geneva: Droz, Paris: Minard, 1957), pp. 9-10. See also Zola, in *Le Voltaire,* Aug. 5, 1879.
17. "Le Premier roman d'Emile Zola," *La Revue illustrée,* IV (Nov. 1, 1887), pp. 297-98.
18. The psychiatrist Jean Vinchon has another explanation for Zola's timidity. He believes that Zola's conduct was determined in large part by the fact that he had a kind of double nature, male and female, which had been produced in him in childhood by a sexual attack on him by a servant. Zola also contracted something of a mother-fixation (his mother had saved him from his attacker) and his wife continued the mother's role after the mother's death. "Zola dîne avec les Goncourt," *Aesculape,* XXXIV, 1 (Jan. 1953), pp. 1-7.
19. This whole aspect of the relationship of the nude with Zola's own work was seen with remarkable clarity by the reporter Vincent, of *Le XIXe Siècle.* Writing as soon as the work was available, on Apr. 17, 1886, he said: "And this work, this grandiose work of Claude's, in which, by a strange and inexplicable obsession, the painter always wants to raise up a nude woman "with enormous thighs," what is that but the very work of Zola? The nude with "enormous thighs" is Gervaise, is Nana, is Pauline, is La Mouquette, all those robust women

with "powerful necks," with "rounded buttocks," who are the mothers, the daughters and the sisters of the Rougon-Macquart."

20. Pp. 218, 253, 310.
21. *Journal. . . .* , XI, p. 14.
22. "Le Divorce et la littérature," *Le Figaro,* Feb. 14, 1881.
23. *Dossier,* p. 316.
24. *Op. cit.,* p. 3.
25. *L'Envers de la gloire,* (Paris: Flammarion, n. d.), p. 82.
26. Goncourt, *Journal. . . .* , X, p. 230 and XIV, p. 104; Alexis, *op. cit.,* pp. 106,170, 200, 204; Lepelletier, *op. cit.,* pp. 82-83; Toulouse, *op. cit.,* p. 256, note; Vallès, "Notes d'un absent—Dickens et Zola," *Le Voltaire,* Feb. 11, 1880; Ernest Seillière, *Emile Zola* (Paris: Grasset, 1923), p. 68; Hemmings, *op. cit.,* pp. 9, 64-65; Vinchon, *op. cit.,* p. 7.
27. *Op. cit.,* p. 211.
28. *Ibid.,* p. 206.
29. *Ibid.,* pp. 208-9.
30. *Ibid.,* p. 210.
31. *Op. cit.,* pp. vi-vii.
32. *Ibid.,* pp. 250-51.
33. "Revue dramatique et littéraire," Dec. 31, 1878.
34. *Op. cit.,* Sept. 24, 1881.
35. *Dossier,* p. 269.
36. *Ibid.,* p. 276.
37. Zola said almost exactly the same thing in almost the same words in his essay on "Le Roman contemporain," *Le Figaro littéraire,* Dec. 22, 1878.
38. *Dossier,* p. 262.
39. *L'Oeuvre,* p. 83.
40. *Ibid.,* p. 321.
41. *Op. cit.,* p. 41.
42. *Ibid.,* pp. 156-57.

CHAPTER VIII

1. *Op. cit.,* p. 189, note.
2. "Claude Lantier," pp. 13-14. André Gill seems to have been first mentioned in connection with Zola by Alexandre Zévaès in 1945 in his *Zola* (Paris: Editions de la Nouvelle Revue Critique), p. 73; but Zévaès makes no mention of Gill as a possible model for Lantier.
3. All the biographical data here come from two sources: J. Valmy-Baysse, *Le Roman d'un caricaturiste* (Paris: Marcel Seheur, 1927), and A. Lods et Vega, *André Gill, sa vie* (Paris: Vanier, 1887).
4. Gill describes these portraits in his *Vingt ans de Paris* (Paris: Marpon et Flammarion, n. d.), pp. 181-88.
5. Alphonse Daudet, *Quarante ans de Paris, 1857-1897* (Geneva: La Palatine, 1945), p. 155.

6. Gill's personality was far different from Claude Lantier's, if Jean Richepin's description of Gill is exact: he was very gay, somewhat boastful (but very timid at bottom, especially when he was with his social "betters"), extremely good hearted and charitable, loving the *peuple,* in short a Romantic who might not have been out of place in Mürger's pages. "André Gill," *Le Figaro littéraire,* July 3, 1886.
7. *Op. cit.,* p. 119.
8. *Op. cit.*
9. *Cézanne, sa vie, son oeuvre, son amitié pour Zola,* p. 303.
10. "Claude Lantier," p. 13. In "Les Clefs de l'*Oeuvre* de Zola," Brady adds one or two more details, p. 262.
11. *Op. cit.,* p. 31.
12. Bibliothèque nationale, Département des manuscrits, NAF no. 24522, p. 165.
13. *Cézanne, son art, son oeuvre,* p. 27.
14. *Op. cit.*
15. "Claude Lantier," p. 13. Rewald also mentions the attempted suicide in *The History of Impressionism,* p. 164.
16. *L'Oeuvre,* p. 135.
17. Quoted in Marc Elder, *Chez Claude Monet à Giverny,* p. 15.
18. Venturi, *Les Archives de l'impressionnisme,* I, p. 45. See also Rewald, *The History of Impressionism,* pp. 148-49, 291-92.
19. Georges Clemenceau, *Claude Monet—Les Nymphéas* (Paris: Plon, 1928), pp. 19-20. For Claude's portrait of his son, see *L'Oeuvre,* p. 290.
20. Rodolphe Walter, "Emile Zola et Claude Monet," *Les Cahiers naturalistes,* 26 (1964), pp. 51-61.
21. Gustave Geffroy, *Claude Monet—sa vie—son oeuvre,* I, p. 218.
22. *Ibid.,* II, pp. 47-63. See also Venturi, *Les Archives de l'impressionnisme,* I, pp. 235-36, 237-38, 250-51, 268, 276, 279, 293-94.
23. *Ibid.,* I, p. 45.
24. Rewald, *The History of Impressionism,* p. 280.
25. *Op. cit.*
26. *Op cit.;* Walter agrees with this identification.
27. *Op. cit.,* p. 142.
28. *Op. cit.*
29. *L'Oeuvre,* pp. 232-33.
30. "Claude Lantier," p. 13.
31. *Emile Zola: Salons,* p. 71; see also p. 131.
32. *Ibid.,* p. 131.
33. *Ibid.,* p. 130.
34. *Ibid.,* p. 131; see also p. 132.
35. *Ibid.,* p. 132.
36. *Ibid.,* p. 240.
37. *Ibid.,* p. 195.

38. Ibid., p. 267. In his "Lettre de Paris" written to *Le Sémaphore de Marseille* for Apr. 30-May 1, 1876, Zola has this to say of Monet: "In landscape painting, he sees clearly, in the full sunlight. These are no longer the browned landscapes of the romantic school, but they show a blonde gaiety, a decomposition of the light nuanced with all the colors of the prism. That is the true originality of the new school, the study of real light and open air."
39. *Emile Zola: Salons,* pp. 195, 239.
40. *Ibid.,* p. 245.
41. *Ibid.,* p. 239.
42. *Ibid.,* p. 132.
43. *Ibid.,* p. 245.
44. *Ibid.,* pp. 266, 269.
45. *Cézanne, sa vie, son oeuvre. . . . ,* p. 309, and *Paul Cézanne,* pp. 146-47.
46. "Emile Zola: From Fact to Fiction," *Modern Language Notes,* July 1948, pp. 407-8. Brady rectifies my observations on several points.
47. "Claude Lantier," p. 17.
48. *Manet et ses oeuvres* (Paris: Gallimard, 1947), pp. 123 ff.
49. *Op. cit.,* p. vii.
50. Cited by Brady, "Claude Lantier," p. 14.
51. Vol. v (1885), p. 35.
52. No. 22, May 31, 1884, p. 175.
53. *Ibid.,* no. 25, July 12, 1884, p. 207.
54. P. 36.
55. This painting was first mentioned as a possible source for "L'Enfant mort" in an article on the exhibition of the Société des artistes indépendants at the Tuileries in 1886, in *L'Art moderne,* VI, 38, (Sept. 19, 1886), p. 301. It was also cited as a possible model by Maurice Beaubourg in his necrological article on Dubois-Pillet, in the *Revue indépendante* for Sept. 1890 (cited by Lövgren, p. 36).
56. "Notes et commentaire" to *L'Oeuvre,* p. 404.
57. Louis Edouard Tabary, *Duranty, 1833-1880* (Paris: Les Belles-lettres, 1954), p. 36, note 86. Alexis also seems to have believed that it was Duranty whom Zola had in mind as he depicted the funeral scene, for to a letter of Mar. 26 (1886) he added this postscript: "I finished *L'Oeuvre* this morning. The cemetery scene is one of your most beautiful pages, and it moved me. Poor Duranty!" Bibliothèque nationale, Département des manuscrits, NAF no. 24510, p. 76.
58. Lövgren, *op. cit.,* p. 38.
59. *Emile Zola: Salons,* p. 132.
60. *Ibid.,* p. 196.
61. *Ibid.,* p. 239.
62. Reproduced in Venturi, *Les Archives de l'impressionnisme,* II, pp. 326-29.
63. Brady, "Les Clefs de l'*Oeuvre* de Zola," pp. 262-63, gives several de-

tails from Renoir's life and artistic career which support the possibility that Renoir was at least a partial model for Claude.

64. Ludovic Rodo-Pissarro and Lionello Venturi, *Camille Pissarro* (Paris: Rosenberg, 1939), I, pp. 35-36.
65. *Emile Zola: Salons,* p. 24.
66. Cited by Rewald, *Cézanne, sa vie, son oeuvre . . . ,* p. 319.
67. Some of them are cited by Lövgren, *op. cit.,* pp. 6-7.
68. *Cézanne,* note to p. 22.
69. A note to him from Zola is dated Apr. 18, 1863. Poulain, *Bazille et ses amis,* p. 166.
70. Emile Zola, *Novelist and Reformer* (London: John Lane. The Bodley Head, 1904), pp. 91-92.
71. *Op. cit.,* p. 204.
72. Jules Breton, *Nos Peintres du siècle* (Paris: Société d'Editions d'Art, 1908), p. 131.
73. *Loc. cit.*
74. *Présence de Zola,* p. 227.
75. *L'Art moderne, Oeuvres complètes,* VI, p. 91.
76. G. Lafenestre, "Marcellin Desboutin," *Revue de l'art ancien et moderne,* XII (1902), p. 406.
77. *Ibid.,* p. 414.
78. Bibliothèque nationale, Département des manuscrits, NAF no. 24517, p. 257.
79. *Op. cit.,* p. 615.
80. *La Vie de Cézanne,* pp. 84-85. Brady also remarks on the possibility that Emperaire may have been a model. "Claude Lantier," p. 11.
81. *Journal,* XIV, p. 109.
82. "Zola et Diderot," *L'Événement,* May 6, 1886.

CHAPTER IX

1. J. Van Santen Kolff remarks in an unpublished, undated letter that Zola told him that he did not use the *Ébauche* when actually writing, relying only on the plans and the notes. Bibliothèque nationale, Département des manuscrits, NAF no. 24524, p. 384. For a detailed and excellent discussion of the *Dossier* and its connection with the final text, see Mitterand, *op. cit.,* pp. 1352 ff.
2. Cf. Chap. II.
3. *L'Oeuvre,* pp. 247-48.
4. *Dossier,* pp. 344-45.
5. *L'Oeuvre,* pp. 117-18.
6. *Ibid.,* p. 124.
7. *Ibid.,* p. 285.
8. *Dossier,* p. 322.
9. *L'Oeuvre,* pp. 231-32.
10. *Dossier,* pp. 439-41.

11. *Ibid.*, p. 18.
12. "Plein-Air" gave Zola a great deal of trouble, evidently, for he wrote a description of it in the first detailed plan of Chapter II, a second description, slightly different, in the second plan of Chapter V, and a third, crossed out, in the manuscript itself before he arrived at the version which now appears in the present Chapter II.
13. Mitterand, *op. cit.*, pp. 1405-85, lists many variants.

CHAPTER X

1. "Courrier de Paris," *Le Matin*, Apr. 10, 1886.
2. *Confessions of a Young Man* (New York: Penguin Books, 1939), p. 100.
3. *Le XIXe Siècle*, Apr. 17, 1886.
4. *Le Siècle*, Apr. 18, 1886.
5. *La République française*, Apr. 28, 1886.
6. *Le Livre*, no. VIII, 77 (May 10, 1886), pp.227-28.
7. *Critique au jour le jour* (Paris: Savine, 1887), pp. 87-102.
8. *La Bataille littéraire*, pp. 112-22.
9. *Notes d'un journaliste* (Paris: Charpentier, 1887), p. 204.
10. *Op. cit.*, p. 332.
11. "Le Crépuscule de l'art pictural," *La Revue des revues*, Apr. 1, 1930.
12. *Revue des sciences humaines*, new series, 65 (Jan.-Mar. 1952), pp. 137-56.
13. *Présentation des Rougon-Macquart* (Paris: Gallimard-NRF, 1964), pp. 269 ff.
14. *Revue bleue*, XXIII, no. 16 (1886), pp. 481-85.
15. Armand de Pontmartin, *op. cit.*, pp. 375-91.
16. *Journal*, XIV, pp. 108-10, entry of Apr. 5, 1886.
17. Lapp, *op. cit.*, p. 97, also see the Pygmalion legend in *L'Oeuvre*.
18. As noted, *passim*, names like Hallegrain, Courajod and Fagerolles have considerable interest and importance.
19. Fosca claims that Zola commits at least three errors in describing Claude's painting technique. (*Op. cit.*, pp. 432-33). Others, notably Gasquet and Vollard, have reflected adversely on Zola's knowledge of the art world.
20. *Correspondance, 1872-1902*, pp. 644 and 656, letters of Aug. 23, 1885, and Feb. 23, 1886.
21. For a discussion of Zola's knowledge of music, see Calvin S. Brown, "Music in Zola's Fiction, Especially Wagner's Music," *PMLA*, LXXI (Mar. 1956), pp. 84-96. Brown is critical of the passages on music in *L'Oeuvre*, apparently in the belief that the nonsense uttered by Gagnière and Madame Jabouille represents Zola's own ideas. But the phrases on music uttered by these characters were taken almost verbatim by Zola from notes given him by Henry Céard and they are so stilted and empty that it is obvious that Zola is using them to satirize a tendency he found around him and which he thought rep-

rehensible. At all events, they are spoken by fictional characters and can scarcely be attributed to Zola as his own without some statement on his part or without some evidence linking him to these characters as autobiographical creations.

22. Guy Robert notes the same tendency in *La Terre:* ". . . . Zola begins with very general intentions, organizes his characters around requirements which are often those of the symbol; such and such a character must represent large scale agriculture, the hope in science, then discouragement; such and such another must render the impossibility of finding in the soil the calm it would give if it were not for the evil of mankind. . . ." *La Terre d'Emile Zola* (Paris: Société d'Edition les Belles Lettres, 1952), p. 229.
23. Lapp discusses the presence of homosexuals in Zola's works, *op. cit.*, pp. 140-42.
24. See note 16, this chapter.
25. *L'Oeuvre,* pp. 349-51.
26. For a discussion of the "femme fatale" in Zola's works, see Lapp, *op. cit.*, Chap. v.
27. See *ibid.*, p. 158.
28. *Op. cit.*, pp. 481-82.
29. So impersonal is Zola's tone throughout that not a single remark in the entire book can be safely attributed to him (as distinct from the narrator).
30. Edmond de Goncourt thought that the opening scene gave the same impression as an opening by Restif de la Bretonne (*Journal,* XIV, p. 76, entry of Dec. 23, 1885) and Zola confessed that it was anything but realistic; he added, though, that he wanted an opening that would give the impression of a Romantic prelude. Interview in *Le Matin,* May 17, 1886.
31. Fernand Henry found this scene both scabrous and lacking in verisimilitude, but thought that Zola got himself out of it with as much skill as delicacy (*op. cit.*, p. 90). Armand de Pontmartin was of somewhat the same mind. Admitting that the chapter contained some fine details, he concluded that it was a real "apotheosis of the flesh." (*Op. cit.*, pp. 376-77).
32. Henry praised this scene as being as delicate as the first chapter and thought it provided a good answer to those who thought that Zola "voyait sale" (*op. cit.*, p. 94). Philippe Gille called it an "exquisite page," a masterpiece of delicacy of sentiment and of expression (*op. cit.*, p. 116).
33. Ricatte sees the Salon scenes as epic; in the first of them the laughter of the crowd has the "resonance of a cataclysm" (*op. cit.*, p. 350).
34. Ricatte notes the "epic" quality of this scene and contrasts Zola's tendencies in this regard with the Goncourts' more purely realistic treatment of anecdote (*ibid.*, p. 347). Henry Céard saw this scene as

particularly sad. (*Lettres inédites à Emile Zola,* ed. by C. A. Burns, Paris: Nizet, 1958, p. 298).

35. Céard praises this scene as striking (*loc. cit.*), but Goncourt was positively enraged by Zola's inclination to make his artists speak a common and crude language. (*Journal,* XIV, pp. 87-88, entry of Feb. 23, 1886).
36. Ricatte praises Zola's skill in revealing the whole administrative process of the Salon, the bargaining, the fatigue, the vertigo that invades the hall. (*Op. cit.,* p. 350).
37. *L'Oeuvre,* p. 140.
38. *Ibid.,* p. 225.
39. For a discussion of the use of antithesis in Zola's works, see Lapp, *op. cit.,* p. 148.
40. For a detailed discussion of these antitheses, see my article, "Antithesis and *Reprise* in Zola's *L'Oeuvre,*" *L'Esprit Créateur,* IV, 2 (Summer, 1964), pp. 68-75.
41. *Le Roman expérimental, Oeuvres complètes,* vol. 39, *passim.*
42. For a discussion of the triangle situation in Zola's works, see Lapp, *op. cit.,* p. 138.
43. See *ibid.,* pp. 24, 48-49, 68, 75.
44. Turnell, *op. cit.,* pp. 126-27.
45. *Ibid.,* p. 124.
46. Lapp, *op. cit.,* p. 150.
47. *Ibid.,* pp. 15-16, 95, 103.
48. *Ibid.,* pp. 133-36.
49. *Ibid.,* pp. 44 ff; see also Turnell, *op. cit.,* pp. 129-30.
50. Lapp, *op. cit.,* p. 95.
51. *Ibid.,* p. 60.

CHAPTER XI

1. *Op. cit.,* pp. 376-77.
2. *Op. cit.,* p. 364, note 159.
3. *Présence de Zola,* pp. 183-89. See also Germain Bazin, *L'Epoque impressionniste,* p. 38.
4. *Cézanne et Zola,* p. 134.
5. *Ibid.,* p. 135.
6. "La Peinture de Claude Lantier," *Revue des sciences humaines,* new series, fascicle 101 (Jan.-Mar. 1961), p. 93.
7. *Ibid.,* p. 101.
8. "Lettre de Paris," *Le Sémaphore de Marseille,* Apr. 30-May 1, 1876.
9. "Notes parisiennes," *ibid.,* Mar. 24, 1877.
10. "Notes parisiennes," *ibid.,* Apr. 19, 1877.
11. *Dossier,* p. 276.
12. *Ibid.,* pp. 300-302; italics added.

13. *L'Oeuvre,* p. 45.
14. See *Emile Zola: Salons,* pp. 193, 226-27, 240-41, for example.
15. *L'Oeuvre,* p. 118.
16. *Emile Zola: Salons,* p. 221; the same idea recurs p. 241.
17. *Ibid.,* p. 126.
18. *Ibid.,* pp. 168, 192, 194-95, 221, 230.
19. *Ibid.,* p. 226.
20. *Ibid.,* pp. 244.
21. *Ibid.,* pp. 253-54.
22. *Ibid.,* p. 168.
23. *Ibid.,* p. 196.
24. *Ibid.,* p. 220.
25. *Ibid.,* p. 222.
26. *Ibid.,* p. 227.
27. *Ibid.,* pp. 242-43.
28. *L'Oeuvre,* p. 197.
29. *Ibid.,* pp. 203-4.
30. *Ibid.,* pp. 296-97.
31. *Ibid.,* pp. 192-93.
32. Henri Hertz reports Zola as saying this: "I not only supported the Impressionists. I translated them into literature, by the touches, notes, coloration, by the palette of many of my descriptions. "Zola témoin de la vérité," *Europe,* XXX (1952), pp. 32-33. See also the excellent remarks of Mitterand, *op. cit.,* p. 1457, on this aspect of Zola's talent.
33. *Emile Zola: Salons,* pp. 267-68.
34. Albert Dethez saw the novel as anything but pessimistic: "A book of pity and love, which proves that in art, truth is justice, as truth is morality; a book that one cannot call pessimistic for in spite of everything it leaves intact in the artist the love of art which torments him, no more pessimistic than that other novel where the writer-philosopher shows that with all the misery, the physical pain and moral torment of which life is made, it is still a joy to live." "Notes et commentaire" to *L'Oeuvre,* p. 400. Henri Guillemin, in *Présentation des Rougon-Macquart* also believes that Zola expressed an optimistic outlook in the novel; he interprets the final line as an expression of hope and courage.
35. *L'Oeuvre,* pp. 392-94.

Select Bibliography

A very large number of works of all kinds deal with L'Oeuvre; *the present references are to books and articles cited in the text. For further references see Henri Mitterand's bibliographical note to the Pléiade edition of* L'Oeuvre, *pp. 1398-1405.*

Adhémar, Hélène and Jean, "Zola et la peinture," *Arts,* Dec. 12-18, 1952.

Adhémar, Jean, "Le Cabinet de travail de Zola," *Gazette des beaux-arts,* Sixth period, LVI (Nov. 1960), pp. 285-98.

Alexandre, Arsène, "Claude Lantier," *Le Figaro,* Dec. 9, 1895.

Alexis, Paul, *Emile Zola, notes d'un ami.* Paris: Charpentier, 1882.

———, "Trubl' au vert," *Le Cri du peuple,* Sept. 2, 1887.

Amicis, Edmondo de, *Studies of Paris,* tr. by W. W. Cady. New York and London: G. P. Putnam's Sons, 1886.

———, *Ritratti letterari,* French tr., *Le Figaro littéraire,* Sept. 24, 1881.

Angell, N., A. Artinian, et al., *Présence de Zola.* Paris: Fasquelle, 1953.

Anon., Review of *L'Oeuvre, Le Moniteur universel,* Aug. 30, 1886.

———, Review of *L'Oeuvre, Le Français,* May 21, 1886.

———, Review of *L'Oeuvre, La Gazette anecdotique,* Apr. 30, 1886.

———, Review of *L'Oeuvre, L'Echo de Paris,* Apr. 6, 1886.

———, Review of *L'Oeuvre, Le Livre,* VIII, 77 (May 10, 1886), pp. 227-28.

D'Aramon, Paul, Review of *L'Oeuvre, La France libre,* Apr. 16 and 24, 1886.

Balzac, Honoré de, *Le Chef-d'oeuvre inconnu,* in *Etudes philosophiques, Oeuvres complètes,* ed. Bouteron and Longnon. Paris: Conard, 1925.

Barbusse, Henri, *Zola,* tr. by Mary B. Green and Frederick C. Green. New York: Dutton, 1932.

Barr, Alfred H., "Cézanne d'après les lettres de Marion à Morstatt, 1865-1868," *Gazette des beaux-arts,* LXXIX (1937), pp. 37-58.

Bataille, Georges, *Manet,* tr. by Austryn Wainhouse and James Emmons. New York: Skira, 1955.

Batilliat, Marcel, *Emile Zola.* Paris: Rieder, 1931.

Baude de Maurcelay, "Un Salon disparu—souvenirs personnels," *Le Figaro littéraire,* Apr. 12, 1890.

Baudelaire, Charles, *Le Portrait ovale,* in *Nouvelles histoires extraordinaires.* Paris: Quantin, 1884.

Bazin, Germain, *L'Epoque impressionniste.* Paris: Editions Pierre Tisné, 1947.

Bergerat, Emile, *Souvenirs d'un enfant de Paris—Les Années de bohème.* Paris: Charpentier, 1911.

Bernard, Emile, *Souvenirs sur Paul Cézanne,* Paris: La Société des Trente, 1912; also in *Mercure de France,* 69 (1907), pp. 387-89.

Bernier, Robert, Review of *L'Oeuvre, La Revue moderne,* May 1886.

Beuchat, Charles, *Le Naturalisme français.* Paris: Corrêa, 1949.

Beucken, Jean de, "Un Portrait de Cézanne," *Illustration,* Supplément théâtral et littéraire, Aug. 11, 1951, pp. 3-32; Aug. 25, 1951, pp. 2-32.

Bibliothèque nationale, *Emile Zola,* exposition organisée pour le cinquantième anniversaire de sa mort. Paris, 1952.

Bigot, Charles, Review of *L'Oeuvre, Le Gagne-Petit,* Apr. 5, 1886.

Blavet, Emile ("Parisis"), "La Vie parisienne: *L'Oeuvre,*" *Le Figaro,* July 22, 1885.

Bowie, Theodore R., *The Painter in French Fiction.* Chapel Hill: University of North Carolina Press, 1950.

Boyé, Maurice P., "Antony Valabrègue, poète et historien d'art," *Rolet,* Dec. 18, 1952; Jan. 1, 8, 15, 22, 1953.

Brady, Patrick, "La Peinture de Claude Lantier," *Revue des sciences humaines,* new series, fasc. 101 (Jan. Nov. 1961), pp. 89-101.

———, "Claude Lantier," *Les Cahiers naturalistes,* 17 (1961), pp. 10-18.

———, "Les Clefs de l'*Oeuvre* de Zola," *Australian Journal of French Studies,* Sept.-Dec. 1964, pp. 257-71.

———, "Les Sources littéraires de l'*Oeuvre* de Zola," *Revue de l'Université de Bruxelles,* new series, XVI, Aug.-Sept. 1964, pp. 413-25.

Breton, Jules, *Nos Peintres du siècle*. Paris: Société d'Editions d'Art, 1908.

Brisson, Adolphe, *L'Envers de la gloire*. Paris: Flammarion, n. d.

Brown, Calvin S., "Music in Zola's Fiction, Especially Wagner's Music," *Publications of the Modern Language Association*, LXXI (Mar. 1956), pp. 84-96.

Burty, Philippe, *Grave imprudence*, *La Nouvelle revue*, V (1880), pp. 583-609, 806-30, VI (1880), pp. 154-87.

Céard, Henry, "Zola intime," *La Revue illustrée*, III (Feb. 15, 1887), pp. 40-45.

———, *Lettres inédites à Emile Zola*, ed. C. A. Burns. Paris: Nizet, 1958.

Cézanne, Paul, *Letters*, ed. by John Rewald, tr. by Marguerite Kay. London: Bruno Cassirer, 1941.

Charensol, Georges, "Zola et les peintres," in N. Angell et al., *Présence de Zola*.

Charvay, Robert, "Zola et Diderot," *L'Événement*, May 6, 1886.

Chincholle, Charles ("Charles"), Interview with Zola, *Le Figaro*, May 2, 1885.

Clemenceau, Georges, *Claude Monet—Les Nymphéas*. Paris: Plon, 1928.

Coquiot, Gustave, *Paul Cézanne*. Paris: Ollendorff, n. d.

Daudet, Alphonse, *Quarante Ans de Paris, 1857-1897*. Geneva: La Palatine, 1945.

Deffoux, Léon, and Emile Zavie, *Le Groupe de Médan*. Paris: Payot, 1920.

Deffoux, Léon, "Emile Zola et ses éditions depuis 1902," *Le Figaro*, Oct. 1, 1927.

———, "Zola à vingt-quatre ans," *Mercure de France*, Dec. 15, 1927, pp. 509-11.

———, "Zola, Chaîne et l'huile d'olive," *Mercure de France*, Dec. 15, 1927.

Desprez, Louis, *L'Evolution naturaliste*. Paris: Tresse, 1884.

Dethez, Albert, Review of *L'Oeuvre*, *Le Siècle*, Apr. 17, 1886.

Dorival, Bernard, *Cézanne*. Paris: Editions Pierre Tisné, 1948.

Doucet, Fernand, *L'Esthétique d'Emile Zola et son application à la critique*. The Hague: De Nederlandsche Boek- en Steendruckerj, n. d.

Dumas *fils*, Alexandre, *Affaire Clémenceau*. Paris: Calmann Lévy, n. d.

Duranty, Edmond, *Le Pays des arts*. Paris: Charpentier, 1881.

Duret, Théodore, *Histoire des peintres impressionnistes*. Paris: Floury, third ed., 1922.

———, *Manet,* tr. J. E. Crawford Fletcher. New York: Crown Publishers, 1937.

Duval, Georges ("Harry Allis"), *Le Quartier Pigalle.* Paris: Marpon et Flammarion, n. d.

Ebin, Ima N., "Manet and Zola," *Gazette des beaux-arts,* sixth series, XXVII (1945), pp. 357-78.

Flaubert, Gustave, *L'Éducation sentimentale, Oeuvres complètes.* Paris: Conard, 1923, vol. IV.

Fouquier, Marcel, Review of *L'Oeuvre, La France,* May 2, 1886.

Français, Maurice, Review of *L'Oeuvre, L'Autorité,* Apr. 5, 1886.

Gasquet, Joachim, *Cézanne.* 2d ed.; Paris: Les Editions Bernheim-Jeune, 1926.

Geffroy, Gustave, *Notes d'un journaliste.* Paris: Charpentier, 1887.

———, *Claude Monet, sa vie, son oeuvre.* Paris: Crès, 1924.

Gill, André, *Vingt ans de Paris.* Paris: Marpon et Flammarion, n. d.

Gille, Philippe, *La Bataille littéraire,* third series. Paris: Havard, 1890.

Girard, Marcel, "Situation d'Emile Zola," *Revue des sciences humaines,* new series, 65 (Jan.-Mar. 1952), pp. 137-56.

Goncourt, Edmond and Jules de, *Les Hommes de lettres.* Paris: Dentu, 1860.

———, *Manette Salomon.* Paris: Flammarion, n. d.

———, *Journal, mémoires de la vie littéraire.* Monaco: Editions de l'Imprimerie nationale, 1956.

Guillemin, Henri, *Présentation des Rougon-Macquart.* Paris: Gallimard-NRF, 1964.

Hamilton, George H., *Manet and His Critics.* New Haven: Yale University Press, 1954.

Hemmings, F. W. J., *Emile Zola.* 1st ed.; Oxford: Clarendon Press, 1953; 2d ed., 1966.

———, "Zola and the *Éducation sentimentale,*" *Romanic Review,* L, 1 (Feb. 1959), pp. 35-40.

Henry, Fernand, *Critique au jour le jour.* Paris: Savine, 1887.

Hertz, Henri, "Zola témoin de la vérité," *Europe,* XXX (1952), pp. 32-33.

Hoche, Jules, "Le Premier roman d'Emile Zola," *La Revue illustrée,* IV, No. 1 (1887), pp. 289-98.

Huyghe, René, *Cézanne.* Paris: Plon, 1936.

Huysmans, Joris-Karl, *En Ménage, Oeuvres complètes.* Paris: Crès, 1944, vol. IV.

———, *L'Art moderne, Oeuvres complètes.* Paris: Crès, 1944, vol. VI.

James, Henry, *The Madonna of the Future,* in *Stories of Writers and Artists,* ed. F. O. Matthiessen. New York: New Directions, 1944.

Jamot, Paul, Georges Wildenstein, Marie-Louise Bataille, *Manet.* Paris: Les Beaux-arts, 1932.

Josephson, Matthew, *Zola and His Time.* New York: Macaulay, 1928.

Jourdain, Francis, "A la Recherche de Cézanne," *Commune,* 68 (Apr. 1939), pp. 433-38.

Kesten, Hermann, Preface to *His Masterpiece,* tr. by Katherine Woods. London: Howell Soskin, 1946.

Lafenestre, Georges, "Marcellin Desboutin," *Revue de l'art ancien et moderne,* XII (1902), pp. 400-407.

Lalo, Charles, "L'Art et la vie II—Le Complexe de Zola," *Revue des cours et conférences.* XXXVIII (Feb. 28, 1937), pp. 508-21.

Lanoux, Armand, *Bonjour, Monsieur Zola.* Paris: Amiot-Dumont, 1954.

Lapp, John C., *Zola Before the Rougon-Macquart Series.* Toronto: University of Toronto Press, 1964.

Larguier, Léo, *Le Dimanche avec Paul Cézanne.* Paris: L'Edition, 1925.

LeBlond, Maurice, "Notes et commentaire" to *L'Oeuvre, Oeuvres complètes.* Paris: Bernouard, 1928, vol. XVIII, pp. 401 ff.

LeBlond-Zola, Denise, "Zola et Cézanne d'après une correspondance retrouvée," *Mercure de France,* CCXXV (1931), pp. 39-58.

———, *Emile Zola raconté par sa fille.* Paris: Fasquelle, 1931.

———, "Paul Alexis, ami des peintres, bohème et critique d'art," *Mercure de France,* Mar. 15, 1939, pp. 293-303.

Lecomte, Georges, "Paul Cézanne," *Revue d'art,* Dec. 9, 1899, pp. 81-87.

Lemaître, Jules, "M. Emile Zola—L'Oeuvre," *Revue politique et littéraire,* XXIII (1886), pp. 481-85.

Lepelletier, Edmond, *Emile Zola, sa vie, son oeuvre.* Paris: Mercure de France, 1908.

Le Roux, Hugues, Review of *L'Oeuvre, La République française,* Apr. 28, 1886.

Lods et Vega, Armand, *André Gill, sa vie.* Paris: Vanier, 1887.

Lövgren, Sven, *The Genesis of Modernism.* Uppsala-Stockholm: Almqvist and Wiksell, n. d.

Mack, Gerstle, *Cézanne*. New York: Knopf, 1935.

Manet, Édouard, *Manet raconté par lui-même et par ses amis*. Vésenay-Geneva: Pierre Cailler, 1945.

Martineau, Henri, *Le Roman scientifique d'Emile Zola*, Paris: J. B. Baillière et fils, 1907.

Massis, Henri, *Comment Zola composait ses romans*. Paris: Charpentier, 1906.

Matthews, J. H., *Les Deux Zola*. Geneva: Droz, 1957.

Mauclair, Camille, *L'Impressionnisme, son histoire, son esthétique, ses maîtres*. Paris: Librairie de l'Art Ancien et Moderne, 1904.

———, "Le Crépuscule de l'art pictural," *La Revue des revues*, Apr. 1, 1930.

Mendès, Catulle ("Jean Prouvaire"), "L'Exposition du boulevard des Capucines," in Venturi, *Archives de l'impressionnisme*.

Moore, George, *A Modern Lover*. London: Tinsley Brothers, 1883.

———, *Confessions of a Young Man*. New York: Penguin Books, 1939.

Moreau-Nélaton, Etienne, *Manet raconté par lui-même*. Paris: Henri Laurens, 1926.

Niess, Robert J., *Emile Zola's Letters to J. Van Santen Kolff*. St. Louis: Washington University Press, 1940.

———, "Nine Letters from Emile Zola to Frans Netscher," *Publications of the Modern Language Association*, XVI (1941), pp. 261-65.

———, "Another View of Zola's *L'Oeuvre*," *Romanic Review*, XXXIX (1948), pp. 282-300.

———, "Emile Zola: from Fact to Fiction," *Modern Language Notes*, July, 1948, pp. 407-8.

———, "Antithesis and *Reprise* in Zola's *L'Oeuvre*," *L'Esprit créateur*, IV (Summer 1961), pp. 68-75.

———, "George Moore and Emile Zola Again," *Symposium*, Spring 1966, pp. 43-49.

Perruchot, Henri, *La Vie de Cézanne*. Paris: Hachette, 1956.

———, *La Vie de Manet*. Paris: Hachette, 1959.

Pissarro, Camille, *Letters to His Son Lucien*, ed. with the assistance of Lucien Pissarro by John Rewald, tr. by Lionel Abel. New York: Pantheon Books, 1948.

Pontmartin, Armand de, *Souvenirs d'un vieux critique*, seventh series. Paris: Calmann Lévy, 1886.

Poulain, Gaston, *Bazille et ses amis*. Paris: La Renaissance du Livre, 1932.

Proust, Antonin, "Edouard Manet, souvenirs," *La Revue blanche,* XII (1897), pp. 125-35, 168-80, 201-7, 306-15, 413-27.

Provence, Marcel, "Cézanne et ses amis—Numa Coste," *Mercure de France,* CLXXXVII (Apr. 1, 1926), pp. 54-81.

Renoir, Auguste ("Un Peintre"), "L'Art décoratif contemporain," in Venturi, *Les Archives de l'impressionnisme.*

Retté, Adolphe, *Le Symbolisme, anecdotes et souvenirs.* Paris: Messein, 1903.

Rewald, John, *The History of Impressionism.* New York: Museum of Modern Art, 1946.

———, *Paul Cézanne, sa vie, son oeuvre, son amitié pour Zola.* Paris: Albin Michel, 1939.

———, *Cézanne et Zola.* Paris: Sedrowski, 1936.

———, *Paul Cézanne, a Biography.* New York: Simon and Schuster, 1948 (also as *The Ordeal of Paul Cézanne,* London: Phoenix House, 1950).

———, *Cézanne, Geffroy et Gasquet.* Paris: Quatre Chemins-Editart, 1959.

Ricatte, Robert, *La Création romanesque chez les Goncourt, 1851-1870.* Paris: Armand Colin, 1953.

Richepin, Jean, "André Gill," *Le Figaro littéraire,* July 3, 1886.

Rivière, Georges, "L'Exposition des impressionnistes," in Venturi, *Les Archives de l'impressionnisme.*

———, *Renoir et ses amis.* Paris: Floury, 1921.

———, *Le Maître Paul Cézanne.* Paris: Floury, 1921.

Robert, Guy, *La Terre d'Emile Zola.* Paris: Les Belles-Lettres, 1952.

———, *Emile Zola, principes et caractères généraux de son oeuvre.* Paris: Les Belles-Lettres, 1952.

Rod, Édouard, *La Nuit vendue,* in *Les Allemands à Paris.* Paris: Derveaux, 1880.

———, *La Femme d'Henri Vanneau.* Paris: Plon-Nourrit, 1884.

Rodo-Pissarro, Ludovic, and Lionello Venturi, *Camille Pissarro.* Paris: Paul Rosenberg, 1939.

Scholl, Aurélien, Review of *L'Oeuvre, Le Matin,* Apr. 10, 1886.

Seillière, Ernest, *Emile Zola.* Paris: Grasset, 1923.

Sherard, Robert H., *Emile Zola, A Biographical and Critical Study.* London: Chatto and Windus, 1893.

Silvestre, Armand, *Au Pays des souvenirs.* Paris: Librairie Illustrée, n. d.

Solari, Emile, "Circonstances dans lesquelles Zola composa ses romans," *Grande revue*, CXIV (June 1924), pp. 603-28.

Tabarant, Adolphe, *Manet et ses oeuvres*. Paris: Gallimard, 1947.

Tabary, Louis E., *Duranty, 1833-1880*. Paris: Les Belles-Lettres, 1954.

Tendron, Marcel, ("Marc Elder"), *Chez Claude Monet à Giverny*. Paris: Les Editions Bernheim-Jeune, 1924.

Toulouse, Edouard, *Emile Zola*. Paris: Société d'Editions Scientifiques, 1896.

de Traz, Georges ("François Fosca"), *Edmond et Jules de Goncourt*. Paris: Albin Michel, 1941.

Turnell, Martin, *The Art of French Fiction*. London: Hamish Hamilton, 1959.

Vallès, Jules, "Notes d'un absent — Dickens et Zola," *Le Voltaire*, Feb. 11, 1880.

Valmy-Baisse, J., *Le Roman d'un caricaturiste*. Paris: Marcel Seheur, 1927.

Venturi, Lionello, *Cézanne, son art, son oeuvre*. Paris: Paul Rosenberg, 1936.

———, *Les Archives de l'impressionnisme*. Paris-New York: Durand-Ruel, 1939.

"Vincent", Review of *L'Oeuvre*, *Le XIXe Siècle*, Apr. 17, 1886.

Vinchon, Jean, "Zola dîne avec les Goncourt, *Aesculape*, Jan. 1953, pp. 1-7.

———, "Un Psychiâtre relit Zola," in Angell et al, *Présence de Zola*.

Vizetelly, Ernest A., Preface to *His Masterpiece*. London: Chatto and Windus, 1902.

———, *Emile Zola, Novelist and Reformer*. London: John Lane, The Bodley Head, 1904.

Vollard, Ambroise, *Renoir, an Intimate Record*, tr. by Harold L. Van Doren and Randolph T. Weaver. New York: Knopf, 1925.

———, *Souvenirs d'un marchand de tableaux*. Paris: Albin Michel, 1937.

———, *Paul Cézanne, His Life and Art*, tr. by Harold L. Van Doren. New York: Crown Publishers, 1937.

Walter, Rodolphe, "Zola et ses amis à Bennecourt," *Les Cahiers naturalistes*, 17 (1961), pp. 19-32.

———, "Cézanne à Bennecourt en 1886," *Gazette des beaux-arts*, Feb. 1962, pp. 103-18.

———, "Emile Zola et Claude Monet," *Les Cahiers naturalistes*, 26 (1964), pp. 51-61.

Wilenski, Reginald H., *Modern French Painters*. 3d ed.; London: Faber and Faber, 1954.

Wilson, Angus, *Emile Zola, an Introductory Study of His Novels.* London: Secker and Warburg, 1952.

Xau, Fernand, *Emile Zola.* Paris: Marpon et Flammarion, 1880.

"Z", "Cabaner," *Le Figaro,* Aug. 7, 1881.

Zévaès, Alexandre, *Emile Zola.* Paris: Editions de la Nouvelle Revue Critique, 1945.

Zola, Emile, Preface to *Nouveaux Contes à Ninon, Oeuvres complètes.* Paris: Bernouard, I (1927), pp. 273-81.

———, *L'Oeuvre,* édition intégrale publiée sous la direction d'Armand Lanoux, études, notes et variantes par Henri Mitterand. Paris: Gallimard-NRF, Bibliothèque de la Pléiade, 1966, vol. IV.

———, *Le Roman expérimental, Oeuvres complètes.* Paris: Bernouard, vol. I (1928).

———, "Le Divorce et la littérature," *Le Figaro,* Feb. 14, 1881.

———, "Le Roman contemporain," *Le Figaro,* Dec. 22, 1878.

———, "Mes Souvenirs sur Gustave Flaubert," *Le Figaro littéraire,* Dec. 11, 1880.

———, *Correspondance, Lettres de jeunesse, Oeuvres complètes.* Paris: Bernouard, vol. 48 (1928).

———, *Correspondance, 1872-1902, Oeuvres complètes.* Paris: Bernouard, vol. 49 (1929).

———, "Le Crapaud," *Le Figaro,* Feb. 28, 1896.

———, *Mes Voyages–Lourdes–Rome,* ed. René Ternois. Paris: Fasquelle, 1958.

———, *Salons,* ed. F. W. J. Hemmings and R. J. Niess, preface by F. W. J. Hemmings. Geneva: Droz, 1959.

Index

Adhémar, H., 172-73, 176
Adhémar, J., 172-73, 176
Affaire Clemenceau, 22-23
"Alexandre," 24, 179-80
Alexis, P., 3, 27-30, 34-36, 42-43, 48, 55, 60, 62, 69, 74, 81, 86, 112, 164-65, 194, 196, 207-8
Allemands à Paris, Les, 17
Allis, Harry, *see* Duval, Georges
Amicis, E. de, 3, 49, 75-76, 166
Anquetin, L., 182
Archives de l'impressionnisme, Les, 174
Assommoir, L', 1, 69, 156-57, 159, 171, 185, 215, 229-32, 234
Au Bonheur des dames, 157, 159, 215 232, 234
Aubourg, P., 15, 25, 50-51

Baille, B., 28-30, 32-33, 60, 63, 69, 74, 84-85, 92, 94, 118, 152, 194, 207
Balzac, H. de, 2, 6-11, 77, 155, 210, 214
Bastien-Lepage, J., 41, 102, 139, 141, 240, 242
Baudelaire, C., 11, 24, 116, 126, 180
Bazille, F., 56, 125, 173-74, 183, 187
Béliard, E., 55-56, 84
Bellot, E., 59, 183, 188
Bête humaine, La, 229
Beuchat, C., 25
Beugnet, A., 51
Bigne, Valtesse de la, 59
Blavet, E., 4
Bourget, P., 38-39, 153, 213, 248
Bouvard et Pécuchet, 47
Bowie, T. R., 12-13, 38, 44
Brady, P., 170, 172-73, 176, 179, 182, 236-38
Brame, G., 39, 51, 53-54
Brion, L., 43
Burty, P., 15-16

Cabanel, A., 44, 57, 118, 141, 143, 148
Cabaner (Jean de Cabanes), 56-57
Carpeaux, J.-B., 49
Céard, H., 2, 5, 36, 38, 197, 217
Cézanne, P., 1, 10, 14, 28-29, 32, 35-36, 38, 56, 58-59, 63-64, 66, 69, 74, 78-86, 87-113, 116-20, 122, 124, 126, 128, 130, 139, 151-53, 156, 170, 172, 178, 183, 185, 187-89, 235
Chaillan, J.-B.-M., 28, 33-34, 194, 196
Champfleury (Jules Husson), 25
Charles, *see* Chincholle, C.
Charles Demailly, 14-15, 25
Chef-d'oeuvre inconnu, Le, 2, 6-9
Chevreul, E., 57, 101, 199, 242
Chien-caillou, 25
Chincholle, C., 4, 38
Chocquet, V., 58
Clemenceau, G., 174
Clésinger, J.-B., 49
Combarieu, F., 181
Confession de Claude, La, 155, 159, 232-33
Conquête de Plassans, La, 73
Contes à Ninon, 67, 161
Contes et nouvelles, 232-33

Corde, La, 24-25, 180
Corot, C., 34, 50, 53, 58
Coste, N., 81
Courbet, G., 17, 44-50, 52-53, 87-88, 95, 123, 142-43, 150, 155, 184, 188, 238, 241
Couture, T., 98, 113, 117, 181, 188
Curée, La, 1, 156, 159

Daudet, A., 5-6, 172, 212
Débâcle, La, 1
Degas, E., 97, 136, 186-87, 189
Delacroix, E., 45, 53, 87-88, 95, 123, 143, 155, 183-84, 238, 241, 244
Desboutin, M., 183, 188-89
Desmoulin, F., 34, 172
Diderot, D., 191
Documents littéraires, 164, 233
Doucet, F., 28, 38, 40, 44, 56
Dubois-Pillet, A., 107, 181-82
Dumas *fils*, A., 22
Duran, C. (Charles Durand), 41, 139-41, 240, 242
Durand-Ruel, P., 50, 53
Duranty, E., 24, 36, 48, 56, 65, 90-91, 97, 121, 139, 182
Duret, T., 51, 80, 90-91, 96-97, 111, 119-20, 136, 239
Duval, Georges, 20-21

Ebin, I., 71, 103, 107, 118, 127, 234-35
Édouard Manet, 103, 116-18, 121-22, 124-28, 135, 143, 164
Éducation sentimentale, L', 6, 24, 47
Emile Zola, notes d'un ami, 27, 34
Emperaire, A., 183, 189-90
En ménage, 19-20

Fantin-Latour, T., 14, 47, 56, 97, 136
Faute de l'abbé Mouret, La, 1, 157, 159
Femme d'Henri Vanneau, La, 17-18
Fiquet, H., 59, 98, 121
Flaubert, G., 6, 25, 36, 44-48, 58, 152, 154, 212, 229
Fortune des Rougon, La, 1, 67, 232
Fosca, F., 14, 38, 42, 127
Fragerolles, A., 20, 40
Français, M., 2, 6, 27, 31

France juive, La, 3

Gachet, Dr. P.-F., 58
Gasquet, J., 28, 43, 81
Gauguin, P., 96, 98
Gausson, L., 57, 101, 197, 199, 242
Gautier, T., 6, 212
Geffroy, G., 2, 90-92, 112, 175, 212
Germinal, 1, 2, 4, 69, 77, 159, 185, 214, 229, 232, 234, 244
Gérome, J.-L., 141, 148
Gervex, H., 29-30, 35, 38-41, 45, 60, 86, 99, 109, 118, 139, 141, 194, 196, 207, 239-40, 242
Gill, A., 170-72
Gille, P., 2, 38, 44, 62, 64, 172, 184-85, 212
Girard, M., 212
Goncourt, E. de, 4-5, 11-14, 49-50, 64-65, 76, 83, 162, 164-65, 190-91, 213-14, 221, 229
Grave imprudence, 15-16
Guillaumin, A., 98, 174
Guillemet, A., 36, 38, 40-41, 50-51, 53-54, 84-85, 95, 97, 99-100, 136, 141, 189, 197

Hemmings, F. W. J., 139, 144, 160, 164, 190
Henry, F., 212
Histoire des peintres impressionnistes, 97
Hoche, J., 160
Holtzapfel, J., 178-79
Hommes de lettres, Les, 14-15
Hoschedé, E., 58
Houssaye, A., 138-39
Hugo, V., 49, 66, 155, 196, 227, 230
Huot, J., 32
Huysmans, J.-K., 19, 66, 153, 187-88, 247

Impressionism, Impressionists, 1, 15-17, 23, 41, 56-57, 82-84, 96-99, 105, 112, 116, 118-19, 131-32, 136-37, 140-41, 143-45, 148, 173, 175, 183-85, 190, 193, 195, 197, 199, 204, 213, 216, 234-46
Ingres, D., 123, 238

Inondation, L', 232

James, H., 9-10, 24, 61
Joie de vivre, La, 1, 73, 77, 159, 232
Jongkind, J. B., 50, 183, 190
Jourdain, F., 124, 197

Lanoux, A., 62, 79-80, 188
Lapp, J. C., 232
LeBlond, M., 28, 38, 40, 42, 62, 81
LeBlond-Zola, D., 36, 62, 80-81
Leconte de Lisle, C., 247-48
Leenhoff, S., 56, 121
Lemaître, J., 2, 62, 212-13
Lepelletier, E., 164, 212
Loti, P., 3
Lövgren, S., 172, 181-83

Madame Bovary, 44, 46-48, 214
Madeleine Férat, 155, 159, 232-33
Madonna of the Future, The, 9-11, 25
Maison du chat-qui-pelote, La, 6
Maître, E., 56
Manet, E., 1, 14-15, 17, 23-25, 29, 36-37, 39-41, 44-48, 50, 56, 59, 63, 78, 81, 84-85, 91, 97-100, 102-3, 112-53, 156, 170-72, 178-80, 182, 184-85, 187-89, 234-35, 240, 242-43
Manette Salomon, 4, 6, 12-14, 191, 213-14
Manifeste des cinq, Le, 39, 159
Marchal, C., 180
Martin, P. F., 15, 50-51, 190
Mauclair, C., 119, 131, 133, 136, 212
Maupassant, G. de, 34, 39, 64, 153-54, 229
Meley, Mlle A., *see* Zola, Mme A.
Mendès, C., 90, 97
Mes Haines, 103, 164
Mes Souvenirs sur Gustave Flaubert, 46, 48, 58
Mes Voyages, 156
Millet, F., 52-53
Mirbeau, O., 175
Mitterand, H., 127
Modern Lover, A., 23-24
Monet, Camille, 174-75, 181
Monet, Cl., 15, 25, 28, 82, 90, 92, 97-98, 102, 107-8, 112, 116, 125, 144-45, 170, 172-78, 185-86, 236-38, 240, 243
Mon Salon, 118, 121, 125, 132-35, 142, 164, 176
Moore, G., 23-24, 83, 210, 224
Murer, E., 58
Mürger, H., 6, 20

Nana, 1, 69, 156-57, 159, 171, 230, 232-34
Naturalisme au Salon, Le, 137, 140, 145, 148, 183, 237, 240-41
Naturalisme au théâtre, Le, 164, 168
Niess, R. J., 144, 178-79
Nos Auteurs dramatiques, 164, 167, 233
Nouveaux contes à Ninon, 66, 76
Nouvelle peinture, La, 139
Nouvelles histoires extraordinaires, 11
Nuit vendue, La, 17-18

Oller y Cestero, F., 174
Oval Portrait, The, 11
Ovid, 214, 219

Page d'amour, Une, 164, 232
Parisis, *see* Blavet, E.
Pays des arts, Le, 24, 90
Pêcheur d'Islande, 3
Perruchot, H., 38, 57, 189
Petit, G., 51, 53-54
Petits poèmes parisiens, 66-67
Pissarro, C., 38, 50, 82, 95-98, 116, 183-86
Pissarro, L., 38, 52
Poe, E. A., 11-12
Pontmartin, A. de, 2, 212-13
Pot-bouille, 1, 73, 159, 229
Proust, A., 114, 118, 120, 123
Prouvaire, *see* Mendès, C.
Pygmalion legend, 8, 193, 214, 219

Quartier Pigalle, Le, 20-21

Racine, J., 219
Refusés, Salon des, 58, 60, 99, 110, 117, 121, 125-26, 132, 134-35, 137, 147, 159, 163, 173, 179, 190, 199, 201, 207, 224-26, 228, 239, 242
Renoir, A., 107, 116, 125, 174, 183-85

Rêve, Le, 56, 164
Rewald, J., 41, 59, 78-80, 91, 93, 95, 103, 118-19, 172, 178, 235-37
Ricatte, R., 14, 235
Richard, P., 181
Robert, G., 169-70
Rod, E., 17-19
Rollinat, M., 20, 157
Romanciers naturalistes, Les, 164, 167
Roman expérimental, Le, 164, 167, 228
Rousseau, T., 52-53
Roux, M., 69, 74
Roybet, F., 38-39, 53
Rozerot, J., 74, 76, 161-62, 247

Scènes de la vie de bohème, 6, 20
Sedelmayer, C., 51, 53
Shaw, G. B., 214
Sherard, R., 64
Sisley, A., 174
Solari, E., 27, 59, 189
Solari, P., 29, 37, 41-43, 69, 74, 189-90, 194

Tabar, F.-G.-L., 183, 187-88
Taine, H., 227
Terre, La, 2, 77, 229, 232
Therbouche, Mme, 183, 191
Thérèse Raquin, 69, 155, 159, 164, 232
Toulouse, Dr. E., 160, 164-65
Trois Contes, 47
Turner, J. M. W., 184, 190-91

Valabrègue, Ant., 28-30, 34-36, 39, 42-44, 58, 66-67, 69, 74, 93, 112, 196
"Valentin," 34
Vallès, J., 164, 171
Van Santen Kolff, J., 5, 81-82
Ventre de Paris, Le, 3-4, 85-86, 157, 159, 171, 173, 195, 244
Venturi, L., 173-75, 184
Vinchon, J., 164, 188
Vizetelly, E. A., 42, 44, 46, 49, 59, 127, 180, 187-88
Voeu d'une morte, Le, 232
Vollard, A., 83, 187
Vollon, A., 18, 118

Walter, R., 152, 174, 176
Wilson, A., 42, 79, 163
Wolff, A., 36, 40-41

Zola, Mme A., 31, 65, 79, 161-62, 232
Zola, Mme F., 30, 65-66, 69